Literary Forensics

How Reading Can Make You
A Better Writer

Gary Alan McBride

Literary Forensics

The web addresses referenced in this book were live and correct at the time of the book's publication but may be subject to change.

First Edition
January 2026

Published by
In Res Media LLC
www.InResMedia.com

Library of Congress Control Number: 2025916924

Paperback ISBN: 979-8-9996598-1-1
Hardcover ISBN: 979-8-9996598-0-4
E-book ISBN: 979-8-9996598-2-8

Cover design by Debbie Lewis
Illustrations by Amanda Sari

Printed in the United States of America

for Deb

POLONIUS: What do you read, my lord?
HAMLET: Words, words, words.
—William Shakespeare, *Hamlet*, act 2, scene 2

There is then creative reading as well as creative writing.
—Ralph Waldo Emerson, *The American Scholar*

Table of Contents

YOUR FIRST CLUE

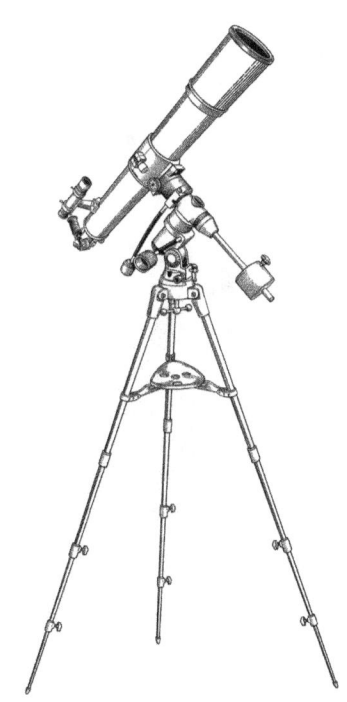

Reading Teaches Writing

Reading teaches writing is not a revolutionary idea. In fact, it's a fundamental principle that all successful writers know to be true.

> I read everything. When I say everything, I read everything: children's literature, Y.A., science fiction, fantasy, romance—I read it all. Each genre fulfills a different need I have. Each book teaches me something.
> —*Jesmyn Ward*

> If you want to be a writer, you must do two things above all others: read a lot and write a lot. There's no way around these two things that I'm aware of, no shortcut.
> —*Stephen King, On Writing: A Memoir of the Craft*

> Reading is also writing. Reading with intention—with attention, with love, and with a seeking nature—is as important to writing as actually putting the words down.
> —*Lauren Groff*

Corner any big-name author at a cocktail party and ask them to recommend the book on craft that made them the writer they are. And every author will reply pretty much the same way: There is no such book. Just read all you can.

You may have heard this before. It sounds so simple. If you want to become a better writer, you must become a better reader. But here's the thing: No one shows you how.

Until now.

My goal in writing *Literary Forensics* was to create a reference book that breaks into simple steps what it takes to become a better reader—that is, to help you read like the writer you want to become. I've done my best to organize this material and make it easy to understand, but know that *Literary Forensics* covers a *lot* of ground. Your journey to becoming a better reader and therefore a better writer will require two things: your time and your attention.

Let's start with time, that most precious commodity. If the average length of a novel is somewhere around 80,000 words, that equates to about eight hours of medium-paced uninterrupted reading. At that rate, you would only have to read about 1,250 novels to achieve Malcolm Gladwell's infamous 10,000 hours[1] and gain the mastery you'll need to read like a writer.

What? You haven't read 1,250 novels? Well, how about 500, or 100? More than a dozen? Two-time National Book Award winner Jesmyn Ward reckons she has read about 1,000 in preparation for each novel she has written. Stephen King wanted to read every waking minute he wasn't writing, so he got his children to read books into a tape recorder so he could listen to them while he drove his car to work or while he attended school events. Lauren Groff says she reads three hundred books per year. Ward, King, and Groff have certainly exceeded 10,000 hours of reading and have attained mastery in their craft.

But here's the kicker: *They continue to read.*

These three acknowledged masters of writing don't see reading as an apprenticeship, or a stage they passed through. They continue to read at the ferocious pace they have always set for themselves, because it continues to benefit their writing. Reading is an essential part of their lives.

Step one in learning to read like a writer is to actually take the time to read.

Read every day.

If you read for just fifteen minutes per day, you can finish a three-hundred-page novel in a month. If you read for an hour every day, you can read a novel a week. Don't have the time to spend reading? Many of us spend hours every day on social media, watching television, or playing video games, time that could be spent reading. And if you suffer from a busier schedule with less free time, reading can be combined with other activities, like eating, commuting, exercising, or winding down before bed.[2] I know many authors with children who get up an hour early to write; you could get up fifteen minutes early to read. Reading is an excellent way to begin your day, and is often more enriching than doomscrolling the news.

The key is to acknowledge how important reading is to your writing and prioritize your time to make room for it. Mark your reading time in your calendar if you have to, but be sure to make it as much of your daily routine as brushing your teeth or eating a meal—or writing. Start today.

The second barrier preventing your reading from teaching you how to write is the lack of a very specific skill. Throughout *Literary Forensics* I'll refer to this skill as *reading like a writer*.[3] Here's my definition:

Reading like a writer means reading with intent and awareness of the craft behind the text, as an author reads to evaluate and edit their own writing.

The purpose of this type of critical reading is to discover how the author did what they did so that you can apply these insights to your own writing. That's the goal.

You may already be asking: How does this kind of reading work? What does *reading like a writer* look like in practice? The answer is in the title of this book.

I chose *Literary Forensics* fully expecting you to think of CSI-style crime investigation. Just as the forensic investigator can determine how the murder was committed from a mere drop of blood and a carpet fiber, so too we study the novel in front of us, and from the smallest of clues—a word, a context, a gap—we can determine how it was created and came to be in the shape we find it.

Spoiler alert: Applying this methodology to the next novel you read will immediately yield writing insights, and you will see new techniques you've learned appear in your own writing with each additional dozen novels you read. You won't have to wait until novel number 1,250 to see results. Nice, huh?

To be clear, like Stephen King said, there is no shortcut to reading hundreds of books. The real improvement to your writing comes when reading like a writer becomes a daily habit, a lifestyle choice. You're a writer, after all.

One more thing about taking the time to read: It's important to remember that 10,000 hours of reading does not automatically grant you writing mastery. It's not *practice makes perfect*, but rather, *perfect practice makes perfect*. Reading without intent, allowing the narrative to enter your brain passively like you'd vegetate in front of the TV, is almost as fruitless as not reading at all. The key to improving your reading skills, more than *what* you read, or the *amount* you read, is in *how* you read—how *conscious* you are while you are reading.

Sounds like a lot of work, right? But it's more of a state of mind than a heroic burst of effort. It's invigorating and addictive. Once you learn how to shine a black light over the pages of a novel, what was hidden now glows, and you can't ever unsee it. Soon you'll crave the thrill of pulling back the glossy sheen of the final edit to uncover yet another authorial nugget of technique, and you'll wonder why you waited so long to read like this. And as can happen when obsessing over your favorite band or sports team, the more you learn, the more you'll want to know.

Mining insights from every work of fiction you read is a skill. Like any skill worth learning, it takes time and requires practice. This is not *Eight Hours to Better Reading*, nor is it *Write Better Fast*. There is no magic pill, nor can I force-feed you the wisdom contained in *Literary Forensics*. But, used mindfully, this book can help you at every step of your critical reading journey.

If you want to improve your writing skills, and you're not reading like a writer, you could be using your valuable reading time far more efficiently. *Literary Forensics* will help you become a more insightful reader and therefore a more effective writer. Reading is not an apprenticeship; it's lifelong learning.

It's also fun! So let's get started.

Four Stages of Discovery

Let's start with the structure of this book. *Literary Forensics* is a reference guide, a set of twenty-five independent chapters, each addressing a different aspect of reading, with exercises. I suggest you do the exercises to build and practice your new skills. It's not enough to merely understand how this works. To get the results you want, you have to apply what you learn. As this is a reference book, take advantage of the table of contents, the glossary, and the index to help you find your way around. Use the endnotes and bibliography to delve deeper into the ideas and sources I present here.

When I first conceived of *Literary Forensics*, I assumed that I would structure it the way many books on writing craft are structured. After all, reading and writing are two sides of the same coin, right? I quickly realized that was not the case at all, however, and the reason surprised me: Novelists are obfuscators while readers are investigators. Much like the differences between perpetrators and detectives, writing and reading require two completely different skill sets. Reading like a writer requires that you pass through four stages of discovery.

Literary Forensics *is organized in the order of our discoveries, rather than in the order of the elements of craft.*

My favorite analogy to explain these four stages is the telescope. The author is like the Big Bang, and in a burst of creative energy they have spread their words across the canvas of the heavens. We readers look up at those points of light through our telescopes and wonder: *How did they get there?* All we have to go on are what we can see and detect with scientific instruments—with very few clues that lead us back to the moment of creation.

I'll take this analogy a little further because it applies to understanding the structure of *Literary Forensics*. We realize as we examine the universe that our perspective is skewed, obscured by Earth's atmospheric soup, and our vantage point is where we stand on a tilted spinning ball orbiting a minor star in a galaxy far from the center of the universe. We first have to correct for these biases before we can hope to gain useful insights.

In the same way, we are all biased readers. We all have unique backgrounds that lead each one of us to perceive identical texts in different ways. The first stage of discovery as you begin to read like a writer is introspection. You need to ask yourself WHAT YOU BRING to the text before you start reading. Correcting for your biases allows you to see the text as clearly as possible. That's the focus of the first section, which contains five chapters.

Our second stage of discovery is to acknowledge our emotions as we encounter the text. Our bodies produce emotional responses much faster than the analytical parts of our brains make sense of what we perceive. Storytelling is an emotive art, and the novelist's skill is in how well they can move us and make us care about their subjects as much as they do. Thus, WHAT YOU FEEL while you read offers you massive clues about the craft underpinning the words. You ignore your own emotions at your peril, both in real life and in your reading. That's the focus of the second section, which contains six chapters.

Once you've corrected for bias and acknowledged how the text makes you feel, WHAT YOU NOTICE is the third stage of discovery; this section contains nine chapters. Here, you hone your ability to analyze the author's tactics and techniques. You can seldom be sure how or why the author chose a given structure or specific words, given your distance from the author, but this third stage of discovery can help you refine your own judgment in making these choices in your own writing. As the detective must understand the properties of a pistol, an axe, a knife, and a rope before they can understand how those weapons might have been used in a crime, so too will you benefit from your knowledge of the specific techniques authors use in their writing. You'll appreciate how language, context, point of view, voice, characterization, structure, pacing, and layering are applied in each novel.

Finally, no text stands in isolation; each piece of writing exists within the wider world. The fourth stage of discovery is about establishing the context in which a novel is intended to be read. For this reason, if you're interested in getting your own work published today, I encourage you to study primarily the most recently published novels. Novelistic forms have changed significantly over the past twenty years, and thematic treatment has changed dramatically over the past five. Today's novels do not resemble the classics, and it's important for critical readers to be aware of the latest developments. This is the focus of the fourth section, WHAT YOU STUDY, which contains the final five chapters.

The graphic above is a visual representation of the four stages of discovery. Moving from left to right, the WHAT YOU BRING section, represented by the luggage, acknowledges the historical and psychological baggage you bring to every novel you read. You then observe your emotional responses to the text in the WHAT YOU FEEL section. You can uncover a great deal of writing craft from these two stages alone, so keep in mind the importance of developing your self-awareness. Once you progress beyond yourself and your emotions, use the telescope of *Literary Forensics* to help you see clearly the effects of the wheel of craft[4] in the WHAT YOU NOTICE section. Finally, beyond considering the novel as a whole (its Gestalt), examine how the novel relates to the rest of an author's body of work, and the worlds of publishing and academia, as well as all the writers, critics, and literary enthusiasts who populate the expanding universe of WHAT YOU STUDY.

In summary, the four stages of discovery are uncovering your biases, tapping into your emotions, noticing craft, and studying a novel's context in the world at large. These relate directly to the four sections of *Literary Forensics*: WHAT YOU BRING, WHAT YOU FEEL, WHAT YOU NOTICE, and WHAT YOU STUDY.

Choosing Your Teachers

Francine Prose, in her book *Reading Like a Writer*, extols the virtues of searching for technical direction or inspiration by serendipitously opening at random books you feel are well written.

> It's a good idea to have a designated section of your bookshelf (perhaps the one nearest your desk) for books by writers who have obviously worked on their sentences, revising and polishing them into gems that continue to dazzle us. These are works you can turn to whenever you feel that your own style is getting a little slack or lazy or vague. You can open such books anywhere and read a sentence that will move you to labor longer, try harder, to return to that trouble spot and rework that imprecise or awkward sentence until it is something to be proud of instead of something you hope that the reader won't notice.
>
> —*Francine Prose*, Reading Like a Writer

Well-written books are the sacred texts of the writer's dark art,[5] so I join Prose in encouraging you to keep this practice alive. In fact, it's the central conceit of this book: that you will be able to find answers to your writing questions not only in well-written books, but in *any* book—even one that's obviously flawed.[6] It's not as crazy as it sounds.

Let's go back to that proverbial cocktail party I mentioned earlier, the one where the successful writer told you to read, read, read. Transform that faceless celebrity into your all-time favorite author. The one you've idolized since your youth or relatively recently—the one you want to be, the one whose writing skills you desperately wish you had as your own. Can you picture who it is? Now imagine working up the nerve to ask them to teach you how to write like they do, to be your private writing coach. Miraculously, they say yes. They agree to teach you all their skills and share all their secrets. But not only that, their fee is insanely modest: the price of one or two of their novels.

Life changing, isn't it? Your favorite author is now your personal writing coach. Sounds crazy, but you're not dreaming. That's what it's like to apply *Literary Forensics* to the works of your favorite authors.

Flush with multiple cocktails, you go one step further, and you ask your favorite author, your new writing coach, for your first reading assignment, your Lesson Number One. They share with you the **First rule of *Literary Forensics***, the foundation from which all the other critical reading tools derive: **Always ask why.**

---

*The **First rule of** Literary Forensics *is **Always ask why**.*

It's important for writers who read to recognize that every author makes hundreds of choices on every page, which should lead critical readers to ask: Why this and not that? Why was this chosen, and that omitted? This **First rule of** *Literary Forensics* is the skill you need in every chapter in this book: the ability to pause at any point within a novel and **Always ask why**.[7]

But while this is the most important tool, it's certainly not the only one you'll need in your investigations. To read like a writer, you'll want to be equipped with the **Seven tools** and the **Three keys** of storytelling from which they all arise.

Notes

1. First defined by Malcolm Gladwell in his 2008 book *Outliers: The Story of Success*.
2. Over her career, the actress Sarah Jessica Parker has had lots of downtime between takes, and she always uses that time to read—in fact, she never goes anywhere without a book in her bag. In spite of not attending college, over the years she has become so well read and so respected by the publishing industry that she manages her own publishing imprint and served as a 2025 Booker Prize judge.
3. I use the terms *reading like a writer* and *critical reading* interchangeably, not in the sense of criticizing, but with *critical* reading as *most important*. For our purposes, they're the same thing.
4. Please note the order of the pie slices in WHAT YOU NOTICE, which have been positioned so that topic is most closely related to the neighboring topics, with some overlap between one chapter and the next. Although "Language" through "Layering" are, by necessity, ordered as chapters 12 through 19, think of the end of chapter 19, "Layering" as leading back into chapter 12, "Language and Grammar."
5. This practice of divination by means of opening a book to a random page to find the answer to a question posed—stichomancy—dates from ancient times, when the philosophical works of Homer and Virgil were used for inspiration. In the more recent past, it was believed that this type of fortune-telling required a sacred text, like the Bible, the I Ching, the Mahabharata, the Talmud, or the Qur'an. Randomly consulting religious texts for inspiration is called *bibliomancy*. Using poetry for divination is called *rhapsodomancy*.
6. In this interview on the topic of reading all the works written by and about a writer, Paul Theroux says, "Bad books are more revealing of a writer's character than the good books." https://www.youtube.com/watch?v=ufFyW9LxBr0
7. George Saunders wrote an entire book describing this rule: *A Swim in a Pond in the Rain: In Which Four Russians Give a Master Class on Writing, Reading, and Life*. He uses short stories from four Russian authors as his example texts and explains in great detail the benefits of periodically interrupting your reading with these questions: What just happened, and why did the author present what they did in the way they did? What do I think will happen next, and why am I being led to expect that? **Always ask why**.

Three Keys and Seven Tools

The reading tools in *Literary Forensics* emerge from the study of the craft of writing. The reason these tools produce results is largely because of the elements of storytelling that exist in every novel: I call them the **Three keys**.[1] The **Seven tools** that derive from these **Three keys** are the most useful and important for you to know, and applying them will make your reading more productive immediately.[2]

---

*The **Three keys** present in every novel are:*
- *Inciting-midpoint-climax*
- *Unspoken contract*
- *Everything serves a purpose*

These elements are so universal that I'm sure you may already be familiar with them. Every novel has an **inciting** incident, a pivotal **midpoint**, and a **climax**. The **unspoken contract** between an author and you, the reader, is that although you may be confused initially, by the end of the novel all will be revealed and the journey will have been worth it. And finally, in novels, **everything serves a purpose** and often has multiple layers of significance.

These are simple truths, yet incredibly useful for our purposes. From these essential precepts derive many more powerful tools for readers. Let's dig in.

The First Key: Inciting-Midpoint-Climax

Every novel begins with a premise, a hook, and an **inciting incident**. The premise is the setup that entices you to open the book—it's the summary (or logline) that describes what novel is about in a sentence or two. The inciting incident begins the protagonist's journey. And the hook compels you to continue reading. These elements constitute the beginning, and they may be combined or appear in a different order, but they exist in some form in every novel.

Almost exactly halfway through the novel at the **midpoint** is the twist. You can visualize it as a fulcrum, like the center post of a seesaw. As you read the first half of a novel, it's like walking up one side of a seesaw. When you pass the midpoint of the plank, the balance shifts underneath your feet, so that what sloped upward now slopes downward. At the midpoint, the seesaw has not metamorphosed into a merry-go-round, nor has the novel ceased to be a novel. But what happens there shifts the balance of everything that has come before, providing a revelation that causes us to question what we thought we knew. That midpoint twist is in every single novel I've ever surveyed. It's not there by accident.

Finally comes the **climax**, or denouement. The climax of the novel should provide the answer to the inciting incident's question, and it's the payoff—the reward for embarking on this narrative journey.

Tool One: Use structure to identify themes

These three elements are the primary structural tentpoles of every novel. When combined with observations at the one-third/two-thirds and the first and third quarters of the book, these markers reveal much about how the novelist formulated and organized their material, what the novel is *really* about, and even why it was written. You can find more on this in chapter 17, "Structure," chapter 18, "Pacing," and chapter 20, "The Gestalt."

The Second Key: The Unspoken Contract

Reading a novel, any novel, requires an element of trust. Whether it's literary fiction, sci-fi, western, thriller, or any other genre, you trust that the author will reward your efforts with a satisfying ending: the hero vanquished, the lovers united, the killer unmasked, or the truth made plain. We all read hoping to experience something that we would not have achieved otherwise: a moment, an amusement, an insight, a feeling.

From the inciting incident onward, the questions pile up: Where are we? What is happening? Who is that? Why are they behaving this way? How can this be?[3] And because the novel eventually answers these questions and provides some sort of resolution to the ensuing conflicts, its overall arc is a progression from confusion to clarity, from chaos to order, from deception to truth, and from darkness to light. Every novel promises a final illumination that will reward the trust we put in its author. That's the **unspoken contract** between writer and reader.

---

*The **unspoken contract** between writer and reader is: Although you may be confused initially, by the end of this novel all will be revealed and the journey will have been worth it.*

However, this final prize cannot be easily won. A skillful author will have developed the ability to hold themselves back and not reveal everything all at once. Readers learn to appreciate the steady drip of knowledge and truth, but are justified in expecting that by the end of the novel, all will be revealed. So, in fact, in the early and middle stages of a novel, it's the author's obligation to deceive you, lie to you, lead you astray, leave you gasping with chapter-ending cliffhangers, and many other sorts of obstacles we would think the author reserved for the protagonist alone.

Understand the consequences of the **unspoken contract** or you'll get played.

Tool Two: Assume you're being played

There's no shame in getting played; in fact it happens to every reader at some point. Any author worth their salt is as skillful as the most devious used car salesman. They're practicing the essential art of narrative: guiding you down the path they intend for you to follow, and coercing you into ignoring everything else. Awkward revelations are *lampshaded*. Plot holes are papered over. Scenes are skipped, timelines compressed, POVs (points of view) switched—all to get you to watch the birdie and ignore the sleight of hand.

So don't take anything within the text at face value, especially in the early chapters, before we've transitioned from darkness to light. What follows are a few tools you can use to cut through the trickery.

Tool Three: Pay attention to POV

One of the most common ways an author can direct your thinking is to feed you the opinions of one of the characters, or the narrator, or even the author themselves when necessary. A useful tool worth developing is to keep track of whose head you're in at any time, and to ask yourself why you think the author has chosen to present this perspective and not any other. Hint: The author is likely hiding something. See chapter 13, "Context in Scene" and chapter 14, "Point of View" for more detail.

Tool Four: What happens is not what's discussed

This reading tool derives from its writing inverse, *Show, don't tell*. When a character says something is so, that doesn't prove that it is so. In fact, it's often the opposite—in fact, all dialogue is suspect. Characters are defined in only one way: by doing—by demonstrating how they overcome the obstacles placed in their way. Observing what a character does is the lodestar that will guide you toward understanding what's really going on. For a deeper discussion of this tool and a character's impact on structure, see chapter 15, "Voice," and chapter 16, "Character Development."

The **unspoken contract** permeates the entire narrative and influences every page of text in ways both large and small. If its residual effects leave you feeling bored, upset, unengaged, or overly confused, those emotions could indicate that the author hasn't held up their end of the contract. When something feels off, it's good to act on those feelings and consult a chapter within the WHAT YOU FEEL section. *X* marks the spot to start digging and uncover what the author was attempting that went sideways.

The Third Key: Everything Serves a Purpose

Every word contained within a novel's 80,000 or so is there for a reason, and every element—both large and small—serves the narrative.

Compact, tight prose is one of those traits of modern fiction that has migrated from the screenplay to the novel, but it looks like it's here to stay. For example, today's average movie length hovers around two hours,[4] which means that a screenwriter has only 120 pages to tell an entire story. That's not a lot of time—but it is enough, especially if the writer is crafty with scene selection and makes each one do double or even triple duty: advance the plot, deepen a characterization or a relationship, and sprinkle in some clues about what lies in store for our heroine.

Our lives are crammed full of responsibilities, activities, and entertainments, all competing for our attention, so for literature to engage us, we expect it to get to the point quickly and use our time efficiently. The modern novel is a streamlined marvel, some say the worse for it, but it's merely the story vessel of our time. Every name, location, object, action, description, and word of dialogue has been carefully selected to serve a specific purpose, and because we know that, it's appropriate for us to question every word. You are already familiar with the tool that's derived from this concept:

Tool Five and *First rule* of **Literary Forensics***:* *Always ask why*

I once attended an interesting workshop given by an editor that involved taking a few pages from classic novels and doing a modern edit. Long gone is the style of Melville or Hardy within which entire chapters could be given over to rumination. Cut. Long-winded descriptions of the landscape? Cut. That C story created to add color? Cut.

This same truth applies to larger elements, including scenes.

Kazuo Ishiguro's 2021 novel *Klara and the Sun* contains a very quiet scene in which Klara stands in a field and ruminates. Only that. I whizzed right by this scene on my first reading, and when I asked myself why it was there, I was stumped. It took a second reading for me to realize that the scene was pivotal, given Klara's nature in contrast to the actual nature she was standing within. In a sense, understanding why that scene was there unlocked so much more of the book. *Of course* Ishiguro wouldn't waste a scene.

Tool Six: Reread

To get everything out of a text you must read it multiple times. I frequently use my first pass through a novel to get caught up in the emotions, to feel the surprise, or shock, or sympathy the author is (mis)directing me to feel—in other words, I allow the author to play me. It's on my second read that I can dig in more deeply. Because I know what's coming, it's much easier for me to see the hints sprinkled, the thematic elements embedded. Because I already understand the context, they pop off the page and glow. I can reread the opening sentence with greater understanding. I can spot the subtle nudges of an author biasing me to feel a particular way about a character or a situation, and I can spot the tiniest clues of what is to come.

Why does it take multiple passes to uncover deeper layers? Let me ask you this: Do you think you're reading the first draft? Of course not! That novel has gone through dozens of versions, sometimes one of more complete rewrites, to get to the state it's in when you find it. Add to that the work of beta readers and multiple editors, and you've got a ton of strata you're attempting to excavate. The symbolism and parallelism you discover on your second or third reading almost never appeared in the author's first draft. Semiotic symbols, by their definition, are also stand-ins for additional context, doing double and triple duty, and they help the author distill their text down on subsequent rewrites. See chapter 19, "Layering," for more detail.

Remember: Novelists obfuscate; readers investigate.

Tool Seven: Rewrite

A powerful tool in determining how the author has put an element to use is to imagine how you'd write it differently. Pause to notice how the author directed your thinking or planted clues. Then consider what you would do next if you were the author. If you have a vague feeling that something must happen, go back and find the moment that thought first occurred to you.

What an author omits from the text is as important (if not more so) than what's on the page, so another great rewrite trick is to fill in what's missing. Consider what has been left unsaid, left undone, a path not taken, or a chunk of time skipped. Imagine how you'd fill in the gaps and you'll have a better understanding of what is in the text and why those gaps exist.

In our novel discussion group, my heart leaps for joy any time one of us says, "Here's how I would have rewritten this...." That's the clearest indication that they have internalized their reading and are applying it to their own writing. They've done it. They're reading like writers.

Seven Tools

Phew—that was a lot to absorb, especially if you're new to reading like a writer. Here are the **Three keys** and **Seven tools** at a glance so you can refer to them later:

Every novel contains the **Three keys**:

- **Inciting-midpoint-climax**
- **Unspoken contract**
- **Everything serves a purpose**

Seven tools of inquiry that derive from the **Three keys** are:

- **Use structure to identify themes**
- **Assume you're being played**
- **Pay attention to POV**
- **What happens is not what's discussed**
- **Always ask why**
- **Reread**
- **Rewrite**

But if you remember only one of these, make sure that it's the most important tool of them all, the **First rule of *Literary Forensics*: Always ask why.**

Notes

1. By this point I've already thrown around a lot of terms you may be unfamiliar with. Don't panic! I've provided you with definitions for the dozens of terms you'll need to know in the glossary, including the **First Rule**, the **Three Keys**, and all the other things I want you to remember. Check 'em out.
2. The complete definition of what constitutes a novel is an essential part of chapter 22, "Other Narrative Forms," in which we consider how those other forms *differ* from the novel.
3. Chuck Wendig bundles these questions into a concept he calls question-driven plotting and identifies them as essential to storytelling. In his craft book, *Damn Fine Story*, Wendig writes, "Questions are the food that feeds the audience. Or, to be more precise: Answers feed the audience, and questions keep them hungry."
4. Actually, the average length of a movie release in the US in 2023 was closer to two hours and twenty-three minutes. Reasons why movies seem to be getting longer are discussed here: https://www.vox.com/culture/24156463/movies-albums-long-songs-scenes-short

Getting Started

Now that you're ready to use *Literary Forensics* as your guidebook to reading like a writer, where do you begin? The answer will be unique to you. Every one of us approaches reading from a different level, with different skills and experiences, so your path will have to be your own. The freedom to choose your own adventure may seem daunting at first, so here are a few common paths to help you get started.

You may opt to dive right in to reading your next novel like a writer without any further preparation. For some people, jumping into the deep end is an excellent way to learn how to swim. As you read, remember the **First rule of *Literary Forensics*: Always ask why**—and the **Three keys** present in every novel: **inciting-midpoint-climax**, the **unspoken contract**, and **everything serves a purpose**. If that's too much to think about at once, don't worry. **Always ask why** is enough to get started. Any time you find something unusual, out of place, or missing, you suspect you're being played, or you find a scene with no purpose or a "rule" seemingly broken, pause, and read the passage again. Begin digging. How do you feel? What did you discover? What do you suspect? What do you think will happen next? Once you've identified what caused you to stop reading, go to the corresponding chapter and work through the exercises. Continue reading your novel, pause, question, and repeat.

But what if you're having trouble hitting pause on your reading?

If getting swept away by the writing is preventing you from getting into critical discovery mode, chapter 2, "How You Read," and chapter 11, "You're Engaged," both go into more detail on methods of reading. The exercises you find there will help you break the spell of passive reading.

Or you may want to take a more measured approach, by studying the methodology first and fully preparing yourself before you read your next novel. Beginning with chapter 1, "Your Point of Reference," and continuing through the five chapters in the WHAT YOU BRING section would be an excellent starting point. Your introspection will give you so much more than just self-knowledge and awareness. Chapters 4 and 5 contain discussions about reading that relate directly to your own writing and what's appropriate to the contemporary novel.

Not sure which novel to read next? Chapter 3, "Choosing What to Read," offers lots of ideas, some that may surprise you. Although this is a book about novels, chapter 22, "Other Narrative Forms," reminds us that we can also apply *Literary Forensics* to whatever narrative we read. Remember this: Writing insights can be gained from any book, so genre, length, or even the quality of the writing doesn't matter.

Or you may consider joining a study group so you can read along with a group of fellow writers. You can follow an agenda similar to that at every *Writers Who Read LIVE!* study group, which is covered in depth in chapter 25, "Your Own Study Group." It follows the four stages of discovery: We first consider WHAT YOU BRING, then WHAT YOU FEEL, NOTICE, and DISCOVER, in that order. But even on your own, you can find inspiration from our group by listening to any episode of our *Writers Who Read* podcast from the comfort of your own home.

The goal of all of these paths is for you to read with intent, to get into the habit of asking *why* instead of reading passively, to thoroughly investigate the text wherever the spirit leads you, and to always keep your eyes open for the unexpected insight.

Well, that's it for the basics—you've completed the introduction to *Literary Forensics*. You're now fully equipped to take advantage of the rest of this book, as you practice reading like a writer.

Happy sleuthing!

WHAT YOU BRING

1
Your Point of Reference

The unexamined life is not worth living.
—*Socrates*

We are all unique individuals, which makes us all unique readers. And because everyone internalizes literature differently, it's important to recognize that positionality—where we stand, shaped by factors like race, gender, and class—inevitably influences our interpretations and conclusions. For example, you may favor or avoid certain genres. You may be writing a novel in one of these genres now. You may know something about the author or the subject matter that colors your reading or causes you to get stuck in your reading, glossing over the actual text instead of digging in. Or your unfamiliarity with a culture, a worldview, or a lifestyle may constitute a bias you bring to your reading on one of these topics.

When our *Writers Who Read* study group meets to explore a novel, before we discuss the book, we introduce ourselves by saying what we thought about the novel *before* we started reading it. We acknowledge *what we bring* to our reading, and it makes for a richer discussion.[1]

Biases are multidimensional and almost infinite in number. Our biases reflect the society within which we were raised, how we were educated, our personal experiences, and to some extent the DNA of how our brains absorb information and how we perceive the world. We all have biases. Our preconceptions and assumptions and reactions to past experiences are part of what makes us who we are. And when discussing literature with others, the way each of us has a unique response and reaction to the text makes our communication that much richer and more insightful.

I'm always tickled when a native English speaker says, "I don't have an accent." It's this point of view, the *I'm normal, and everyone else talks funny*, that exposes a lack of self-awareness. Without being able to notice one's own quirks and biases, we find conversations about the merits of literature devolving into argument. Because our examination of novels is predicated on being as clear-eyed as possible, it's necessary to lay all our weapons on the table before we begin so that we don't accidentally shoot one another (or ourselves in the foot) with our preconceptions.

I'm not suggesting that you eliminate your biases—which is impossible—but rather that you notice and acknowledge them. It's an essential first step in learning how to read like a writer. Just like the astronomer who needs to compensate for the fact they are standing on a spinning Earth in a remote corner of the universe, you need to know exactly how your biases tilt your point of view, so when you encounter unfamiliar or uncomfortable writing, you will be better able to course-correct and see the author closer to where they are.

Understanding who you are and what baggage you bring to a text is the critical first stage of discovery in *Literary Forensics*. Learning how to recognize the biases you bring to a text and how to overcome them is the purpose of this chapter.

Eisegesis

You may be familiar with the term *exegesis*.[2] It's routinely applied to the study of religious texts, but it really means a critical explication or interpretation of *any* text. *Eisegesis*, on the other hand, is what happens when you interpret a text to conform to your biases. It's also called "reading into the text." When this occurs, you may experience confirmation bias and find in your reading the "proof" you sought with regard to an intellectual theory, a political movement, or a current life issue, whether or not that topic is actually covered in the novel. All of us read our own experiences into text—we can't avoid it. But why?

We do it because the author invites us to do so.

That's how fiction works. An author sketches a scene on the page but cannot possibly fill in every visual aspect for you; a novel is not a movie. So unless you suffer from aphantasia—the inability to see things in your mind's eye—you generate a movie of the novel you're reading in your own imagination. And, quite naturally, you populate scenes with people, places, and things from your life and the movies you've watched. We all fill in the narrative gaps with archetypes. Is a character scatterbrained? We reach for a stereotype. Are they lazy, dishonest, deceitful, manipulative? Ditto.

You can't help but interject your own experiences into the novels you read. It's part of the natural process of absorbing and internalizing. But you need to be aware that you're doing it. And through your awareness you will observe when you start adding elements that don't belong there. Permit me to modify St. Augustine's most famous quote about moderation to my purposes for my thesis statement:

We seek moderation in all things in order to be free of **eisegeses** *that prevent us from being free to* **observe author and novel**.[3]

Here's an example of eisegesis from my study group's reading of Gail Honeyman's *Eleanor Oliphant Is Completely Fine*. You may encounter something similar to this in your own reading.

It doesn't take an MFA to guess that the title is hyperbolic and that Eleanor is actually the opposite of *completely fine*. But what ails her? Eleanor has led a challenging life with a specific traumatic event that is pivotal to the plot. (No spoilers here.) I interpreted her behavior as exhibiting signs of PTSD. Two members of my reading group who have children on the autism spectrum interpreted Eleanor's behavior as evidence of autism, however. I could not find anything within the text to confirm that Honeyman intended her main character to have autism. In fact, Honeyman said in interviews she was inspired to write her novel on the theme of crushing loneliness. Eleanor had a tragic life and experienced pain that was difficult to bear, so she shut herself off from the world. Because of that she has difficulty making friends. But inferring that the character has autism is an eisegetical reading of the text.

The remainder of this chapter covers how you can approach reading novels and avoid eisegesis. The goal is to arm you with a practical framework that you can use every day. Here we cover:

- **Self-assessment**: Identifying what you bring to your reading
- **Horizon of expectation:** Recognizing how the literary canon, multiculturalism, and marketing influence your responses to a novel
- **Contextual awareness:** Understanding why your interpretation of any text will be unique to you

Self-Assessment

The first step toward self-awareness is to take an inventory of your background, your experiences, and your personal baggage—everything that made you who you are today. The exercise at the end of this section is one of the most important in the entire book, and I hope you do it.

I don't want you to feel squeamish about doing a little self-examination. This isn't some wishy-washy New-Age pseudoscience I'm proposing here. Performing a self-assessment in relation to literary analysis actually has many decades of solid academic literary theory behind it, which I describe in greater detail in chapter 23, "Academic Disciplines."

Although we all have individual histories that have given us our biases, here are some things we share: We all have a gender (or not). We all have opinions about postcolonial theory, and if we are Americans, we must also consider African American history and our current collective culture. The same with feminism, LGBTQ+ issues, and politics. Some of us have more than opinions—that is, we may have experienced others' biases *as members* of one or more of these groups. I believe that you ignore these topics at your own peril as you attempt to open yourself to receive any novel you want to read and to understand.

Inventory

I ask you to be honest with yourself when you do your own personal inventory, and because I won't make you do anything that I haven't done, below are my personal biases.

I'm a white, cisgender, heterosexual American male. Through my father's family, my surname was brought over to the colonies before the Revolutionary War from my Scots-Irish ancestors. As such, some of my forefathers had direct contact with the slave trade, and have benefited from that American brand of colonialism. Through my mother's family I also have nineteenth-century Swiss-German heritage. I was raised Lutheran but am now an atheist. I have a university degree, but not an advanced one. I have worked for a few decades in the IT industry as a coder and now as a data scientist, so I have a near-obsessive appetite for quantitative and qualitative precision.

Although I once harbored conservative views, I have since encountered many different cultures through my travels, my music-making, and my work. Now I skew liberal, and I consider myself a feminist. I try my earnest best to meet everyone at their level, and my sincerest wish is to play nice with whomever I meet. But I am flawed. I have my biases. I can't help it. So I do what I can to self-correct when I read fiction critically.

Remember that the ideas expressed in this book are better than their author. I detailed my origins with a single purpose in mind: to give you an example of what I hope you will try for yourself in the exercise that follows.

What you bring to your reading

While examining your life in general is of obvious value, learning to apply more specific self-examination to your reading is the focus of the entire WHAT YOU BRING section. Every time *Writers Who Read* study a new novel, each of us takes stock of the baggage we bring to that specific book. In that spirit, I'll share what I bring to *Eleanor Oliphant*.

Honeyman's novel is set in Scotland, where I have ancestors, and where I've worked and vacationed numerous times. It was originally targeted for a UK audience and I've lived in England, so I feel I have some insight into the culture. I have experienced feeling like an outsider in an office setting, and although I've never suffered from disfiguration or full-blown PTSD, I have known stress and trauma. My parents died a few decades ago, and so I know what it feels like to lose them, although I was an adult when that happened and I have never been in foster care, nor have I been a ward of the state. I enjoy reading mass-market fiction and literary fiction—I feel this book crosses over into both—but because this was Honeyman's debut novel, I had not read her writing before this.

That covers my relationship to the author, the novel's setting and themes, stylistic treatment, and genre.

EXERCISE 1

Reflect on yourself in relation to the novel you are now reading. What baggage do you bring to this book? What expectations, what life experience, and what biases? Identify yourself, as accurately as you can. Take your time and maybe write down your self-assessment, as I have done. Reflect on assumptions you might be making about the author based on their age, their race, where they grew up, or their social status.

Horizon of Expectations

The horizon of expectations is what you perceive the novel to be about, before reading even a single word, and it will certainly influence the way you investigate the text. A more academic description: The horizon of expectations is the "set of cultural norms, assumptions, and criteria shaping the way in which readers understand and judge a literary work at a given time,"[4] and it refers to the set of expectations you bring to a text based on your prior knowledge and life experiences.

This concept, developed by philosopher Hans Robert Jauss and fundamental to his reception theory, suggests that readers interpret and evaluate a work through the lens of these expectations, which evolve as we encounter new genres or styles.

Authors may play with or subvert these expectations to surprise or challenge you, often creating deeper meanings or new interpretations of the text. Contributing factors include:

- The canon
- Multiculturalism
- Marketing

The canon

The pantheon of Great Writers and their Masterworks was, until fairly recently, populated almost exclusively by dead white guys. From Plato to Shakespeare to Philip Roth, the canon was faithfully taught in university programs across the United States. The most recent academic to promote the hegemony of the canon was Harold Bloom in *The Western Canon* and later, *The American Canon*. Who determined which works were included in this canon, and who chose which authors were so honored? Bloom did—Bloom and a host of other white guys before him. For the last few centuries, our society tacitly accepted that the experts know what is beneficial for us to read better than we do ourselves.

The situation has improved greatly with the rise of female writers and people of color taking their rightful positions in our largest publishing houses and universities. The path to publication has widened to a larger number of authors who are—and always have been—as good or even better than their white male contemporaries. So let's address the persistent shadows cast by academic gatekeepers and the power of the Master of Fine Arts degree.

One member of my reading group is not only a wonderful visual artist but also a gifted storyteller and podcaster. Their mastery of the story form is clearly evident in every episode they narrate, edit, and produce by themselves. And yet, when analyzing works of literature, they qualify their response with a "Well, I didn't go to college, so I probably don't get it." My wife, who has zero musical training, has just as good an ear for music as I do, a conservatory-trained musician. Nevertheless, the influence of the academic pedigree and the authority of the so-called literary canon remain long and imposing. These continue to influence how many of us receive and perceive novels we are *supposed* to like and understand but somehow don't.

To that I say, life is short. Read the books that bring *you* insight and fulfillment. You do you; don't worry about advanced degrees and the "accepted" canon. After all, we writers are artisans, and wherever we are, each of us must still put in the thousands of hours of hard work.

Multiculturalism

In the centuries before the airplane and the Internet, people weren't as mobile, and it could take decades for their ideas to circulate farther than a few miles from their origin. Writers could be confident in their audience's worldview, education, and cultural norms. The myth of a common readership existing somewhere out there persisted long after novels could be distributed widely and quickly.

That world is gone.

Modern culture is no longer a common culture, and the good news is that different voices are finally being heard. The bad news is that, accelerated by social media, we often find ourselves in balkanized enclaves of like-minded readers. What in the past was thought of as common knowledge or common sense is no longer common to all readers in a culture, community, or even group.

Tommy Orange, in his 2018 novel *There There,* describes the lives of a dozen Native Americans on their way to a powwow in Oakland, California. Orange cannot be certain that every reader would know that thousands of his ancestors were massacred by white settlers, or that the white man's hegemony over the native continues to this day. Orange opens his novel with an entire section dedicated to relating this history, and in this way sets the table for his masterful story. He does it again at the midpoint to ensure that no reader can forget it. The presence of these explanatory sections are a direct result of present-day multiculturalism.

What Orange is doing to curate our horizon of expectations is to relieve the reader of the burden of having to research the time, place, and cultural norms necessary to understand the themes of his novel.

Marketing

How do you appraise a novel, even before you open it and read it? Don't tell me you don't do this. Despite the adage, we all judge books by their covers.

You can't help being heavily influenced by a book's packaging, its shelf place-ment, or that review you read in the *New York Times* or *Kirkus Reviews*. That is to say, your initial introduction to the book you are about to read is a product of the publisher's marketing campaign. Another way you are influenced could be through the recommendation of a trusted friend. But how did *they* first encounter this novel? Most likely also through some aspect of marketing.

You cannot escape the capitalist marketing machine—it is a ubiquitous and necessary evil if you want to be sure that authors get paid to continue writing books. But this marketing comes with a price, which is that it ignores the idea that every work of fiction is unique.

Part of the marketing is to cover a book with art that evokes a certain sentiment so that readers will self-select what they find most appealing. Unfortunately, this means that sometimes the cover is misleading. Bonnie Garmus complained about the US publisher's romance-inspired cover of her 2022 novel *Lessons in Chemistry*; she felt the image detracted from its main theme, female empowerment.[5]

Another aspect of marketing is to tag a novel with a variety of categories, simply to make it easier to shelve with other books in the same category. For online booksellers, these tags drive the search algorithms that lead shoppers from one book to another. This may position a title in a way that doesn't represent what it's about or makes it difficult to find.

The final aspects of marketing are the book blurb and the critic's review, which further induce potential readers to believe that they will find a certain something within the book, whether it's there or not. All marketing relies on the same psychology that drives our decision making, a notion explored in greater depth in chapter 3, "Choosing What to Read."

EXERCISE 2

Pick a novel you haven't read and take a look at it online or in a bookstore. What do you think you know about this book, and how did you learn it? Would you like to read it? Why? Or if the book doesn't appeal to you at all, why not? What aspects or features influence your feelings and decisions about whether to read it? Your answers may also reveal your own tastes and biases.

Contextual Awareness

John Cage's *4'33"* is a piece of classical music for solo piano that has flummoxed audiences for decades. To perform it, a pianist walks onstage, receives the audience's applause, sits down at the piano ready to play, and then, for the next four and a half minutes… does nothing. The pianist then indicates that the performance has ended by standing up, taking a bow (to applause or stunned silence), and exiting the stage.

What just happened? Cage was making the point that no piece of music is enjoyed in a vacuum, and by forcing an audience to deal uncomfortably with silence from the stage, the hope is that they will notice all of the external noises, fidgeting audience members, and other ambient sounds that are present in every performance of every piece of music.

The same is true with the way you receive a novel. Although you may try to focus on the text, your brain is constantly churning. You try to get into the zone of the story, but perhaps you're distracted by your children, that chore you're putting off, the unresolved work issue, and other forms of background noise. These things absolutely influence your point of reference, whether you realize it or not, and it's important to acknowledge them.

Your perception of a novel is always in relation to the world around you, which changes over time, just like you do. Some books I enjoyed in my youth now seem trite; my perspective has shifted. Novels I found life-changing in my twenties have been become part of my consciousness, and they never land quite the same way when I reread them.

A number of people read J.R.R. Tolkien's *The Lord of the Rings* every year. Others annually reread[6] *The Immortals Quartet* by Tamora Pierce, or Bram Stoker's *Dracula*, or *The Book Thief* by Markus Zusak. Rereading can bring you back to your happy place, but it also can provide you with something new to discover within a cherished work. Of course it's not the book that's changed; it's you and your awareness of the world you live in.

Interpretation

Emojis exist for an important reason, and that is: Writing, especially the casual type of writing found in an email or text, is open to an amazing array of interpretations. Emojis help the writer set the intended tone. Because novels are also dependent upon a reader's approach to the written world, they too are open to many different interpretations.

The novelist writes to connect with readers by hoping they will understand their words, feel the emotions they hoped to invoke, and internalize the themes they explored. But sometimes readers reinterpret the text, experience feelings the author never intended, and veer off on tangents of their own, widening the gap between author and reader. Novels translated from different languages suffer from additional encodings and decodings on their journey from author to reader. Much like a game of Telephone, the author's intent and message is almost certain to have been garbled by the time it reaches you.

These mismatches are the result of incongruous points of reference between writer and reader. Notice how a variety of points of view affects the production of stage plays.

> Each audience member will view the action of a play through the lens of his or her personality, beliefs, experience, and culture.... The best theatre thrives on ambiguity, not certainty; it succeeds by prompting or provoking audience members to ask questions, rather than by convincing them to accept the artists' predetermined answers.
> —*Robert Knopf*, Script Analysis for Theatre

Ambiguities are unavoidable when a story is translated from the page to the stage, just as when a novel migrates from the author's pen, through the gauntlet of editors, publicists, and critics, and into the reader's hands. Partially because of the inevitable variability of interpretations, the most reliable goal of any narrative form is not to indoctrinate or educate, but rather to help its audience have an *experience* that they can share with each other.

How you experience a novel and how you translate a novel's world into something that holds meaning for you is unique to you. It's important to remember that even if others relate experiences that are similar to yours, they are not *exactly* your experiences. Your interpretation of what you read is yours and yours alone, and that's what makes reading novels such a powerful tool for personal introspection.

EXERCISE 3

What do you look for in the novels you read? Entertainment? Enlightenment? How do you feel about stories that don't end with a bang? Are you okay with novels that are about an idea and end ambiguously? How important do you think characterization is to storytelling? Think about what range of storytelling feels "acceptable" to you, and what falls outside those boundaries. Would you be willing to experience other genres you're unfamiliar with?

Think about any book you're reading, or are considering reading (or definitely are *not* going to read). What parameters do you accept, and which are turnoffs? And most importantly, what do those choices say about *you*?

Notes

1. For the complete agenda of our monthly *Writers Who Read LIVE* meetings, see chapter 25, "Your Own Study Group."

2. You will find a definition of *exegesis* in the glossary at the back of this book, which includes more terms used in *Literary Forensics*.

3. St. Augustine's original quote (translated from the original Latin) is, "We seek moderation in all things to be free of attachments that prevent us from being free to serve God and neighbor."

4. Chris Baldick, "horizon of expectations," in *The Oxford Dictionary of Literary Terms*, 4th ed., (Oxford University Press, UK, 2015).

5. Readers complained when the protagonist's love interest made an exit early in the novel. Their expectations of a romance were thwarted because of the book's misleading cover.

6. https://www.reddit.com/r/booksuggestions/comments/gms5za/whats_that_one_book_you_have_to_reread_every_year/

2
How You Read

Hermes was an ancient Greek deity—the one with the winged sandals—who was the messenger of the gods. According to myth, Hermes also invented language and speech. Being a wily ambassador, he was also an interpreter, a trickster, and a liar.[1] To me he sounds like the ultimate novelist.[2] We should all aspire to be as clever as Hermes, whose name forms the root of the word used to describe the theory and methodology of interpretation: *hermeneutics*.

Analyzing how we read is almost as old as the written word itself. Aristotle's *On Interpretation* covers the basics: identifying parts of speech, affirmations and negations, and then the logical or rhetorical inferences that can be made with the piece parts. Aristotle's text takes less than an hour to consume, and it does not cover anything more than the basic grammar and syntax typically taught in elementary school.[3] I assume you already know the basics of language—after all, you're reading these words, so let's move on.

Modern hermeneutics includes the study of verbal and textual communication (covered here), presuppositions (covered in chapter 1, "Your Point of Reference"), and semiotics (the study of signs and symbols, covered in chapter 19, "Layering"). For this chapter, let's take a closer look at four key elements of textual communication—how you read—which may lead you to very different interpretations of the same text:

- **Intention**: Why you read
- **Distance**: How carefully you read
- **Cadence**: When you read
- **Resistance**: Internalizing what you read

And to illustrate the nuances within these different types of reading, I'll use as my source text a Bjørk sofa assembly instruction manual.

Intention

In his classic text *How to Read a Book*,[4] Mortimer Adler describes four levels of reading:

1. **Elementary:** Using the basics of vocabulary and grammar, similar to what Aristotle's *On Interpretation* covers
2. **Inspectional:** A quick scan
3. **Analytical:** The focus of this chapter, section, and most of this book
4. **Syntopical:** Using other books to supplement what you read[5]

Each of these levels describes *how* you approach a text, and implicit within each of these definitions is *why* you would read in this way.

Inspectional reading

Say your intention is to assemble a Bjørk sofa. At some point, you may have decided this will be an easy task, so you barely glance at the instruction manual's hieroglyphics before applying the hex wrench to your creation.

As Adler mentions in his book, inspectional reading is a quick scan of the text that does not engage one's critical faculties. If you read novels for pleasure, your conscious mind flits over the surface of the text, taking in just enough to grasp the plot without pausing to ponder any deeper meaning. You're on a fun ride, and if words you don't fully understand fly by, it feels like a drag to pause the ride and find a dictionary. Ugh.

This surface-skimming method of reading a novel may also serve you on your first pass (as it does me), as you glean the overall structure and key emotional beats. But this method of reading won't teach you how to write. For that, you'll need a second, more analytical reading.

Back to our Bjørk sofa. It's not going well, as you can imagine.

Analytical reading

You disconnect the sofa's Part A from Assembly F and lay all the pieces on the floor. Perhaps it's time to analyze all the components before you begin again.

Has a text ever left you stumped? Has it challenged your assumptions about what you thought you knew? If so, you've just moved beyond inspectional to the realm of analytical reading, which forms the core of *Literary Forensics*. Two entire sections of this book, WHAT YOU FEEL and WHAT YOU NOTICE, are based on understanding what analytical reading is and how it works.

You analyze the text in order to grasp its deeper meaning, and in doing so you learn new things. As when you assemble a sofa, you read a text with an analytical mindset because you're doing it to learn. Your reading has a purpose.[6]

Syntopical reading

It turns out that while you've been focused on our Bjørk sofa, you should have been paying closer attention to your cat, who was swiping at the nuts and bolts. You've lost a few key parts and now must visit the hardware store to buy new ones.

Syntopical reading, as described by Adler, is using outside texts and resources to further enhance our understanding of the text at hand: looking up unfamiliar words in a dictionary, searching the Internet for external references, or, like me writing this book, following the rabbit holes of research to find original sources of information.

In my preparations for leading my monthly book group, I often consult online author interviews, articles, or even entire topics the author has referenced that I'm unfamiliar with, all to understand the author's perspective, and, by extension, their novel's inner workings. Because it is so useful for writers who read, I have included an entire section in this book dedicated to syntopical reading: WHAT YOU STUDY.

EXERCISE 1

Think about the novel you have just finished reading, or one you're now reading. How in-depth was your reading? Did it stay at an inspectional level, or did you dig deeper, looking up words, phrases, or cultural references? Did you find any recurring themes? Did you wonder why the author wrote the novel? Were you struck by the language—a turn of phrase or a poetic sentence?

Do you mark up your books in the margins or take notes? If not, why not? Are you reading purely for pleasure, or do you intend to use the book you've just read as a study guide? And if so, do you think that your level of reading matches your intentions?

Distance

From this point on, I will assume your reading intention is analytical. Let's consider different perspectives on analytical reading, from close to distant.

Close reading

Close reading arose in 1920s Britain as a new technique to study fiction, replacing the impressionistic view of literature dominant at the time with close attention to word selection, syntax, and the ordering of ideas. By the 1930s these techniques had crossed the Atlantic, and America's New Critics were also using them to study authorial intention, cultural contexts, and ideology.[7] Close reading is, today, the standard for analyzing text within the contexts of academic research and literary criticism. One of the most frequent questions I get when describing *Literary Forensics* to a civilian is: Isn't that just close reading?

Well, not quite.

Close reading's original primary goal, through uncovering the *meaning* of a text and the *intention* of its author, was to evaluate its *merit*. Most academic literature on the subject of close reading today is focused on instructing elementary- and secondary-school English teachers to teach how to read for *comprehension*,[8] because every scholar must be able to read analytically to be able to further their own education.

Literary Forensics uses close reading as a means to unravel the author's artifice, and so to uncover the structures and techniques contained within. Our goal is not to judge but to observe and to probe. And although it is certainly a useful technique, close reading alone is insufficient for our wide-ranging investigations.

As we look again at our Bjørk sofa's instruction manual, we begin to notice the subtle differences between Parts F, G, and H and their variously sized connector bolts. We reflect on each piece as we investigate its purpose. Surely close reading alone is what we need to understand our sofa's construction, right?

Nope. Not even close.[9]

Distant reading

And along came the post-structuralists.

Up until the 1960s and 1970s, the literary canon was considered to comprise perfectly-formed expressions of Art—pearls of wisdom to be carefully studied and emulated. By the end of the twentieth century, however, the focus of literary theory shifted toward analyzing texts through cultural and political lenses. No longer considered in isolation, novels were evaluated by their subjectivity, their authors' identities, and their portrayals of worldly power and knowledge. All works were being considered in relation to the real world outside the text.

A new focus on critical reading was proposed by Franco Moretti in 2000: distant reading.

> Distant reading: where distance... is a condition of knowledge: it allows you to focus on units that are much smaller or much larger than the text: devices, themes, tropes—or genres and systems.
> —*Franco Moretti,* Conjectures on World Literature

Close reading was myopic in both its granular treatment of text and the narrow band of "acceptable" texts worthy of study. Subsequent literary theories such as semiotics, New Historicism, deconstructionism, feminism, critical race theory, postcolonial criticism, and queer theory blew the doors off stodgy New Criticism and its ancient canon and opened up *all* texts to serious criticism.

Through this plethora of poststructuralist disciplines, micro-, macro-, and meta-perspectives are now an essential part of any serious literary inquiry. Hence, distant reading.

Let's turn back to your Bjørk sofa. Having laid all the pieces on the floor, you begin to see patterns in the number and size of the parts, and you realize that only a certain number of configurations make sense. Some parts have been mislabeled, and when you turn to the last page of the instruction manual, you discover why: Every word was translated into English from the original Norwegian by a Chinese company.

Close and distant reading

Close reading is still a very valuable discipline that you can use to dissect novels *for the purposes of reading like a writer*. Distant reading introduces the idea that no text can exist in a vacuum and that its position within its culture must also be considered when evaluating it. But even with distant reading, *Literary Forensics* is not concerned with passing judgment on novels, nor is it a goal that you become a literary critic.

You should however be keenly interested in observing what's happening between the covers and in positioning the text within the real world so that you can discover techniques you can use in your own writing.

EXERCISE 2

Reread: Pick any spot in a novel you're reading now. Analyze one paragraph, paying close attention to who is addressing you, the reader, and what *exactly* they are saying. Is it a bit of dialogue? Narrative? Action? Backstory? What is being communicated, and what exact words were chosen to convey it? Is it in the voice of the author or indicative of their specific culture?

Rewrite: Now consider when the author wrote their book. When—in what year or decade—was it published? What is it about the text that pins it to its time and place? Is it the vocabulary, situations, relationships, or are there other cultural markers? Could it have been written the same way today?

Cadence

Reading, because we control it, is adaptable to our needs and rhythms.
  —*Sven Birkerts*, The Gutenberg Elegies[10]

This and the following sections are about the decisions you make when you read a novel. You may pore over every word or you may skip entire sections. You may read in short bursts or long stretches, and you may pause your reading frequently or stop only at the end of a chapter or section. You may begin many novels you do not finish, or consume two or three at once, switching between them.

These choices determine how these stories interact with your conscious and subconscious brain, and how easy or how challenging you make it to learn anything from the text.

When and how

We all have circadian rhythms that affect when our bodies find it most natural to wake up, take our meals, crave exercise, and feel peak mental freshness. When I was younger, my peak mental hours were from 10 a.m. to 2 p.m. Because I was practicing to become a concert pianist, I scheduled my most difficult study between those hours. These days my most strenuous mental activity is writing this book, and I find that it requires a more pliable brain—something that occurs naturally for me between 5 a.m. and 9 a.m. (It's 6:30 a.m. on a Sunday as I write this.)

The activity determines the appropriate timing. Think about when you get hungry. That's your body craving food. But other parts of our bodies need to be fed, too. And the brain craves mental challenges just as much as the stomach craves food.

If you have a job, think about what your brain craves after a stressful day at work: mental and emotional rest. Many of us turn to the TV at that time as a way to relax and quiet our brains. If you choose to read when you are emotionally drained, your reading may be inspectional at best.

I prefer to do my critical reading in the evening, after the cares of the day have faded somewhat. I relish stepping into a different world for a while, and even if I'm reading critically, it somehow calms my brain. When I was younger, I could read until dawn. Lately, I'm lucky to get through an entire chapter before I get sleepy, because I like to read in bed. If instead I read in a comfortable chair, even having the same energy level, and at the same time of day, I tend not to fall asleep. (Go figure.)

Be aware of when and how you choose to read, especially if you're trying to use a novel as a textbook. Remember to use good posture and proper lighting, stay hydrated, and try reading in short bursts or take short breaks. Study requires a significant amount of brain power, so prepare yourself accordingly.

The Bjørk sofa instruction manual has now been repurposed as a cocktail coaster on your nightstand. Perhaps you'll read it tomorrow.

Optimum cadence

For some of us, the times when we can read and how we read are dictated by our schedules. The office worker may read on a lunch break; work-from-home parents may be able to carve out time only when their children are engaged in other activities; or perhaps you crave a good book after exercise or a meal.

Regardless of your situation, notice the amount of time you've budgeted to read, and how much reading you accomplish before you set the book down and return to your real life. Some of us can read for hours at a stretch; others in fifteen-minute sprints. The brain also needs to take a break periodically. I have an e-reader that interrupts me after an hour with a one-minute countdown timer that obscures the screen, reminding me to look away and refocus my eyes.

I suggest taking note of your own reading habits so you can learn how your brain reacts to books. Try to increase the percentage of your time spent in close reading, which is more beneficial to your studies and ultimately a more efficient use of your time.

Hitting pause

The most useful feature of my TV remote is the pause button. I stream every movie and TV show I watch, so I can pause a video drama exactly as I would set down a book to ponder it or set it aside for a while.

George Saunders, in his informative book on reading and writing, *A Swim in a Pond in the Rain*,[11] recommends hitting pause after reading the first page of a story, and periodically thereafter. The purpose of these pauses is to take a breath, give your brain a chance to absorb what you've just read, and begin to ask the essential questions:

- What just happened?
- How do I feel about it?
- What do I think will happen next?

It's easy and fun to practice this skill while streaming TV and movies, and my wife and I do this now, almost every time we watch something together. We pause in the middle of a scene and ask: What is this scene's function—why is it here? Then we make predictions: What happens next? What obstacles will befall this character? And in doing so, while we play this game, we briefly become writers ourselves. When we resume the video, we see whether we were right. (I admit that my wife is much, much better at this than I am—and she's not even trying to become a writer.)

Another good reason to take your novel reading in doses rather than continuously has to do with our natural inclination to skip things and fill gaps using our imaginations. We start doing this as children. Unable to understand the world, our young brains invent answers. The game of peek-a-boo is compelling to a toddler because they haven't yet grasped the idea that when something is out of view, it's actually still there. Closing one's eyes means the rest of the world has ceased to exist.

We fall into that pattern so easily if we skip over words, get bored, and move ahead a few pages without realizing that we may have missed something critically important. We're playing peek-a-boo with a novel.

Here's another way to hit pause: by reading the text aloud. Your internal reading voice is simply not as judgmental as your ears, and when you vocalize the words on the page, you can better appraise their content, intent, smoothness/awkwardness, and meaning.

Hitting the pause button frequently this way in your reading serves to negate that childish impulse of clumsy invention, and instead forces you to register what has just happened and engages your imagination like a writer to think through the narrative logically. Are you able to pause your reading at will? It's an important skill to cultivate as you learn to read like a writer, and you can find exercises to help you learn how in chapter 11, "You're Engaged."

You've decided to resume work on your Bjørk sofa over the weekend after you've had a few days to calm down and refocus.

Finishing the book

I used to read four or five books at once. I'd start one, get distracted or bored, pick up another for a while, then go to another. Sometimes I let so much time lapse between reading sessions that when I picked up a neglected book, I had forgotten many of its salient points. I'd have to go back five or ten pages to get a rolling start, and sometimes I'd have to read it again from page one. I left many, many books unfinished.

If you read multiple books at once, I'm not suggesting that you change your ways. But I don't do that anymore, and here's why: Finishing a book is more important to me now than finding it interesting. I'll explain.

Before I cared about using novels as a way to learn writing, I read mostly for fun. Even if the text was challenging (like Faulkner's *The Sound and the Fury* or Joyce's *Ulysses*), I felt intellectually satisfied by completing it. But I'd abandon any text that wasn't in the literary canon and therefore wasn't explicitly "good for me" if it didn't capture my fancy.

No more.

Even with a novel that I'm not excited by, I will read it to its conclusion because today I am just as interested in the entire shape of the story as I am in the plot and the characters. If you don't finish the novels you read, I'll bet you're less likely to finish writing your own, if only because you haven't read as many endings.

In other words, the more novels you finish reading, the more data points you get on how novels are completed, which may further inspire you to push on to the end of that ugly first draft.[12]

By the way, congratulations on refocusing your efforts on fully understanding what you've read and applying that knowledge to finishing your task. As it happens, you're reading these words from the comfort of your brand-new Bjørk sofa! So stylish.

EXERCISE 3

When do you like to read, and for how long? Do you make it to the end of a chapter or section before you set the book down? Do you find yourself pausing for days, and then having to turn back a few pages to pick up any confusing threads? What and where would be your ideal reading time and place?

Do you finish every novel you start reading? If not, pick your current favorite and try reading all the way to the end. Did reading all of it teach you anything new about form?

Rewrite: How often do you pause and ponder what might come next? Try this with something you're reading now, and ask yourself one more question: If I could finish writing this paragraph (or chapter or book), where would I take the story?

Resistance

I'll admit that I'm one of the worst people to sit next to at the theater, because I want everyone to be as invested in the performance as I am. Because it takes some effort for me to suspend disbelief and get swept away by whatever is being presented on the stage or the screen, I resent interruptions created by other patrons who are just not that into it. I *want* to be carried away into whatever drama is on display. To me, that's the entire purpose of attending, and I want to get my money's worth. Why else would you be there?[13]

I know, I know. There are lots of reasons people buy tickets beyond merely enjoying a performance, but since you're here to learn to read more deeply, I ask that you consider the reader who is *not* accepting what's on the page. Let's examine mental barriers that create distance between you and a novel.

Suspending disbelief

Because I love the spectacle of live performance, movies, and novels, and I am willingly swept away, I can't watch horror films. I believe they're real, at least while I'm watching them. The horror is excruciating for me, not entertaining. I suspect that those who love horror approach their reading and viewing with some side-eye. If something gruesome can be entertaining, it follows that the reader enjoys the thrill of encountering something awful *happening to someone else* while at the same time realizing that it's not real and will not affect their lives at all. The horror has not been internalized and so can be dealt with at a distance. The distance that the viewer or the reader maintains from the source material is the flip side of suspending disbelief.

Novel reading is unique among storytelling forms in that we readers create the movie within our own brains. We are director, cameraman, lighting director, music editor, costume and set designer, makeup artist, and casting agent, all rolled into one. It's a highly personal experience and one that can bring us very close to the source material if we allow ourselves to be vulnerable and open.

But other times we are resistant to what we read. Perhaps something doesn't make sense to us or what we're reading contradicts what we believe to be possible or true, so we find the text difficult to accept. To learn more about what triggers this distance between the reader and the text, look at chapters in the section WHAT YOU FEEL.

It's our conscious engagement with the novel that is critical to our acceptance of it. We ask ourselves, consciously or not, would this character really behave in this way in this situation? And the way we judge what we read is to seek out comparable examples from our own life, or from the lives of people we know or have heard about. It's actually in our nature to resist the words we read.

> SOCRATES: How real existence is to be studied or discovered is, I suspect, beyond you and me. But we may admit so much, that the knowledge of things is not to be derived from names. No; they must be studied and investigated in themselves.
> —*Plato*, Cratylus[14]

In Plato's dialogue above, Socrates reminds us that we cannot rely on the meaning of words alone to understand the essence of a thing, and also that words "have the power to reveal, but they also conceal; speech can signify all things, but it also turns things this way and that."[15]

Every word is suspect.

Remember the ancient Greeks had language deriving from Hermes, who was a trickster and a liar. Yet Hermes also was the messenger of the gods, who occasionally delivered the truth. The lesson here is simple: Trust, but verify.[16]

Real experiences

> [T]here is a difference between inferring that something is the case and, for example, seeing it to be the case.
> —*Wilfrid Sellars*, Empiricism and the Philosophy of Mind[17]

As a young man, I realized that much of what I thought I knew about the world was what I had gathered by watching TV or movies and not from personal experience. As I got older, my life filled with more people; with a broadening range of experiences, I was able to replace my childlike peek-a-boo formulations with facts. I now wonder what my life would have been like had I not experienced so many things and met so many people. I am certain I would have been less accepting of novels containing stories that didn't align with my own.

Theory of mind is the research area that investigates folk psychological concepts for imputing mental states to others and to oneself—what we know, think, want, and feel, and what we imagine others know, think, want, and feel. Which ideas (e.g., justice, fairness, equality) have seeped into our consciousnesses because they are thought to be common knowledge or folk wisdom, and which ideas have we arrived at through our lived experiences?[18]

All the thoughts we experience or infer inform our worldview as we attempt to comprehend and interpret the written word. We absorb a novel not with a single eye, but through the filter of our multifaceted ideas and experiences, like an image refracted through a kaleidoscope. Psychological insight is therefore a useful tool for us: Readers and novelists alike benefit from the broadest possible range of understanding of the human condition, especially when it lies beyond the realm of our own lives. For example, author Eleanor Catton spent two years researching family psychology and psychopathy[19] before she wrote a word of her 2023 novel *Birnam Wood*.

Because honestly, who in their right mind would ever think that it's easy to assemble a Bjørk sofa? Not me! Not anymore.

EXERCISE 4

Reread: Pick any passage from a novel you're reading, and ask whether it relates to any of your own life experiences. Is it something you've experienced personally, or is it something you learned from a friend, or saw once in a movie? Can you quantify the distance from that passage to your own life?

Rewrite: Are you resisting what's on the page? Do you find yourself pulling away, losing interest, or actively arguing with what is written? How dissonant or consonant do you find the text? Would you have written it differently? If so, how?

Notes

1. In *Circe*, Madeline Miller's meticulously researched 2018 novel, the god Hermes is a meddling gossip. Hermes's Roman equivalent was the god Mercury.
2. This refers back to the **assume you're being played** tool described in YOUR FIRST CLUE, in which I compared a novelist to a used-car salesperson who is directing your attention toward only what they want you to see. Do you think this is a good comparison?
3. *On Interpretation* is the fourth-century BCE equivalent of Strunk & White's *Elements of Style*.
4. Mortimer J. Adler and Charles Van Doren, *How to Read a Book*, revised and updated edition (Simon and Schuster, New York, 1972).
5. This comprises the entire section WHAT YOU STUDY.
6. If you're ready to shift your reading from inspectional to analytical, then head over to chapter 11, "You're Engaged," once you've completed this chapter.
7. Gerald Graff, *Professing Literature: An Institutional History* (University of Chicago Press, Illinois, 1987).
8. One useful attribute of close reading as used in teaching pedagogy details how to annotate a text. Marking where something occurs and making notes on your thoughts and responses as you read is a valuable record of how a narrative is perceived, at least by one reader (that is, you).
9. Pun intended. Sorry.

10. Sven Birkerts, *The Gutenberg Elegies: The Fate of Reading in an Electronic Age* (Faber and Faber, Massachusetts, 1994).

11. George Saunders, *A Swim in a Pond in the Rain: In Which Four Russians Give a Master Class on Writing, Reading, and Life* (Random House, New York, 2021).

12. If you're here because I directed you here from chapter 11, "You're Engaged," you can return to that chapter now. You're not experiencing reading resistance.

13. I try hard not to be that guy who shushes complete strangers, so these days I usually fortify myself with alcohol to abide any noisy neighbors.

14. Plato, *Cratylus,* trans. Benjamin Jowett (Project Gutenberg, Illinois, 2008). Written c. 375 BCE.

15. David Couzens Hoy, *The Critical Circle: Literature, History, and Philosophical Hermeneutics* (University of California Press, California, 1982).

16. A rhyming Russian proverb that President Reagan repeated so often during nuclear treaty negotiations with the USSR that Soviet leader Mikhail Gorbachev said he got tired of hearing it.

17. Wilfred Sellars, *Empiricism and the Philosophy of Mind* (Harvard University Press, Massachusetts, 1997). First published 1956.

18. Suzanne Nossel, the former executive director of PEN America, is able to precisely identify the exact scenes and scenarios she grafts onto her novel reading: "A novel has to be immersive, and a world needs to come to life, drawing on places I have been or can imagine. I set Elizabeth Strout's books near a summer camp in Maine where I was a counselor. My setting for Mohsin Hamid's *Exit West* was Hong Kong. I can conjure the image of cabins in the woods at Camp David that lodged in my head when I read Lawrence Wright's *Thirteen Days in September.* That said, it's hard to inhabit a different geography and world by reading just a few pages a night. I need a certain amount of time for the landscape of the book to set up camp in my brain." https://www.nytimes.com/2024/07/18/books/review/suzanne-nossel-pen-america-interview.html.

19. From "The Center for Fiction Presents Eleanor Catton on *Birnam Wood* with Meg Wolitzer," YouTube, March 8, 2023. https://www.youtube.com/watch?v=wfgA9z4M0MU.

3
Choosing What to Read

In 2017, data scientist Seth Stephens-Davidowitz accessed a huge tranche of Spotify music listening data, and from it he determined the most important period in men's and women's lives for formulating musical tastes.[1] For men it's between ages thirteen and sixteen, and for women it's between ages eleven and fourteen. Because we live in a world of self-reference-boosting algorithms, for many of us these tastes are never challenged; through services like Spotify you can relive the music of your youth forever. Nothing compels you to check out what the kids are listening to these days if you remain in your own musical bubble. That's sad.

Consider classic *anything*. Part of the road to becoming a classic artifact was to be, at one time, merely one of many similar things.

Classical music? Bach, Mozart, and Beethoven had hundreds of contemporaries, and yet it's *their* masterworks that continue to be performed today. Classic rock? Rockabilly artists abounded in the 1950s, and yet most of us have heard of the kid from Tupelo with the blue suede shoes. The Fab Four are revered, and the Rolling Stones gather no moss; as of 2025 they're still touring. When I mention the Purple One, it's easy to envision the Minneapolis guitarist with the regal name.

Of the millions of novels published in the twentieth century, those by Virginia Woolf, Ernest Hemingway, F. Scott Fitzgerald, William Faulkner, George Orwell, and Vladimir Nabokov are considered classics. Why is that?

It's so much easier to look backward in time and recognize who stood above their peers and who has been remembered than it is to critically evaluate artists creating in the here and now. It takes more work to find a living writer worthy of your admiration, and it's also difficult to find your writing tribe. But if you take the time and make the effort, you will be richly rewarded. I follow dozens of contemporary authors, and I am delighted when a new novel of theirs is published. But

I'm also on the lookout for debut authors, new voices, and innovative storytelling. Would you like to do the same?

Like hanging out at the local music venue or record store (remember those?) eager to catch the next wave and experience something new, you don't need to be a teenager to become a fanatic. You can begin your next literary obsession today.

This chapter discusses some of the practical steps you can take to find a novel to study that's right for you. It covers some of the traditional methods of selecting a book and then explores how to break out of a rut if you find you're in one. Topics include:

- **The Canon:** What is the canon, are there new canons, and who are the gatekeepers of modern publishing and tastemaking?
- **Genre:** What is genre, how are genres being mixed, and how does genre relate to gender?
- **Favorite Topics:** How to move beyond plot, break old habits, and find new novels to read.
- **Other Sources:** Use reading groups, prize recipients, and social book review sites to discover what novels are hot, respected, and worth your time.

The Canon

> The Canon is loaded.
> —*Percival Everett*[2]

Harold Bloom in his 1994 *The Western Canon* named twenty-six "immortal" authors that he felt should be studied, and a list of works[3] that he considered canonical. Let's break apart the four things in that last sentence that are completely at odds with culture in the twenty-first century.

The gatekeepers

Until the beginning of this century, there was a general acceptance of literary canon curation, and, in the specific case of *The Western Canon*, the curator was humanities professor and literary critic Harold Bloom. The formation of canons continues at the university through elementary-school levels by necessity, as educators and their governing bodies must determine their curricula.

The American Library Association reports that the number of banned books has risen sharply in the US in this decade, and that 2022 saw nearly twice the number of demands to censor books over the 729 challenges reported in 2021.[4] Censorship is generally predicated on a book's subject matter and not the quality of the writing found within. Repressing certain types of stories and people appears to be more important than considering the impact of this censorship on the quality of elementary and secondary schooling. This is the will of some present-day gatekeepers.

Multiple canons

For all practical purposes, the canon[5] is whatever your state school board says it is. What is taught in schools, then, is whatever teachers believe they can reasonably offer while trying to avoid censorship from the educational boards mentioned above. Also, more than ever, librarians are coming under fire for daring to shelve a wide variety of perspectives and worldviews.

Immortality

As a literary critic, Harold Bloom concerned himself with determining which books would survive the test of time. As a result, he was quite confident in placing within his canon works by Sappho, Shakespeare, and Strindberg, and admittedly less confident about including works he published during his lifetime.

For our purposes, however, it's not important to assess novels we read in this way. Our primary concern is whether the work contains writerly teaching moments, and I assure you, every single novel contains lessons for you. Therefore, whether a book is perceived as a masterwork should neither sway us in favor of nor dissuade us from reading it like a writer.

Because it's good for you

There is a huge difference between saying we could all benefit from reading more novels and me telling you what I think you should read. I wouldn't presume to be so insensitive. Only you can decide which works speak to you and what books you consider to be a worthwhile investment of your time. I will, however, presume to present you with a list of options and suggest places to look for new novels, and I will share with you titles that I've found valuable. This manual is full of references to these novels, and you can find the complete (and ever-growing) list of these novels online at https://LiteraryForensics.org, under "Resources."

EXERCISE 1

That novel you're reading right now—how did you select it? Did you read a critic's review, or get a recommendation from a friend? Did you find it by browsing at your local library or bookstore? What caught your attention? Was it the cover, blurbs, or a clerk's recommendation?

What is most important to you when selecting what to read? Is it the entertainment value? Something you think is "good" for you? Is it the title or the author who speaks to you more? Is the novel a prizewinner, or on some influencer's must-read list? Or have you read this author before? Is the book part of a series? And if so, how did you happen upon the series?

By analyzing your selection criteria, you can learn how to broaden your search and cast a wider net to find additional titles you find worth your time.

Genre

You may be thinking: I'm writing a thriller, so I should be reading thrillers. Nothing wrong with that. You can certainly read a few dozen examples and then emulate what you have found inside. It's a good starting point, especially if your writing fits neatly into the industry-defined definition of your genre. But what if it doesn't? If your writing seems to defy genre then you might benefit from this brief discussion about what genre is.

Did you know that the words *gender* and *genre* share a common root? I bring this up to expand the way we think about genre when we apply it to selecting the novels we choose to read. Genre is a type, a category, a box. The idea of only reading within one genre can be just as limiting as, say, selecting books only based on the gender of their author. Or their age, ethnicity, political or religious bent, or any other nonliterary characteristic.

> [L]iterary genres are historical inscriptions, not only in terms of ideas and themes but also in their matrices of time and space, which Bakhtin calls "chronotopes."
> —*Daphna Erdinast-Vulcan*, Borderline Subjectivity: The Futurity of the Present in Bakhtin's Work[6]

I'm stymied every time I try to come up with a good definition for genre. I suppose the best I can give you is similar to what constitutes a canon these days:

Genre is whatever its readers say it is. Genre evolves over time and is bolstered by the categories created by publishers and booksellers to group and shelve novels to efficiently get them in front of their eager readers.

If you're looking to genre as a means to categorize different types of novels, though, you may get frustrated very quickly. I know I have. Beyond a few obvious story contracts like the romance and the whodunit, the waters quickly get murky. That's why I sometimes use Shawn Coyne's Five-Leaf Clover, which defines genre based on the five parameters of content, structure, style, reality, and time.[7]

Rather than attempting to pigeonhole an entire novel into a simplistic one-word phrase, understand that there are multiple axes along which you can categorize a novel. For example, what is its *chronotope,* or space-time location? Is it on Earth in the present day? Or in France during the time of Joan of Arc? Then, what is its thematic content? Its intent? What is its form—archplot, short form, or something else?

Picking genres

When we're asked what we like to read, how many of us resort to one of two answers: 1) I like to read [insert genre here]; or 2) I've read [insert novel titles here]? Instead, why not compile a list of genre characteristics that resonate with you. Maybe you're into speculative history, or family-based stories, or novels that tackle philosophical themes. Once you identify your reading preferences, you can venture out into adjacent genres and try them on for size.

In chapter 4, "Your Novel," I'll also ask you to think about how your own novel would be categorized. The results may surprise you and lead you to discover novels you wouldn't otherwise have considered reading.

Mixing genres

Inventive novelists have been mixing genres for centuries, even though there was a stronger divide between genres because publishing and bookstores had such highly structured disciplines. Cross-genre work existed (Kurt Vonnegut's sci-fi satire, Shirley Jackson's literary horror), but it wasn't common or expected. Genre-blended books were often rebranded into one dominant genre for marketing and shelving in bookstores. As recently as ten to twenty years ago, genre-mixing was growing, but it was still considered niche or risky. For example, Margaret Atwood and Kazuo Ishiguro have blended genres, but that was often seen as literary experimentation. The market was still segmented, so a publisher had to choose one shelf for their author's book: sci-fi or romance, but not both.

Today, though, genre-mixing in novels is much more common and accepted today than it was even five years ago. Why? Digital publishing and self-publishing broke down many barriers, and in an online bookstore, writers don't have to pick a dominant genre to fit their book onto a physical shelf. Online communities, which allow users to categorize books with an infinite number of descriptor tags, allow authors to promote unique genre blends. And the rise of fan fiction has normalized the idea of narrative mash-ups.

As a result, today authors and publishers are intentionally blending genres more than ever before. Independent and self-published authors are especially adventurous because they aren't limited by traditional publishing norms. And readers are more open to cross-genre books, so long as the story is compelling. Cross-genre examples from the 2020s include:

- *Iron Widow* by Xiran Jay Zhao: sci-fi + fantasy + feminist dystopia
- *Fourth Wing* by Rebecca Yarros: military fantasy + romance
- *Mexican Gothic* by Silvia Moreno-Garcia: gothic horror + historical fiction + social commentary

EXERCISE 2

What novels do you like to read, and how do you describe them? By topic or plot? By your favorite genre? Try to quantify your tastes more precisely. What strikes you as completely out-of-bounds? What looks similar enough to what you enjoy that you might want to give it a read?

What are you reading now, and why? Author Deborah Harkness found that after recovering from cancer, she wanted to read only historical nonfiction, and not novels.[8] Is anything in your life right now determining your reading habits?

What genre best describes your own writing? Do you explore a wide range of styles, or do you stick to something more familiar? Try asking a critique partner how they would categorize your writing, and offer to do the same for them.

Favorite Topics

When you shop around for your next novel to read, how do you go about choosing? Do you enjoy coming-of-age stories, romance novels, thrillers, historical fiction, fantasy, mysteries, or literary fiction? Or do you look for plot details, like, it's about my hometown, about WWII espionage, or about an intergenerational family? Would a favorite topic be enough of a reason for you to check out an unfamiliar author? Or have you already identified which authors are writing stories with plotlines you enjoy?

I used to select my reading using just such criteria. But after years of studying writing craft, I now crave different things: balanced pacing, unusual characterization, and good sentence construction. I look for how efficiently an author describes a scene: that is, what's said, what's left out, and what's truly necessary without using too many words. This has changed what I enjoy reading so much that now the surface subject matter of a work has faded into insignificance.

I'm reading novels today I would have never considered reading ten years ago.

Plot is skin-deep

The chapters in this book that cover plot, chapter 16, "Character Development" and chapter 17, "Structure," tie story structure directly to character journey, and tie organizational structure to thematic development. Plot, in the sense of moving characters around like chess pieces, is actually a byproduct of character development. Think about your own writing process and how you develop your stories: First, you have an idea—a topic or theme you'd like to explore. From your inspiration arise characters and their voices, you put them in scenes, string the scenes together, and *voila!* You have your plot.

You can also imagine that when an author writes a novel it's something like making a stack of pancakes. The first pancake is their motivation for writing. As they create their characters, scenes, and themes, those pancakes stack up. And their top-most pancake—the one you see—is the plot.

When you consume their novel, or stack of pancakes, you're always looking at the plot. The plot also helps you to organize the material you discover further down the stack and to keep track of the characters and the scenes. That stack of pancakes represents the difference between how you perceive a novel when you read it and how an author conceived of that novel when they wrote it.[9]

Here's another analogy: If you compare a novel to a body, although you may imagine that the plot is the skeleton, it's actually the skin. The true skeleton of any novel consists of the ideas, observations, themes, and worldviews that led an author to write their book in the first place. If you're choosing your reading by plot type, then you may not be optimizing the opportunity to use a novel to learn how to write.

I invite you to dig deeper into the novels you already admire and ask yourself what was going on under the surface that worked its way inside your head and your heart. I'll bet it was more than the plot elements alone.

Punching above your weight

We are what we read. While every individual is unique, all of us possess unlimited potential. Eat well and you will be healthier.

> Exercise well and you will be stronger. Read well and you will be...
> what? Smarter? Maybe. More informed? Surely.
> —*Robert DiYanni*, You Are What You Read[10]

Professional athletes typically work out with heavier weights and stronger bands of resistance than would be required on the field, the mat, or the court. Why is that? It's because the most efficient engine is one that coasts, one that does not need to use all its energy at every minute. That way, when extra effort is required, the power is there in reserve.

Your writing muscles need a similar workout. You'll want to load up on reading that goes beyond what you would expect of yourself when you write your own novel. I hope you discover more difficult techniques, more arduous plotting situations, more complex prose in your reading than you require in your own writing. This is what will bulk up your writing muscles.

Your own investigative reading is personal, of course—there are no right or wrong books—but I'd like you to be aware of the old software developer's adage, *"Garbage in? Garbage out!"* (GIGO for short.) Which echoes the old saying, "You are what you eat."

You can't hope to pen a Pulitzer Prize–winning manuscript if you're spending your time watching TikTok, or hope to win the Hugo if you're only reading the backs of cereal boxes. Nothing against TikTok creators or cereal marketeers, but if you want to create writing of quality, the best use of your time is to read the novels you aspire to emulate.

Breaking the habit

If you're still not inspired to broaden your reading habits, then let's pull focus away from you for a moment. Stop to consider what other people are reading, and why. The next section covers a number of resources to discover what other people are reading and how highly they value a particular book or the works of an author. While the only arbiter of your own personal taste is you, it will broaden your world to consider the fashions of others, if only to discard them for something you like better.

People vote with their pocketbooks, and so you may want to seek out sales rankings within your genre, topic interest, and other categories. There's a lot of information freely available on *Goodreads* and *Amazon*.[11]

EXERCISE 3

Pick any book you love. What is it about this book that sparks such affection? Why did you enjoy reading *that,* and not something else? Does it have anything to do with your background, education, life experiences, circle of friends? Is it the intricacies of the plot? The subject matter? The main character?

What are your favorite topics or plot types? Spy novels? Romances? Books about farmers, difficult families, or science fiction? Try to pinpoint how you identify the types of books you enjoy, and try to find common threads between them, if they exist.

Now imagine something you would *never* read. Try to find the quintessential example of that book, and crack it open. The idea here is to venture outside your comfort zone.

Other Sources

Here are some resources that I've used to discover new authors and new novels.

Social media

The bookish corners of the Internet include Fable,[12] StoryGraph[13] with its AI recommendation engine (which, unlike that titanic stalwart Goodreads, is *not* owned by Amazon), LibraryThing,[14] Litsy,[15] and others. Literary channels that reside within existing social media platforms include Bookstagram[16] (on Instagram), BookTok[17] (on TikTok), and BookTube[18] (on YouTube). Of course, you'll need to mess with their algorithms to get to something new and interesting. You can follow hashtags that are unrelated to your genre, or follow your favorite authors and see what they're reading, or notice which accounts are posting together or tagging each other, and follow them.

Podcasts are also a huge source of information about books, genres, authors, their process, and the craft of writing. For the craft of *reading,* I recommend the podcast companion to this book, *Writers Who Read,*[19] available wherever you get your podcasts.

Bookstores and libraries

Yep, actual brick-and-mortar buildings you have to travel to IRL. They do still exist. A bookstore's staff picks, new releases, and curated displays are useful ways for you to find a book that you may not have come across otherwise. Also, you'll be supporting the local economy.

And of course, take advantage of your local library. Librarians are full of useful information about the latest titles and are happy to help you find something new—it's their job! Even if you'd like to stay home, most public libraries subscribe to EBSCO's NoveList database of book recommendations, which you can sign into online by specifying your local library[20] and using your library card.

Prizes

Every year dozens of novels are honored by being shortlisted for a major prize, making an influencer's reading list, or being included as a best book of the year on various publication's annual lists. The ones I usually follow include the *National Book Award*, the *National Book Critics Circle Award*, the *Pulitzer Prize*, and the *Booker Prize*.[21] Other prestigious genre awards include the *Hugo, Edgar, Nebula, World Fantasy Award, Newbery Medal, PEN/Faulkner*, and many more.[22]

I can't list them all here because there are too many, and of course it goes without saying that they're all selected by humans and therefore their selections are subjective. But most of the prize committees are interested in using their prestige to help further the career of a writer they deem worthy, and that's a noble cause. For that reason, these prizes offer a place to start if you want to understand what today's literary critics consider quality writing.

Top-ten lists

These are the annual recommendation lists compiled by the major newspapers, magazines, and media outlets. It also includes book club lists, such as those curated by NPR, Oprah, Reese Witherspoon, Jenna Bush, Barack Obama, Bill Gates, and other famous people and entities. Again, you can find lots of books here you might not have found elsewhere.

I also like to read the *New York Times Book Review's* weekly *By the Book* on the reading habits of a single author or tastemaker. I've found many new books and authors there that I'm willing to try, especially if I resonate with the interviewee.

I've also found a quite a few interesting books on the *Goodreads* best-of lists that come out at the end of the year. These books are voted on by readers, and include books that haven't necessarily been critics' darlings but have gained a solid readership. The *Book of the Month Club* also offers a surprisingly diverse array of titles.

Your favorite search engine is also your friend. Try various word combinations to discover Internet bloggers or Substack writers who make lists of their favorite novels.

Book groups

Every town has a book club or two. Some meet at your local public library, but many others meet in people's homes, and still others meet online. There is a book group out there somewhere that has similar tastes to your own—it's up to you to find it, or create it. Meetup.com is a good place to start.

Ancillary to this book are the dozens of novels I've selected for my *Writers Who Read* study group.[23] Presentations for all of them are available for your free use online,[24] and you can also use selections from this list to curate your own discussions. See chapter 25, "Your Own Study Group."

New canons

If you'd like to know what's being promoted as today's New Literary Canon, you can access the reading lists from various university English departments. You can also search the Internet to see which authors have been hired to teach and where, and I find YouTube a valuable resource for virtually attending their latest lectures.

You should also be aware that it's considered bad form for one author to give an unfavorable review of another's work, so you won't likely find much dirt. But pay close attention to who is presenting together, or who is interviewing whom at an online bookstore event. You can use these connections to find veins of interesting writing and clusters of authors who admire each other's work.

In today's brave new world, there is no right or wrong canon, and that's not a bad thing. With the demise of the traditional canon, dozens of new ones have arisen that are interesting and take into account so many more points of view than the individual curators of the past could manage. Of course, it's up to you to find a curator you trust and consider to be your touchstone.

EXERCISE 4

From the many resources listed in this section, pick one or two and see if you can find any new novels there that interest you. You may discover a motherlode of riches from an unexpected source. Just like a friend whose tastes you trust, you may find common ground from a critic, a book-club curator, or the editorial committee of a local newspaper or national periodical.

I hope in this way you will find an author or two to follow, and maybe even discover a cluster of writers whose novels you want to study.

Notes

1. Seth Stephens Davidowitz, "The Songs That Bind," Opinion, *New York Times*, February 10, 2018, https://www.nytimes.com/2018/02/10/opinion/sunday/favorite-songs.html.

2. Eliana Dockterman, "Percival Everett Is Challenging the American Literary Canon," *Time*, February 6, 2025, https://time.com/7210599/percival-everett-james-literary-canon/.

3. Harold Bloom, *The Western Canon*, Robert Teeter's Home Page, accessed May 20, 2025, http://sonic.net/~rteeter/grtbloom.html#chaos.

4. "American Library Association reports record number of demands to censor library books and materials in 2022," on the American Library Association website, accessed May 20, 2025, https://www.ala.org/news/press-releases/2023/03/record-book-bans-2022.

5. An interesting article about Bloom's literary canon: https://www.tckpublishing.com/the-literary-canon/.

6. Daphna Erdinast Vulcan, "Borderline Subjectivity: The Futurity of the Present in Bakhtin's Work," *Partial Answers: Journal of Literature and the History of Ideas* 8, no. 1 (2010), 169–183.

7. "Genres of Writing: Definition, Examples, and 12 Types," on the Story Grid website, accessed May 20, 2025, https://storygrid.com/genrefiveleafclover/. (Scroll down on this web page to see the detailed graphic.)

8. "Deborah Harkness Has Never Read Jane Austen. Really," By The Book, *New York Times*, August 8, 2021, https://www.nytimes.com/2024/08/01/books/review/deborah-harkness-all-souls-black-bird-oracle.html.

9. When I first presented *Literary Forensics* at writers conferences, I made a big deal about Aristotle's six elements of drama and the order in which they're written: Thought (*dianoia*), Character (*ethos*), Diction (*lexos*), Melody (*melos*), Spectacle (*opsis*), and Plot (*mythos*), as opposed to the order in which they're consumed by readers: Plot, Spectacle, Melody, Diction, Character, and finally, Thought. Aristotle did present them in that sequence, true, but I no longer need to stick to his order.

10. Robert DiYanni, *You Are What You Read: A Practical Guide to Reading Well* (Princeton University Press, New Jersey, 2021).

11. For more on finding freely available industry data, see chapter 21, "The Publishing Industry."

12. https://fable.co/

13. https://www.thestorygraph.com/

14. https://www.librarything.com/

15. https://www.litsy.com/web/home

16. https://www.instagram.com/bookstagram/?hl=en

17. https://www.tiktok.com/tag/booktok

18. https://www.youtube.com/hashtag/booktube

19. https://WritersWhoRead.com

20. https://www.ebsco.com/novelist/find-my-organization

21. Find a more complete list of literary awards here: https://en.wikipedia.org/wiki/List_of_literary_awards.

22. https://www.google.com/search?q=novel+genre+prizes

23. You can find our upcoming books and meeting registration information at https://WritersWhoRead.com/live.

24. https://writerswhoread.com/books-alphabetical/ and https://writerswhoread.com/authors-alphabetical/

4
Your Novel

Here's the real reason you want to read like a writer: You are a writer, and you're writing a novel. If you're not a writer, then you can skip this section—it's not for you. If you are a writer but you're not writing a *novel*, I recommend reading this section anyway, and also consulting chapter 22, "Other Narrative Forms."

So you're writing a novel. Then… what are you doing? Don't you know no one has the attention span for more than a fifteen-second TikTok video or at most an action-hero movie? And who has a spare eight to twelve hours to read novels these days? Who reads, period? It's common knowledge that literature is no longer relevant in modern society. And besides, the novel died years ago—replaced by [*fill in any supposed novel-killing technology here*].

Am I wrong? If you think so, that's good! You've passed the test.

Now that we've established that you are writing a novel and believe the novel is alive and well, flourishing as a storytelling form, and relevant in the twenty-first century,[1] I have one more test for you. This is trickier, and requires some introspection on your part.

Why are you writing your novel?

Why are you writing this specific novel? What do you hope to achieve? I'm not talking about fame, wealth, or the admiration of your peers. Although these are wonderful things, they exist outside of the novel itself. No, I'm asking you what you're hoping to achieve *inside* your novel.

The possible answers to this question form the foundation for this chapter, which is about studying your own novel for the missing elements you hope to find in the other novels that you read. It's kind of working in the opposite direction from the focus of all the other chapters in this book. That is, the goal here is to identify those qualities you hope to create in your own writing, and to make a plan[2] to seek out those specific elements in the novels you read.

I am not an ornithologist. I am a bird.
—Saul Bellow

Bellow was lucky. He had natural talent oozing out of his fingertips and famously proclaimed that he didn't feel the need to study himself or his writing habits—that was for others. But most of us are not so lucky, and we need to learn how to study our craft.

Stephen King is a prolific and successful author, but his memoir *On Writing* was deeply frustrating to me because at the end of the book, when he illustrates his own writing process, he lays down a regimen that almost none of us can follow:

- He writes two thousand words a day, a sprinter's pace in a marathon event.
- His first draft looks better than my twenty-seventh draft, and then he shows off by improving it further.
- He reads hundreds of books a year.

The other 99.99 percent of us who struggle with our writing cannot take King's methods as a blueprint. Most of us are simply not that talented, nor have we yet put in the decades of hard work that King has to further refine his talent, so we already have two strikes against us.

Therefore, you have to be clever with your limited time. You must pinpoint what you know you need to learn, and direct your reading in such a way that you're always aware when an author does what you want to do so that you can study it and learn from it.

In other words, you'll need to fine-tune your studies toward specific lessons. And as you do that—hopefully with the aid of this book—your writing will improve. The learning strategies covered in this chapter fall into four categories:

- **Root cause:** Discovering motivation
- **End-means:** Working backward
- **Heuristics:** Testing formulas
- **Serendipity:** Random brainstorming

Root Cause

Why do you write? Understanding why you are driven to write your novel will help you learn what you hope to achieve. And by locating as precisely as you can the root causes of why you write, you will also be able to identify the fears, phobias, and shortcomings that stand between you and success. Knowing what you lack will help you craft a study plan to bridge the gaps, but it only comes with an honest look back at your history and by taking lessons from your experiences.

Were you bullied as a child? Did you have a lot of friends? Did you grow up in a safe environment, or was there trouble at home? Did you survive tragic circumstances or a traumatic event? Are you in therapy now? Are you defined by your past, or do you live in the present? Do you still dream about what the future might hold?

And what about your reading habits—do you read a lot? Do you consider yourself a bookworm, or a bookish person? Do you read more than your friends? Reading is often the gateway drug to writing, but if you don't read a lot, then you've come to writing by a different path. What were the steps that led you to want to be a writer and to attempt tackling the long form of the novel? What's in your head as you write? What motivates you to sit down and spill your thoughts onto the page?

George Orwell, in his essay "Why I Write," identified four primary motives—aside from the need to earn a living—that he believes exist in varying degrees in every writer: sheer egoism (the quest for fame and admiration); aesthetic enthusiasm (joy of writing for its own sake); historical impulse (the need to set the record straight); and political purpose (the desire to influence others). Which of these traits exist in you, and to what degree?

To help you figure this out, let's do a little visualization. What does your completed novel look like? Whom do you imagine reading your work? What does success look like? The answers to all these questions will be different for each one of us, and if you haven't already grappled with them, I suggest you take a moment right now to consider your own root causes.

My motivation

In the spirit of not asking you to do anything I wouldn't do myself, I'll share with you what motivates me. The reason I'm giving you my personal example is to help you in case you're stuck trying to answer the questions in the paragraphs above, or you don't understand what I'm asking of you. Remember that your journey is unique and what I'm about to share with you is in no way a suggestion that you should be like me. In fact, I hope you're *not* like me, because my route to the book you're now reading has not been the most direct or the most advantageous for a writer.

My father was in the Air Force, so he thought that his son should have a crew cut like he did. This was in the 1970s, when *everyone* had long hair, so I got picked on a lot for my haircut. Oh, and my mother made my clothes—also very uncool. To defend myself, I developed a sense of humor so that I was able to parry the worst of the insults. I also had a lot of natural musical talent and I played the piano, which led to more awkward social situations, of course. My problems were exclusively of the first-world variety, so my childhood wasn't tragic. But I did learn what it means to be an outsider and to be picked on for my differences. This led to my lifelong empathy for other outsiders.

When I got to university, I discovered this entire group of people who were *well read*, which I discovered for the first time meant that it wasn't *what* they had read, but that they read *a lot*. I wanted that for myself, but the investment of time seemed awfully high. Besides, I was having too much fun playing the piano, and so I continued my habit of reading only sporadically.

Beginning in 2015, when I decided that the third act of my creative life would be as a novelist, I started reading *seriously*, more regularly, and with purpose. Setting out to become well read, I discovered many contemporary authors whose work I wanted to explore further, and even larger numbers of writers whose voices were underrepresented. It also marked the first time I had ever systematically searched for new authors to emulate. This is something that now, ten years later, I do all the time.

My life as a truly discerning reader began then, decades later than most. That's why when a member of my reading group suggested I write this book, I thought they were joking. I imagined all the super-intelligent people who were much better suited, talented, and situated to write this book than I was. It's for this reason that I work extra hard to research every topic presented here, to avoid missing key points or misrepresenting them.[3]

Fear is a strong motivator, and it's the reason I originally decided to pursue the traditional publishing path with an agent and an established publishing house. I needed validation every step of the way that my ideas are not crazy and that not just my friends but a wider circle of strangers would think my efforts are worthwhile.

I am also motivated to write this for everyone, not just for academics. Underpinning my work is the assertion that all of us are on equal footing as writers who read—I don't want anyone to feel like an outsider. I foster that inclusiveness in my reading group, and I hope you can feel that warmth come off the page. I want everyone—even the fuzzy-wuzzy budding pianists who had to develop a sense of humor to survive grade school—to feel welcome.

That's my motivation.

EXERCISE 1

Look into your life for the *real* reasons you're writing your stories. Be honest with yourself, and don't ignore the embarrassing experiences. I have found the challenging parts of my life are actually stronger motivators for me than the pleasant bits. I don't believe that all artists are tortured, but I do believe that all artists have a bee in their bonnet, a grain of sand irritating their shell that propels them to act. Identify exactly what drives you to *write* instead of pouring your creative energies into anything else, because it's important to incorporate those decisions and that specific set of desires into your reading for the best possible results.

End-Means

As a child I loved solving mazes. It didn't take me too long to discover that mazes were constructed to be the most challenging when encountered start to finish, that is, via the proscribed entry point. But when I attempted to solve a maze backward—that is, starting at the exit and tracing a path toward the entrance—it would often be much easier to solve. The obstacles and dead ends simply weren't oriented that way, and so the connected path was much more direct and easier to find.

I have the same hope for your encounter with *Literary Forensics*. Because we're all trying to work our way through the same maze—writing a novel—it sometimes benefits us to approach the problem from the other end of the pipe and look through it backward.

Backward design

The father of educational evaluation and assessment, Ralph W. Tyler, first formulated the concept of backward design in 1949, although his paradigm wasn't given that catchy title until the 1990s. It's a planning framework that starts with the end in mind, setting goals before choosing instructional methods and assessments. At its worst, this methodology is used by educators to "teach to the test." But at its best, it has led to instructive curricula and has spawned commercial design principles embraced by Steve Jobs at Apple and today's product designers at Amazon. It works like this:

- Identify your target audience and the results you hope to achieve.
- Quantify your ability to meet your goals and establish tests.
- Design activities that will make your desired results happen.

For writers, this should be easy to visualize.

First, envision where you'd like your book to appear in the marketplace. Give your novel a memorable title that will appeal to your intended audience. Identify competitive titles and determine whether you can carve out a unique niche that your story will fill. Write your dream jacket-cover blurbs and the back-cover synopsis. In screenwriting, this is called "creating your logline." If you have any difficulty with this step, think about the mash-up approach popular in moviemaking that weds two unlikely concepts. For example: Thor at Club Med, or Jack Reacher raising bees, or Jane Austen's zombie apocalypse (this one was actually published). In other words, visualize your published novel and the reception you hope for. For example, do you want it discussed at book clubs? Do you want people fangirling about it on Instagram?

Next, take note of the precise details of your final creation. What emotional impact do you hope to achieve? How do you see it stacking up against competing titles? How does your novel distinguish itself?[4] What specific niche is your target audience? How does your novel address current social and societal trends? Where does it land on the scale of literary to mass-market fiction? Do you want to have a speaking career or other educational aspect tied into it? Do you want it made into a movie or TV show? Is critical acclaim or commercial success more important to you? What are the best- and worst-case outcomes of your endeavor? And what idea motivates you so strongly that you are willing to take the risk of failure?

Along the way, it's important to stress-test your assumptions about the progress you feel you have made, and the most common way to do that is to present your writing to a critique group. The feedback they provide is invaluable to knowing whether or not your innovations have landed in the way you hoped. This is an iterative process, and it requires you to identify the gaps between where you are now and where you want to be by the end of your editorial process. Identify your strengths and weaknesses; from those you can create a study plan that helps you to write your way out of ignorance.

In my own study plan, I like to tackle the most gnarly problem first, understanding that this issue will likely require the most amount of time to overcome and that I probably won't be able to fix it all in one pass. I visualize my work as a Gantt chart with parallel task timelines that I can approach simultaneously. By the way, this book is organized into similar parallel topics that you can explore in your own way.

Librarian metaphor

It's trite to say that Google's search algorithm has changed our lives. At this point, we expect to be able to have the answer to any question at our fingertips, just a click away. But the idea that all answers are available to us is illusory, because a mere search of terms will not answer any of the most important questions, like: What themes underpin my writing? What's the impact if I have character *X* do activity *Y*? How will I finish my first draft?

ChatGPT and other AI-based algorithms have created an enormous splash since being released to the general public in 2022. In fact, Bing or Bard may be able to give you some useful advice to the question, how will I finish my first draft? But as helpful as these agents are in synthesizing concepts and spitting them back as cogent English sentences, truly they are advanced versions of the librarian metaphor.[5] In other words, ask a librarian about a topic, and they will return with a stack of books.

Neither Google search nor ChatGPT is truly creating anything beyond a clever synthesis of ideas assembled from all the text the artificial intelligence has ever ingested. The biggest issue with AI is that by asking the question, you have already limited the possible results. And much like the computer in Douglas Adams's *The Hitchhiker's Guide to the Galaxy*, if you want a better answer than *42*, you need to be asking better questions about life, the universe, and everything.

Find your tribe

> What has been will be again, what has been done will be done again; there is nothing new under the sun. Is there anything of which one can say, "Look! This is something new"? It was here already, long ago; it was here before our time.
> —*Ecclesiastes 1:9–10*

What is your goal? I suggest that you focus on the desired result of your writings and find other authors who are aiming for the same thing. If you can't find any other author on your path, I would suggest that you haven't looked hard enough to find them. They're out there.

All I'm saying is: There is truly nothing new under the sun, except for your own unique voice. Don't attempt to reinvent the wheel. If another author has written a book that has cleared a path for you, I suggest you read their work. You can learn so much from studying their writing, even if you don't care for it, or imagine it's of inferior quality. Actually, if you find someone on your path who writes poorly, you've just struck gold! Study where they failed, but also study where they succeeded. Piggyback on their learnings and write something better. That's a much easier path to take than striking out into the wilderness without a plan.

Besides, before you can market your novel, you'll need to identify who's most likely to read it. Seek out your tribe now.

EXERCISE 2

Try backward design on your novel by imagining the physical book's location in your favorite bookstore. If that's online, then imagine which other titles would be recommended next to yours. Who is reading it? What impact has your novel made on your target audience? And ask yourself: Are you ready to write that book today? If not, then make a list of things you need to work on, including technical writing skills as well as research topics. Make a plan about how to address the gaps between where you are today and that bright, shining future you imagine for your creation.

You may want to use the *Appendix B: Reading Worksheet* to help you organize your study plan.

Heuristics

Another popular method of problem-solving is by testing hypotheses. This is the opposite of end-means because it is working through issues in a forward direction. I placed this section after the one about backward learning because I believe this process is not as efficient. If you remember the maze example above, solving a maze backward leads to a more direct solution. Solving the maze from the beginning and testing various path hypotheses will inevitably lead to dead ends.

This is similar to what the "pantser"—the novelist who writes as they go, as opposed to the "plotter," who outlines first and writes to fill in their schema—experiences when writing initial drafts. Pantser novelists describe throwing away hundreds of pages of their writing, huge sections of completed novels, and in some cases, abandoning entire concepts that stubbornly resist coming to fruition.

But the heuristic method can work if you doggedly refuse to give up. Thomas Edison famously tested thousands of materials before he landed on the right filament for his light bulb. And frankly, many authors enjoy the experimental process and wouldn't trade it for anything. You may be one of these people.

Experimentation

To formulate an experiment, you need to identify a problem and name some possible solutions that you will test. I have rewritten an entire novel in third-person perspective when I realized first-person narrative wasn't working. I've also elevated minor characters to major status.

I'll suggest that before you do a complete rewrite that you try to tackle individual issues, to see if you can save your story. Here are some simplified examples of what I mean.

Your protagonist is a self-centered sociopath, and you need your readers to identify with her.

Possible experiments include:

- Craft a "save the cat" moment.
- Put your character into an easily-relatable situation.
- Lean into the crazy and go over the top.
- Inject comedic elements for relief.

Your story takes place on twenty-fifth-century Mars, and you need to create a believable world.

Possible experiments include:

- Take a city or country you know and write life on Mars like that.
- Take focus away from arcane technologies by leaning more on human interactions.
- Research historical explorers and see what you can extrapolate.

You need your characters to speak different languages in a seamless way.
Possible experiments include:

- Write conversations with indirect attribution (without quotation marks).
- Inject a few foreign words into the text to give the reader hints.
- Focus more on actions and less on speech.

I've offered just a few ideas with just a few possible experiments for each, but of course the issues are legion, and the possible solutions are infinite. To run your experiments, though, I don't need to remind you that you'll need to write a lot. To evaluate the results, you'll want to share them with your critique group and see how they are received. It's also very important that you take note of what feels good to write as you're writing, because the solutions to your problems can also be found that way.

Correlation is not causation

My beloved Colorado Rockies have never won a World Series. Heck, over the first thirty years of their existence, they've never even won their division. But I go to games, and I root for them anyway. Sometimes, when they're trailing in the late innings, I'll flip my cap inside out and turn it into a rally hat. Then, when they mount a comeback and win the game, I can take partial credit for their success.

Even in the superstition-laden major leagues, though, I doubt any player has ever attributed a win or loss to their fans' rally hats. And yet we cling to our false concepts of how one thing leads to another, imagining that correlation indicates causation.

What are your writerly superstitions? Do you write sequentially? Always construct exactly eleven plot points? Save the cat? Does your writing require music or candles or a special chair? Are you allergic to adverbs?

Don't get me wrong. None of these things are bad. In fact, they're all useful. But none of them is absolutely necessary. Keep in mind that correlation does not imply causation—that is, just because two things exist side by side, that doesn't prove that one caused the other to happen. Don't be afraid to try something new.

EXERCISE 3

Reread and Rewrite: Ask the tough questions, formulate your experiments, and write, write, write! If you're looking for litmus tests to determine whether your experiments were successful, examine your writing through the lenses of some of the chapters of this book.

Serendipity

A story is always talking to you; you just have to learn to listen to it.
—Stuart Dybek

It took me about twenty years to learn how to practice the piano. I'll explain.

Piano came too easy for me, and I was able to master my initial assignments with a minimum amount of practice. I thought I was clever, but what I was really doing was sowing the seeds of later headaches. I never practiced regularly—I'm talking four to six hours per day, every day—until I went to college. Now the heat was on: I needed to learn a lot of music and with strict deadlines. The problem was, I didn't know how.

I assumed that my natural ability would see me through, but it didn't. I needed to learn how to learn, and I had developed no tools. I floundered.

Fast-forward to when I was teaching piano in Thailand. Yes, I had achieved some proficiency through sheer force of will, but I couldn't say that I was using my practice time efficiently. That is, until I allowed my intuition to dictate my schedule and the way I practiced. Strangely, I started progressing at lightning speed. I was even able to predict, within a few hours, how long it would take me to master a piece of music I'd never studied. Remarkable, but true.

Sometimes writing a novel may seem like an impossible undertaking. There is so much to learn and the topics are so deep that even identifying what it is you know or don't know seems impossible.

That may be why you're here reading this now. You're here to learn, and we all have to start our journey somewhere. So start anywhere. It truly doesn't matter where. Indulge your imagination, tap into your subconsciousness, and follow your gut. Open this book, close your eyes, and point.

Begin there.[6]

A few caveats

This method of entrusting your writing to your daily whims is not for everyone. It requires a few things that most of us do not possess.

1. A certain level of mastery. This is not for beginners. It requires relying on your own subconscious to guide you in the right direction. If you have no experience writing or are still a novice, then your subconscious reasoning faculty cannot be fully trusted. It may even lead you astray.
2. Confidence that you're not trying to sabotage your own writing. This requires a certain level of self-awareness that can only come through introspection. Is your desire to write genuine? Do you *really* want to succeed? Can you trust yourself fully to commit to the hard work?
3. A regular writing schedule. What I'm proposing here is no magic pill. It is certainly not a shortcut to good writing, nor does it replace years of study and practice.

Postlude

A few words on my practice, which I continue to this day in both my writing and music-making. In the past I would come to a practice session (or a writing session) with predefined goals. I decided I would spend my time learning this measure, this phrase, this page. I would work sequentially. I would work backward. I'd separate left and right hands. Whatever. All of it was worthless.

Today I approach each session with a blank mind. I work on the first thing I think of, and then the next, and then the next, without fear of deadlines. If on a particular day I can't focus, I close the piano lid or the laptop and do something else. And I do this without fear of deadlines, because I know this to be true: Playing what doesn't want to be played or writing what doesn't want to be written will actually set me back a day, and it will take me another full day to get back to where I was before I tried to force it. This is where my confidence that I'm not self-sabotaging features most significantly. I am confident that I *do* want to complete the writing, that I *do* want to master the music, but my subconscious brain is telling me, *not today.*

I always listen.

EXERCISE 4

Take a moment to ask yourself what's keeping you from finishing your novel. If it's external issues, I can't help you. But if it's something technical—if your writing isn't landing the way you'd hoped, if you're struggling to move your plot along—try this: Open this book to any page, read until you are inspired or you get to an exercise, and then do the exercise.

It can't hurt.

Notes

1. It turns out you're right! The written word is alive and well. See https://www.nytimes.com/2022/07/10/books/bookstores-diversity-pandemic.html and https://www.cnn.com/2024/11/16/business/barnes-and-noble-is-back-again/index.html.
2. The worksheet in Appendix C is designed to help you organize your thoughts and design a study plan.
3. https://en.wikipedia.org/wiki/Impostor_syndrome
4. To answer some of these questions about your novel, you can take advantage of the resources listed in chapter 21, "The Publishing Industry."
5. Noam Chomsky, "The False Promise of ChatGPT," *New York Times*, March 8, 2023, https://www.nytimes.com/2023/03/08/opinion/noam-chomsky-chatgpt-ai.html.
6. See also the "Choosing Your Teachers" section in YOUR FIRST CLUE.

5
What Should You Write?

The quick answer is: Write whatever you like. Who am I to say? Find your bliss.

Because this is a book about reading, a better answer is, as you write, 1) know your readers; 2) be aware of your effect on readers; and 3) be a more appreciative reader yourself. How an author's writing affects their readers is explored in more detail in the sections WHAT YOU FEEL and WHAT YOU NOTICE, and is covered more succinctly in chapter 14, "Point of View" and chapter 20, "The Gestalt." Chapter 21, "The Publishing Industry" also has useful information on marketing, genres, and topics.

But this chapter is focused on you and your writing.

> Eat to please yourself, but dress to please others.
> —Benjamin Franklin

First of all, I'm not attempting to teach you how to write—there are a gazillion craft books out there for that. Nor am I trying to preach conformity or limit your freedom. But because the central theme of this book is enlightenment through reading, I hope that you read and write with your eyes wide open, aware of the implications of what you are reading and the ramifications of what you are writing.

Some stories cannot be written—that's an issue of craft. But other stories should not be written—and that's a matter of judgment. For example, Salman Rushdie knew exactly what he was doing when he portrayed the prophet Muhammed in his 1988 novel *The Satanic Verses*. He anticipated that his depiction of the most revered figure in the Muslim faith would cause a stir, but he decided to poke the bear anyway in hope of stoking a broader conversation. What followed instead was a religious fatwa calling for Rushdie's death that forced him to go into hiding for decades and required round-the-clock protection. This fatwa remains in place to this day; it sparked a 2022 attack that almost took his life.

> The writer can choose what he writes about, but he cannot
> choose what he is able to make live.
> —Flannery O'Connor

So you have to be you, and you have to tell your story—you have no choice in either. I get it. But one of the greatest benefits of reading as many contemporary novels as you can is that it will hone your sense of what is being published today and why. Racial stereotyping and ethnic slurs are out, and, frankly, better narrative and descriptive passages can be crafted without them. Agatha Christie's *Hercule Poirot* and *Miss Marple* mysteries have been rewritten[1] to accommodate modern tastes. New editions published by HarperCollins have removed most references to ethnicity, descriptions of a judge's "Indian temper" and a hotel worker's "lovely white teeth" were cut, and instances of the word "natives" have been replaced by "locals." Even more recently published works are being revised.

The remainder of this chapter takes a look at the ramifications of any writer's authorial choices, as well as how those decisions are received by readers.

- **Appropriation:** Recognizing whose story is being told, and how various cultures are represented
- **Sense and sensitivity:** Understanding the norms of fiction through societal trends, considering readers' reactions, and choosing your best options
- **Mass-market fiction:** The interplay of artistry and commerce, and finding quality writing
- **Inside baseball:** Becoming a more appreciative reader by digging deeper and understanding more about how novels are constructed

Appropriation

> The alternative to appropriation is a world in which artists only
> reference their own cultures.
> —*Gabrielle Zevin*, Tomorrow, and Tomorrow, and Tomorrow

Consider the raw materials of storytelling: words, phrases, places, people, situations, feelings, form, and more. We didn't invent any of those things, and none of them belong to us. Think about it. Even the memoirist, who certainly owns their life story, must use other people's words, and depict people, places, and things that do not belong to them to tell their story.

Everything is borrowed, and all art is a remix.[2] Nothing is one hundred percent ours except our own perspective. Furthermore, it's a time-honored tradition for novelists to borrow from the people they know, and present them as characters in their fiction, either thinly or thickly veiled.

But where does the publishing industry draw the lines? What is appropriate for my story, and what is appropriation?

Whose story to tell?

The topic of cultural appropriation is a big one today, and at its best it helps to redress centuries of literary misrepresentation of characters from other cultures. At its worst, though, it can stifle your storytelling to the point that you become afraid to write any character who doesn't walk, talk, and act like you. Absurd, right? Stories require contrasting characters arising from a variety of backgrounds and situations, with a variety of opinions and worldviews; otherwise they'd be boring as hell. You know this is true.[3]

The topic of literary appropriation is also a hot one right now, and a few recent novels have addressed the issue head-on. Jean Hanff Korelitz's 2021 fun romp of a novel *The Plot* considers whether or not a plot outline—just the outline—is copyrightable. (It's not.) More seriously, R. F. Kuang's 2023 novel *Yellowface* considers whether or not a non-Asian author passing off a complete novel by a recently deceased Asian author is both literary and cultural appropriation. (It is.) One white guy stealing another white guy's outline and turning it into a manuscript is very different from a non-Asian author trying to pass themselves off as Asian for the purposes of publishing a stolen manuscript. (Boo!)

Those are extreme cases, yet they are worth considering because they represent edge cases on a continuum of appropriation. Pulitzer Prize–winning author Paul Harding said of his 2023 novel *This Other Eden,* about an African American family evicted from an island in Maine, a story that resembles the real history of Malaga Island: "I'm not the person to write the history of Malaga Island; I have no organic connection to it; I didn't grow up there," he said. "Those people's personal lives are not mine to take up."[4]

Harding is very conscious that he is not African American himself and that their stories are not his to tell; he also feels he can imagine his own version of a story that is based on historical events. For better or for worse, many readers continue to consider the author an integral part of what they write.

Authors know that readers also judge them on the basis of their gender, so quite a few authors have disguised theirs, through initialisms: (J.K. Rowling; S. E. Hinton; L. M. Montgomery; J. D. Robb), by pretending to be men (George Eliot;

George Sand; Currer, Ellis, and Acton Bell; Isak Dinesen; Robert Galbraith), or by pretending to be women (Edith Van Dyne; Deanna Dwyer; Leigh Nichols; Marilyn Ross; and perhaps Elena Ferrante).[5]

Representation

> Acknowledging the ways in which we deviate from so-called normalcy is an important step in learning to write the other.
> —*Nisi Shawl and Cynthia Ward*, Writing the Other[6]

Fiction involves a variety of characters who may have different backgrounds from one another, each ideally having a unique voice. As you read published works to discern what appropriate representation means in your own work, ask the following questions:

1. Does the author exhibit an understanding of the culture being represented, or do the characters lack dimension and reinforce existing stereotypes?
2. What is the context of the cultural representation—that is, does it feel essential to the work, or is it tacked on?
3. What does the author's representation actually say about the culture? Is the message positive, negative, or neutral? And is the culture itself being used as a stand-in for something else, for example, character development?

In your reading, seek out alternative representations of the story you need to tell and the characters you want to write. It's important to understand what's already been written and gauge your own reaction to other perspectives, especially if you find an author writing about something you know very well. Evaluate for yourself whether or not the author has represented a cultural aspect appropriately. Compare your views with others. The best-case scenario is discovering, through your reading, an author's treatment that you would like to replicate in your own work.

Alternatively, if the author has upset your sensibilities, see chapter 7, "You're Upset." If they have left you confused, see chapter 9, "You're Confused." Or, if the author has navigated the difficult waters and has brought home an accurate representation of another culture, see chapter 11, "You're Engaged."

EXERCISE 1

Reread: How do you describe yourself? How do you identify? Have you ever seen a character like you represented in a work of fiction? And if so, what about the representation was accurate, and what was not?

Rewrite: If you were rewriting that story, how would you modify that representation? Also think about putting yourself into an existing novel, any novel, as a main or supporting character. How differently would you need to write this character to make yourself come alive on the page? What elements of your character would you include to signal who you are? And how would you change the contours of the plot or setting to reveal more about your character?

Sense and Sensitivity

Much of what upsets a reader's sensibilities overlaps those hot topics you want to avoid at holiday gatherings. You know what they are. But the specifics within those topics are constantly evolving.

The Overton window

The range of acceptability of political ideas to the majority of a population at a given time is known as the Overton window, or the window of discourse, here shown along a spectrum from *unthinkable* to *policy*:

Unthinkable → Radical → Acceptable → Sensible → Popular → Policy

This window has shifted dramatically over the past decade, such that some political actions and types of public discourse that were at one time considered unthinkable are now much more commonplace. But enough about political animals acting out their grievances. What about human-to-human contact, between you and me? Has that also changed drastically?

I'm afraid that answer is also yes. Social media platforms have circulated new ideas and new ways of interacting with each other that, again, would have been unthinkable as recently as a decade ago.

But is all this change negative? Hardly.

We're still human beings. Maslow's hierarchy of needs has remained constant throughout history. We all need to breathe, to eat, to enjoy shelter, to feel safe, to belong to a tribe, to be loved, and also to feel good about ourselves. Beyond that arise more intellectual and spiritual needs, including self-actualization and transcendence. I do not think that these fundamental needs will ever change or go away, and furthermore, it's this bundle of desires, hopes, and dreams that identify us as human. Anything outside that—including political movements, media trends, and fashions—is like a tribal robe or a ceremonial cloak we wear. External needs can be significant, but I don't think they fundamentally change what defines us as human beings.

The novel remains one of the primary vehicles for describing the humanity wrapped inside the contemporary concerns of the author, who is trying to express those concerns in a way that readers will understand and accept.

> The realm of literature and more broadly of culture (from which literature cannot be separated) constitutes the indispensable context of a literary work and of the author's position within it, outside of which it is impossible to understand either the work or the author's intentions reflected in it.
> —M. M. Bakhtin, Forms of Time and of the Chronotope in the Novel

To read a novel is to be introduced to its author on very intimate terms. To read a novel is to understand the culture within which it was created. But to read a novel is also to glimpse ourselves and those needs and desires common to all of us, because without that connective tissue, authors could never hope to reach their readers.

Sensitivity readers

It's standard practice these days for authors and publishers to employ sensitivity readers who are well versed in the specific milieu covered within the novel. Sensitivity readers, who live and breathe the culture being represented, can pass judgment on whether details of characterizations and social interactions have been represented correctly.

This is also something that we do, consciously or not, with every novel we read. We compare topics and situations that arise with our own experience of the world, checking for authenticity or artificiality. Over time, these judgments inform our own writing, but this process can be accelerated with mindful reading.

What about you?

You and who you are may be a hot topic, and the act of writing about your own beautiful self may cause a stir. Let me say this about that: Anyone who objects to a person or a group of people who are simply being themselves (and not attacking anyone else) is wrong, wrong, wrong, wrong, wrong!

Nevertheless, cliques of people exist who demonize and ostracize others. Here in the US, book banning is on the rise, and it makes me sad to think that our noble librarians on the front lines are under attack simply for trying to offer up the widest possible array of perspectives for their communities. It makes me sadder that entire segments of writers and many topics of discussion are actively being attacked.

Whatever you do write about, I hope you will want to present your best face to the world. But be aware that whatever you write will be perceived differently by others. Like an emoji-free email, it will be open to interpretations you can't possibly anticipate without the help of other readers. Nevertheless, there are ways to detect triggers in your reading that you can use as tests for your writing. To learn to separate your personal reading experience from how others will receive this work see chapter 14, "Point of View" and chapter 20, "The Gestalt."

More options

Because societal change seems to be ever accelerating, there are more and more choices for both writers and readers. It's so last century to frame things in binary terms: gay or straight, good or evil, wrong or right. The more of us who approach novels from our separate points of view, the more the old tropes will no longer work. Rather, every novel becomes its own island with its own language, customs, and norms. Instead of grafting old meanings onto modern novels, it helps to think of every element and every position within the novel as pointing in a certain direction, like the needle in a compass. Individual objects or actions may be totems with assigned values. It's less about any inherent or imagined quality of the thing itself, but rather a question of whether its inclusion here, right here, points toward the novel's goalposts, or is a distraction that leads you in a different direction.

Any element, sacred or profane, can find a place in a work of fiction. It's not the thing itself that matters as much as the effect that's created when it's in context. Also see chapter 13, "Context in Scene."

EXERCISE 2

Reread: Pick a novel with ethnic or racial topics or characters that relate to your own life and experiences in some way. How sensitive is the author to cultural characteristics or norms that you know to be true? Are the representations authentic? Was this writing a product of its times?

Rewrite: How would you rewrite an offending passage to temper it? Is the offense timeless, or is it only part of your contemporary world? How does the way you interact with society affect your own writing?

Mass-Market Fiction

> There are no inferior types of fiction, only inferior practitioners of them.
> —*David Morrell*

Think of novel genres and book distribution channels as swim lanes. The reason those rows of pool buoys exist is to help make swimming laps as frictionless as possible. A novel's marketing and distribution work the same way. By labeling a book mass-market romcom, publishers are hoping to elicit a positive response from readers who seek a story that occupies that lane.

But those labels don't tell the full story of what's between the covers, nor do they say anything about the quality of the writing. They are just the buoys guiding a novel through distribution, shelving, and marketing. It's so easy to get caught up in labels and forget that they don't indicate at all whether you'll enjoy a given book.

Frankly, the labels mean less and less each year, especially with the rise of metatagging and search algorithms. After all, it's online behavior analysis that determines which books pop up as recommendations on Amazon or Barnes and Noble's website. Yet a different set of rules determines which books end up at Costco, Walmart, or other sales outlets.

Blazing a trail

Sometimes authors come along and create their own lanes. Colleen Hoover self-published for years and built up a substantial following before a traditional publishing house started distributing her novels. In 2023 Hoover owned five of the top ten best-selling novels in America. She charted her own path, and she delivers content that her readership laps up.

Andy Weir's *The Martian* was originally published on Weir's blog in serialized form. It became so popular that a traditional publishing house purchased the distribution rights three years later. It's a well-crafted book, and it made for an entertaining movie. Quality writing can be found anywhere.

Romance novels have long been considered to be the least deserving of the literary genres. After a 120-year silence, the *New York Times* only started reviewing romance novels in 2017, and even then only sporadically. But successful romance novelists as a group are by far the best compensated, both with legions of adoring fans and piles of money. Rebecca Yarros's best-selling 2023 novel, *Fourth Wing*, and its sequels have taken romantasy sales into the stratosphere. Is that really so undeserving?

And finally, of the dozens of novels I've studied with my reading group, the one I recommend the most to my non-writing friends is the 2017 mass-market novel *Eleanor Oliphant Is Completely Fine* by Gail Honeyman. It's funny, it's tragic, the characters are well drawn, and the plot is as tight as a drum. It's as well crafted as any work of literary fiction we've surveyed, and yet it can be enjoyed by a wide cross-section of readers. It's no criticism of Honeyman that you can buy it at Target.

The herd

Occasionally a number of similar novels are published at the same time by different publishers. That's because of the massive lead time required for books to work their way from manuscript submission to printed book. What this means is that two years ago, there was buzz around a specific person or topic or theme, and the requests went out for works of that nature. Or that novels were green-lit because they were "of the moment." It's easy for readers to infer that these themes or topics are critical to get their own novels published today, but this isn't necessarily true. In fact, that data is often two years out of date!

Don't get thrown off your path. If you find something fascinating, or insightful, or meaningful, then that's what needs to be the focus of your reading and writing, fashion be damned. Understanding why this or that publisher would be willing to take a financial gamble on a specific story is a type of advanced calculus that is beyond your control, so I don't recommend wasting time trying to understand it. Writing to what you believe the masses want will take you down a rat hole, and it requires wasting a lot of good writing time trying to understand the market.

EXERCISE 3

Reread: Pick up any novel you have available to you. Where did you buy it? Did where you bought it influence your decision to purchase it? What defines airport bookshop books? What do you think defines mass-market fiction?

Rewrite: Would your novel be sold at a superstore? Why or why not? Is writing commercial fiction important to you?

Inside Baseball

Reading improves writing, which improves reading, which improves writing, and so on.

Reading and writing form a virtuous circle. Experience with each magnifies your appreciation of the other and your recognition of the craft and energy required to complete a manuscript. I always get a thrill of recognition when something created by another writer mirrors whatever I'm working on myself.

A growing number of podcasts are dedicated to backstage stories—inside baseball—on a variety of topics. It's a survey of creative minds, and I find inspiration across many disciplines, not just writing. I don't have plans to produce a TV series, but I'm still interested in learning about camera angles, editing, and sound design because I can relate these to the construction of POV. Many aspects of good storytelling contribute to a well-crafted narrative, and I find inspiration in many unexpected places.

I used to follow the makers of *The West Wing* and their podcast, as they meticulously examined every single episode over their seven-year run. I also enjoy other podcasts dedicated to the makers of *Saturday Night Live*, featuring cast members, writers, and guests who describe how that show gets made.

I also voraciously consume *New York Magazine*'s Vulture articles, and I am proud to be a Gilmore Guy. (Long live Amy Sherman-Palladino!) Cultivate your storytelling obsessions and geek out, I say.

Watching the credits

Raise your hand if you watch the credits of a TV show or movie. Bonus points for sitting in the theater after the staff have turned on the lights and started sweeping up the popcorn. I always look there for connections. You'd be surprised how many minor contributors to a movie have the same surname as the director, producers, or sometimes the stars. I'm not going to trash nepo babies here, but I enjoy spotting familiar names in interesting places. It tells me something about how the movie was put together and also which people had the greatest influence on the production.[7]

We get the same list of credits for free at the end of every novel. It takes a village to feed and foster the literary urges of an aspiring writer, and I'm eager to learn their names.

I used to skip the acknowledgments section, but now I read it closely. As an author yourself, especially if you feel some resonance between the novel you've just read and your own work, you may want to learn the names of the agent, any editors, and the publisher, because any one of them may be interested in your writing as well. Your next step, dear readers, is to go straight to the latest *Writer's Digest* directory to look them up. Isn't it time to send out those query letters?

As a writer I hope you're also interested in studying the publishing industry, which is covered in greater detail in chapter 21, "The Publishing Industry." Unless you've already published your novel, you probably don't yet know the steps of seeing your creation through to market. Whether you self-publish, strike a deal with a small imprint, or land a contract with one of the major publishing houses, there's a routine known only to the initiated.

Finding an agent who believes in you, working with that agent to shop your manuscript, finding a publisher, the back-and-forth with an editor over the course of months or even years, and, finally, the release of your book, and then working with a publicist on interviews, readings, book signings, etc., is the inside baseball I'm talking about. To me, it's endlessly fascinating.

It's also of critical importance to any author.

Who, why, how?

I'm constantly wondering how an author came up with their story, and how they handled the germination of their ideas. Today, thanks to the magic of the Internet, we can get better answers to these questions than we could from any previous generation of authors. Many authors curate their newsletters, blogs, and social media with the hope of building a platform, mostly by writing about their own process. Major bookstore author events and interviews are streamed online, recorded, and published on YouTube.

Learning about authors and how they write allows you to compare them to your own path and gauge how far you have to go. It also increases the possibility that you can find an author on a similar path to yours or one who has written a book you wish you'd written. From there it's on to an analysis of why their book was published, at that time, in that country, and by that publishing house.

As you relate the novels you read to your own writing, I'm hoping that through the virtuous circle of reading, writing, reading, writing, and reading some more, the writing will become easier, and the reading will become more reflective and instructive.

That's what I'm banking on. It's the belief that fuels this book.

EXERCISE 4

Reread: Do you regularly read feature articles about authors? Book reviews? Do you subscribe to any writing podcasts? How did you find the authors you follow—by reading their books, or through someone else's recommendation?

Rewrite: Which author's writing is closest to your worldview? Whose writing do you emulate when you write? Think of an author you would like to learn more about and see what you can discover about their writing process that you can use in your own writing.

Notes

1. "Agatha Christie classics latest to be rewritten for modern sensitivities," *The Telegraph*, March 25, 2023, https://www.telegraph.co.uk/news/2023/03/25/agatha-christie-classics-latest-rewritten-modern-sensitivities/.
2. https://www.everythingisaremix.info/watch-the-series.
3. Lionel Shriver famously took a stand on cultural appropriation by wearing a sombrero while giving a keynote speech at the 2016 Brisbane Writer's Conference. You can find the full transcript of her speech at https://www.theguardian.com/commentisfree/2016/sep/13/lionel-shrivers-full-speech-i-hope-the-concept-of-cultural-appropriation-is-a-passing-fad.
4. "Paul Harding Captures the Quiet Side of Calamity," *New York Times*, January 22, 2023, https://www.nytimes.com/2023/01/22/books/paul-harding-this-other-eden.html.
5. Ferrante's real identity has remained a closely guarded secret for over thirty years.
6. Nisi Shawl and Cynthia Ward, *Writing the Other: A Practical Approach* (Aqueduct Press, Washington, 2005).
7. Sometimes the music behind the credits is wonderful.

WHAT YOU FEEL

6
You're Bored

The most useful definition of *boredom* I have found for the purposes of evaluating writing is this: *Boredom* is "the aversive experience of wanting, but being unable, to engage in satisfying activity."[1] To be bored, you must be denied a satisfying activity.

When reading a book, your desire is to be transported by the narrative, and so boredom is what you register when that is being thwarted.

But boredom is not the same as experiencing frustration or anxiety. Boredom is merely the failure to engage. It is not your subsequent conscious reactions, either mentally or physically, that might arise from that failure to engage. Boredom arises from the subconscious, and is therefore often tricky to diagnose.

Tell me if the following scenario sounds familiar:

CHILD (prone on the floor, head in hands): I'm bored.

PARENT (trying to solve the problem): Why don't you play with your toys?

CHILD (rolling over): I don't want to play with my toys.

PARENT: Why don't you ride your bike?

CHILD (sharply): But I don't want to ride my bike.

And the child will continue to be bored until the parent finally thinks to ask the child exactly what it is that they *do* want to do. From the psychological description of boredom above, we know that the child *wants to engage in something*. But because boredom operates at the subconscious level, it requires extra effort to identify *what* is desired, let alone to understand *how that desire is being thwarted*.

Matrix of intent versus obstacle

> [W]e read literature to have a good time. Not an easy time, nec-
> essarily, but not a hard time and not a bad time.
> —*Martin Amis*[2]

When you read, you want to be engaged with the text on your own terms. Like Goldilocks, you want an experience that is *just right*: not too challenging, poetic, or exotic—which can be off-putting—and yet challenging, poetic, or exotic enough to pique your interest and keep you engaged. For example, you may want to:

- Learn something new, perhaps through insightfulness, or by traveling to exotic locations and distant times
- Be entertained, through humor, plot twists, or a feeling of wonder and awe
- Feel communion with a character or characters, empathizing with deep emotions, such as love and sorrow
- Experience poetic, stylish writing
- Encounter an intellectual challenge arising from complexity
- Enjoy a frictionless ride, the opposite of being challenged

If you don't find what you want—if your expectations are thwarted—you may find yourself bored. But those elements relate directly to voice and tone, and so are integral to the overall character of the narrative. Not engaging for these reasons is partially due to what you bring to your reading. (See also chapter 2, "How You Read.")

But your boredom may be a result of flow, interrupted—you find you just can't get into the novel. This can happen when you encounter the following:[3]

- **Monotony**: Writing that is predictable and repetitive
- **Non-specificity:** Writing without description
- **Simplistic content:** Overexplaining, requiring no engagement from the reader
- **Passivity:** A lack of action
- **Coldness:** A lack of emotion or engagement of the senses
- **Inconsistency:** Lack of structural clarity or clear transitions
- **Complexity:** Misused syntax and unfamiliar vocabulary

There you have it: six different reading experiences you may desire, and seven potential barriers preventing you from fulfilling those desires. Your relationship to any work of fiction, therefore, becomes a matrix of different elements from these two lists. Because you're mining literature for insights that will help you write engaging, not boring, prose, you should identify exactly what you want from the text, and what in the text has induced boredom, so you can understand *why* you are bored.

The rest of this chapter will explore those seven barriers to flow. If you're not sure which one applies to you, it may help to scan the lists of symptoms.

Monotony

SYMPTOMS

- Insipid story
- Uninspired word choice
- No rhythmic variety
- Breaking the rule of threes

> Geoff drove home. So did Pam. They ate lunch. It was good.
> —*Anonymous*

Sorry for that awful prose, but it's to prove a point. Are you still with me? Good. Hemingway this is not, and here's why: These are four (not three) sentences, each made up of three monosyllabic words. Eek!

In short, it's monotonous. Monotony can, and does, exist within larger structures, too, expanding on each of three sins: A scene may be insipidly wooden; words may be repeated, or the wrong words used; and paragraphs may all be of similar length—that is, everything is exposition, or it's all dialogue.

An editor once told me she can get a pretty good idea of the quality of prose just by scanning the layout of words on the page. If there is a mixture of text and white space, a balance of description and dialogue, if the paragraphs are of a pleasing mixture of sizes and shapes—in other words, if the text exhibits sufficient variety, there's a good chance the actual writing may be inspired, precise, and have an interesting rhythm.

The key word here is *variety*.

Monotony can be found at any level: the word, the sentence, the paragraph, the scene, the chapter, the book. It's the feeling of sameness that may pervade any work written in a formulaic way.

Each chapter may contain these elements: setup, action, cliffhanger; setup, action, cliffhanger; setup, action, cliffhanger, etc. If this is the structure, no matter how skillfully each paragraph was written, the reader may soon experience ennui. It's too predictable, and predictability kills any story.

There's also the rule of threes. That is, humans crave pieces of information delivered in groups of three (and no more): "It's late; I'm tired; and I'd kill for a beer." If an author attempts longer groupings, or goes to the well too often, the resulting text can read as monotonous, even absurd. This absurdity, if acknowledged, can be useful, but it's rarely effective. Andrew Lloyd Webber and Tim Rice[4] pulled it off by describing Joseph's coat of many colors in this way:

> It was red and yellow and green and brown and scarlet and black and ochre and peach and ruby and olive and violet and fawn and lilac and gold and chocolate and mauve and cream and crimson and silver and rose and azure and lemon and russet and grey and purple and white and pink and orange and blue.[5]

EXERCISE 1

Reread: Open any novel and find a page that has several paragraphs that appear to be of similar length, then read those paragraphs. What do you find? Is the writing interesting? Is it engaging? Does it make you want to read more? Does it show any of the symptoms listed above? If not, how does it avoid them?

Rewrite: If you find these paragraphs dull, how would you modify them?

Non-Specificity

SYMPTOMS

- Too much dialogue
- Floating sensation
- Difficult to visualize
- Banal situation

The human brain craves facts and engages with details.

If I meet you at a party and tell you I know some guy who started his own company, your natural inclination, if you haven't already turned to talk with someone else by now, might be to ask, Do I know him? Or: What kind of company? Or: Why are you telling me this, and why should I care?

But what if I say, "My childhood friend Dave, the one who worked as a firefighter for twenty years, finally founded his own fire mitigation consultancy, advising towns all over Colorado. In fact, he's in such demand that he's hired a staff of twenty."

Isn't that second story much more interesting?

Comedians understand this well. Instead of telling stories about other people, so many stand-up routines consist of stories directly involving the comedian—things that happened to them, and their reactions. Because they are relating the precise details of their experiences, they make the connection between performer and audience much more real, more immediate, and more intimate. Their stories land.

Another common problem found in prose is when an author has miscalibrated the ratio between the expression of ideas and the description of action. Too much dialogue can induce the feeling of floating in a scene, of not being able to envision characters' actions or location. Readers get lost and may forget where they are, or even why they're there.

EXERCISE 2

Reread: Find a page that contains all dialogue, if possible, or at least a lengthy conversation. Start reading where the quotes begin and try to determine these characters' location in space and time. See if you are given enough information to determine what they look like and what they are doing—sitting, standing, running, in a car, or maybe doing something else.

Rewrite: Try to identify the missing details that untethered the characters from a specific physical location or activity. What would you have the characters doing that would have made their conversation more interesting?

Simplistic Content

SYMPTOMS

- Too much explaining
- Failure to engage the intellect
- Wooden characters
- Condescending tone

The secret of boring people lies in telling them everything.
—Anton Chekhov

Simplistic content in a novel can result from oversharing or from writing down to the reader. The first is a product of a writer's naivete; the second stems from hubris.

Oversharing is common among inexperienced writers. I found myself doing this while writing my first novel, wanting to fill the page with *all* the fruits of my research. More experienced writers learn what to omit from a narrative to convey only the necessary elements, and they trust the reader to fill in the gaps.

Writing down to a reader is when a writer assumes their readers lack the education or sophistication to grasp a narrative without additional help. One contemporary thriller author—I have read and enjoyed every one of his best-selling novels—writes like this. Unfamiliar people, places, or events are always introduced with Wikipedia-like entries. This tells me that the author does not trust his readership to be as sophisticated as he is, and this condescension infuses every chapter. He writes a damn taut plot, though, so I let it go. Other readers are not so forgiving.

The key to fixing this is to write *accessibly*, not *simplistically*. There's a huge difference.

To write accessibly means to give the reader a fair chance at understanding the narrative, even though it may be complex and sophisticated. This is accomplished by using common vocabulary, basic syntax and grammar, and reasonably sized sentences and paragraphs. This opens the writing to a wider range of readers, but doesn't dumb down the prose. Hemingway and Steinbeck followed these precepts in their clean, direct prose, but no one would call their writing simplistic.

Great examples of *not* writing simplistically or writing down to the reader come from well-written young adult fiction such as the *Harry Potter* series by J.K. Rowling or *The Hate U Give* by Angie Thomas. Both works are targeted at teenagers, and yet both also have a significant adult following. Think also about Pixar movies, made for children, but enjoyed equally by adults. How do they do this?

Good writing, no matter how nuanced and complex, is always accessible.

EXERCISE 3

Reread: You're here because you've just read a passage that offers too much detail. Review it closely to figure out why. It could be clunky writing, needless repetition, or overexplanation. Is the text lacking sophistication (by that I mean lacking realistic life experience)? Do you feel you are you the intended audience for this story? Why or why not?

Rewrite: How would you fix this passage? Would you do a simple edit or deletion, or do you feel you would have to rewrite the whole book to fix it? In other words, does this problem seem limited to this passage, or does it seem to permeate the entire book?

Passivity

SYMPTOMS

- Lacking concrete action
- Pages filled with thoughts and reflections
- Indirect grammar
- Too much backstory

> Action is the very basis of our art, and with it our creative work must begin.
> —Konstantin Stanislavski

Show, don't tell. Avoid the passive voice. A thousand books on writing extol the virtues of action. Novels *depend* on characters taking action, because it's the way readers know what a character is capable of—and action propels the plot. For more on why this is important to a novel, see chapter 16, "Character Development."

Theatrical action is "what the characters do to each other to get what they want from each other," according to Robert Knopf in his Stanislavski-inspired book on script analysis.[6] *What the characters do to each other.* If that sounds confrontational, it is! Conflict and friction propel narrative fiction, and without action, any narrative seems limp. (You can find more on slow-moving novels in chapter 18, "Pacing.")

Passivity can be the product of having too much backstory and not enough story. Even though some ferocious actions may have occurred in the narrative's past, it qualifies as passive because *it's not happening now*. A tale of a dragon previously slain does not engage you the same way as if you are staring down the flaming nostrils of the scaly beast towering over you right now.

Literary fiction often gets maligned for having a higher ratio of reflection to action, and for some readers, that lack of action reads as passivity. The more time a character is not *doing something*, the more they are allowing things to happen to them. But even the action-packed thriller requires a mix of action and reflection. In fact, *all* fictional characters need to experience at least *some* introspection—at least enough for them to feel real, to express what motivates them, and to convince the reader to care enough to read on.

Passivity can also be a product of grammar and syntax. This includes forms of the verb *is* plus a gerund (a verb ending in *-ing*, as in "she is walking"). *Am, are*, and *is* state that something exists as if frozen, which halts the action on the page. Gerunds take a concrete action and turn it into a static noun, removing its position in time, and obscuring when it *is occurring* (as in this phrase). Action can also be stifled through too much dialogue. Remember **what happens is not what's discussed**, from the **Seven tools**? Talking isn't doing; in fact, it holds up the action.

It's important that a novel conveys the intentions of its characters through action. This makes the characters seem real, and it propels the plot. It's also necessary for characters to reflect on what they will do or have done to others, and what others have done to them—no novel can do without some of this passive narrative. But how much passivity is too much? That's really up to you to decide.

EXERCISE 4

Reread: Refer to a passage in any novel that you feel lacks action, and take a quick survey. Can you determine where we are and what's actually happening in the scene? If that's difficult to answer, you may be looking at a reflective scene. Is it a result of passive voice? If so, why do you think the author is not involving their characters in an action?

Are you looking at backstory? If so, do you feel the story is spending too much time in the past? Are there enough action scenes to balance the reflective passages?

Rewrite: Make a passive section active. Consider how much backstory you would cut to do this, or how you would transform it into interactions between two characters in the present, further adding tension and defining relationships.

Coldness

SYMPTOMS

- You don't care about the characters.
- You can't distinguish the characters from each other.
- The characters aren't behaving logically.
- You can't imagine the scene.

By coldness I mean narrative lacking the warmth of emotion, failing to engage the senses, leaning too heavily on action or plot at the expense of reflection, or featuring flat or wooden characters. *Coldness* represents the opposite ratio of action-to-reflection explored in the previous section, "Passivity."

A novel's cold tone can be the result of sparse prose, an ironic or dispassionate voice, or themes that prioritize abstract ideas, philosophy, or social critique over emotional resonance. Or it may have to do with its meager use of the five senses. Good narrative puts you in the scene: You hear the thuds of the dragon approaching, and it's so close you can smell its awful breath. When you feel the heat of its flames enveloping your body, you taste your own coppery blood as your face melts away. Action is not just visual.

It's also possible that you're experiencing monotony. If you have problems distinguishing one character from another, if every character seems to speak with the same voice, the author may not have written each character's inner lives and motivations in a way that believably brings them to life. It could also be that those characters have not been imbued with anything visual, auditory, or tactile that would make them feel more real.

EXERCISE 5

Reread: Find a boring passage in a novel you're reading. Paying attention to POV (point of view), examine how fully the character with the POV experiences their surroundings. Can you see the character in every scene? Are their motivations and their emotional responses authentic? Or is the POV set at a distance from the action, and if so, what purpose does that serve? Is the cause of your boredom something else?

Rewrite: What elements are missing from that scene? What emotions or sensations would you add to make the scene and its characters come alive?

Inconsistency

SYMPTOMS

- You feel dizziness or a lack of ground under your feet.
- You can't tell where you are.
- You don't know who is talking.

You're here because of the feeling when reading a novel that something has shifted, maybe without your noticing—that something feels *off*. This sensation could be due to inconsistencies of timeline, tone, continuity, dialogue attribution, historical inaccuracies, plot holes, or *head-hopping* (shifting POV). Many of these are discussed in more detail in chapter 7, "You're Upset."

For this section, though, we'll limit our discussion to how inconsistencies affect various POVs and the timeline, which are the most common issues you'll encounter.

We'll start with POV. It's common to find multiple points of view in a narrative. Omniscience can also be written well. What's not good is when multiple characters get jumbled in the reader's mind to the point of confusion. Problems sometimes arise around unclear transitions and structural inconsistencies, also known as head-hopping. Clearly delineated points of view are absolutely necessary for the reader, and the following often indicate transitions between POVs:

- Chapters are titled with the name of the character whose POV is used.
- A dinkus (* * *) or spatial break separates different POVs within a chapter.
- The paragraph in which a character's POV begins features that character's name in the first sentence.

Clear, consistent POV markers from page one forward allow your reading to migrate from POV to POV seamlessly so the context shifting isn't jarring. Inconsistent POVs will definitely trip you up.

Let's also talk about inconsistencies found in a novel's timeline.

Beginning a novel *in medias res*—in the middle of the action—is so popular today that the technique has migrated from the thriller into many other genres. Grabbing a reader's attention by placing them at the midpoint or even the climax of the story in the first chapter is certainly effective, but it can creates a few challenges with form. An author needs to establish clear markers of past, present, and even future narrative. Sometimes the author deliberately switches verb tense, but tense isn't always enough of a temporal locator, as dialogue contains its own variety of tenses, potentially confusing the reader.

Moving backward and forward in time also requires the reader to work harder to keep track of who knows what and when. In this scene, was this or that already known or had that not yet happened? If not, then how does this character know about that situation?

To make matters even trickier, authors sometimes blur the lines between POV and time setting *on purpose*, to create a cloud of uncertainty within the reader's mind. This was the intent of George Saunders in his novel *Lincoln in the Bardo*. Many ghosts inhabit this narrative, ghosts who have a lot to say. But, of course, ghosts have no corporeal form, nor are they bound by the traditional space-time continuum. Saunders accomplished this nifty trick by delaying narrative attributions until the ends of sections, leaving the ghosts' words to shimmer in our minds before we know who said what, to whom, or even why. This has a magical effect, but it also can leave some readers confused. And confusion can lead to boredom.

EXERCISE 6

Reread: Open a novel with multiple POVs to any section and figure out the POV on that page. This may not be easy, because POV is almost never overtly stated in the middle of a passage. You'll likely need to search backward for a while, and this should give you a sense of how far an author is stretching the reach of a single POV. This will help you identify the initial marker that indicates a POV.

POV is one of the most difficult skills to master, and you may find this exercise difficult, but don't be discouraged! Getting better at tracking down POV in your reading will pay dividends in your writing. Remember, always **pay attention to POV**.

Rewrite: Figure out why the passage you identified was written in the POV of that particular character. How would the scene work differently from a different POV?

Complexity

SYMPTOMS

- Discomfort
- Confusion
- Where are we, and what's happening?
- Feeling lost

Boredom pervades the opening sentence of Lewis Carroll's *Alice in Wonderland*:

> Alice was beginning to get very tired of sitting by her sister on the bank, and of having nothing to do: once or twice she had peeped into the book her sister was reading, but it had no pictures or conversations in it, "and what is the use of a book," thought Alice, "without pictures or conversations?"

Here's another Alice with a similar issue in the first sentence of Lisa Halliday's *Asymmetry*:

> Alice was beginning to get very tired of all this sitting by herself with nothing to do: every so often she tried again to read the book in her lap, but it was made up almost exclusively of long paragraphs, and no quotation marks whatsoever, and what is the point of a book, thought Alice, that does not have any quotation marks?

A book without pictures or conversations, or with long paragraphs of dialogue but without attributions or quotation marks (I'm lookin' at you, Cormac McCarthy) can be challenging to read. And what's challenging to a reader can quickly induce boredom.

How about this passage from postcolonial theorist Homi Bhaba?

> If, for a while, the ruse of desire is calculable for the uses of discipline, soon the repetition of guilt, justification, pseudo-scientific theories, superstition, spurious authorities and classification can be seen as the desperate effort to "normalise" normally the disturbance of a discourse of splitting that violates the rational enlightened claims of its enunciatory modality.[7]

I'm not sure what Bhaba is saying here. I fell asleep midway through the passage. He might be describing his lunch, for all I know.

Academic writing tends toward the obfuscatory, partially when arcane vocabulary is required to express complex ideas, but mostly because non-literature-focused writers in academia often underestimate the difficulty and the time required to write comprehensible prose.

It's never a good idea to use a big word when a small one will do, just as it's risky to construct complex sentences and assume that readers will be able to follow them. The average reading level for the vast majority of current literary fiction that I've surveyed over the past seven years is seventh grade. How do I know that? Many online tools[8] are designed to help English teachers vet the texts they plan to teach in their classes. Grade levels and reading ease or complexity scores are derived from average word length, average number of syllables per word, length and complexity of sentences, and the number of paragraphs. A low Lexical Density score (from 1 to 100) and a high Flesch Reading Ease score (also from 1 to 100) indicate a text that's easy to comprehend. The fact that Literature (note the capital *L*) that wins prestigious prizes has a seventh-grade reading level on average means quality writing doesn't need to be difficult to read.

These simplistic reading-level tests are not sophisticated enough to take into account emotional heft and symbolic layering, but rest assured, modern Literature has not yet slipped to the level of *Dick and Jane*.

Let's talk now about that final bugaboo: nonstandard punctuation and unfamiliar grammar. Jane Austen overused double negatives, Emily Dickinson famously invented her own punctuation marks, E. E. Cummings used unconventional orthography ("e.e. cummings"), and William Faulkner often used no punctuation at all! To some, these writers' innovations expand the English language; to others, they're just confusing.

Authors who paddle outside the standard English swim lane risk alienating their readers, and the four authors above, along with Lewis Carroll and Cormac McCarthy, are respected and even revered. But they are only six voices out of the thousands who innovated and have never been heard from again.

EXERCISE 7

Reread: In any novel, find a sentence that confuses you. Hint: Look for a long one—it's the most likely to suffer from complex syntax. Ask yourself why the author chose to write such a complex sentence or paragraph. Where they balancing other, shorter sentences for rhythm? What's the effect of such a sentence? Does it feel poetic, soaring?

Rewrite: Try simplifying a complex sentence you've found. Maybe break it into smaller chunks, reorder the clauses, or use simpler words. Does doing this change the underlying focus or meaning? If so, how?

Notes

1. John D. Eastwood, Alexandra Frischen, Mark Fenske, and Daniel Smilek, "The unengaged mind defining boredom in terms of attention," *Perspectives on Psychological Science* 7 (2012), 482–495.

2. "Martin Amis Is Committed to the Pleasure Principle in Books," By The Book, *New York Times*, October 22, 2020, https://www.nytimes.com/2020/10/22/books/review/martin-amis-by-the-book-interview.html.

3. Shahram Heshmat, "Eight Reasons Why We Get Bored," *Psychology Today*, June 16, 2017, https://www.psychologytoday.com/us/blog/science-choice/201706/eight-reasons-why-we-get-bored.

4. https://en.wikipedia.org/wiki/Joseph_and_the_Amazing_Technicolor_Dreamcoat

5. Note the alternating duples (trochees) and triples (dactyls), their spacing, and the way they pile up. It's no accident that "orange and blue" feels like a satisfying ending.

6. Robert Knopf, *Script Analysis for Theater: Tools for Interpretation, Collaboration and Production* (Methuen Drama, UK, 2017).

7. Homi K. Bhaba, *The Location of Culture* (Routledge, UK, 1994).

8. I use this one: https://www.online-utility.org/english/readability_test_and_improve.jsp

7

You're Upset

Upset is one of those wonderful words whose meaning has evolved into its opposite. Originally a portmanteau of *up* and *set*, it once meant to construct or to erect. Now, of course, it means to topple. But it's important to remember that to be upset, you must first be set up. In other words, to experience disappointment, you must first have expectations that are frustrated.

The state of being upset is parallel to what happens when you experience boredom (see chapter 6, "You're Bored"). Psychologists describe boredom as frustration, with *low* arousal, while being upset is frustration, with *high* arousal.[1] Think of feeling bored as more unconscious frustration and feeling upset as fully conscious frustration. One benefit of the immediate realization that you're upset is that it's easier to identify the trigger within the text that made you feel this way.

Feeling upset covers a broad range of emotions from mild disquiet to queasiness, shock, offense, pain, and anger. Anger, though, is described by the latest medical research[2] as a secondary emotion. In other words, while you may feel hurt or offended while reading a text, to experience anger requires a judgment about how to react, and you choose anger.

Reacting to a novel in anger—the sharpest secondary emotion to feeling upset—helps you see how you read and what baggage you bring to your reading. It can serve as a clue to your relationship with the text and how deeply your reading affects you.[3] After all, you could have channeled being upset into astonishment, bemusement, or even laughter.

Once you notice that you are upset by a setup, it's time to find the root cause in the text. Upsetting the reader may have been intended by the author, it may result from your personal expectations, it may indicate a flaw in the writing, or any combination of the three. When you feel upset by your reading, it's important to immediately identify what you were expecting.[4]

This rest of this chapter focuses on identifying the various setups that could have been upset, which include:

- **Genre:** Story types are constructed around the expectation of a certain conclusion.
- **Consistency:** The universe of the story and its worldview are logical and consistent.
- **Representation:** Values are assigned to characters, objects, or places.
- **Agency:** Characters have self-awareness and the ability to control their situations.
- **Morality:** Stories reveal or challenge personal and societal norms of what's right and wrong.
- **Trust and truth:** The **unspoken contract** between writer and reader promises you will learn the truth whether or not **you're being played**.

Genre[5]

The Book Industry Study Group[6] lists 88 genres and 355 fiction subjects. Amazon—the largest bookstore in the English-speaking world—categorizes its books with more than sixteen thousand distinct labels, and authors can choose up to ten of these for each book.[7] From obvious genres like Thriller, Mystery, Western, and Sci-Fi, to hyperspecific labels like Viking Historical Romance, Amazon allows authors to describe a book in relation to many different categories.

It's a great system, except for one small problem: It's often misleading.

For example, Jessamine Chan's 2022 novel *The School for Good Mothers* describes a dystopian near-future world, much in the way that Margaret Atwood did in *The Handmaid's Tale*. I would think that lovers of one would enjoy the other, but Amazon has different ideas. *School* is tagged with Women's Domestic Life Fiction, Family Life Fiction, and Literary Fiction, while *Handmaid* is tagged with Dystopian Fiction (accurate), Dystopian Science Fiction (Atwood might have a problem with that), and Literary Criticism & Theory (huh?), a category within which it was the number-one bestseller.

Genre, for most novels, is an artificial construct foisted upon readers by publishers' marketing departments and booksellers in an attempt to categorize and arrange like-topic books. In brick-and-mortar bookstores, this serves a practical purpose: It indicates where to shelve the book. But beyond obvious genres like Thriller, Mystery, Western, Sci-Fi, or Romance, genre designations get murky quickly.

It's a mistake to believe that genres were ever set in stone. It's more like publishers and booksellers have back-constructed categories for what writers have already written, much like the "rules" of grammar, riddled with inconsistencies, were back-constructed from the way we actually use the language. (For more background on genre, see the "Genre" section in chapter 3, "Choosing What to Read.")

Regardless of how a novel is shelved, once a novel is labeled with a genre, readers expect the author to fulfill the **unspoken contract** of that genre. Women's Fiction tells us women's issues will be explored. Romance tells us that lovers will connect. Cozy Murder Mysteries will end by identifying and apprehending the killer. Now imagine a Romance unrequited, a Mystery unsolved, a tragic Comedy, or any novel mis-shelved or mislabeled. I'd be upset too.

Cover design

The next setup facing you is the set of promises displayed on the book jacket: namely, its cover art and the blurbs of praise. A misleading book cover can definitely set you up to be upset.

Let's begin with the art. Exterior book design conveys a lot of information about a book's intended audience through the use of color, shapes, layout, typefaces, and just a few words. There are good designs and bad designs, and I don't mean bad design in reference to awful art, horrible layout, or tragic typefaces, although that makes for an entertaining side discussion. No, bad art design misleads the reader, whereas good design tells you what to expect inside the book. Examples of good cover design include both *The School for Good Mothers* and *The Handmaid's Tale* (and the iconic bonnet design on Atwood's sequel, *The Testaments*). They feature abstract graphics, indicating a fable—that is, an abstraction of a complex social situation—and are drawn with bold, solid colors and outlines like an instruction manual, both of these dust jackets give you a hint of the broad brushstrokes contained within—the universality of these women's tales.

Misleading cover designs include the Amazon makeover of Luis Alberto Urrea's *The House of Broken Angels*, transforming the original evocative yellow cover featuring a hummingbird (good) into a circus of Mexican designs, featuring a silhouette of an old man with a child (so wrong!) hovering over a Mexican village. You might expect a Mexican pastoral parable, but in fact, it's about a sprawling family living in modern-day urban San Diego, California. Amazon must have bet that ethnicity sells, even though the cover has almost nothing else to do with the novel.

Another poorly conceived cover is the American version of Bonnie Garmus's *Lessons in Chemistry*. While the UK cover got it right—blocks of primary colors behind a 1950s housewife holding a black-and-white TV—the US cover is more contemporary, featuring a cartoon-style woman's face displaying side-eye, in the style of modern romance novels. Many readers were upset to discover a quarter of the way through that *Lessons* is definitely *not* a Romance novel.

Then there are the blurbs on the cover or just inside: praise from critics or fellow authors. Overenthusiastic reviews by fellow authors can be suspect because most authors do not want to attack the work of their fellow writers. When I read the weekly "By the Book" interview feature in the *New York Times Book Review*, I always smile when an author is asked to name any books they found disappointing. Not one contemporary author is ever named, and for good reason: No one wants that criticism to bounce back onto them.

Book blurbs can be very useful, however, especially when coming from a critic or an author who aligns with your sensibilities. For example, Tana French was ecstatic when Stephen King called her novel *The Witch Elm* "extraordinary," because King's imprimatur is one of the gold standards for suspense and crime.

Inaccurate or misleading quotes, however, set up false expectations for a novel that is eventually likely to upset you.

EXERCISE 1

Reread: Take a novel that you've recently read and look at its cover, the blurbs, and even read a critic's review or two. Were they accurate? What did they get right, and what was misleading? Was the tone of the book different from what you expected? Did this book fit into a genre, was it a mixture of genres, or was it uncategorizable?

Rewrite: How would you have categorized this novel? Would you have shelved it where you found it? Can you write a better synopsis than the one on the inside cover? What else would you have written differently?

Consistency

Authors can innovate in countless ways: Reordering events, introducing random characters, and subverting genre are just a few. But the universe of the story should be logical and consistent. Characters' names should not change without warning, nor should the attractions that connect characters, places, and worlds switch on and off without explanation. Needlessly jumping around in time and space also can lead readers to confusion and frustration.

Consistent settings, characters, and themes spanning an entire novel—called *world-building* in science fiction—combine to form an immersive alternate reality. N. K. Jemisin, in her Hugo Award–winning trilogy *Broken Earth,* created an unstable world of earthquakes, which logically spawned creatures suited to that environment: Stone Eaters and Obelisks, with the power to control seismic energy, Orogeny, and from *that* the Fulcrum and Guardians. Because Jemisin bound these elements together logically and organically, they form a believable world.

The craft of world-building actually applies to all novels. Every author paints their version of reality differently, and relates their vision to every element within the narrative, from the world, to the characters within it, down to the mechanics driving individual scenes. Consistency within a scene is also called *continuity*, an important concept in the film world with its different camera angles, edits, and multiple takes. Was the table by the fireplace now under the window? If Rajiv just drove away, why is he now standing next to Zoe? Wasn't her dress a different color? Why is the male dog now female?

Consistency of character requires consistent behavior, at least until a significant force compels them to change. In fact, most novels dedicate hundreds of pages to describing exactly how much angst a protagonist can endure before (finally!) changing their ways. Having Cyd overcoming her lifelong shyness within one scene is not believable. She has to earn her deviation from consistency as much as the author needs to carefully take her there.

We also expect consistency within genre. A common term for crossing a line or going too far afield is *jumping the shark*. This term originated from the 1980s sitcom *Happy Days*, centered on the adolescent children of a wholesome family in 1950s Milwaukee. The episode when The Fonz water-skied over a shark in Hawaii was when many fans decided the series had lost its way.[8]

Cognitive dissonance

This is the psychological discomfort caused by contradictory information and the mental strain of trying to resolve the contradiction in your mind. When an author unwittingly presents multiple realities through inconsistency, your struggle to comprehend the passage may register as boredom, irritation, or frustration.

This unease can be caused by contradictions within environments, characters, and plots, but also by the contradictions between ideas, beliefs, and values. Saying black is white or up is down or that good is evil may work in context, but if doing so upsets the established worldview, as a reader, you will struggle to understand why. Interestingly, the notion that the author may have goofed may be farthest from your mind, but your reading skills will improve if you always consider the struggles of the writer.

When you discover such confounding contradictions, remember the **First rule of _Literary Forensics_**: **Always ask why**. What are these two opposites doing here? What is the author trying to achieve? Is this dichotomy consistent with this world, this scene, this character—or has the author _jumped the shark_?

Although your first inclination might be to try to explain away such inconsistencies or to ignore them altogether, don't let up. You've just uncovered an excellent place to dig in and study.

EXERCISE 2

Reread: Look again at passage containing the inconsistencies that are making you upset. Are they inconsistencies of world-building, of continuity, character, theme, voice, or of something else? How do these contradictions affect the characters or the plot, and do you feel they were included by mistake or deliberately? If you think the author included them on purpose, do they feel necessary? What have you learned about the writer's style or techniques from these inconsistencies?

Rewrite: Fix the passage by cleaning up the inconsistencies. Has your fix changed anything outside of the immediate scene? Was anything lost?

Representation

Alexander Grothendieck was one of the most celebrated mathematicians of the twentieth century. Since his death in 2014, he has appeared in at least two recent novels: _When We Cease to Understand the World_ by Benjamín Labatut, and _Stella Maris_ by Cormac McCarthy. In McCarthy's novel, Grothendieck is presented as a friend of the protagonist, but in a very insubstantial way. He is mentioned only tangentially, and perhaps the author is using Grothendieck's name as a way to confer status upon the main character. In Labatut's novel, Grothendieck is a central character, and we get a close third-person peek into his mind. This is a very different use of a real person.

Has either author misappropriated Grothendieck's identity? Should the members of his family sue for libel? How much or how far should an author be allowed to fictionalize the life and thoughts of a real person without at least some attempt to obfuscate their identity? Does an author have any moral obligation to accurately represent historical figures? What about historical movements? Religious figures?

If we have knowledge of a specific person, or of a society, a race, a sexual orientation, a religious belief, a philosophical dogma, a mental condition, a field of study, or professional expertise, then we probably have an opinion of how each should be represented on the page. The more we know of a topic, the more critical becomes our eye for detail. Each of us considers ourselves to be an expert at *something*, be it life in Southwest Denver in the 1970s (me!), or anabelian geometry (Grothendieck), or the best locally brewed IPA (me again!). We are willing to let much of the rest of a narrative pass, but we tend not to tolerate a misrepresentation of what we *know*.

Beyond appropriating real historical figures in a distorian (history-distorting) way, in what other ways can authors misrepresent activities, professions, objects, or places? There are no bounds. It's fiction, after all. Every author of fiction is free to use contrafactual information if they feel it advances their story, including misrepresentation of minorities, hate speech, fetishism, religious viewpoints, or foisting agendas onto their readers. The question is, however, to what purpose is this invective being used? Is it intended to harm, control, or mislead readers, or is it integral to the storytelling for some other reason?

Presentism

Wikipedia contributors are cautioned not to judge historical events by current standards.[9] This applies especially to subjects determined to be "politically incorrect" by today's moral standards. Whitewashing by omission is just as inaccurate as bowdlerizing original source material. Presenting historical elements as though they conformed to today's societal norms is called *Presentism*, and scholars generally avoid it.

But is using a Presentist lens inherently wrong for the creator of fiction, and should an author avoid it altogether? Well, let's look at this issue another way. What would historical fiction look like if it did not account for its readership living in the present day?

Mostly unintelligible.

In *Burma Sahib*, Paul Theroux did an admirable job of mimicking George Orwell writing his autobiographical novel, but by presenting early twentieth-century colonialism, racism, and fetishism by using an authentic Anglo-Indian vocabulary, Theroux made his book more difficult for modern readers to read. On the flip side, twenty-first-century sensibilities drive the 1950s protagonist of Bonnie Garmus's *Lessons in Chemistry* and the thirteenth-century protagonist of Lauren Groff's *Matrix*, but those choices make the challenges faced by the women of those times easier for today's readers to understand.

To represent another era in fiction requires the author to skillfully weave the historical into what a modern reader can recognize. The historical accuracy of fiction only needs to go far enough to give the reader a taste. Novels are not textbooks, after all. This means it's up to the reader to determine how well the author has represented the past. For more on issues of representation, see chapter 8, "The Spell Is Broken."

EXERCISE 3

Reread: Recall something within a novel you've read that you feel has been misrepresented. Does the characterization of a person, place, or activity feel like a stereotype? Is its tone disrespectful to the disenfranchised? On a scale of one to ten, how dangerous do you believe this characterization is to its intended audience? Consider your perspective. Might others react in a different way? If so, why?

Rewrite: How much work would be required to rewrite the offending passages? Would it be a minor fix, or does the issue permeate the entire novel? If the solution is to change some minor characteristics of the environment or modify minor characters, think about how this might alter the overall tone, themes, or direction of the book.

Agency

The agency of characters is their degree of freedom and ability to achieve their goals—to slay their dragons or conquer their inner demons, for example. Are they given the opportunity to learn the truth, or are they encumbered with misinformation? Confusion and muddleheadedness can be just as enslaving as being chained to a rock or being as weak and dependent as a three-year-old.

When the Internet and then cell phones came into general use, writers of all genres groaned. How could their characters ever again be uninformed, misdirected, deceived, or left in the dark, if all the answers (and their phone's flashlight!) were already right there in their hands? The bad news for humanity, as we now know, is that just as much disinformation as information is available to us today, and most of us cannot tell the difference between the two. And the good news for writers is: well, just that.

Consider also the restrictions that various occupations impose upon their workers: The scientist must be objective, the scholar needs to be thorough, the judge must be fair. Then there are the limits that society itself imposes on its citizens. Various caste systems, the repression of minorities, poor treatment of women—the list goes on. An anthropologist once told me that the effect of culture on its people is to restrict them to a limited set of options.

Other barriers to agency include characters' ability to be self-aware, to recognize their situation, their limitations, or the power they have to effect change. This manifests itself in mistaken identities, misunderstood actions, and deceptive motivations, all of which have been dramatically deployed to confuse characters. How many romcom plots are based primarily on these premises?

A character who experiences some form of internal or external conflict that limits their agency and prevents them from progressing in their personal journey or achieving their goals is known as a *stuck character*. In her 2023 novel *Let Us Descend*, Jesmyn Ward tackles a seemingly impossible task: How do you give a protagonist agency when she is a nineteenth-century American slave? Although Annis has almost no control over her situation, her actions, or her body, she demonstrates her agency in the way she interacts with the spirit world, and this becomes the key to her freedom.

Status

Status refers to a character's social, economic, or hierarchical position within a fictional world and encompasses external factors such as wealth, rank, and profession, as well as internal perceptions like reputation and respect. Status can be static or fluid, even shifting from one character to another within a single scene.

Status shapes the power dynamics and relationships of every character in every scene, and is exhibited by the power a character or a group has over others. Therefore, status directly impacts a character's agency—what they are able to do, or not do.

And one more thing to keep in mind about status: No two characters in any novel have equal status—ever—that is, the status of every fictional character can be directly compared to any other.

Access to information, or knowing something another character doesn't, contributes directly to their status, as does possession of something another character desires. Status is also reflected in what a character is allowed to get away with, which is related to privilege. Think of Larry David in *Curb Your Enthusiasm* flaunting his white privilege in the most annoying ways possible, until the end of every episode, when he gets his comeuppance, and his status is instantly reversed.

EXERCISE 4

Reread: Find a passage concerning a character's agency that has left you upset, or open any novel to any scene that has two characters interacting with each other. Which one has higher status, and why? Think about the degree of agency of each character. Do their power dynamics set limits on what either character can do, or is their agency controlled by other internal or external forces? What about this power dynamic is upsetting to you, if anything?

Rewrite: Flip the status of the two characters in that scene. How does this status manifest itself, and what is the newly elevated character able to do or say that they weren't allowed to do or say before? What about the demoted character—how has their agency been curtailed? Has rebalancing their status changed how you feel about the scene?

Morality

Morality is knowing the difference between right and wrong and choosing to do what's right, even when it's hard or no one's watching. Treating others with kindness, fairness, and respect comprises the moral compass that guides us to take responsibility for our actions, forgive wrongs, and have the courage to do the right thing, even in the face of danger.

Honesty, the paramount attribute of moral behavior, is so important that it gets its own section, below: "Trust and Truth."

Morality governs individual conduct, and so shapes the judgments, decisions, and actions made by every character you will find in a novel. A good rule of thumb when evaluating a character's morality is to ask yourself whether, given the same situation, you would do the same thing. If not, then you may have good reason to be upset.

Gray areas

> "Save the Cat!"
> —Blake Snyder

If you write screenplays, you are probably familiar with Snyder's book, but did you stop to think about the title? Why is saving the cat the right thing to do? Are there cats that don't deserve to be saved? Shouldn't they be left to suffer or die in horrible ways? I can see you wincing. *Of course* you shouldn't harm a helpless pet.

Now let me rephrase the same question. Are there *people* who don't deserve to be saved? Shouldn't they be left to suffer or die in horrible ways? Some of you are nodding your heads. And I'll bet most of you were at least willing to consider the proposition. Cats aren't even our own *species*, and yet we feel instinctively more protective toward them than toward our fellow humans. What's going on here?

You're experiencing the mercurial nature of morality, and how it changes depending on who is involved, their level of agency, and other extenuating circumstances.

Let's consider some absolute no-nos. Murder? It's condoned by the state when a soldier goes to war. Theft? Taking what you can from "the man" may be considered virtuous, Robin Hood being a popular example. As for inbreeding, I'll just say that Adam and Eve, the mythical parents of us all, shared identical DNA. It's right there in Genesis.

If you find yourself upset by the immoral behavior you encounter in a novel, it's important to consider the situation, and how far a moral compass can be bent before it breaks. Even Save the Cat can be turned upside down. The very first scene of the US version of the television series *House of Cards*, Season One, introduces Francis Underwood, a generally horrible human being. He hears a dog get hit by a car and when he goes outside, he finds the animal in anguish. Instead of trying to rescue the dog, he kills the dog.

Ethics

Morality is the individual's personal compass of right and wrong, while ethics are the rules or principles we follow in a group, profession, or society. Let's say I know a secret about Jake that he doesn't want me to tell you, but I want to share it with you. If I'm your best friend and the secret is that Jake has a crush on you, that's one thing. But if I'm Jake's psychiatrist or his lawyer, revealing anything of my client's confidential conversations is both illegal and unethical. Or if Jake's secret is that he's planning to shoot up a school, and you're the police, it's my *ethical obligation* to tell you, professional relationship or not.

If morality can be fluid, then ethics are a raging river of changing context. Here's an example of "correct" social behavior that has completely changed during the years of COVID: cell phone usage in public places.

When smartphones started to become ubiquitous a few decades ago, certain social norms developed around what was and what was not appropriate. In the last few years, however, even the sanctity of the concert hall has been invaded by phones. A recital series I regularly attend has a single program posted outside the hall for patrons to photograph, with a QR code to access the program notes, which are not available any other way. The concert producers are actually encouraging their audience to keep their phones active throughout the performance, potentially disturbing the performers onstage, behavior I would have considered wrong as recently as only a year ago.

Social norms change.

It's important to keep track of what is considered polite, appropriate, or even allowable. What was once considered obscene now regularly appears on our TV streaming services, reminding us that ethical content is constantly in flux.

Sometimes an author may push the boundaries of moral or ethical behavior in service to their narrative. Presenting unethical behavior as "right" can also be used to tweak the reader into a reaction: It may upset you.

EXERCISE 5

Reread: Find a passage in a novel you've read that contains questionable moral or ethical actions. Did it involve characters behaving badly in service to the narrative, or do you sense that the author's worldview is not in tune with yours? Are you feeling nostalgic for the olden times, when people were nicer, right defeated might, and everyone just got along? Do you honestly believe that the world was ever a nicer place for everyone?

Rewrite: How would you represent the events portrayed in the book? Imagine an immoral or unethical action that would be the right thing to do in the situation and try to write those gray areas convincingly.

Trust and Truth

Storytelling is an act of delivering satisfaction in the most meager doses possible.
—*Chuck Wendig*, Damn Fine Story

All readers are vulnerable in the hands of a writer, because all relationships—including this one—are based on trust. The **unspoken contract** between writer and reader is that in spite of being played through misdirection, an unreliable narrator, gaslighting, lampshading, plot twists, cliffhangers, and coincidences, you trust that the writer will eventually drop the obfuscation, remove the barriers between the characters and their destinies, and reveal to you The Truth.

We all bring our own set of expectations to a novel: a good time, an exciting journey, morality explored, interesting relationships. We trust the author to deliver whatever has been promised on the jacket cover or through the contract of its genre. The author's job, however, is to continually deny you your pleasure, take you down pathways you had not expected, and guide you on your journey—in other words, to manipulate you. This can be upsetting.

Sometimes an author paints themselves into a corner and has to resort to extraordinary means to wrap up the plot and fulfill the **unspoken contract**. That sudden jolt you feel when enemies suddenly become friends, when issues quickly get resolved, and when the solution appears without warning, was given a name by J.R.R. Tolkien: *eucatastrophe*. It's also known as *deus ex machina*: the god from the machine.[10]

When this happens in a narrative, as a contemporary reader of novels, you're likely to feel cheated, and rightfully so. You have a right to expect the text to be peppered with clues—real clues—about where the story is going. The ending, while surprising, must be at least plausible—a natural extension of what has gone before.

I have read books and I have seen movies where it's obvious that the writer ran out of time and suddenly finished the story, logic and credulity be damned.[11] In 1950, director Alfred Hitchcock provided a new and sinister twist to eucatastrophe. In his movie *Stage Fright*, having run out of suspects for the murder back in Act I, he revealed that the murderer was with us all along, and that the movie's opening was itself a "lying flashback" designed solely to fool us into eliminating him from our suspicions. Moviegoers cried foul, and I don't blame them. Hitchcock crossed the line between unreliable narration and outright lies, seriously weakening his own movie.

Fake news

Unreliable narrators are legion. Two popular examples are Amy in Gillian Flynn's 2012 novel, *Gone Girl,* and Rachel in Paula Hawkins's 2015 novel, *The Girl on the Train*. Taffy Brodesser-Akner, in her insightful 2019 novel, *Fleishman Is in Trouble*, has a double twist of deception going on, involving both the titular character (which Fleishman is in trouble?) and the narrator (who is narrating here?). You're led to believe that the book is about one thing, then another, and finally another. I marvel at the skill with which the author gives a master class in POV, reminding us that things aren't necessarily what they seem, especially when experienced through the eyes of another person.

Another marvel of shape-shifting is Susan Choi's 2019 novel, *Trust Exercise*. Each of the three sections is told from a different point of view, à la Kurosawa's *Rashomon*, in which various characters provide subjective, alternative, and contradictory versions of the same violent event. However, in Choi's story, we also question whether there was an event at all, with the truth revealed only in the final scene.

Remember that *everything* presented to you at the outset of any novel should be carefully considered. It's as if you've walked into a theater mid-scene with every trick of lighting, sound, and spectacle on full display. It's up to you to remember that you're witnessing a play, that you're reading a novel. The truth is this: Being misled, amazed, and fooled can be enjoyable, but only when by the end of the book you are in on the game.

EXERCISE 6

Reread: Find a novel that you feel goes too far with deception, plot twists, or an untidy ending. Identify exactly which of your expectations were upset, and consider how it happened. First, identify the section, paragraph, or sentence where a piece of fake news was presented; then, go to the page where it was revealed to be false. Did the author write a deliberate lie, or did they present an ambiguous situation or condition that you made assumptions about and used to incorrectly fill in the gaps? Do you feel this misdirection was intentional, or did the author make a mistake?

Rewrite: If the novel has an unconvincing ending, identify the untidy elements and consider how you would have wrapped them up differently. The fix may require looking earlier in the novel. Was the author too ambitious, presenting too many threads or too many plot twists? To get a sense of the novel's pacing and how you might streamline the story or change its shape, consider the length of the chapters and the amount of new information presented in each chapter. Nothing is out of bounds—consider everything.

Notes

1. Edwin A. J. van Hooft and Madelon L. M. van Hooff, "The state of boredom: Frustrating or depressing?" *Motivation and Emotion* 42, no. 6 (2018), 931–946. https://doi.org/10.1007/s11031-018-9710-6.

2. Patrick M. Reilly and Michael S. Shropshire, "Anger Management for Substance Use Disorder and Mental Health Clients: A Cognitive-Behavioral Therapy Manual," US Department of Health and Human Services; Substance Abuse and Mental Health Services Administration; Center for Substance Abuse Treatment, (Rockville, Maryland, 2019; first printed 2002). https://store.samhsa.gov/sites/default/files/d7/priv/anger_management_manual_508_compliant.pdf.

3. If you feel your emotions are getting in the way of your reading, it may help you to read chapter 1, "Your Point of Reference" and chapter 2, "How You Read," and conduct a self-assessment. Identifying your triggers is the first step to mastering them.

4. This is a callback to the "Horizon of Expectations" section in chapter 1, "Your Point of Reference."

5. For other angles on the makeup of genre, see the "Genre" section in chapter 3, "Choosing What to Read," and the "Marketing" section of chapter 21, "The Publishing Industry."

6. https://www.bisg.org/

7. Find a much deeper discussion of fiction categories in the "Marketing" section of chapter 21, "The Publishing Industry."

8. The fact that this turning point did not occur when the *Happy Days* family were visited by an alien (Mork from Ork) is beyond me. Both of these fictitious events had to be cries for help coming from the writers' room.

9. https://en.wikipedia.org/wiki/Wikipedia:Presentism

10. In the final scene of many early seventeenth-century operas, a (usually Greek or Roman) god would descend from the rafters on a wire controlled by machinery, to wave their magic wand or finger or sprinkle dust or strum their lyre and fix every problem on the stage. Talk about a cheap trick!

11. Writing the ending of a novel is one of the most difficult skills for writers to master, and this is why it's so important for you to read a novel all the way from beginning to end. I believe the more novels you finish reading, the more likely you will finish writing your own novel.

8
The Spell Is Broken

Sometimes you're reading and encounter something strange, unusual, or wrong that causes you to stop and wonder: What just happened? What *was* that? Any number of things can trip you up, popping you out of your flow state and back into the real world, startled. Let's call these *jagged edges*.

Often the jagged edge is a word that looks odd or out of place, something improbable or impossible. It's jarring enough that your subconscious ejects you from the story. Poof! The spell is broken. If you've encountered this in your reading, this chapter is for you.

There's not enough room in this chapter to talk about every variety of jagged edge, so I've narrowed it down to a factual mistake or something that doesn't feel right, based on your experience. Other issues can jar you out of your reading zone, of course, so here are some incongruities covered elsewhere:

- Is something unclear or confusing? See chapter 9, "You're Confused."
- If the culprit was poor word choice or awkward sentence structure, please refer to chapter 12, "Language and Grammar."
- Does something within a scene feel out of place? See chapter 13, "Context in Scene."
- Are characters not acting naturally or realistically? See chapter 14, "Point of View," chapter 15, "Voice," or chapter 16, "Character Development."

Are you still here? Good. It's time to start hunting for the improbabilities and impossibilities that create those jagged edges.

Probable impossibility

> With respect to the requirements of art, a probable impossibility
> is to be preferred to a thing improbable and yet possible.
> —*Aristotle*, Poetics

For millennia, audiences have been able to *suspend their disbelief* and accept a narrative that contains seemingly impossible elements, but only if they are probable and derive logically from the premise. Aristotle described these events that, while not possible in reality, seem convincing and natural within a story—like magical creatures or supernatural powers—as *probable impossibilities*. And we readers accept these probable impossibilities all the time: vampires, zombies, and the belief that two lovebirds can live happily ever after.

Good storytelling emphasizes emotional resonance and internal consistency over literal truth, making these imaginative elements more compelling for readers. Let's look at a few probable impossibilities to see how they hold up.

- Is it possible that the Millennium Falcon can zip from one end of the universe to the other? No. Nothing can go faster than the speed of light. But, *given the Star Wars universe*, is it probable that hyperdrive works? Yes, of course. Success.
- Is it possible that Forrest Gump could have been in all those different places at the exact moment when those historic events took place? No way. *Given Forrest's special gifts*, is his story probable? Yes, as would be any obviously fantastical fable. Success.

Now let's examine a few Aristotelian no-nos: scenarios that are possible but improbable.

- Is it possible that Serena Williams could have won every tennis tournament that she ever entered? Yes. Is it probable? No. We all instinctually understand that not even one of the greatest players ever can win one hundred percent of the time. Fail.
- Is it possible that world leaders will all, at some point in the future, embrace world peace? Yes. Is it probable? Uh, I don't think so—have you ever met human beings? Fail.

If an impossibility is presented logically—a marionette becoming a boy, a nutcracker wooing a girl—and the reader can accept it, then following the logic of the premise can make for a satisfying story. Consider the outrageous impossibility of King Oedipus killing his father and marrying his mother. *If you can accept that*, then the rest of the story follows logically.

To take Aristotle's lesson further, let's tease apart the story of the world's most famous archaeologist Indiana Jones, who is himself a bundle of probable impossibilities.

We'll begin with the elephant in the room. All of the adventure, all the fun scenes audiences enjoy arise from the fact that Indiana Jones is essentially a grave robber. Would an audience cheer on someone who gleefully desecrates human remains? Not so possible. Therefore, the writers made him a college professor, who steals artifacts not for himself, but to add to his university's museum collection for the greater good. That is more probable.

Now let's consider the impossibility of Indiana Jones's expertise. He has a genius-level fluency in a number of languages and understands more deeply than any other expert on earth the fine details of a number of cultures, a feat that would have required a few lifetimes of study. And he also is never wrong about a single historical detail—not ever. Much like Dan Brown's semiologist Robert Langdon in *The Da Vinci Code*, Jones instantly arrives at insights that would take a normal expert in the field months, if not years to decode, and he is able to do this while fending off snakes or evading a giant boulder. Possible? No. But given that impossible expertise, is it probable that it was he who discovered the Ark of the Covenant when no one over the past 2,500 years had done so? Yeah, sure.

On to Indiana Jones's professional career. He should have been made head of his department by now, right? But that wouldn't do, because the additional administrative responsibility would tie him down to the campus. Jones needs to be able to, at the drop of a fedora, gallivant across the world. Therefore, he must have some character flaw that has hampered his career, like being the classic rogue cop, right? Relationship issues, a drinking problem, or maybe a severe aversion to the rule of authority. But the writers' hands are tied: Jones can't appear to have any of these problems, because remember, they're trying to redeem a grave robber. So he has a boss and is respectful of his authority and the "rules" of antiquity collection (which don't really exist). Impossibly, we are asked to believe that he never rebels, is completely subservient to authority, and understands right from wrong. But once we accept Jones as a moral character, is it probable we will cheer his exploits? You tell me.

Areas of expertise

While we often embrace probable impossibilities in storytelling—cheering for grave-robbing professors or believing in faster-than-light travel—there are other areas where suspending disbelief becomes more challenging. Some narrative elements, especially those rooted in the real world, are subject to greater scrutiny. When a story touches on actual history, specific cultures, relatable life experiences, or familiar professions, readers can become far less forgiving.

Let's explore how these factors, ranging from historical accuracy to personal identification, influence your willingness to believe and engage with a narrative. I'll group these jagged edges into five areas and cover each topic in greater detail:

- **Historical eras:** Challenges in realistically representing to a modern audience a historical epoch that is unfamiliar to most readers.
- **Location and culture:** Translating unfamiliar places and peoples to a general readership.
- **Life experiences:** When we encounter experiences similar to our own, we become hypercritical.
- **Professional expertise:** Our perception of professions and hobbies colors our reading.
- **Physical predisposition:** We may resemble characters who are not portrayed sympathetically.

Historical Eras

In the late 1990s, I picked up a best-selling novel about an amazing prophecy contained within an ancient Peruvian text dating back to about 600 BCE that predicted a "massive transformation in human society in the last decades of the twentieth century." Time was being measured in millennia. When I read that passage about the Peruvian prophet who had no knowledge of the Christian Era system of numbering years, I closed the book and threw it in the trash. That single glaring anachronism broke the spell so completely that I could not continue reading the story.

I'm a history nerd, and I enjoy the four-dimensional chess required to picture ancient times or alternative societies, as both a reader and a writer. I appreciate how difficult it is to accurately portray a distant time and also to translate that experience into a story a modern audience can comprehend and appreciate, without tipping too far into presentism.[1] I'm always on the lookout for clunkers. Here are a few of many I've encountered over the years.

Anachronisms: The presence of a color TV in the early 1950s took me out of one novel completely, and I had to check it out. For context, my middle-class family didn't own a color TV until the 1970s. Score: B-. Color TVs did exist at that time, but broadcasts were rarely in color. Because the television was in the story only to denote wealth and status (and had no bearing on the plot), I think it would have been better to use something less startlingly odd.

Modern conveniences: Here's a general nit. In period westerns, horses are often used like cars are today: always ready and fast with limitless energy. In real life, they weren't.

Hunky-dory race relations: Thank you, Toni Morrison, Jesmyn Ward, and Ta-Nehisi Coates, for writing historical fiction that cuts to the bone. We should never forget that people can be unspeakably cruel to those they consider to be outcasts. Whitewashing this cruelty in historical fiction does not make it better; it serves only to make the writer look foolish. (Shame on you, *The Legend of Bagger Vance*.[2])

Everyone speaks a common language: As recently as a few hundred years ago, dialects and languages were translated far less frequently, so cross-cultural communication was rare. I do like Lauren Groff's solution in *Matrix* to her twelfth-century nuns communicating in a pastiche of regional French, English, Gaelic dialects, Latin, and Greek: She uses indirect attribution (no direct quotes) exclusively, sparing the reader the more accurate, but tedious language-switching. In *The Name of the Rose*, Umberto Eco found another solution in a similar epoch: He merged the pastiche of languages into the mouth of a single character who was understood by all, contextualizing the common language used by the other characters and throwing it into relief.

Getting a distant time and place right is notoriously difficult; translating that experience so a modern audience can understand it accurately is next to impossible. And who can really say how accurately this is represented, because none of us was there. It's easy for an author to make a misstep and create that jagged edge for the reader.

EXERCISE 1

Reread: In a contemporary novel, a work of historical fiction, or a fantasy novel, pick a detail at random and ask: How certain am I that this is possible, given the time and place? What might be wrong about it? Theorize about why the author has landed on using that specific detail and not any other.

Rewrite: How would you fix the inaccuracy? What is possible? Is an anachronism integral to the plot, or would a different detail get the point across better?

Location and Culture

The more one is able to leave one's cultural home, the more easily is one able to judge it, and the whole world as well, with the spiritual detachment and generosity necessary for true vision.
—*Edward W. Said*, Orientalism

Spirit of place refers to the qualities that make a specific location uniquely meaningful and emotionally significant to you. Your sense of a place is shaped not only by its physical elements—landmarks, landscapes, architecture—but also through its culture—traditions, festivals, cuisine, technology, fashion, arts, music, and stories.

The place where we grow up shapes our lives, and its tribal, religious, and political beliefs form who we are. What's considered cool, who has power, and what really matters to our peers, controls what we do and why we do it.

A huge barrier to writing believable contemporary fiction is the fact that a significant number of readers will be familiar with that location or culture, and they will know immediately whether or not a given scenario, activity, or character has been portrayed accurately.

An author's engagement with the greater world contributes to their worldview and informs how sympathetically they are able to imagine or portray a location and culture not their own. If a story travels to distant lands, then having more than a passing knowledge of location and culture is crucial to keeping it real.

In some novels, the location itself takes center stage: the Hotel Metropol in Amor Towles's *A Gentleman in Moscow* stands in for the deprivations of Stalinist Russia; the road in Cormac McCarthy's *The Road* represents our culture's path toward destruction; and Elena Ferrante's Neapolitan novels could not exist without Naples.

Of course, a novel can also be about the decimation of location, like Native American tribal land in Tommy Orange's *There There*, or the use of teleportation devices in Mohsin Hamid's *Exit West* that render location meaningless, reminding us that no matter how long we live anywhere, we are all immigrants.

EXERCISE 2

Reread: Find a novel with at least one scene set in a location or culture you're familiar with. Are the conflicts between characters personality-driven, or are they rooted within local cultural or societal norms? Is the setting integral to the story, or does the location not matter? Are the setting and its culture accurately depicted?

Rewrite: Within a scene, fix any inaccuracies directly related to its location and culture. Would that same scene work if depicted within a different society, culture, or location? Why or why not? Try writing a scene set in a different milieu.

Life Experiences

A mullet competition in Michigan in 2020 quickly expanded to become a national event, and today men and women vie to be recognized for their hair. It's a thing people do. If you own a Harley-Davidson motorcycle, no one needs to explain to you the significance of Sturgis, South Dakota. Music lovers understand the shorthand of experience implied just by naming important events: Coachella, Glastonbury, Stagecoach, Newport, KAMP, Tanglewood, Woodstock, and hundreds more.

If you are a parent, you know all about the Terrible Twos, and you may cringe as your own parents spoil your kids rotten. Younger siblings endure elder brothers and sisters, and vice versa. Dealing with pushy cousins, wacky uncles, and estranged relationships is the stuff of millions of stories, and will inspire millions more.

You may have gotten a tattoo (or twenty), been to Burning Man, ridden in a helicopter, or surfed in Hawaii. A growing number of us have experience with drugs, legal or not, prescribed or selected, and we understand the distinct effects unique to each.

A large part of our lives involves the people we meet, the friendships we make, and the loves we share. Our animal beings crave contact with other humans (or our pets), which is critically important to our health, our mental well-being, and ultimately our survival. I do not think that the human race will ever tire of reading about friendship and romance.

These are our life experiences, and these are the subjects, the topics, and the backdrops and foregrounds of the stories we read and write. And when an author writes what they know, they can never go too far astray, right?

Yet having an experience does not necessarily make it a universal experience. An event significant to one person may be almost meaningless to another, even if they are experiencing the same event! A well-known, seemingly universal experience distilled down to shorthand implying a point of view or a state of mind or a level of education or intelligence risks becoming a cliché, or worse, a stereotype.

It's important to remember that an event or experience is one thing; whereas the value ascribed to the event, or the social marker implied by the experience, is a very, very different thing: a product of someone's judgment.

When a singular character in a novel passes judgment on events or situations, that's a device pulled out of the author's character-constructing toolbox. When a narrator or the voice of the author expresses that same cliché or stereotype, however, we see the author revealing their own narrow worldview. An author's treatment of life's varied tapestry is multilayered, and it may mean different things when expressed through different voices:

- Individual character
- Group or tribe
- Narrator or author

If the judgment is made at a single character's level, it could introduce a potential conflict with another character. If expressed by the group, the judgment can reveal the biases and mindsets of those in power.

EXERCISE 3

Reread: Are you here because you were struck by a cliché? A stereotype? An inaccurate portrayal of a life experience you've had? Do you sense prejudicial treatment—overly positive or negative? What about characters' interactions with each other? Do their motivations seem real? Are their reactions to hardship or success believable? Are you rooting for the hero, or for someone else?

Rewrite: In that same passage, would you express any judgment or preference differently, by softening the tone or changing the description altogether? How would that change the voice of the narrative?

Professional Expertise

I think we all enjoy reading about experts doing expert things: entrepreneurs amassing their empires, sports teams executing their game plans, researchers curing diseases and discovering new medicines, and hundreds of other topics. Part of the thrill is exposure to the professionals' inner lives: peeking behind the scenes, understanding the landscape and obstacles to success, hearing their jargon, and being slightly confused but giddy. The onslaught of unique words, expressions, and situations makes the writing feel more authentic, and the best writing of this type puts you in the room where it happens.

But because real professionals spend months, years, and decades doing what looks to an outsider like boring, repetitive things, and it would be most authentic and realistic to show them doing those boring, repetitive things, how can a writer make an expert's life interesting and yet authentic at the same time? The answer is through artifice. Through a careful balance between the probable and improbable, and between the possible and the impossible.

Each of you has your own expertise that deeply influences how you accept or do not accept what's presented to you in the text of a novel. Are you a computer expert? You'll notice when software is supposed to be doing something it can't do. An EMT? You'll be hypercritical of lifesaving techniques. Run a restaurant? There's no way that many people can be served that quickly.

I, for example, am a classically trained pianist, conductor, and composer, so I am hypersensitive to music and rhythm. When I watch a movie, I can't help but judge the soundtrack. If an actor is pretending to play the piano, I notice how far their hands are from the keys that generate those notes. For the life of me, I cannot understand how much money goes into period costumes, hair, makeup, sets, and props, and how little attention is paid to period music. It drives me nuts when they get it wrong, which is often.

EXERCISE 4

Reread: Find a novel you've read centered on an area of your expertise. Did they get it right, or does it feel false? If it's inaccurately portrayed, do you think the author was ignorant of the subject, or could it be that their mistake was a choice— to move the story along, or to reveal something about character, for example?

Rewrite: Create a more authentic portrayal of someone in that profession and observe how your fixes change scene tension, character motivation, or even the plot. Is your fix easier to read, or have you made things more complicated in your quest for accuracy?

Would it make more sense for that character to practice a different role within the same profession, or a different profession entirely—which would work better? Maybe the head coach ought to be the linebackers' coach; or the neurosurgeon should be the anesthesiologist; or the orchestral conductor should be the principal violinist.

Physical Predisposition

> I look to a day when people will not be judged by the color of their skin, but by the content of their character.
> —*Dr. Martin Luther King Jr.*

Who you are and what you look like shouldn't matter, especially if you believe as I do that we are all created equal. Unfortunately, as George Orwell put it in *Animal Farm,* some of us are more equal than others. It's sad, but that's the way the world works.

The 2010s marked a time of many advances in gender and sexual equality, and also much societal backlash. As a result, as I write this in the 2020s, these topics are currently politically fraught and emotionally charged. Add the topics of medical conditions, including substance addiction, physical and mental disabilities, as well as those of race, culture, and class, and you've got many reasons to be pulled out of the text you read when any one of those subjects is misrepresented.

This topic, more than any other, is why I select for my study group only novels published within the past twelve to eighteen months. It is so important to see and understand how humanity in all its flavors is being portrayed today, because physical depictions are fraught with difficulties for the writer.

Is an author remaining neutral when designating the physical attributes of their characters, or are they using appearance as shorthand for a stereotype? And, naturally, if we possess any combination of those physical characteristics (and that's all of us), we are sensitive to writing that portrays the group we identify with less than equitably.

One last thing: It's important to separate the novel from the novelist. (This topic is also covered more broadly in chapter 5, "What Should You Write?") Knowing the race, gender, sexual orientation, or any other characteristic of the author will, for better or worse, inform how you receive their writing. But it shouldn't *limit* how you receive what they write.

Don't be guilty of limiting the content of an author's characters by judging the color of the writer's skin, their gender, sexual orientation, or by any other physical predispositions. Be sure to treat all authors equally, just as you would expect them to represent their characters with fairness and respect.

EXERCISE 5

Reread: You're here because the physical portrayal of a character in a novel was so jarring that it made you jump out of the narrative. Was that character's appearance important to the story, or did it distract from it? Was it necessary to know their medical condition, drug habits, sexual orientation, or race?

Rewrite: See if you can rewrite the offending passage in a more sympathetic way. If you can't, think about how the story would change if that character's physical characteristics weren't described at all, or kept to a minimum, of if they looked completely different. Would that character's function in the story remain the same? Why or why not?

Notes

1. See also the "Presentism" section in chapter 7, "You're Upset."
2. A 2000 sports film starring Will Smith as Bagger Vance, a sort of golf shaman. Set in segregated Georgia in 1931, it was released into theaters at a time when even Tiger Woods was not allowed to be a member of Augusta National Golf Club because of the color of his skin, a particularly egregious example of revisionist history.

9
You're Confused

'Twas brillig, and the slithy toves
Did gyre and gimble in the wabe:
All mimsy were the borogoves,
And the mome raths outgrabe.
—*Lewis Carroll, "Jabberwocky"*

You're here because the novel you're reading has left you feeling confused. Unclear, disorganized, or flawed writing can lead to confusion, but confusion can also be the result of a deliberate choice made by the author to engage with you, to encourage critical thinking, and to evoke an emotional response.

Remember the **unspoken contract**: the progression from darkness to light, from chaos to orderliness, and from confusion to enlightenment. Confusing you may be exactly what the author intended, as Lewis Carroll did in his nonsense poem "Jabberwocky." Confusion that eventually yields to clarity can make for a satisfying reading experience.

To be certain you're in the chapter that best applies to your reading experience, let's compare confusion with dissonance. Chapter 8, "The Spell Is Broken," covers the five types of jagged edges that can prevent you from suspending your disbelief. Those dissonances arise when a novel is in conflict with our experience of the real world. Confusion, on the other hand, arises from within the narrative: from ambiguities, contradictions, unfamiliar terms, or poor organization. Unlike feeling bored (see chapter 6, "You're Bored") or finding the spell has been broken through dissonance with the real world, feeling confused does not necessarily indicate a failure on the part of the novelist. The author may be deliberately leading you on a journey from confusion to enlightenment.

Before we investigate specific categories of confusing text, let's first address root causes of confusion that can appear in any of the following areas.

Contradictions

Let's say that a character's name changes mid-scene, or their dead aunt is suddenly alive, or someone's emotion doesn't match how they behave.[1] These inconsistencies are all evidence of poor writing or careless editing.

But sometimes contradictions are necessary to the story, a good example being the unreliable narrator. That's when you are fed contrafactual information by a main character whose intention is to obfuscate and confuse. Of course, if your confusion isn't resolved by the end of the novel, feel free to pass judgment on the author.

Poor organization

This can be anything from awkward sentence structure to scenes presented out of order to an entire plot that seems to make no sense. Also watch out for switching POVs or head-hopping, moving backward and forward in time, or characters and scenes presented without explanation. Sometimes, however, an unusual format or structure is intentional, so you must determine whether it supports the overall effect the author intended.

Unfamiliar symbols and practices

Long words, foreign phrases, obscure customs, and esoteric motives can all make a novel difficult to read. So does anything obscure that an author expects you to understand but doesn't explain. Part of the writer's craft is in knowing what is common knowledge and what is not, and in giving you subtle hints when presenting something out of the ordinary. Overexplaining is pandering, but under-explaining is confusing. It's a balancing act.

Ambiguity

The most common source of confusion arises when there aren't enough concrete details provided by the author to ground you within the narrative. Omitting critical details, such as in a scene that hasn't been properly set, or from descriptions of characters, or when indicating who is speaking, can leave you wrestling with multiple interpretations and contradictory readings. Economy of words is a virtue, but too few words leave the text too vague to be understood.

Cognitive overload

A novel can also be too much—that is, stuffed with too many characters, too much detail, or too many storylines. Some novels could benefit from serious editing. On the other hand, sometimes complexity is exactly what the author intends, as in the case of Jennifer Egan's 2022 novel *The Candy House*. Egan presents the reader with so many characters in so many scenarios that it becomes clear this overload is intentional and conveys one of her novel's main themes, the brain's response to social media.

Long sentences and long chapters can also lead to mental strain. When section breaks, chapter breaks, or plot points are set too far apart, the distance between them can fatigue and disorient the reader.

Missteps like these can occur anywhere within the novel, from word choice and grammar to characterization, scene, plot, and the novel as a whole. The root causes of confusion will likely fall into one or more of the following categories:

- **Vocabulary and grammar:** Unattributed dialogue, mangled grammar, unfamiliar words, or foreign phrases
- **Culture and history:** Unfamiliar places, events, or symbols
- **Characters and point of view:** Head-hopping or psychological incongruities
- **Scene and plot:** Unclear primary action or motivation, unexpected or unexplained gaps in the narrative, or too many twists and turns
- **Distancing effects:** Writing that breaks the norms and seems experimental

Vocabulary and Grammar

Sometimes an important scene hinges on a single word, and you've never read that word before, so you wonder whether it was misspelled. Perhaps a description is missing, or actions are described out of order, or the sentence's syntax is garbled. You reread the passage again and again, but it refuses to make sense. What's going on?

You're looking at poor word choices that may have resulted from other choices that led to this awkward moment. Maybe the author wanted to express two ideas that should have been stated separately, or the material itself might have benefited from a different introduction or a different point of view.

We've all experienced this awkwardness in one novel or another. By spending a few extra minutes to discover possible meanings of the word or passage, you can usually figure out what the author intended to say. Your next step, as a student of good writing, is to think of a clearer or less clumsy way to say it.

Mangled grammar

Subject-verb disagreement, dangling modifiers, too many subordinate clauses, phrases that don't fit together, incorrect use of commas or apostrophes—we've all seen these grammatical errors. Other times a writer may be overly ambitious, attempting to cram too much information into a single sentence. As a general rule, the longer the sentence, the more clauses you must track and the greater the potential for confusion.

Sometimes grammatical issues arise when an author is trying to be ambiguous, for example by hiding the gender of a character, or merely hinting at their presence in a scene. Or a sentence may flow smoothly but its content is vague. In both of these situations, whether the sentences seem to be overloaded with too much information or almost devoid of specificity, the author is calling on grammar to do the heavy lifting that would have been better left to scene setting, context, or plotting.

Technical jargon or foreign phrases

Sometimes you'll see profession-specific lingo that is not intended to be clearly understood but is there only for effect. Obscure words or dense acronyms can indicate that Skippy Sailor is an expert seaman or that Joe Grunt knows his way around a battlefield. Other times an author will use foreign words or entire phrases to indicate a character's fluency in another language. You are expected to understand the Frenchman's *je ne sais quoi* or the German's *schadenfreude* without a dictionary.

Within the proper context, a foreign word or two can go a long way to set a tone. But the text can become confusing when understanding a scene depends on decoding the meanings of unfamiliar words. Some authors address this by immediately following unfamiliar words with an explanation in English. This can give the reader a hint of foreignness and a bit of education in the same paragraph.

Other novels, like James Joyce's *Ulysses* or Paul Theroux's *Burma Sahib*, are so saturated with unfamiliar words and phrases originating in languages other than English that most readers can't hope to understand them without the help of a dictionary or search engine.

Dialogue and attribution

A frequent source of confusion comes in the middle of a section of dialogue, when you've lost track of who is saying what. This may be due to a lack of attribution ("he said," "she said") in the text. Sometimes characters in conversation seem to be speaking with the same voice, which also makes it difficult to differentiate between them. Lack of attribution stems from a desire to streamline the text, because too many attributions—although clarifying—can annoy some readers.

Removing attributions can also be an aesthetic choice, more about creating a stream-of-consciousness effect than about limiting word count. George Saunders cleverly used this technique in his 2017 experimental novel, *Lincoln in the Bardo*, which is chock-full of ghosts. To achieve the magical effect of having them float in front of us, he began their dialogues without any attributions at all. He assigned attributions much later in the section, leaving readers initially confused about who was saying what. In this case, the lack of attribution was *intentional* and integral to the storytelling; it created a sensation that could only arise through the medium of words.

Now let's consider dialogue without attribution and also without quotation marks. You might think it would be more difficult to read than dialogue with quotation marks, yet often this indirect attribution forces the writer to make the question of who is speaking clearer to the reader than passages without any attribution at all.

Action attributed to a specific character can also be interspersed into dialogue, in place of using the word said. *Monica set down her glass*, or *Greg did a spit take*. I like to see an action by a character inside the same paragraph as what they just said, tying the action and the quote together and making it clear who's saying and doing what. Not every writer does that, though, which can make the dialogue more confusing. Also, what is being said can sometimes indicate who is saying it, but that's not always the case.

EXERCISE 1

Reread: In the novel that had you confused, or a novel in a genre you don't usually read, about a topic you don't know, or set in a place you've never visited, look for confusing sentences or unfamiliar words, place names, or events. Are terms explained or described, at least the first time they occur, or does the author expect you to know their meanings without any assistance? Think about how many words or phrases per page you are willing to look up. Do the unfamiliar terms on these pages exceed that number?

Rewrite: Do you understand what's going on well enough to relate the story to someone else? How would you rewrite a challenging passage to make it more understandable? Would your changes alter the narrative voice?

Culture and History

The sum of human wisdom is not contained in any one language, and no single language is CAPABLE of expressing all forms and degrees of human comprehension.
—Ezra Pound, ABC of Reading[2]

Years ago, I read *Snow Country*, a classic Japanese novel written by Yasunari Kawabata published in 1948 (and later translated into English by Edward G. Seidensticker). During its climactic scene, the protagonist refers to his geisha girlfriend as a woman instead of a girl. Apparently, that's the moment she knows their romance is doomed, but I did not understand the significance of that one word, or that era of extreme class disparity, and so its importance flew right over my head.

Translated novels, lifted from one culture and filtered into the language of another, are diminished by even the most artful translation. That's because readers who are not multicultural (that's most of us) can't begin to fathom the subtle ways that different locales, belief systems, and societal norms affect the stories of the people who live in those places. We may find ourselves lost in translation.

Milieu

Novels from your own culture but set in a different time period or social context may contain language or references that are unfamiliar to you. Think of all the different subcultures that exist today: military, athletic, financial, agricultural, medical, technological, political—the list goes on and on and on. About any of those groups, what would they have been doing differently, and how they would have communicated differently twenty, fifty, or one hundred years ago? Confusion can arise when a novelist tries to translate archaic activities and speech patterns into a modern vernacular.

Symbolism

As discussed in chapter 19, "Layering," your novel-reading experience is greatly enriched when you can spot the themes and symbols embedded in the narrative. But what happens when you aren't familiar with the symbols an author uses, or the ambiguous elements are not clearly defined or explained? That might lead you to misinterpret a novel's underlying messages, contributing to your confusion.

When reading Lisa Halliday's *Asymmetry*, it helps to have read *Alice in Wonderland*. Madeline Miller's *Circe* benefits from some knowledge of Greek and Roman mythology. A common trope for English and American writers for the past few hundred years is to model dramatic elements on Shakespeare's plays, or to utilize Judeo-Christian symbolism. If you don't know your Shakespeare, then the titles of Gabrielle Zevin's *Tomorrow, and Tomorrow, and Tomorrow* and Eleanor Catton's *Birnam Wood* won't land as intended. And if you haven't read the Bible, references such as the title of William Faulkner's *Absalom, Absalom!* or the opening line of *Moby Dick* ("Call me Ishmael") will fly past you.

EXERCISE 2

Reread: Pick up a novel about a culture or setting that you know nothing about. Read until you encounter the first activity or bit of jargon that's confusing to you. How effective do you think the novelist is at describing what's happening? Do you understand what's going on?

Rewrite: Using the same passage, change the culture or setting to one you're familiar with, using lingo and symbols you know well. How much do you have to explain to make it understandable or relatable to any reader?

Characters and Point of View

Say Jessica appears in a scene you're reading, and she's written in a way that indicates you should already be familiar with her, but you can't remember who she is or why she's there. Has this happened to you?

It's confusing when characters resemble one another, especially in stories with a lengthy cast of characters. But many times, when you can't remember who is who, it's not necessarily your fault; this might be an authorial shortcoming. There are so many ways an author can distinguish every character, making them unique and easy to visualize, that no two characters should feel interchangeable.

A writer can evoke multiple senses to differentiate a character's role, position, or relationship to the main character and the action, keeping those essential descriptions coming throughout the novel. A character may have a special look, a habit, a verbal or physical tic, or a way of dressing or moving or sighing that signals their appearance in the story. Characters without any of these distinctions become just as unmoored and ghostly as the phantoms in Saunders's *Lincoln in the Bardo*.[3]

Some characters are differentiated with a unique name, feeling, or even a single recurring description. For example, the *"crapulent major"* in Viet Thanh Nguyen's *The Sympathizer* made an indelible impression on me, especially because of Nguyen's use of an unfamiliar word, "crapulent." That word accompanies the major every time he appears in a scene, and it perfectly describes him.

Head-hopping

A scene in a novel should be easy to visualize, and it's the author's job to help you to create that movie inside your head. You should know where each scene is physically located at every moment, which characters are present, and what is happening. It should be clear whether you are viewing the action from above, omnisciently, or if you are inside one character's consciousness.

Shifting the POV from one character to another is quite common in modern fiction. Most of the recent novels I have surveyed have multiple POVs, but these shifts need to be handled with care. A change of POV to that of a different character is almost always marked with that character's name, which is usually found in the chapter heading, or in the first sentence or paragraph. Poorly executed context switching, that is, frequent changes of POV without clear or consistent markers, is known as head-hopping, and it almost always leads to confusion.

An example of an omniscient POV done well is Ann Patchett's novel *Bel Canto*, in which the narrator's perspective floats like a spirit to inhabit the mind of one character after another. But Patchett provides easily identifiable markers so that it's clear where you are within each scene at any given moment.

Psychological incongruity

The American psychologist Robert Plutchik spent his career studying and quantifying human emotions, building upon Charles Darwin's study of the physical predisposition of emotions.[4] The connection between emotion, facial expression, and action is clear: One signifies or represents the other. Plutchik's wheel of emotions[5] identifies eight basic emotions and their opposites. For example, the opposite of anger is fear, and not sadness or joy. Therefore, a character can't be angry and afraid simultaneously.

Sometimes an author portrays an emotion in a confusing manner. That raised eyebrow, indicating surprise, interest, or skepticism, doesn't jibe with the same character's yawn of boredom, or otherwise clashes with what they're saying and how they're saying it. A character's motivations and desires can also be at odds with their actions and desires. Maybe the characters themselves are confused, or perhaps they're lying to themselves or others.[6]

EXERCISE 3

Reread: Open a novel to any page and read a few paragraphs. Is it clear where the action is taking place, who the characters are, and how they relate to each other? Are the characters interacting in a natural way? Can you identify which character's point of view the narrative is centering, or are you seeing the action from an omniscient point of view? If any of these things are confusing, note how many pages you have to go back to find the necessary context.

Rewrite: Where would you add indications that clarify whose perspective you're seeing? Remind the reader frequently who a character is by describing attributes unique to them, like what they're doing, what they think, and what they want. Would fewer POVs make the narrative easier to understand?

Scene and Plot

Confusion in novels isn't always caused by poor writing or editing. Sometimes the author is being too clever or showing off their vocabulary to the extent that not even their keenest readers can follow what's happening. When the writing gets too fancy, an author is burying their original premise under a number of unnecessary layers. In comedy writing, this is called *putting a hat on a hat*. One hat is enough to tell the story. Wearing more than one hat becomes confusing.

Starting in the middle

A popular storytelling technique is to begin a novel *in medias res*, or mid-scene. The opening scene is usually a pivotal one, full of action and importance. It's a way to quickly submerge you in the story, but if not done properly, it can also confuse.

If you've ever given a speech, you're likely familiar with the three-point rule of oration: 1) tell them what you're going to say, 2) say it, and 3) summarize what you said.

This advice can also apply to novels. You can 1) foreshadow the action, 2) show the action, and 3) reflect on the action. Here's a romance novel trope that explains what I mean. The climax of any good romance is sex. But sex without foreplay or aftercare is empty and potentially abusive. Therefore, your story needs an overture *and* a postlude to fully convey the entire erotica symphony.[7]

Twists and turns

Who doesn't love a good thriller or a juicy mystery? A clever narrative that keeps you guessing up until the final page is fun to read, but only if you can keep up with the twists. The double-agent betrayal, identity reveal, time loops, and false realities (dead all along, it was just a dream, and the unreliable narrator) are common ways to create the necessary twists and turns. Gillian Flynn's novel *Gone Girl*, for example, has become the acknowledged gold standard of unreliable narration, even though it contains a massive plot twist.

When a novelist makes their plot realistic and clear, and you're willing to suspend disbelief, it's a fun ride. But sometimes the leaps taken by the author go too far, plunging some readers into bafflement and frustration. Two of my favorite novels, Lisa Halliday's *Asymmetry* and Susan Choi's *Trust Exercise,* contain double twists of such magnitude that I find them satisfyingly clever and daring, but they leave some readers confused.

Charles Yu's National Book Award–winning 2020 novel *Interior Chinatown* is structured like a screenplay, blending satire, fiction, and cultural critique. With no fewer than seven different frames of reference,[8] the novel constantly shifts between tones and genres in a way that can throw readers off balance. Jennifer Egan's masterworks, *A Visit from the Goon Squad* and *The Candy House*, present many characters and interlocking storylines that give readers a lot to track.

Beginning a novel *in medias res* requires the author to work backward and forward in time, creating a nonlinear structure that can be confusing if it is not clearly explained. Add an unreliable narrator and some plot twists to the mix and the likelihood of confusion becomes much greater. These techniques constantly challenge your understanding of the plot, events, and character motivations, requiring careful interpretation and analysis.

Narrative gaps

To my knowledge, *Mad Men* was the first episodic, long-form narrative TV drama to take giant leaps in time between episodes within a single season. Those leaps left huge narrative gaps; many plot points were omitted. These omissions left viewers wondering whether between episodes a character had gotten married, divorced, been fired or promoted, or how the Madison Avenue ad agency's work had progressed. The episodes answered many of these questions indirectly, but some plot threads were dropped without warning or explanation.

The **unspoken contract** in novels stipulates that eventually every question will be addressed and that every gap will be filled—or at least explained. Anything left unresolved by the end of the novel may frustrate or confuse the reader.

Sometimes a novelist will jump months, years, or decades between plot points, using the gaps to focus your attention on the common elements, cueing you to ignore other threads. The narrative of Colson Whitehead's 2020 Pulitzer Prize–winning novel *The Nickel Boys* alternates between 1964, 1968, 1988, 2014, and the present day. The four sections of Hernan Diaz's 2023 Pulitzer Prize–winning novel *Trust* not only leap across decades, but also switch narrators, points of view, and writing styles. You need to pay close attention to understand how everything fits together, but Mildred explains all in the final section.

The opposite of good narrative gap management is the *plot hole*, which is a gap, inconsistency, or contradiction in a story's logic, events, or character's behavior that breaks the internal coherence of the narrative. Filmmakers can get away with plot holes much easier than novelists can because a quick edit to a new scene can easily distract your attention from a movie's faults. Novel readers, on the other hand, have plenty of time to pause and think about what might be missing in the novel.

EXERCISE 4

Reread: Choose a thriller or any novel that begins *in medias res*. An easy way to spot a novel that jumps forward and backward in time is if the chapter titles or subtitles include dates and times. Stop after reading the first page and ask yourself: What are some possible backstories? Where do you think the plot will go next? Where would you *like* it to go?

Now read the rest of the first chapter. How accurate were your guesses?

Rewrite: Try to predict the remainder of the plot, and any remaining backstory elements that explain the current events. Estimate how many pages you would spend on character development or backstory to ensure that the plot makes sense.

Distancing Effects

Beyond the **Three keys—inciting-midpoint-climax**, the **unspoken contract**, and **everything serves a purpose**—novels sometimes follow their own unique inner compass, and that's part of what makes them so rich—and sometimes so challenging. While many readers expect a novel to follow a familiar pattern—archplot form, consistent characters, or a linear timeline—some novels deliberately depart from that structure. Others may blur the lines between fiction and nonfiction, or even question what a "story" is in the first place. For readers used to more traditional narratives, these choices can be disorienting or even frustrating.

These unconventional novels often reflect a different kind of artistic intention. Instead of simply telling a story, the author might be exploring an abstract idea, playing with language, or challenging the reader's assumptions about reality, identity, or meaning. This kind of experimentation can be powerful, but it can also leave readers wondering what they're supposed to "get" from the text. Understanding that novels come in many forms and that not all are meant to be read the same way can help open the door to deeper engagement with even the most complex or unconventional works.

The fourth wall

> It is of course necessary to drop the assumption that there is a fourth wall cutting the audience off from the stage and the consequent illusion that the stage action is taking place in reality and without an audience. That being so, it is possible for the actor in principle to address the audience direct.
> —*Bertolt Brecht*[9]

Thai *Likay* is a dramatic form that features actors, singers, and dancers wearing traditional costumes, accompanied by a small Thai classical ensemble that appear to be presenting an ancient folktale but are actually improvising interactions with the audience. British *Panto*,[10] performed every Christmas season, and staged performances of *melodrama* in the US also allow the audience to participate, breaking down traditional theatrical barriers. When the German playwright Bertolt Brecht attended a Chinese theater, it inspired him to innovate a new style of dramaturgy[11] he called the *distancing effect,* which not only breaks the fourth wall but, as *metafiction* can, highlights the artificiality of the narrative.

In a similar way, the author can manipulate the fourth wall—that imaginary boundary between the novel's characters, narrator, and novelist, and the reader. Martin Amis and Colum McCann make appearances as themselves in their own novels, *Inside Story* and *Apeirogon*, respectively. Rachel Cusk, Karl Ove Knausgård, and Jon Fosse write in a style that's a combination of autobiography and fiction, what we now call *autofiction*. For them, barriers between the characters, the narrator, and the novelist don't exist.

When an author breaks the fourth wall by directly addressing the reader or drawing attention to the fact that they're telling a story, it can disrupt the immersive flow readers expect from a novel. This technique can be playful, thought-provoking, or intentionally jarring, but it often catches readers off guard. While some may find it engaging or clever, others might feel confused or unsure how to interpret the shift. Recognizing that this is a deliberate stylistic choice, rather than a mistake or inconsistency, can help readers better appreciate the layers of meaning and intention behind the narrative.

Novelty

From the metafiction of the earliest modern novel-within-a-novel, part two of Cervantes's *Don Quixote*, to George Eliot sharing her opinions of her own characters in *Middlemarch*, to Jennifer Egan's PowerPoint presentation within her novel *A Visit From the Goon Squad*, authors have long found and will continue to find innovative ways to communicate with readers.

We shouldn't be surprised; the word *novel* itself derives from *novus*, Latin for "new." Even the earliest novelists used techniques we would call radical or modern. In other words, invention has always been at the core of long-form storytelling, and today's variations are really just a continuation of that tradition.

Tommy Orange's novel *There There* presents a dozen characters in seemingly unrelated short stories, with two historical essays on the plight of the Native American over the past five hundred years at the beginning and the midpoint of the book. The level of detail Orange uses to describe the individual characters and their stories pays off spectacularly when they all come together at a powwow in Oakland, California.

At first glance, Lisa Halliday's novel *Asymmetry* appears to be two novels in one, followed by a transcript of a radio program. Halliday uses a highly unusual binary form to challenge the reader to find the similarities between two different narratives, and in doing so uncover deeper truths about the main characters.

Susan Choi's 2019 novel *Trust Exercise* gives the reader three completely different views of the same event, as is done in Akira Kurosawa's 1950 film *Rashomon*, demonstrating that truth has different meanings for each of the characters.

The table of contents of Hernan Diaz's 2022 novel, *Trust*, makes the novel appear to be a collection of short stories, but as you read the book, you discover the four sections are actually a novel-within-a-novel, followed by the outline of an autobiography, then a memoir, and finally a series of diary entries. Each section was written in a different style, from the perspective of a different character, that presents—as Halliday and Choi do in their novels—very different views of the same narrative, as a prism separates light into many colors.

Although an unfamiliar technique or concept can certainly be confusing at first, I offer a simple solution: Read, read, read, and read some more. And when you find something unusual, I hope you have the fortitude to work through your confusion until you find delight in the novelty of it.

EXERCISE 5

Reread: If you've never read metafiction, stream of consciousness, or auto-fiction (all defined in Appendix A: Glossary), visit the Wikipedia or Spark Notes websites to read the synopses of a few of these novels. Are the plots action-based or more internally focused? What makes them unique? Timeless? Start reading one and ask whether this compels or intrigues you.

Rewrite: Think about your own novel, and the way you've approached your subject matter. Have you considered alternative approaches, similar to ones you discovered in this exercise? Are there any elements you might add?

Notes

1. See Charles Darwin's seminal work on the visual manifestations of human emotion, *The Expression of the Emotions in Man and Animals*, as described here: https://en.wikipedia.org/wiki/The_Expression_of_the_Emotions_in_Man_and_Animals.

2. Ezra Pound, *ABC of Reading*, (New Directions, New York, 1934).

3. Saunders was fully intentional when writing this way, to brilliant effect.

4. Charles Darwin, *The Expression of the Emotions in Man and Animals* (D. Appleton and Company, New York, 1899).

5. Robert Plutchik, "The Nature of Emotions: Human emotions have deep evolutionary roots, a fact that may explain their complexity and provide tools for clinical practice," *American Scientist* 89, no. 4 (2001), 344–350.

6. Pamela Meyer, in her excellent book *Liespotting*, gives readers great tips on how to spot liars and the yarns they spin using clues from their physical movements to the compositions of the stories themselves. Truthful stories are mostly "critical events," while fabrications tend to be much more prologue than significant details. Pamela Meyer, *Liespotting: Proven Techniques to Detect Deception* (St. Martin's Press, New York, 2010).

7. Apologies to Beethoven.

8. They are 1) the narrator talking to you; 2) historical essays on immigration; 3) Willis's second-person voice; 4) the fictional world of Black & White; 5) the real-world production of Black & White; 6) the script; and 7) the real lives of Willis and his family. It's a lot to track.

9. John Willett, *Brecht on Theatre* (Hill and Wang, New York, 1964), 136.

10. See https://en.wikipedia.org/wiki/Pantomime for a more detailed description of this uniquely British tradition.

11. Some commentators cite Brecht's theatrical innovations as the most significant since Aristotle. https://en.wikipedia.org/wiki/Epic_theatre

10
You Figured It Out

The **unspoken contract** describes the journey from darkness to light; from chaos to order; from misdirection to truth. This gradual revelation of facts forms a common thread across all fiction. An inciting incident occurs, and although you are initially in the dark, you are intrigued enough to want to understand what just happened and why. As the novel progresses, you discover new things—you uncover characters' true identities, motivations, and affections—all of which leads you to the denouement of resolution, understanding, and, hopefully, satisfaction.

This thrill of discovery and the satisfaction of resolution after a long journey is why you came to fiction and why you have kept reading novels throughout your life.

So far, so good. But what if you can see through the darkness at the outset? What if, by the end of the opening section, you already have a good idea of whodunit, or you know why the inciting incident happened, or you have figured it all out? What if, midway through, you can see the twist coming? What if the text progresses in such a straight line that the outcome has become obvious and you feel it's unnecessary to read to the end?

If you find yourself in that situation, you're either exceptionally clever or the author has done a poor job of handling their story's journey from darkness into light. These stumbles actually happen quite often and may have been the result of one or more missteps. Let's explore each one in greater detail.

- **Underestimating Readers:** Simplistic, unsophisticated writing
- **Oversharing:** More information than you need
- **Relying on Formulas:** Creaky prose that unintentionally reveals its plot structure
- **No B-story:** A lack of necessary contrast to the primary plot, timeline, or POV
- **Chekhov's AK-47:** A ham-handed execution of Chekhov's gun that gives away the plot

Underestimating Readers

There are many canny and clever readers out there, so woe to any author who assumes that you lack sophistication. You expect that an author (or their publisher, if it's not the same person) is aware of other titles in their genre, and society at large, and is able to write to the level of a discerning reader. Furthermore, it's insulting if they write down to you.

Sophistication versus complexity

Sophisticated writing is clear, nuanced, and elegant, showing depth of thought and precise word choice without being unnecessarily complicated. It avoids clutter and jargon, focusing instead on rhythm, tone, and layered meaning, making it easy to read but rich in insight. In contrast, complex writing often involves dense structure, heavy vocabulary, or convoluted ideas that can obscure meaning. Sophistication is about refinement and clarity, not difficulty.

Writing an interesting and multilayered narrative that leads the reader to unexpected places and keeps them engaged is not the result of large words or long sentences. For example, Hemingway's prose is simple and direct—and also very sophisticated. J. K. Rowling's *Harry Potter* series, written for adolescents, has engaged and entertained millions of adults. This is also true of the best young adult (YA) fiction.

The average American adult reading level is sixth grade, and my studies of even the most sophisticated contemporary fiction (including literary fiction) reveal that these novels are, for the most part, being written to that same grade level. How can this be? It's because complexity and sophistication are completely separate and operate along different axes.[1]

For example, Douglas Stuart's *Shuggie Bain* and Damon Galgut's *The Promise*—both recent Booker Prize winners—are written at a seventh-grade reading level, while Dan Brown's *Origin*—a mass-market thriller—requires tenth-grade reading skills.[2] Why?

It's all about vocabulary.

Dan Brown wants to dazzle his readers. He peppers his texts with unfamiliar words to give the reader the sensation of entering a secret society. Brown's sentences and paragraphs are of average length, but he includes Wikipedia-like descriptions of historical people and places to ensure that his readers can follow along. A text that challenges the reader in this way tends to score much higher on grade-level testing tools, even though it is easy enough for the average reader to consume without feeling fatigued. And because Brown writes fast-paced thrillers, he needs to cover a lot of ground very quickly to keep the plot moving and to keep the cliffhangers coming. He's made a stylistic choice.

Sophisticated writing

Enough about word choice, sentence length, and reading grade level. What *does* make writing sophisticated? It certainly starts with a solid understanding of twenty-first-century culture and twenty-first-century readers. A novel needs to:

- Engage with readers on their level—that is, provide adult text for adults, nonspecialized text for nonspecialists, and offer just enough detail to be interesting, because too much would produce clutter.
- Be clear and realistic enough so that readers can visualize what is happening in their mind's eye.
- Hold key elements out of view until the appropriate moments, but not so far between plot points that the reader loses interest and abandons the book. (See chapter 18, "Pacing.")
- Ensure that every revelation changes the balance or the tilt of the narrative, but not be too obvious. Unexpected yet inevitable is the goal here.
- Take into account today's society, today's norms, and the most recent fiction in its genre.

As you read, stay alert to how a novel meets you at your level—whether it is clear, vivid, and engaging without adding overwhelming detail. Pay attention to the twists that shift the story's direction, see if its pacing keeps you hooked, and consider whether the narrative reflects the world where you live. Sophisticated writing should deepen your connection to the story, meet you at your level, and be clever enough to hold your attention through the final page.

EXERCISE 1

Reread: In a novel you figured out early on, try to locate the exact page and paragraph when the ending dawned on you. What did the author unintentionally give away? Did you feel the text was too simplistic? Was the author writing down to you?

Rewrite: How would you have written it differently to keep the reader's attention without giving too much away? Or is a lack of sophistication woven throughout the text? Is the text irredeemable? If so, why?

Oversharing

Nature is wont to hide herself.
—Heraclitus

A novelist must walk a fine line between richness and restraint, providing enough detail to spark the reader's imagination and create a vivid world, but not so much that details clutter the narrative or stifle the reader's interpretations. It's about trust: trusting the reader to fill in the gaps, and knowing when to guide and when to let go.

Too little information in a scene can leave you floating in midair, unsure of where the action is taking place, who just said what, or how the scene fits into the plot. This informational gap can create confusion or even cause you to lose interest altogether. Oversharing comes with its own risks, though, leading to reader fatigue, or blurring the narrative so that you lose the thread of the scene or the momentum of the plot. It can also give away too much, too soon, arming you with enough clues to see the ending coming well before the author intends. Worse, when everything is explained outright, there's no need for the reader to stay mentally engaged. If you're not asked to connect the dots—if you're not picking up on cues, filling in blanks, or drawing conclusions—then the act of reading becomes passive.

While a novel should not leave you confused (see chapter 9, "You're Confused"), neither should you be flooded with too much information, especially at the beginning of a novel. Oversharing is also the mark of an inexperienced writer, one who has not yet mastered the requirements of the **unspoken contract**. Excessive backstory or unnecessary details also disrupt the narrative's rhythm (see chapter 18, "Pacing").

Oversharing may be the result of an author wanting all their research to end up on the page, or it may attempt to compensate for a lack of action or character development (see chapter 16, "Character Development"), or structural flaws in the plot.

Red herrings

To make a scene feel realistic, writers sometimes add lots of characters and activity—but this can overwhelm the reader. In movies, a busy setting works because the eye takes it in instantly, while in writing, describing all that action takes time and words. What feels like natural background on the screen can become confusing and distracting on the page. Crowded, fast-moving scenes are something films handle more easily than novels.

Sometimes authors include *red herrings,* extra details inserted explicitly to mislead the reader. While they can be useful in thrillers and mysteries, these extra threads can confuse readers if they're not skillfully woven into the novel. If readers expect to be misled, red herrings can backfire and focus readers on the wrong aspects of the novel entirely.

Postcards

Here's an example of a passage that provides additional information *without* oversharing: a *postcard*. A postcard[3] in this context is a reflective passage found most often within literary fiction that deepens your understanding of characters and relationships without advancing the plot. These powerful, evocative sequels are intended to leave a lasting impression, often evoking an emotion or visual image that stays with you.

Postcards expand your knowledge of a person, place, or thing, but they aren't examples of oversharing because they focus on evoking emotional depth, not including exhaustive detail. These scenes aim to capture a *moment that matters*—a memory, image, or feeling so powerful it could fit on a postcard and yet resonates deeply with the character's inner life. Instead of bogging down the narrative with excessive description, postcards serve to distill the scene to its emotional core, letting subtext and implication do the heavy lifting. It's not about telling the reader everything; it's about showing the *right* thing at the *right* time, with just enough clarity to stir the reader's imagination and empathy.

In Gabrielle Zevin's 2022 novel. *Tomorrow, and Tomorrow, and Tomorrow*, a postcard moment is when Sam and Sadie, childhood friends and game designers, sit on the floor of their tiny apartment, surrounded by scattered sketches and half-eaten take-out food. Basking in the glow of a computer screen, they're building a world both for their game and for their futures together.

In Delia Owens's 2018 novel, *Where the Crawdads Sing*, a postcard moment occurs when Kya sits alone in a tiny boat at dawn, watching the mist lift from the water as fireflies flicker above the reeds. The image captures both the wild beauty of her world and her profound loneliness, a snapshot of isolation and belonging in the same breath.

EXERCISE 2

Reread: Find a scene or a narration in a novel you're reading that gave you more information than you felt was necessary. Did it restate the same point already made, or provide you with anything that wasn't relevant to the story? Did it give the plot away, or did it provide emotional insight, like a postcard? Was it backstory or foreshadowing? And if it was foreshadowing, how much did it give away?

Rewrite: What would you have cut? And how much could you cut without disrupting the story?

Relying on Formulas

It's a rare narrative that delivers such an inventive twist that it ends up changing the landscape for all the works that follow. In theater, the whodunit *The Mousetrap* has such a clever ending that, aside from the COVID hiatus, it has remained on the London stage continuously since 1952—and it shows no signs of closing. For movies, the twists at the ends of *Body Heat*, *The Crying Game*, and *The Sixth Sense* have spawned countless imitators. More recently, the novels *Gone Girl* and *The Girl on the Train* have taken unreliable narration to a new level.

In 2004 Christopher Booker published *The Seven Basic Plots: Why We Tell Stories*, the result of more than thirty years of study. His thesis is that all stories are variations of these basic seven. University-based research[4] into thousands of novels culled from Project Gutenberg[5] has yielded six unique emotional arcs. The number of basic story types depends on how they are categorized, whether it's thirty-seven, ten, seven, six, four, or even one. But regardless of the number, the conclusion is the same: There are no new stories under the sun.

Most fiction draws on familiar tropes, story structures, and well-known plot types—not necessarily a bad thing. Since it's rare for a novel to hinge on a groundbreaking twist or an unforgettable hook, most successful stories rely on the strength of their characters and their unique situations to make the reading experience engaging and meaningful. It's less about the destination, and more about the journey—*how* a story unfolds—that engages readers and keeps them guessing.

> Contradictions are what make writers interesting; consistency is for cooking.
> —*James Wood*[6]

Every author is unique, and every book has its own tone, its own style. If you encounter formulaic writing, your reaction to it may be less about the formula and more about the lack of a distinctive voice. Wooden storytelling exposes its gears and makes visible its architecture. Vibrant, quirky, authentic representation gets you to focus less on the structure and more on the characters. What you perceive as formulaic may be a symptom of bland writing.

Think about the various clichés you've encountered in novels: the thriller's perfectly functioning technology, the romance's *meet cute*,[7] or the cozy murder mystery's neighborhood know-it-all. There are too many to name,[8] but you know them when you read them. Consider how they came to be clichés in the first place. As with stereotypes, clichés spring from the desire for shortcuts, if unimaginative.

Now think of some famous characters: Jack Reacher, Stephanie Plum, or James Bond. While their stories often follow familiar formulas, their authors make them compelling through strong, consistent characterization. In fact, part of the appeal is that we believe we know how these characters will react in any given situation, yet they still manage to surprise us. Their enduring popularity, reflected in strong sales and loyal fanbases, proves readers keep coming back not just for the plot, but for the characters themselves.

The number of possible storytelling formulas is finite. But the specific details of the narrative, the strength of the author's voice, and the richness of their characters combine into infinite possibilities. If a novel seems so familiar that you know exactly where it's headed, the author has not created characters or situations interesting enough to divert your attention away from the timeworn tropes.

EXERCISE 3

Reread: Identify any formulas used to create the novel you're reading now. Is it genre fiction? A hero's journey? A romance? Do the characters engage you, or do they feel inauthentic? Have you figured out the ending? If so, how?

Think about any genres you enjoy reading. Are you able to ignore poor writing or overlook certain genre conventions? Investigate your favorite books to identify any blind spots in your reading.

Rewrite: In the novel you're reading now, how would you turn a cliché or a writing formula upside down? Could you do it in a way that enriches the characters?

No B-Story

Antecedent and consequence, action and reflection, scene and sequel—fiction is filled with pairings. To truly shine, a protagonist requires an antagonist not only to provide a necessary foil, but also to show the protagonist in a favorable light. To reinforce a novel's primary plot, a parallel B-story can reinforce and enhance major themes within the work. If the novel is about creating video games, as in

Gabrielle Zevin's *Tomorrow and Tomorrow and Tomorrow*, contrast is provided through the real-life relationships of its characters. Kazuo Ishiguro's *Klara and the Sun*—primarily about Klara and her relationship to the Sun (of course)—is deepened by the B-story about Josie's illness.

A novel without a B-story often moves too directly from point A to point B, making the narrative feel predictable or one-dimensional. The B-story adds texture, depth, and contrast—it introduces subplots, emotional stakes, or thematic echoes that enrich the main arc. Without it, a novel can feel like a straight road with no detours, missing the complexity and layered tension that keep readers fully engaged.

Time and POV

Let's think of B-stories more broadly: as anything in a novel that creates contrast or offers an alternative angle. These could be side plots, changes in time, different points of view, or even shifts in tone or storytelling style. Just like moving between past and present, or jumping between characters, these shifts break up the main storyline and keep the reader engaged by adding variety and complexity.

Using multiple timelines, perspectives, and narrative techniques not only enriches the story's themes but also expands the possibilities for how events can unfold. While not every novel needs one or more of these, once you notice these elements in stories, you'll also notice when they're missing, often in books that feel too straightforward or whose endings feel too easy to predict. Switching focus keeps readers guessing and helps prevent the story from becoming too linear.

For example, in *Apeirogon*, Colum McCann breaks the narrative into 1,001 fragments, giving a fresh structure to a real-life story and making it feel unpredictable. Similarly, Charles Yu's *Interior Chinatown* plays with multiple layers of storytelling—mixing screenplays personal history, and direct narration—to create a reading experience that's surprising yet emotionally true. You don't see where it's going, but when it gets there, it just feels right.

EXERCISE 4

Reread: Is there a B-story in the novel you're currently reading? If not, does it have more than one POV, or changes in the timeframe, different points of view, or even shifts in tone? Have you already figured out the ending?

Rewrite: Pick any secondary character in the book and construct a B-story for them that mirrors the protagonist's journey or acts as a counterpoint. Does the side character's new arc change the plot? Does it reinforce the protagonist's story?

Chekhov's AK-47

If in the first act you have hung a pistol on the wall, then in the following one it should be fired. Otherwise don't put it there.
—Anton Chekhov

Ideally, the clues an author leaves behind are subtle—easy to miss, but powerful in hindsight. The best ones create a subconscious sense of anticipation, so when something major happens later, it feels both surprising and inevitable. Eleanor Catton's *Birnam Wood* offers a great example: An early mention of a pistol is so brief that it's easy to overlook, until it is fired late in the story. That's Chekhov's gun done well.

On the other hand, some clues are anything but subtle. They're loud, obvious, and impossible to ignore—more like Rambo charging in with two AK-47s than quiet, strategic moves. These moments can feel like clumsy plot setups, signaling the hand of an inexperienced writer. Strong storytelling doesn't march in a straight line; it explores possibilities, builds tension naturally, and avoids drawing a neon sign around every important detail.

Chekhov's advice—to use the gun if you show it—is a reminder to follow through on what's been included. But you should also be wary of setups that are too obvious. Overloading the beginning of a story with dramatic elements can be a red flag for a lack of subtlety elsewhere, like over-the-top characters or a plot that moves too predictably.

Eucatastrophe redux

Chekhov's gun doesn't always go off in the middle of a novel—sometimes, it gets fired at the end. You might read a book and, nearing the final chapters, get the sinking feeling that there's no way the author can tie up all the loose threads. And when the story suddenly veers in a strange direction, it often reflects the writer's last-ditch effort to force an ending that doesn't quite fit. Twists always come with a cost, and too often, it's the reader who pays—especially when those twists rely on a *deus ex machina* or feel like a repeat of earlier missteps.

When an author hasn't built a foundation of inevitability, a story's ending can feel jarring or unearned. It raises the question of whether the author resisted where the story wanted to go. Maybe they had a different plan in mind and couldn't let go of it, even when the writing itself pointed to another, more fitting outcome. Sometimes, writers force a twist simply to avoid an ending that feels too familiar or too neat, even if it's the one that makes the most sense.

I once read a widely praised novel that fell into this trap. For most of the book, the writing was quiet, confident, and masterful. I could see where it was going, and I was satisfied just waiting for the resolution to unfold. But in the final pages, the author swerved into an unrealistic happy ending. The characters all survived, despite everything suggesting they wouldn't. The ending felt completely out of step with the rest of the story—thirty pages that undid the strength of the previous three hundred. It's disappointing when a novel loses its footing at the finish line, but it happens more often than it should.

EXERCISE 5

Reread: Go back to a novel you've read with an ending that didn't feel right or didn't feel earned. Think about where you expected it go, and what clues in the text made you feel that way. Were these clues scattered evenly throughout the book?

Now identify where the author changed direction and veered from the inevitable conclusion. How does the writing feel different? Did the pace increase, and did the twists and revelations pile up quickly? Do you feel the writer was under pressure to wrap up their novel?

Rewrite: How would you have ended the novel? Would a more natural conclusion have been more satisfying? Can you come up with a surprising ending that still seems inevitable?

Notes

1. While existing tools can measure the grade level necessary to comprehend vocabulary and sentence structure, we don't yet have a way to measure sophistication. AI is getting cleverer every year, but as of this writing, it's still not smart enough to measure a passage's sophistication level. One will likely be developed in the coming years, though. See chapter 24, "Digital Humanities."

2. For my reading-level evaluations, I used the Readability Calculator found here: https://www.online-utility.org/english/readability_test_and_improve.jsp.

3. For a good description of postcards, see literary agent Donald Maass's essay at https://writerunboxed.com/2016/06/01/what-makes-fiction-literary-scenes-versus-postcards/.

4. Andrew J. Reagan, Lewis Mitchell, Dilan Kiley et al., "The emotional arcs of stories are dominated by six basic shapes," *EPJ Data Science* 5, no. 31 (2016). https://doi.org/10.1140/epjds/s13688-016-0093-1.

5. *Project Gutenberg* is an online collection of free fiction that is out of copyright and in the public domain. https://www.gutenberg.org/

6. James Wood, *Serious Noticing* (Farrar, Straus and Giroux, New York, 2019).

7. https://en.wikipedia.org/wiki/Meet_cute

8. A list of tropes culled from TV shows (you can lose yourself here for days, and I have): https://tvtropes.org/

11
You're Engaged

You're relaxed, sitting or lying down, a book in front of you, and breathing very slowly. You're almost completely still, except for the occasional hand reaching up to turn a page. And then… more stillness, more silence, until… another page. This goes on for a long time.

Hey, you! Over there! Snap out of it!

I know you're not reading this chapter because you're bored or upset or confused. Maybe you're curious about why it exists, or maybe you opened to this page by accident. Well, you're here now, and to this I say, game on.

You're already aware that reading the best writers can teach you how to write, and so you've been reading your favorite author. You got all the way to the end of another delightful novel and—*poof*! You didn't learn a thing.

Well, we're going to put a stop to that right now. I don't mean you should stop reading for enjoyment, because what you'll cover in this chapter, if you do it right, will add to your pleasure and make reading even more enjoyable. Being in the headspace of the author might even make you feel like a collaborator in the creation of their story, instead of a mere consumer. It will certainly make you read like a writer.

It begins with *how* you read, and a quick visit to chapter 2, "How You Read." If you haven't already read that chapter, please do so now. I'll wait for you right here.

Have you read chapter 2? Good. And what did you learn? Yes! Your reading has been inspectional and not analytical, right? Well, we're here to change that. First, we're going to review the important skill of *hitting pause*, in case you're not already adept at this. Then we'll play some games that exercise that skill.

Hitting Pause

Nirvana for a reader is the flow state we enter when the writing pulls us into another world. As writers ourselves, we must strive to understand this process, which means that we need to cultivate the ability to have two parts of our brain operating simultaneously. We can still enjoy what we read, sure, but we also need to be cognizant of that enjoyment *while it's happening*.

Our worst critic

I'm going to ask you now to engage with that awful part of your brain: the judgmental part. The voice that hovers over your shoulder and judges your crappy writing. The one who is always second-guessing you. Yeah, *that* smart aleck.

Don't be afraid. Go ahead and wake them up. It doesn't matter if they're cranky. The crankier the better, in fact, because the reason you're summoning them this time is not to judge you or your writing. Oh, no. They're here to judge the novel you'll read. Isn't that a relief?

And you'll need that judgmental jerk to go full snark all over the text if you're to have any hope of snapping yourself out of your flow state for the milliseconds it takes for you to be aware of the elements of the novel you're reading *as you encounter them*. Feel free to engage with this inner voice. That twit will try to find fault with everything, every detail, and faults there may be. All good. As you read, observe what's at fault, and try to figure out why it came to be what it was. Try a quick rewrite, if you can. If you can't, then the flaw may be deeper, or broader, and may require a more comprehensive rewrite.

Other times the writing is so transcendent that you'll need to push back on that snarky voice until they admit that, yes, a particular passage is masterful. *Et voilà!* Instead of rushing past good writing, you've paused long enough to uncover a gem. It's time now to dig into what makes this passage so good. Voice? Tone? Poetry? Juxtaposition? What made it stand out to you, and how can you apply that special sauce to your own writing?

Mental cues

Sometimes engaging your judgmental voice isn't enough to pull you out of the story and get you thinking about the qualities of the writing as you're reading. If that's the case, then you can preload your short-term memory with one of more of these prompts:

- **Your own arm:** When you're at the end of a page, you are momentarily aware of the need to turn to the next one. If you've decided to pause after every page, you can use this flow hiccup to ask the important questions about the page.

- **A new section:** Again, if you have enough self-discipline to pause at the beginning of a new section within a chapter, you can ask the important questions about that section.
- **A new chapter:** Ditto for pausing to reflect on the entire chapter, although in some novels this may be too large of a chunk of text to be useful for your explorations.

Because you're taking artificial breaks in your reading (and not pausing because you've been jarred out of your flow state), it's necessary to perform a general survey to make sure you take note of what's important within the text. These are the questions you'll need to ask:[1]

- What just happened?
- Why was it written as it was?
- How does that serve the story?
- Has it changed what you know or WHAT YOU FEEL?
- Would you have written it differently?
- What do you think will happen next?

Feel free to ask additional questions that pertain to your course of study, such as ones you may have picked up from any of the other chapters of this book. For example: Why these words, and in this order? What's the ratio of dialogue to narrative? What informs the tone, or the voice, and has there been a register shift? What obstacles have been placed in a character's path? Were there any interesting juxtapositions or contextual framing? Was the scene a seduction, negotiation, or argument? How was the pacing? Did you spot any symbols or metaphors?

Outside help

Maybe you can't come out of your flow state, and you can't control the pages whizzing by. You look up and—drat!—you've read another five chapters without taking note of any techniques. Maybe it's time to bring in some heavy machinery: the clock alarm.

Every cell phone has an alarm feature. You can set yours to interrupt your reading after, say, five, ten, or fifteen minutes. It depends on your reading speed, but I caution you against programming an alarm for less time than it takes you to read a page, and more time than it takes to read, say, five pages. Too large a chunk of reading is too much to analyze all at once. Small is good in this case. Take baby steps at first.

Other things that will interrupt your reading, of course, include looking up an unfamiliar word in the dictionary, being interrupted by a family member or a friend, or any other outside random event. But these things aren't predictable or reliable.

It's important to develop a routine that is predictable and reliable. This artificial outside help should be used only temporarily until you can discipline yourself to take breaks at your chosen intervals. Use the clock alarm if you find that useful. But it's important to learn to rely on your inner voice, because this observer will always be there, eager to pop into action.

EXERCISE 1

Using any novel as your guide, read a few pages to see which technique reliably makes you pause. Is it the judgmental voice? Are you disciplined enough to pause after every page, section, or chapter? Or do you need to use your phone alarm? It doesn't matter how you do it, but you must pause and ask the six vital questions listed above. Return to this exercise after every game to see if you've been able to progress toward the ultimate goal of being able to read and notice yourself reading at the same time.

Game Time

Now it's time to treat reading like a game. Doesn't that already sound like fun? The rules are simple: They're the **Three keys and Seven tools** you learned from *YOUR FIRST CLUE*. First, remember the **Three keys** that define every narrative:

- **Inciting-midpoint-climax**
- **Unspoken contract**
- **Everything serves a purpose**

Here are the **Seven tools** that derive from those keys:

- **Always ask why** (which is also the **First rule of Literary Forensics**)
- **Assume you're being played**
- **Pay attention to POV**
- **What happens is not what's discussed**
- **Reread**
- **Rewrite**

If you're not sure what they mean or how to use them, then go back and read that section now. Here's a brief summary.

Remember that embedded within the novel is the promise that no matter where we start, no matter how confusing the circumstances, we will journey to a place that shines a light on what has come before, and everything between the beginning and the end of the novel is there for a reason. The beginning of a story sets us up for everything that follows, so the opening of any novel bears very close reading. All of it deserves close attention, but especially the first chapter.[2] Everything in the text serves a purpose, so pay attention to what characters actually do versus what they talk about. Question every element and ask why it is there and what purpose it serves. And, finally, know that a single pass through the text won't cut it. You will need to read it more than once to actually learn anything from it about the craft of writing.

Phew! Got it? Good. Once you learn how to pause your reading reliably, you're ready to play any of the dozen games in this chapter that are divided into three categories:

- **Scene Games:** Why does this scene exist? Scene position. It's not normal. What's next?
- **Character Games:** Introduction. Intent. Obstacles. Bad choices.
- **Plot Games:** Thriller & whodunit. Romance & buddies. B-stories. Cut, cut!

All set? Okay, let's go.

Scene Games

Because the storytelling techniques of movies and episodic television shows are similar to what you'll find in novels, and easier to identify, especially if you have no prior experience, I'll use these in my examples. Of course, you can directly apply each of these games to your reading, but I'd like to start with some streaming video. I think it's a good way to begin.

To play, you'll need either a novel you haven't read or a movie you've never watched on your on-demand streaming service, cable, satellite—or DVD, if you're old school. For these games, broadcast TV (that is, live television without a pause button) won't work because you'll need to pause frequently. You may also need to rewind. Pausing and rewinding are no problem with a novel, of course.

Remember that the goal for all of these games is to eventually apply them to novels, so you shouldn't focus on video for too long.

Game 1: Why does this scene exist?

The opening scene of a movie, or the opening scene of the first episode of any series, is likely an introduction to the setting and the main characters.

Sometimes the opening scene is *in medias res*, which is intended to excite and titillate more than to inform. A good example is the opening to most thriller novels and every James Bond film, which shows our hero fighting villains. This is designed to make us curious about what will happen next.

Every scene throughout a novel and a movie has a purpose. I like to hit pause somewhere in the middle of a movie or a novel, long after the primary characters and their motivations have been established. I ask myself why this scene exists—that is, what is it doing to move the story forward? Are we learning more about a character, a relationship, a flaw of the antagonist, or do we learn something else that's important to the plot?

Think hard, dig deep, and remember that **everything serves a purpose**. There's no way the scene is doing *nothing*.

Game 2: Scene position

Why is this scene here, and not anywhere else? For this game, I like to hit pause at the very top of on the scene, so the only clues I have are the location and the characters in that place. What are they doing there? And I don't mean what is the plot point that brought them to this place, but what's *really* going on? Will a character reveal their flaw? Will characters swap status? Will we see a seduction, a negotiation, or a fight?

Here's an example. Let's say we're watching a heist movie, and we know that the next scene takes place on the morning of the job. What is the next scene? Is it set in the gang leader's apartment, does it unfold outside the bank as the gang moves into position, or is it inside the bank lobby? Each of these gives us very different clues about where the story is headed. The first scene is more about the leader, the second is about the team, and the third is about the victims. It's up to you to evaluate what each of these setups means.

Here's another example. On the dance floor, two strangers lock eyes. We must already know one of them, otherwise the scene doesn't make any sense. Why show this, and why have this interlude at this specific point in the story? Would this potential hookup mean something different if it came at the beginning of the story? At the middle? The end? Also, if nothing is random in making a movie, why include a random moment like this? Is it to underline the characters' nonchalance, or could it be that they aren't really strangers, and had planned their rendezvous in advance? The tone of the story that's already been established holds a lot of weight when you evaluate these possible explanations.

Game 3: It's not normal

An important feature of fiction is worldbuilding, even if the events take place in a familiar environment in the present day. It's important for the reader to grasp this particular world's salient features as a precursor to understanding the action that will follow.

We have to suspend our disbelief. Most readers and viewers do this subconsciously, but because our task is to uncover the mechanics of this suspension, we need to be aware of the aspects of any scene that facilitates it. Hint: This is usually accomplished through the shorthand of describing a scene in such a way that the reader fills in the gaps with experiences from their own life.

For example, it's too much of a coincidence for any one person to witness dozens of murders in their lifetime. If you're reading a cozy mystery series, then you have to suppress the thought that perhaps the detective is, in fact, a serial killer. Thirty seasons of Inspector Morse and its spin-offs may lead you to believe that Oxford, England, is the murder capital of the world. The point is, there are things any author wants you to ignore, and other things they want you to focus on, for the purposes of telling their story.

Your job in this game is to pause in any scene and identify what unusual things are present, and notice what's missing from the scene that would normally track to reality. Pay close attention to what's *not* there, too.

Game 4: What's next?

This requires you to hit pause right at the end of a scene before catching sight of the next one. This skill requires the sense of timing of a film editor. Once you feel the rhythms of the camera cuts within a scene, you start to get a sense of when that editor will end the scene. By the way, these rhythmic cuts also exist in prose, so if you begin to recognize scene endings on video, you may start to recognize when scenes end on the page.

Rhythm also extends to large and small ensembles. Scenes that contain many characters should be interspersed with more intimate scenes featuring one or two people. Too many characters on-screen all the time would be tedious, and difficult to follow.

So what's next? Imagine that you're writing this drama, and for this you need to have a sense of where you'd like this story to go. Even if you're not sure, you may be wondering what's up with character X or Y, and decide that it's time to check in with them.

Extra credit to you if you get it right: That means you're starting to merge with the mind of the storyteller.

Character Games

Characters have different arcs depending on the form and genre of the story. Characters in one-off stories like novels and movies may transform dramatically. Recurring characters in episodic TV usually remain static, but the modern style allows for characters' growth over the course of one or more seasons. Keep this in mind as you parse a minimum of information to predict what happens next. For more information on character arcs, see chapter 16, "Character Development."

For each of the games in the following section, you'll want to pause early in the scene.

Game 5: Introduction

Closely observe who is in a scene, how they enter, in what order, and with what point of view. You may not have been introduced to them yet, or they may be familiar to you. By simply noticing what they wear, what they do, and how prominently they occupy the space, when you pause, your job is to guess who is in charge or has status, identify their motivation (if you can), and try to predict something about their story arcs.

It may be something small: These two don't like each other, or this character acts while others react, or one is wearing a provocative outfit. It may be large: That one's getting murdered, that one will probably face tragedy, or those two will end up together. Depending on where in the novel or drama you pause, you may already have more information and can make a more accurate prediction.

Also be aware of how the writer *wants* you to feel about a character. I enjoy watching short-form police procedurals or one-hour murder mysteries. By design, you never have enough information at the beginning to be able to make a good prediction, and the writers are throwing red herrings in your path. Knowing the conventions of the genre, you may be able to further refine your assessments.

Here's one example from the much-maligned TV situation comedy (also known as a sitcom), which can actually be a treasure trove of storytelling techniques. Twenty-two minutes in length, each story needs to be introduced immediately with a minimum number of words, sometimes a single line of dialogue (leaving room for jokes). There is always an A- and a B-story, and sometimes a C-story. For instance, A says, "I still don't know what I'm wearing to the Halloween party tonight." B says, "I can't even think about that right now—my sister arrives in town in an hour." Boom and boom. We know what will occupy those two characters in this episode. And then we get to predict how these stories will collide and what situations the characters will find themselves in.

In a novel, the author usually spends more time on crafting the first chapter, the first paragraph, and the opening sentence, than on other parts of the novel. See what you can divine about the entire novel from just the beginning. Many times, it's all there on page one.

Game 6: Intent

In this game you will identify what each character wants.

The setup is similar to the previous game, but this can be played at any point in the story. What does each character want, and how badly do they want it? What a character *wants* is often very different from what they *need*.

Remember that if a character wants nothing, they're a placeholder within the drama. The doorman, the waitress, the other minor characters should all want something, even if that desire isn't apparent. It motivates how they approach each situation. The doorman might want to be liked, so he's sunny and friendly even in difficult situations. The waitress might want respect, so she despises interruptions when she recites the evening's special dishes.

Good writing means that everyone wants something. Go explore!

Game 7: Obstacles

Have you wondered why characters in fiction are called *characters* and not *people* or *roles*? It's because a character is nothing more than the embodiment of character. And character is always revealed to the reader by how they deal with the obstacles in their story. Every author and every writer's room spends hours, weeks, and months dreaming up obstacles for their characters.

The first step for every reader and every writer is to identify what each character wants. If the character doesn't want anything, they're not a character, they're a cutout, and we may be looking at poor writing.

One way to think of an obstacle is like a wall. What a character encounters over the course of a narrative could be *wall, wall, wall, wall, wall, DOOR!* There may be more or fewer walls, but if you've paused in chapter one or only five minutes into a drama, the character is certainly going to be encountering a wall next, not a door. What appear to be doors early in a story are often walls in disguise.

You'll need to pause once you've identified a character's intent or desire, which is going to be early in the story. You must know what a character wants before you can predict what obstacles the writer will put in their way. This is a fun game to play anywhere in a story, because inherent to the nature of any fictional character is the fact that obstacles will *always* be put in their way.

Find them.

Game 8: Bad choices

Sometimes a character gets in their own way and creates their own obstacles. When presented with two options, they instinctively choose the wrong one.[3] This character's worst enemy may be their own bad habits and desires, diminishing the writer's need to create an antagonist against which the character can reveal who they are.

These characters can be stubborn, clueless, or cruel, but a common thread is that they are not self-aware, nor can they imagine the bigger-picture consequences of their actions. A string of these poor decisions may take the form *bad choice, bad choice, bad choice, bad choice, GOOD choice!* These arcs may be resolved in a variety of ways, including:

- One of their bad decisions ends up being a good decision for reasons beyond their control. This results in a character still not self-aware of their flaws, someone who "fails up."
- Recognition of their own self-destructive behavior may eventually lead to a good (or less-bad) decision. This may need to be balanced with yet another bad yet much less destructive decision because, while characters may evolve, making bad choices may be rooted in their DNA.

After you've paused in a scene, your job is to try to predict which options will be made available to a character. No extra points for predicting that they will choose the bad option.

Plot Games

The scope of these games encompasses multiple scenes and multiple characters. They are about the plot as a whole, where it's headed, and where every character ends up by the end of the narrative.

Game 9: Thriller and whodunit

Horror, espionage, and mystery are genres with a few characteristics in common: mysterious backstories, unexpected revelations, and red herrings (or MacGuffins). From the opening lines, the writer is attempting to give you just enough information so that you continue to read, but not enough information so that you can predict every twist and turn.

For example, in murder mysteries and police procedurals, the writing is shaded so that there's an obvious candidate for the murderer or an obvious solution to the conundrum that occupies the main characters. But rest assured, things are almost never what they seem. It's the writer's job to keep the reader in the dark but without making the reader feel they're being played, even though they are. It's a difficult balancing act, so it's possible to spot flaws in the plot logic.

Sometimes massive plot holes or threads are abandoned. Your job in this game is to identify the markers that cause your thinking to move in a certain direction. Then you'll need to evaluate those false flags: Are they clever or banal, effective or easy to dismiss?

Game 10: Romance and buddies

Romances and buddy stories are similar in the affection or affinity that exists between the main characters. In this game, we'll be identifying the familiar tropes of the genre and whether they are played straight or with a twist.

Even buddy movies have their own version of the meet-cute, although that may exist in their backstory, and buddies often become allies because of shared adversity. But it's there, and you can uncover it.

Wants and desires. It's almost certain that at the story's outset, both of the main characters are pursuing separate paths. Even if they're competing for the same job, they'll want it for different reasons. There must be a contrast drawn between the two. What is it?

Estrangement. Even buddies go through rough times, and the "boy loses girl" part of a buddy movie may have more to do about external events or differences in moral compasses than about a severing of ties or a loss of obligation to the other.

Giving up something for each other. This tracks equally well in both genres. What each of the two protagonists *think* they need from the other will be subverted in this, the penultimate section before the final union.

As you read or watch, identify how the two main characters begin with contrasting goals or desires. What separates them at the start? Then, look for the moment of sacrifice or compromise: What does each character give up or learn so they can truly connect by the end?

Game 11: B-stories

Multithreaded stories—those with A-, B-, and sometimes C-stories—require keeping every subplot in motion for the duration of the story. The first step in this game is questioning why these subplots exist at all. Usually they mirror the A-story in some way that provides contrast and counterpoint to the main action. Authors use subplots to throw the main action into sharp relief without requiring too much explanation.

The second part of this game is about proportion and timing. Pause anywhere and ask why certain plots were backgrounded, and for how long. Why do you think certain scenes were in a particular sequence? What purpose does that order serve? And what about the timing or spacing? Why did certain plot points occur at those moments, and not earlier or later?

Also, mark the exact point when you started wondering what happened to X. Or why you haven't seen Y in a long time. Did the author stretch the timeline too far? And what purpose might that serve?

Game 12: Cut, cut!

This game must be done closer to the end of the story because it requires you to wear an editor's hat. You're here to identify what was necessary and what wasn't. What went on too long, or what should have been expanded? Which elements were necessary, and which ones distracted from the story?

About scenes: Could that scene have been cut? Did you need to see it? Conversely, was a scene missing that would have explained something essential?

About timing: Did a particular scene go on too long? Was a scene too brief, or was an emotional moment cut short? Did something interfere with the storytelling to an extent that it became too fuzzy or muddled to understand? For a deeper discussion of narrative rhythms, see chapter 18, "Pacing."

About characters: Was every character necessary, or was one character so much like another that they could easily have been removed? Conversely, did one character carry too much weight and need to be split into two characters?

About threads: Did every subplot land? Was each one's purpose adding to the emotional weight? Did it act as comic relief? Or was it in contrast to the protagonist's journey, showing where a different path would lead?

Pause at the end of the story or close to the end to ask these questions while you can still remember the answers.

Notes

1. George Saunders gives similar advice about how to read like a writer in his insightful *A Swim in a Pond in the Rain*.
2. The first chapter of any novel is certainly the most revised and polished. It's what gets submitted most frequently to critique groups, coaches, agents, editors, and competitions as the best indication of what the novel is about and what's to follow.
3. This could be the wrong dress, wrong friend, wrong job, wrong college major, wrong love interest, and so on.

WHAT YOU NOTICE

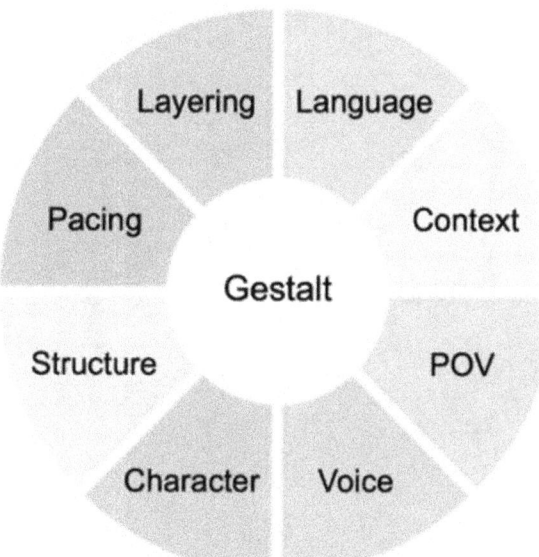

12
Language and Grammar

What's strange is how many beginning writers seem to think that grammar is irrelevant, or that they are somehow above or beyond this subject more fit for a schoolchild than the future author of great literature.
—*Francine Prose*, Reading Like a Writer

Believing that you understand how language works just because you use it every day is an illusion. Yes, you may *understand* what you read, but the majority of ways that you express yourself during an average day is little more than small talk.[1] Think about it. *Good morning! How are you? Did you catch the game? Eat your peas. Be home by ten. I'm beat.* We spend our lives perfecting the simple interactions we learned as children, and many of us do not feel we have much of a grasp of the incredible power of language. Therefore, vocabulary and grammar merit further study.

Because this is a book on reading—not writing—this chapter will *not* cover everything you need to know about word usage and grammatical structure. For that you're better off spending time with language mavens *Strunk and White*[2] and *Garner.*[3] We will instead take advantage of the amazing work done by discourse analysts—those people tasked with interpreting what people say and how they use language to say it. After all, your job is to back-construct intent from your reading, which, although easier than writing, still requires you to have a solid foundation in the techniques writers use to tell stories.[4]

The tools you will employ to investigate the language and grammar found in the novel are:

- **Vocabulary:** Why studying and understanding all types of words is important for readers, including their derivations and usage, whether it's prosaic or poetic.

- **Intonation:** How word usage sets a tone or employs a dialect, or how the sounds of words influence our perception, and how characters' verbal tics tell us who they are.
- **Subjects and Predicates:** Word order, which influences anchoring, action, status, focus, and intent.
- **Person, Place, and Time:** The basic ingredients of POV.
- **Integrating Information:** How bunches of words are used together in phrases and clauses, or through topic chaining, repetition, and callbacks.

Vocabulary

I urge my students to get a usage dictionary.... To recognize that you need a usage dictionary, you have to be paying a level of attention to your own writing that very few people are doing.... A usage dictionary is [like] a linguistic hard drive.... For me the big trio is a big dictionary, a usage dictionary, a thesaurus—only because I cannot retain and move nimbly around in enough of the language not to need these extra sources. As a teacher, about 90% of my job is getting the students to understand why they might need one.
— *David Foster Wallace*, Quack This Way[5]

Words form the building blocks of every story you read, while grammar is the mortar that cements them in place. Words and grammar together are the foundation upon which all novels are built. And we've all seen what happens to buildings with poor foundations. If you're going to be an effective reader and writer, you must do the two things that 99 percent of humans never do: fully understand the meaning and usage of every word you use; and master grammar.

While living in Thailand and attempting to speak Thai, I learned a valuable lesson about the flexibility of the English language. Needing to borrow a sledgehammer from the groundskeeper, but not knowing the word, I asked him for a tool to break concrete. I mimed swinging a sledgehammer.

Confusion. I knew the words for *tool* and *concrete* so I realized that the problem must be the verb. I tried another word meaning *break*. Another blank stare. After asking a friend for help (in English), she giggled and suggested a third word for *break* I hadn't learned, but one that was appropriate to what I was asking for. The next day, when I used *that* verb for *break* between *tool* and *concrete*, the groundskeeper came back immediately with a sledgehammer.

Thai is a formulaic language, meaning that there are many situations within which only one word or combination of words will do, and I wasn't applying them correctly. When I thought I was communicating with the groundskeeper, I was actually speaking gibberish. To English speakers this seems absurd, but only because we have a different type of language. And because English has twice as many words as any other language (the result of the contributions of many world languages over time) words such as *break, shatter, smash, crack, snap, fracture, fragment, splinter, disintegrate, split, burst, tear, rend, sever, rupture, separate, divide*, and *bust* can be used almost interchangeably, depending on the context. We think nothing of this flexibility in usage, because from an early age we have been trained to expect alternate words and not rigid formulas—that is, nothing is set in concrete.

Your brain on poetry

Take the phrase *sun-kissed orange*. English, in addition to allowing for infinite word swapping, also excels in unexpected word juxtaposition, otherwise known as poetry. Of course, we are aware our sun is a star, and is not capable of kissing anything, especially an orange. But since we also know that oranges require sunlight to blossom and mature, the image of an anthropomorphic glowing orb planting a radiant kiss on a citrus fruit is more adorable than crazy. The unfamiliar pattern of words sparks associations between what it means to express physical warmth and emotional warmth, both of which nurture growth.

Back to Thai, a language capable of expressing ambiguities impossible to express in English. But the poetic expression *sun-kissed orange* directly translated would produce gibberish worse than my sledgehammer example above. In fact, it would create a cognitive dissonance: The sun is a red star; people kiss; followed by a color or a fruit, neither of which is red. What's going on?

All words—even unfamiliar or nonsense words—tickle our brains and evoke certain shapes, images, and qualities. In 1924, a Georgian psychologist first observed what came to be known as the Kiki-Bouba effect,[6] further proof that word choice matters! Comedians already know this.[7]

> Fifty-seven years in this business, you learn a few things. You know what words are funny and which words are not funny. Alka Seltzer is funny. You say "Alka Seltzer" you get a laugh.... Words with "k" in them are funny. Casey Stengel, that's a funny name. Robert Taylor is not funny. Cupcake is funny. Tomato is not funny. Cookie is funny. Cucumber is funny. Car keys. Cleveland... Cleveland is funny. Maryland is not funny. Then, there's chicken.

> Chicken is funny. Pickle is funny. Cab is funny. Cockroach is
> funny—not if you get 'em, only if you say 'em.
> —*Neil Simon*, The Sunshine Boys

Oh, and the least-favorite word in English seems to be *moist*.[8] (Eew.)

Latinate and Anglo-Saxon words

Aid and abet, assault and battery, breaking and entering, will and testament—every *legal doublet* contains a Latinate and an Anglo-Saxon word meaning the same thing. These redundant phrases were created centuries ago, when English had not yet coalesced into its modern form and there was a need for the law to be comprehensible both in Latin and in the vernacular Germanic-based language.

Although English has subsequently absorbed vocabulary from hundreds of languages, this dichotomy of Germanic and Romance language words remains one of the most important to the writer. Short, blunt Anglo-Saxon words are often used in fast-paced scenes to describe decisive action, while Latinate words, being longer, are useful to depict reflection by subtly slowing the reader down or evoking an aspect of the words' origins.

The title character of Gail Honeyman's 2017 novel, *Eleanor Oliphant Is Completely Fine,* is shown, through first-person POV, as evolving from a worldview of blind certainty to introspection through the progression from Anglo-Saxon to Latinate words. At the inciting incident, the protagonist uses these verbs: *Found. Saw. Knew.* Anglo-Saxon words all. But at the climax she uses: *Firm. Measured. Certain.* These are Latinate words. Eleanor Oliphant's worldview has shifted, revealed to the reader not only through the actions of the plot but also through the very words she chooses to describe her situation. Masterful.

Vernacular

> But no living word relates to its object in a singular way.... It is
> precisely in the process of living interaction with this specific
> environment that the word may be individualized and given sty-
> listic shape.
> —*Mikhail Bakhtin*, Discourse in the Novel

Of course, there are many more English words than those with Anglo-Saxon or Latinate roots, and some are not yet in any dictionary. Language constantly evolves, new words are coined, some accumulate additional meaning, others change meaning or fall out of common usage. Think of these common words that have recently acquired new meanings: *woke, goat,* and *they*. We also have completely new words such as: *woot*, *stan*, *bae*, and *zir*. Some words have fallen out of favor, such as *groovy*, *hussy*, and *blockhead*.

Military and governmental agencies are constantly coming up with acronyms or portmanteaus (word pairings) that sometimes form new words. Examples include *snafu*, *awol*, and *humvee*. Jargon from specialized practices can seep into common usage, too: *bomb cyclone*, *red zone*, *gaslight*, and *snoot*.[9]

As a reader, it's important for you to keep up with current word usage, and to gauge whether the words narrating the story or spilling from characters' mouths are appropriate. Many words carry additional freight; likewise, a word out of place will upset as much as the perfect word will delight.

Finding the perfect word

Because English is such a rich language, there's no excuse not to use the right word in every situation. Choosing the perfect word sharpens meaning, shapes voice, and deepens emotional impact—making the difference between a flat sentence and one that resonates. In writing, as in craftsmanship, the right tool—in this case, the right word—elevates the entire piece.[10]

Sometimes English is not enough, and authors will invent the words they need. I know it's difficult to grok,[11] but finding the cromulent[12] word isn't a catch-22.[13] Other times an author may overdo it with *de trop* foreign phrases, eliciting *sangfroid* from the *hoi polloi*.

Illegitimi non carborundum, okay?[14]

Clichés

Avoid them like the plague.

Clichés aren't just a sign of lazy writing, but they also remove specificity from a narrator or character's voice. For a detailed discussion of how clichés and formulaic writing disrupt a story, see the "Relying on Formulas" section of chapter 10, "You Figured It Out."

EXERCISE 1

Reread: Slow down—you're reading too fast! Stop right now, take a moment, and examine the last sentence you just read in your novel. Why did the author use those specific words and not any others? Any passage will do, because word choice identifies an author as precisely as a fingerprint.

Do you find yourself glossing over words, unsure of their meaning? Or ignoring foreign phrases? You'll be doing yourself a lifelong service if you look them up. Look up familiar words, too. You'll often find a new or obscure meaning for a word you thought you understood. English is as deep as it is wide.

Rewrite: Within that sentence you read, which words or phrases would you have swapped out for something different, or do you think all of the words were perfectly chosen? If so, are you reading a cliché? Always be on the lookout for things expressed uniquely, even poetically. Examine these shining examples of craft closely to learn from them.

Intonation

Intonation refers to the distinctive rhythm, tone, and flow of how characters and narrators express themselves. You hear it in their vocabulary, slang, speech patterns, and level of formality (or *register*). It reflects their backgrounds, personalities, and emotional states, helping readers "hear" voices on the page and distinguish them from others.

Getting the right tone with the right words, sentence structure, and voice is a little like mixing paint. When the mix is just right, readers can sense the subtle shades, and the characters come alive on the page. But when the tone or dialogue feels off, it's hard to figure out why—like trying to re-create a paint color without knowing which colors were blended to make it.

I can't think of a more illustrative text to demonstrate this than Mark Twain's *The Adventures of Huckleberry Finn*. Let's consider the vocabulary of one of its main characters, Tom Sawyer.

> Right is right, and wrong is wrong, and a body ain't got no business doing wrong when he ain't ignorant and knows better.

When adults write characters who are very different from themselves—like forty-nine-year-old, educated, witty, well-traveled, heterosexual, cisgender white Mark Twain writing about an uneducated boy from a rural background—they must strike a balance between keeping the character's behavior and speech believable and keeping the story moving. Readers often overlook small inconsistencies, but these choices are worth examining more closely.

Ignorant is an awfully big word for Tom Sawyer, and yet Twain put it in his mouth. The sentence performs perfectly well without *ain't ignorant and*. *A body ain't got no business* is a turn of phrase Tom might have heard from his Aunt Sally, so it fits coming out of the mouth of a boy. Also, the bromide *right is right, and wrong is wrong* is something Tom had doubtless heard and internalized.

But it's the use of that word *ignorant* that signals the author's voice bleeding into Tom's dialogue, changing the intonation a shade. Perhaps that was Twain's intention all along.

Dialect

When I started this section by quoting *Huckleberry Finn*, I bet you thought I was going to focus on dialect like *alwuz, 'bout, dat, dey,* and the infamous n-word, which has *always* been freighted with meaning and subtext. Twain certainly had his methods,[15] one of which he described in a preface to his novel titled *EXPLANATORY*.

> In this book a number of dialects are used, to wit: the Missouri negro dialect; the extremest form of the backwoods Southwestern dialect; the ordinary "Pike County" dialect; and four modified varieties of this last. The shadings have not been done in a haphazard fashion, or by guesswork; but painstakingly, and with the trustworthy guidance and support of personal familiarity with these several forms of speech. I make this explanation for the reason that without it many readers would suppose that all these characters were trying to talk alike and not succeeding.

Part of Twain's genius was his gift for regional dialect, and his works remain the most enduring attempts to capture exactly how people of the time talked. However, how many of us today can differentiate between a backwoods Southwestern and a Pike County dialect or any of its four varieties? And more importantly, how important are all of those parochial shades to the telling of Twain's story today?

My answer is: not much, if at all. But when it was published, those dialects were both a cause for alarm and a powerful selling point: For the first time, Americans saw characters in a novel who talked like they did in real life.[16] Today's readers intuitively understand that good characterization is less about dialect and more about performance—what a character actually does. Readers can find dialect too cumbersome and distracting.

Be on the lookout for stereotyping if you feel an author is relying too much on dialect as a substitute for characterization. Using just a few unique words can effectively suggest a character's difference or background, but using too many can slow down the story and distract the reader.

The rule of thumb when using dialect is: Less is more.

Code switching is when a speaker alternates between two or more dialects or language varieties, and a mashup of two languages can also qualify as its own dialect. Think Spanglish, Yinglish, Ebonics, or advertising English, bureaucratic English, corporate English, or hipster English, especially how they contrast with standard English. And because this section began with a quote from *Huckleberry Finn*, let's close with Percival Everett's 2024 novel, *James*, which is the story of Huck Finn as told from the perspective of the enslaved man Jim. Chapter 2 contains the most delightful takedown of Twain's study of dialects, as James teaches his children how to code switch for the benefit of the white folks: by never admitting they know how to speak proper English, and by never contradicting their masters (even when they're obviously wrong) but letting them believe all the good ideas are theirs.

Sound symbolism

Words whose sounds suggest extra meaning or context belong to a group known as *sound symbols*. Sound symbolism is how we attach concepts and meaning to the way a word sounds. Think about when an author uses swear words for emphasis. The actual meaning of the word is often less important than the formation of the word: which strong consonants and vowels are used, or how it feels to say or hear. A clever writer, if desiring enhanced emphasis but not wishing to offend, might instead use words that only sound like they're dirty.[17] Techniques poets use that you should be familiar with include:

- **Onomatopoeia**: Words that sound like the expression or effect they're meant to evoke. For example: *oink* or *whoosh*.
- **Ideophone**: Repeating words as a way to increase their emphasis or strength. See the "Repetition/callbacks" section below for more.
- **Phonesthemes**: Groups of similar-sounding words that imply a class of meaning: For example, *gleam*, *glow*, and *glare*.
- **Deictic symbolism**: Where in the mouth the word is formed. The sounds of words formed with sibilant consonants or farther back in the throat or on the palate may be linked by meaning. This can span multiple languages.
- **Tactile sound**: How it feels to enunciate the word. It feels different to utter a swear word, with its plosives and hard consonants, compared to saying soothing sibilants to a worried child or pet.

Verbal tics

Good writing clearly and quickly defines who a character is. A character may be associated with the use of a particular word, or they may stutter, or begin their sentences with a *So…* or finish them with a *yeah*. They may use fractured syntax, or mix their metaphors, or deliver their dialogue slowly and with rhythmic pauses in between phrases.[18] Verbal tics can help you recognize who's speaking or which character's perspective you're in, which is helpful—as long as the author doesn't rely on them as a shorthand in place of deeper character development. See chapter 16, "Character Development."

Focus shifting pronouns is another verbal tic—one I associate with professional athletes. See how many interviewees use the word *you* when talking about themselves and the game they've just played. Similar to using passive voice, it puts distance between the athlete and their actions.

EXERCISE 2

Reread: Pick a section of dialogue between two characters. Without attribution, can you tell who is saying what? Look for any verbal tics, including dialect and tonality.

Find a section of narrative that presents the thoughts or actions of a particular character. Again, what is it about the text that identifies who is doing what? Is it word choice, dialect, syntax, rhythm, or some other marker? Is the author striking a serious, jocular, or condescending tone, or are they playing with register?

Rewrite: Use whatever verbal indicators you found and compare them with the way characters speak in your own novel. Have your discoveries inspired you to modify how any of your characters talk?

Subjects and Predicates

Let's begin with the classic word order of English sentences: subject, verb, object, or SVO. Someone (S) is doing something (V) to someone else (O). Your investigation of even the simplest of sentences should lead you to ask at least five questions:

- **Anchoring:** What's the word order—what comes first, or is most important?
- **Action:** Who is exercising their agency?
- **Status:** Who is in control?
- **Focus:** What is most important?
- **Intent:** What is the subtext?

Deixis refers to words or phrases whose meanings depend on context. Even the simplest sentence can only be fully understood when deixis is considered. Take this example: *Sally asks Jim.* It seems simple—subject, verb, object. Clear and straightforward, right? But let's take a closer look at *Sally asks Jim.*

Anchoring

The first word in any sentence anchors what follows in our brain. The first word here is *Sally,* and so we build the rest of our mental image around her. Regardless of what follows, even if the sentence is two pages long, we should remember where we began, because the author began there as well. Note that this sentence could be shortened to *Sally asks* or even *Sally* and retain its meaning so long as the asking and the direction of the asking are understood. The sentence *The asking is being done by Sally* also puts her in the driver's seat, but at a distance. Although the action is similar, the passive voice moves the anchor of the sentence to be *The asking* rather than Sally.[19]

Action

Who's exercising their agency? Remember that they may be different from the Subject. Even though the Subject is *The asking* in the sentence *The asking is being done by Sally*, it's still Sally who's doing the asking, even though she's not the subject, as in *Sally asks Jim*. The passive voice serves also to mute the immediacy of Sally's action. It's still happening, but at a distance, and so her asking is not as visceral as the direct statement.

Status

Who is in control? That may be Jim, depending on the meaning of the word *asks*. Remember that status is different from action. Although Sally may exert crazy agency by asking again and again for a response from Jim, if he refuses her requests, her status is diminished. Jim may have higher status because he has information that Sally lacks, or she may be asking him for assistance. Conversely, as a teacher she may be telling her student Jim to shut up, or her question may be a rhetorical one that Sally already knows the answer to, thereby establishing her dominance. We don't know without the context.

Focus

What is the most important idea in the sentence *Sally asks Jim*? It's where the emphasis is placed, which again depends upon context. Is it that *Sally and not anyone else* asks Jim? Or is it that Sally *asks* Jim instead of *telling* him or *hitting* him? What about Sally asking *Jim* instead of asking Jerry? Although the three words remain the same, identifying the most significant word or clause leads to completely different meanings, which leads us to our last question: intent.

Intent

What is the subtext? What is the story behind the sentence? It could be that Sally is mute until the moment she asks Jim, which is a miracle. Jim may be Sally's dead husband, and the sentence implies that she's talking to someone who isn't there. Perhaps she's hallucinating. And lastly, the sentence is missing an object complement. Sally asks Jim… *what*, exactly? The reader is left hanging.

EXERCISE 3

Reread: Pick a sentence, any sentence, from a novel you're reading. Work through the five questions listed above. Imagine if the answers to each of the five questions were different.

Rewrite: Is there a way to reword the sentence to eliminate all ambiguity? How would you change the sentence to make it more ambiguous? Imagine a situation in which you'd prefer ambiguity. Imagine when you'd want a single interpretation.

Person, Place, and Time

The most popular narrative perspective across novels of every genre is third-person past tense. First-person present tense is surging but will never overtake the favorite. Second-person past, present, or future tense is used very rarely, brought out only on special occasions.

Why is that?

It relates to how each combination gives the author certain freedoms or places specific limits on the narrative. By closely examining the text, we can infer the author's thought process and understand why they made the choices that appear on the page.

In this section, we're presuming a single person is narrating. First-person plural[20] is sometimes used for a chapter or section to signify the voice of the community, third-person plural is even rarer, and second-person plural is virtually nonexistent.

Third person

When you read about *him, her,* or *they,* you should take notice of the distance between you and the characters. Where have you, the reader, been positioned within the scene relative to the action? You can be as close as inside a character's head, or as far away as outer space, looking down on those characters as dots on the planet. You should expect to travel, much like a movie camera on a dolly, back and forth, up and down, in and out. You may also be asked to focus on more than one character at a time.

Third person allows for the presence of a narrator—who could be the author, an all-knowing observer, or even a character within the story. With a flexible point of view and a range of narrative styles, third person offers authors the greatest freedom in how they tell their story.

First person

This confines you to the inside of a single character's head, peering out at the world through their eyes. First person comes with some rules: *I* am in every scene, and as a result *I* cannot know anything that *I* have not experienced myself or heard about from others, nor am *I* able to know for certain what any other character is thinking or how they are motivated, or even how this world works.

I knows *nothing* for certain because the perspective of this *I* is so limited.

This requires the author to shape the plot and narrative within those limits. So why choose first person? Because it delivers the most immediate and immersive storytelling, making it feel like the character is personally telling you what happened to them. The narrator and protagonist are one.

Second person

Authors use second person to put some distance between themselves, their characters, and their actions. It's quite the jujitsu move to displace this responsibility onto the reader!

You become the narrator. The story is placed wherever *you* are.

Use of second person is rare, but I'm seeing an uptick. Authors like Jennifer Egan and Tommy Orange have used second person for a chapter or two in their recent novels, creating a striking contrast with the rest of the narrative.

Charles Yu's 2020 National Book Award–winning novel *Interior Chinatown* is that rarest of birds: It uses second person throughout the entire book as a way to get the reader to identify with the plight of its Chinese American protagonists. Before *Interior Chinatown*, the most famous second-person novels were Mohsin Hamid's *How to Get Filthy Rich in Rising Asia* (2013) and Jay McInerney's *Bright Lights, Big City* (1984).[21]

Mixing persons

Novels that mix first and third person should make you ask why. Is focusing the reader's attention in this way necessary to the storytelling, or is it a distraction? What is gained by shifting perspective? And what is lost? Recent examples of first and third person mixed well include: Susan Choi's *Trust Exercise*, Ocean Vuong's *On Earth We're Briefly Gorgeous*, and Martin Amis's *Inside Story*.

Past tense

Most novels are written primarily in the past tense—third person, past tense—but even then, around 50 percent of the verbs are present tense. That's due to dialogue, which contains a lot of present-tense verbs. Maybe we should call this tense "past-focused" or "primarily past," because it's not a pure usage. This mixture provides yet another reason that past is novelist's favorite tense: Nothing prevents them from using present- and even future-tense verbs.

Present tense

Books with 75 percent or more present-tense verbs are definitely written in the present tense, and often also written in first person, but not always. Present tense is therefore as impure as past tense—lots of past tense words intrude, which in this case indicates backstory.

Present tense is visceral, creating tension and anticipation for the simple reason that we readers can't predict what will come next. Using present tense creates some restrictions for the author that we readers need to be aware of, including:

- There is little to no opportunity for foreshadowing.
- Point of view tends to be close.
- Verbs can imply ongoing action instead of momentary action. Example: *I live.*
- It tends toward a linear narrative, due to the immediacy of perspective.

Future tense

Future tense is rarely used, and found mostly in experimental fiction.

EXERCISE 4

Reread: Pick any passage in a novel you're reading, stop, and note the person, place, and tense. That is, which person—first, second, or third—is used? How close or distant to the characters are you placed? And which verb tense is being used? Do you think these choices are the most effective for the story being told?

Rewrite: Would you have made a different choice of voice or tense? Consider altering the scene's point of view, thinking of it like a camera angle: How about a close-up, a two-shot, or a wide angle that takes in an entire room, town, or planet?

Compare this passage to something similar in your own novel. Do you remember how you chose which voice and tense to use? Was it conscious, or is that how you write naturally? Which novels gave you the idea to write that way?

Integrating Information

Now that we've explored the basic building blocks of language and grammar, let's move on to how they combine to form larger structures—clauses, phrases, sentences, and paragraphs. As always, we're focusing on what can be clearly observed: the results of skillful language use.[22] These observations can be grouped into the following categories:

- Main and subordinate clauses
- Topic chaining
- Repetition/callbacks

Main and subordinate clauses

English is highly flexible, so authors often rearrange words, clauses, and phrases to suit the context and their intent. A sliding scale of grammatical complexity exists between prose and poetry, with prose usually being more straightforward and direct. But any and all poetic techniques can be employed by the novelist at any time, and so it's important to be aware of any unusual usage. Anything out of the ordinary becomes a marker, a starting point for your investigation.

Some quirks flow better than others when used adroitly. I've crafted each of the examples that follow by using a sentence formed by the technique described. You may need to reread these to see the connection.

- SOV—Subject, Object, then Verb—confusing to many readers can be.
- A technique often found in newspapers, an appositive phrase before the subject can read awkwardly.
- Run-on sentences tend to disorient the reader by cramming too much information into a single sentence with one clause following another almost willy-nilly until the reader gives up in frustration because it's important to break up longer expressions with shorter ones which will serve a variety of purposes including keeping the reading grade at an easily consumable level and providing a sense of rhythm and flow proving less taxing for the reader. Like this sentence.

- Incomplete sentences? Perfectly acceptable. Sometimes. But not too often.
- Using gerunds can be obfuscating and result in distancing action away from the reader and pulling them out of the narrative, while action verbs land.
- While a subordinate clause assumes, a main clause asserts!

When important ideas are buried in subordinate clauses, they lose impact. Main clauses carry more weight. It's up to the novelist to recognize how their ideas are positioned and to align those decisions with their intentions.

Topic chaining

For a novel to make sense to readers, each scene must follow a clear thread of ideas that establishes a central focus or purpose. How those ideas are arranged—within sentences, between sentences, and across paragraphs—shapes the reader's experience. Building a tone or emotion, like fear or love, requires deliberate layering: Fear must steadily increase to create tension, while love should show up not just on characters' faces, but in their words, actions, and how the world feels through their eyes.

Scenes are built by chaining together topics, characters, symbols, and emotions sentence by sentence, paragraph by paragraph. Each scene centers on a conflict, plot point, or idea, and you understand its meaning based on how the information unfolds. Here are some of the elements that go into creating a topic or theme:

- **Setting**: The jumping-off point for the scene, prompting the reader to focus on a character (or characters), a place, and a time
- **Catalyst**: What happens to the focal character within the place and time
- **Crisis**: The situation or issue that creates tension (because, as we know, every scene needs to contain conflict)
- **Evaluation**: Not necessarily the resolution, which might come much later, but how much or little this scene affects the focal character

A topic or theme shouldn't be stated outright—instead, it must unfold gradually through a chain of connected ideas to feel real, believable, and moving or relevant to you. See also chapter 13, "Context in Scene."

Repetition/callbacks

> Can I hear an Amen? [Amen!]
> —*Anonymous*

> Hi-de-hi-de-hi-de-ho! [Hi-de-hi-de-hi-de-ho!]
> —*Cab Calloway,* Minnie the Moocher

Stand-up comedians often use callbacks: They introduce an image or activity early in their set and then bring it back later for a punchline. This technique is similar to Chekhov's gun, but applied at a smaller scale—within a single paragraph or section of a novel.

Great speakers, like rappers or preachers, also rely on call-and-response to unite an audience around a single phrase, creating a shared sense of purpose. A similar micro-callback in writing involves repetition—repeating words, phrases, or even sounds like vowels and consonants. Here are six key techniques a writer can use, which are essential for readers to recognize. I'll highlight these through the examples I've provided.

- **Anaphora**: Repeating words at the beginnings of phrases. Repeating them often. Repeating them until you understand their importance.
- **Epistrophe**: The flip side of anaphora: repeating words at the ends of phrases, as in, "The truth. The whole truth. And nothing but the truth."
- **Assonance**: Resemblance of sounds within their vowels. "His tender heir might bear his memory" —William Shakespeare, *Sonnet 1*
- **Consonance**: Similar to assonance, consonance repeats consonants inside words.
- **Alliteration**: Continuously curated consonants at the *beginnings* of words. Peter Piper picked a peck of pickled peppers. Booth led boldly with his big bass drum.
- **Rhyme**: The same vowel sound in **places**: the *ends* of words or **phrases**. I'll construe you knew this, too!

EXERCISE 5

Reread: Pick a sentence within a novel that contains more than one clause, one with a number of commas. You don't have to diagram the sentence, but it wouldn't be a bad idea.[23] Find the main clause and any subordinate clauses. Where's the focus? If it's not clear, then consider the order in which the clauses are laid out, giving priority to the one presented first. Their order matters!

Now choose a paragraph, or section, within a page. Identify the key idea being conveyed, and observe the topic chaining. Does it use repetition or callbacks?

Rewrite: Think about how the passage would land differently if you rewrote it in your own style. Is the original sentence or paragraph structure similar to your writing style, or is it dramatically different? Would you be willing to use what you found in your own novel?

Notes

1. Much of this small talk contains *phatic* expressions. For more on this topic, see: https://en.wikipedia.org/wiki/Phatic_expression.

2. William Strunk Jr. and E. B. White, *The Elements of Style* (Pearson/Longman, UK, 1959).

3. Bryan A. Garner, *A Dictionary of Modern American Usage, 3rd ed.,* (Oxford University Press, New York, 2009).

4. For this section, I'm building directly upon the work of James Paul Gee and his seminal discourse analysis toolkit, James Paul Gee, *How to Do Discourse Analysis: A Toolkit* (Routledge, New York, 2005).

5. Bryan A. Garner and David Foster Wallace, *Quack This Way: David Foster Wallace & Bryan A. Garner Talk Language and Writing* (Rosepen Books, Sedona, 2013).

6. https://en.wikipedia.org/wiki/Bouba/kiki_effect And here's a fun test you can take that measures the effects of "Kiki" and "Bouba" on your brain: https://www.nytimes.com/interactive/2023/06/28/arts/kiki-bouba-effect.html

7. An excellent overview of what makes certain words funny: https://en.wikipedia.org/wiki/Inherently_funny_word

8. "Words Came In, Marked for Death…" *New Yorker*, April 23, 2012, https://www.newyorker.com/culture/culture-desk/words-came-in-marked-for-death.

9. Coined by David Foster Wallace, *SNOOT* is a self-describing acronym of *Syntax Nudnik Of Our Time.*

10. Some examples of unfamiliar words an author might choose include: *peplum, calutron, matrix,* and *polder*. Each of these words apply to a specific thing or situation, and using them relieves the author of having to write a dozen other words. When, in your reading, these alternative words pop into your head (is *that* what the author meant?) or if you find the same words being used too often not to be noticed, congratulate yourself, for you have gained another tool to help you read like a writer.

11. Robert Heinlein, *Stranger in a Strange Land* (G. P. Putnam's Sons, New York, 1961).

12. "Lisa the Iconoclast," *The Simpsons* season 7, episode 16, https://www.merriam-webster.com/words-at-play/what-does-cromulent-mean.

13. Joseph Heller, *Catch-22* (Simon & Schuster, New York, 1961).

14. https://www.merriam-webster.com/words-at-play/the-hilarious-history-of-ok-okay

15. Amina Azzouz et al. "African American Vernacular English Examination in Mark Twain's Huckleberry Finn," *Ennass Journal* 8, no. 1 (2021), 558–569.

16. The very colloquial dialect got Twain into trouble. Only two months after its publication in 1885, librarians in Concord, Massachusetts, deemed it "trash" and "suitable only for the slums." The New York Public Library once banned it from the children's reading room because Huck scratched when he itched and said "sweat." See also: https://www.pbs.org/wgbh/americanexperience/features/banned-adventures-huckleberry-finn/ and https://firstamendment.mtsu.edu/article/adventures-of-huckleberry-finn/.

17. "Curse Words Around the World Have Something in Common (We Swear)," Elizabeth Preston, *New York Times*, December 6, 2022, https://www.nytimes.com/2022/12/06/science/swearwords-sounds.html. Also, Shiri Lev Ari and Ryan McKay, "The sound of swearing: Are there universal patterns in profanity?" *Psychonomic Bulletin & Review* 30, no. 3, (2023), 1103–1114. https://doi.org/10.3758/s13423-022-02202-0.

18. David Owen, "The Objectively Objectionable Grammatical Pet Peeve," *New Yorker*, January 12, 2023, https://www.newyorker.com/culture/annals-of-inquiry/the-objectively-objection-able-grammatical-pet-peeve.

19. By the way, the English "norm" of expressing a subject first, followed by a verb and then an object (SVO), is the structure of only 42 percent of the world's languages. Most prevalent is SOV, at 45 percent—placing the subject and its predicate next to each other, with the verb describing what the subject is doing to the object coming last. The remaining four combinations of the order of S, V, and O represent the normal order in only 13 percent of the world's languages. Here's more information than you will probably ever need to know about verb-object word order: https://en.wikipedia.org/wiki/Subject%E2%80%93verb%E2%80%93object_word_order.

20. An example of an entire novel told in first-person plural is Jeffrey Eugenides's novel, *The Virgin Suicides* (1993).

21. And, of course, Laura Numeroff's children's classic *If You Give a Mouse a Cookie* (1985).

22. For further study, I recommend a compilation of grammatical patterns and how they appear in the works of contemporary professional writers: Virginia Tufte, *Grammar as Style*, (Holt, Rinehart and Winston, Inc., New York, 1971).

23. ChatGPT is really good at diagramming sentences, by the way. Just use the following prompt: "Diagram the following sentence: [insert sentence here]." For more on how other LLM chatbots can help your reading, see chapter 24, "Digital Humanities."

13
Context in Scene

Context[1] refers to the background information—such as setting, character relationships, past events, and emotional tone—that helps readers understand the meaning and significance of what's happening in the moment. It's the invisible framework that gives a scene depth and clarity, allowing the reader to interpret dialogue, actions, and tension within a broader narrative. Without context, scenes risk feeling disjointed, confusing, or emotionally flat.

This chapter will look at context within *scene*, and only in scene. If you're interested in exploring the way scenes and chapters work in context with each other, please refer to chapter 17, "Structure." Or to study the context of an entire novel within the literary and publishing landscapes, see chapter 4, "Your Novel," chapter 20, "The Gestalt," chapter 21, "The Publishing Industry," and chapter 23, "Academic Disciplines."

Mise-en-scène

Mise-en-scène, or *setting the stage*, is what theater and film professionals call set design and the placement of actors, props, and visual and sonic effects within that design. Context is what I'm calling the study of mise-en-scène in novels, because novels contain additional layers that cannot be realized in the visual arts. The key difference between theater and film, which you experience by seeing and hearing, and novels, which you read and visualize within your head, is that the author controls the revelation of elements within a novel's scene. The slow reveal is a well-used novelistic technique: First, the author tells/shows you one thing, and then another, and another, each revelation altering the context or the meaning of the previous elements, casting those elements *in a different light*.

Here's an example from Gail Honeyman's *Eleanor Oliphant Is Completely Fine*. Honeyman has written *Eleanor* from the title character's point of view, and because she rarely looks at herself in a mirror, she isn't self-regarding. Instead, we experience how Eleanor appears to others, first through her interactions with her fellow office workers. From those exchanges, we form a certain opinion about Eleanor's character; Honeyman keeps our focus on that aspect alone, in part by using humor. In our mind's eye, we think we know exactly how Eleanor appears to her officemates. It comes as a shock when we discover that we got it wrong, which of course was Honeyman's intention all along. The author has given us just enough information for us to construct Eleanor in our mind, but not enough information for us to understand everything. That comes later.

To attempt this visual misdirection in the theater would be impossible. You'd know exactly how Eleanor appears the moment she walks onto the stage.

Sometimes these misunderstandings happen by accident; I can't tell you how many times I've missed a key word or phrase of description in a novel, certain I'm constructing the image correctly in my head, only to have it undermined a few pages later. I used to think that all of those mistakes were my fault, and probably most of them were. But not all of them. Some of those miscues are the writer's doing, and they are also worth studying. See chapter 9, "You're Confused."

A little story

To illustrate how important context is to understanding how a scene works, let's consider this short story I wrote and your reactions to it. Please pause after each numbered statement to answer the question: *Did I spend too much for that car?*

1. I bought a car for $200,000. Do you think I spent too much? That's a lot of money for a car, isn't it?
2. What if I told you the car I bought was an Aston Martin Valkyrie, which at the time I write this, retails for $3.5 million. *Now* do you think I spent too much?
3. I should probably admit to you that I'm working a minimum-wage job, that I have four children and a wife to support, and that there's no way I can pay all our bills on my meager income. Do you think I was wrong to spend that much on the Valkyrie?
4. Now I tell you my rich uncle gave me a million dollars to spend on something that would make me happy. I paid off all my debts, set up trusts for my wife and children, and have a few hundred thousand left over, even after buying the car. My wife loves it. Do you still think I spent too much?

I hope my little parable had you seesawing between yes and no, between approval and reproach. That was the idea. I wanted to demonstrate that, depending on the context, that same fact (the car purchase) can be seen as wasteful, crafty, irresponsible, or justified. I'll refer back to this story throughout this chapter to frame how context within a scene is formed by these four types of relationships:

- **Facts**: The raw elements, the positive and negative charge of those elements, their ordering and pacing, and the way that the meaning of an element can change throughout the scene, or relative to the overall narrative.
- **Juxtaposition**: The meaning or significance of individual elements and whether they work in harmony with each other or create conflict. This includes characters and objects, their relationships to each other and to their surroundings, and their relative power/status markers, significance, and inevitable conflicts.
- **Order:** Having a piece of information first, or last, or somewhere in the middle changes its charge, its power, and often its meaning. Where a fact is introduced affects how it received by the reader. Here we look at different orderings of the same information to understand the subtle shadings at work.
- **Intention**: The purpose of a scene—why it exists, and why it was placed here.

We'll investigate how this scene figures within the chapter, examining a few different constructs: scene and sequel; action versus reflection; categorization as a fight, seduction, or negotiation; and its focus on milieu, idea, character, or event.

Facts

The most granular example of context is what I'll call the context of facts. The only information, in the example that I gave you initially, was that I bought a car, and how much I spent on it. Now two hundred grand is a heck of a lot to spend on an automobile, or at least it is in 2025. Oh, and I guided you in a certain direction, reinforcing the idea that even I, the narrator, thought that it was a lot of money. So, without anything more to go on, you judged me. Can you remember what you thought? Did you think I was wasteful? Maybe you thought I was one of those rich authors living the high life. (Ha!) Either way, how you judged me is influenced by what you bring to the text, covered more in chapter 1, "Your Point of Reference."

The upshot is that I didn't provide you with any context. I only gave you three facts: I bought a car; it cost $200,000; and $200,000 is a lot of money. Without giving you anything more to go on, I, as a storyteller, encouraged you to fill in the gaps of my situation, which led you to ask certain questions, and maybe you arrived at certain conclusions.

When you read a naked statement of facts like that in a novel, pause and ask yourself why the author did that. I chose a very large price for that car on purpose; I wanted it to be a cost out of most people's reach. I set a marker, saying: *super-large purchase here*. That purchase may have sparked envy, or concern, or pity (who would waste that much money on a car?), or outrage (a sports car contributes to global warming, and there are certainly more useful things to buy).

Sometimes an author gives the reader raw data like that to jump-start our imagination. Salman Rushdie's *Satanic Verses* begins with a man falling out of an airplane at 30,000 feet, which brings up all kinds of questions in the reader's mind, most immediately, *Is this real?* Rushdie is content to let the reader stew for at least a chapter before providing any context at all. He is inviting us to search for answers to the conundrum he created.

Often an author wants to set up the reader with a scenario where all is not what it seems. This deliberate misdirection is always used in a whodunit, nearly always appears in romances, but it shows up across all genres.

Filling in the gaps

The beginning of Act VII in Charles Yu's 2020 novel, *Interior Chinatown*, opens to Phoebe and an unnamed man who's wearing a forty-year-old shirt sitting on upended plastic crates in the kitchen and laughing. Without a direct quote of the passage, know those are the only details the author provides to set the scene.

Although I've read this novel a number of times, I can't remember the context of this scene exactly, which works for our purposes. Even so, I have a mental image of a man, likely an older man because he's wearing such an old shirt, and Phoebe, both of them sitting on crates in a kitchen. Somehow, I'm thinking the kitchen is industrial, like one you'd find in a restaurant, because they're sitting on crates and not on dining chairs. I don't think I've ever had crates in my kitchen at home, and certainly not two of them that I'd wanted to use as chairs. But I'm not you; maybe you have.

I also notice that the author doesn't name the man but refers to him with the pronoun "he." That level of familiarity gives me some indication of his closeness or importance to the narrative. Could "he" be the protagonist's father? Boss? Antagonist? We don't have enough information.[2]

In this scene, I imagine both "he" and Phoebe are dressed casually. I decided that they might be working in that kitchen and taking a break. I imagine a loose strand of hair and a bead of sweat dripping down Phoebe's forehead. How did I make that leap? I think it's because I'm imagining a restaurant kitchen, and I'm assuming that it's uncomfortably hot. But that strand of hair? I have no idea where that came from. Welcome to the inside of my head.

He and Phoebe could just as easily be guests at a wedding, dressed to the nines, and in the kitchen because they've been searching for a spare bottle of champagne. The kitchen could be in someone's house, and the crates the ones used by caterers. But I envision these two characters more humbly, and I'll hold that image in my head until the author tells me otherwise.

EXERCISE 1

Reread: Find a novel you haven't read and open it up to any page deep in the story. Read a sentence or two until you can find some statement of fact in the scene. Try to picture the scene in your head. Is there enough information on the page to do that, or do you seem to be floating in midair? As your mind's eye fills in the gaps in the text, take note of what you added to it. What assumptions did you make about the scene?

Rewrite: Taking note of what you added to the scene, read a little farther to see if you got it right. If not, then what facts would you add to the original scene to make the context clearer?

Juxtaposition

The priming effect

Priming is a psychological phenomenon where exposure to one stimulus influences the response to a subsequent stimulus, even if the person is unaware of the connection. In reading, when two descriptions are "placed" near each other, the first description can "prime" the reader's perception or interpretation of the second, shaping how the second description is understood or felt. This usually happens to you subconsciously, but it's a common trick of writing you need to be aware of, and one that, once you start to recognize it in the novels you read, can be a valuable addition to your toolkit.

Let's refer back to the second passage of my car-buying story. On its own, the only information conveyed is that an Aston Martin Valkyrie retails for $3.5 million. That information alone will probably not evoke much of an emotional response.

Rich people need expensive things to buy, and watchmakers, home builders, and automobile manufacturers are only too happy to oblige.

However, when you place that statement just after the previous statement, which says I paid only $200,000 for that car, the second statement about the true value of the Valkyrie should set off bells in your head. Surely, I'd scored an amazing deal on the sports car. But I hope you're also wondering: Who is this guy who can buy such an expensive automobile? And who would sell such a car for less than ten percent of its value? Is the seller fencing stolen goods? And what about me—am I in on the scam, or am I some naive rube who stumbled into a chop shop and whose life is now in danger? If not, then surely I'll be going to jail before act two.

That's the power of two pieces of information in close proximity.

Here's another example, from *The Female Persuasion* by Meg Wolitzer, that I've been thinking about ever since her novel came out in 2018. Greer, a vegetarian, has been invited to dinner at the house of her hero, Faith, who is cooking steaks in the kitchen. Greer glances out the kitchen window and at that very moment sees a wild deer prance into the light of a single floodlight, oblivious to anyone watching.

That's quite a juxtaposition. The vegetarian, trapped in the kitchen of her meat-serving host, sees the very reason she doesn't eat meat appear under the floodlight as if on cue. Wolitzer underlines Greer's plight in that moment, and the deer sighting ends the chapter. And, of course, it's symbolic of the relationship between the women.

EXERCISE 2

Reread: In a novel you're reading, look for two seemingly unrelated things—adjectives, objects, or people—placed in close proximity to each other. What does each one mean separately, and how does their meaning change when they're put together?

Rewrite: Go to a passage you're currently writing and put two seemingly unrelated things next to each other to see their effect on each other. You can use a random word generator for inspiration.[3]

Status and power

In Judeo-Christian philosophy, there's an idea that all people are created equal. But in Thai culture (which I know well) and in other East Asian cultures (which I know less well), the concept of equality doesn't really exist. No two people are ever on equal footing. The gap between them might be small, but it's always there.

Even saying something as simple as "Hi! How are you?" requires knowing your status relative to the other person—the language demands it.

In fiction, that sense of relative status is even more pronounced—there is no such thing as true equality between two characters in a novel. So the real question becomes: How is that status expressed?

Karl Marx says power reflects social class. Paul-Michel Foucault ties it to money. But power can come from a lot of places: emotional influence, social rank, age, position, or even location. It can also be physical—brute force, coercion, subjugation, violence.

In any scene with two or more characters, someone has the upper hand. But who? And how?

Take the Wolitzer example above. Faith has the upper hand over Greer because of her position, influence, and the fact that they're in her home. Together, they hold power over the deer, through force.

Now imagine this: A king sits on his throne, speaking to a serf kneeling before him. On the surface, the king clearly holds the power. But what if the "serf" is actually a knight in disguise, who's arranged for the king to be alone—and has allies hidden, ready to strike? Who is really in control now?

Power also shows up in action. Who is doing something, and who is passive? Between two people in a car, the driver has control, right? But what if the passenger is holding a gun to the driver's head?

EXERCISE 3

Reread: In a novel you're reading, find a two-person scene. Who has the power, and how do you know they have it? Is their power overt or subtle? And does the power emanate from physical characteristics, social status, sexual prowess, access to knowledge, or something else?

Rewrite: Edit the scene to show power shifting from one character to the other. Consider replacing one type of power with another.

Order

The anchoring effect is the cognitive bias that occurs when you rely too heavily on the first piece of information you encounter within a text (the "anchor") when making decisions or judgments about the text that follows. This initial information can influence subsequent emotions and opinions about people, places, things, and situations encountered in the novel, even if the initial information is irrelevant or unreliable.

Let's go back to my little car-buying story. Now imagine I started it by telling you about my rich uncle and how I was setting aside all this money for my family. Then I filled in the details: I work a minimum-wage job, and I got a great deal on an Aston Martin. Suddenly, the story feels kind of. . . boring, right? But why?

You might think it's because I gave too much information up front—but that's not it. It's the same information as before, just in a different order. The problem is in the sequence. To make a story compelling, the information should build, from light to heavy, from vague to specific, from sparse to dense.

Think of a classic whodunit. The author doesn't dump all the facts on page one. Instead, they give you just enough to spark curiosity, then layer on clues one by one. That slow reveal is what makes the story exciting. An early reveal that a character had a grudge against the deceased makes you suspect them as the murderer. That's a result of the anchoring effect, even though this suspect is probably a red herring.

The slow reveal is also important for romance novels. Right in the middle—between the meeting of the lovers and the happily-ever-after—comes the misunderstanding or heartbreak moment. That tension is only satisfying because the author holds back information. Sometimes, the characters are confused too, and that's intentional. The emotional payoff comes after that uncertainty has been fully explored.

In short, what an author reveals—and when they reveal it—matters. That's what keeps readers turning pages.

EXERCISE 4

Reread: Choose a descriptive scene from any novel. Pay close attention to the order of the details: What does the author describe first? What comes next? What's saved for last? Is the point of view zooming in from a wide-angle view to a close-up? If so, where does the focus finally land, and why?

Rewrite: Now imagine if the order of the scene were different—would it change how you picture it? Would it shift how you feel about it? Try rearranging the elements yourself and see how the emphasis, focus, or emotional tone shifts.

Next, just for fun, try adding unexpected elements to the scene. What if there were a Martian? A ticking bomb behind the door? An apple pie cooling on the windowsill? Or even Benjamin Franklin strolling in? Let your imagination run wild.

Intention

Every scene in a novel serves a specific purpose—whether it's to reveal character, build tension, advance the plot, shift relationships, or deepen the emotional stakes—so that every moment moves the story forward in a meaningful way. To understand the purpose of a scene, why it exists and what the author hoped to accomplish from it, we'll need to broaden our understanding of how writers structure scenes.

Here are three ways three different artists categorize the purpose of a scene. Whether it's director Mike Nichols describing interactions between characters, Dwight Swain's differentiation between action and reflection, or author Orson Scott Card's focus on subject matter, these give you a few of the many ways that the intention of an author can be discovered.

Fight, seduction, or negotiation

The late director Mike Nichols has said that a scene can only be one of three things: a fight, a seduction, or a negotiation.[4] Thinking about scenes in this way gives us a useful tool to help uncover an author's intent. Let's consider each of the three types.

A fight can be a conflict between two people, two armies, a melee in battle—these are the obvious fights. But a fight can be between a person and their uncooperative laptop, or between a person and the thunderstorm that's ruining their picnic, or between a dog and a cat, or between a tectonic plate and the fracking crew. It's conflict.

A seduction may be what popped into your mind first—that is, a scene between two potential lovers. But it can also be a con artist working his mark, or the patient elementary school teacher trying to get Jimmy to learn his times tables. It's one person or thing manipulating another.

A negotiation can be two parties hashing out a peace treaty, or someone on a diet trying to convince themselves to avoid potato chips. It can be two sisters sharing their wardrobes, or the inner dialogue of someone deciding whether it's time to service their car.

Let's go back to my car story. Since there's only one character in the narrative (me), let's consider my interaction with you, the reader. Did my monologue strike you more like a negotiation, a seduction, or a fight?

EXERCISE 5

Reread: Pick a scene from any novel and decide whether it's a fight, seduction, negotiation, or some combination of the three.

Rewrite: Change the intent of that scene, transforming a negotiation into a fight or a fight into a seduction. How does this change the characters' motivations? Can you modify the intent of a scene without changing what its characters really want?

Scene and sequel

Dwight Swain introduced the terms *scene* and *sequel* in storytelling. A scene is where the action happens, and a sequel is the reflective passage that follows, allowing characters (and readers) to process what just occurred.

It's essential to pay attention to this rhythm in your reading. Authors stacking one action scene after another can create two problems:

1. The reader gets overwhelmed by nonstop activity.
2. There's no time to absorb the significance of what just happened.

For example, if a warrior slays a dragon, it's a mistake to jump straight to them slaying an ogre in the next scene. That dragon moment should matter. Shouldn't there be a reward? A celebration? Some emotional or physical fallout? Without a reflective beat, the impact of the action is lost.

Balance is key, between movement and meaning, between event and emotional context.

Francine Prose, in *Reading Like a Writer*, shares a story about struggling to write a fight scene. To fix it, she studied one written by a favorite author and made a surprising discovery: The fight scene was preceded by a calm, reflective moment—a quieting of the nerves and a slower pace. That contrast made the action more powerful.

Think of the biblical story of Jesus's execution, one of the most intense scenes in literature. It's not preceded by violence but by a quiet prayer in the Garden of Gethsemane, a moment of stillness that heightens the drama that follows.

Would you consider my car-buying story more scene or sequel? If you think it's scene, then where is it taking place? And if it's sequel, do you find evidence of self-reflection?

EXERCISE 6

Reread: Pick a scene in any novel. Determine whether it is a *scene* (action) or *sequel* (reflection), referring back to what just happened, or forward to presage an upcoming event. (If it's neither of these, could it be a postcard?)

Rewrite: Is there a sequel following the action scene? What does it do, or why isn't it there? Could you safely remove it without affecting the plot?

Milieu, idea, character, or event

Orson Scott Card proposes that every novel can be categorized by one of four primary focuses:

- **Milieu:** Centered on a sense of place
- **Idea:** Exploring a philosophical or conceptual question
- **Character:** Following a character's internal journey
- **Event:** Built around a significant event, like a death, revolution, or major change

If this theory holds, then most of the scenes within the novel should reflect that same focus.

Take *The Vanishing Half* by Brit Bennett, a novel that engages with the idea of racial passing and assimilation in white society. While not every scene explicitly centers on that theme, traces of it are woven throughout. This consistent thread allows the author to convey the novel's deeper meaning and vision.

So even if a scene doesn't address the theme directly, it should still resonate with the novel's core focus in some way, whether through imagery, conflict, character choices, or tone. What was the focus of my car-buying story? Was it the event of the purchase, the idea of moral or immoral action, or did it focus more on my character?

EXERCISE 7

Reread: Think about a novel you've already read, or know from its marketing, reviews, or author interviews, and identify what the book is about. Does this work fit into Card's theory that it will be about one of four themes? If not, which of the four—milieu, idea, character, or event—makes the most sense? Then examine a random scene to see if you can find traces of that context.

Rewrite: Which of Card's four categories best describes your novel?

Notes

1. For far more about linguistic context than we have room for here, see https://en.wikipedia.org/wiki/Context_(In linguistics).
2. One further note: The narrator is using second-person present tense, and so is speaking directly to the reader, a topic covered in chapter 12, "Language and Grammar."
3. I use this one: https://randomwordgenerator.com/.
4. Dana Stevens, "The Three Types of Scenes According to Mike Nichols," *Slate.com*, November 20, 2014, https://slate.com/culture/2014/11/mike-nichols-dead-at-83-watch-three-of-his-best-scenes-from-the-movies-video.html.

14
Point of View

Point of view (POV) is the perspective from which a story is told—essentially, whose eyes and mind the reader is experiencing the events through. It shapes your connection to the story, how much you know, and what you feel. POV can range from the micro to the macro—from the intimate thoughts of a single character to the broader perspectives of families, cities, or nations. It can even reflect a narrator's entire worldview or on any perspective in between.

POV is complex and challenging to write, demanding the full range of an author's skills. Understanding its layers requires you to look deeper into the text and expand how you interpret what's happening. To help make sense of these layers, let's compare them to the elements involved in making a movie.

Think about a memorable scene in your favorite movie and ask yourself what made it work so well. Was it the characters, the setting, or the dialogue? Maybe the cinematographer contributed to the overall effect with striking camera angles; or the set designer skillfully deployed fog, symbolic colors, and lighting; or the costume and makeup departments gave the production an authentic look and feel. What about the rhythm of the visual editing and the sweep of the music and sound effects? The crews of those departments each had a hand in the final product, in addition to the contributions of the actors, directors, writers, and producers.

Constructing a novel's point of view requires that the novelist possess the skills of all of those artists. But a novelist's work is made even more difficult by two additional factors. The first is that in addition to the cinematic visual and auditory experiences, a novel depicts tastes, smells, tactile sensations, and the very thoughts of its characters. The second is that the novel needs to be relatable to *you*, enough so that—unlike a movie, which can remain alien to your experience—the novel triggers a suspension of the here and now within your mind so that you can imagine the action playing out inside your head, with you participating in the story.

A novel is so much more than its cousin, that skeletal script of stage and screen, which contains only two elements: dialogue and stage direction. All of the meat on the bones of a novel, that is, all the connective tissue between dialogue and stage direction within a novel, is part of POV. This requires a novelist to master skills similar to all of the artisans who translate a play from the page into a production.

Therefore, your ability to evaluate a POV—which is multifaceted—depends on mastering a considerable number of tools. But you can start with two simple questions:

- Where are we?
- Whose story is this right now?

This chapter covers the component parts of POV at the micro level. To explore a novel's macro POV—the conceptual or thematic point of view that spans chapters or an entire novel—see chapter 15, "Voice" and chapter 20, "The Gestalt."

If you haven't already read chapters 12, "Language and Grammar" (especially the "Intonation" and "Person, Place, and Time" sections) and 13, "Context in Scene" (all of it), I suggest you do so before tackling this chapter and the next.

Person, Place, and Distance

> If we think through the many narrative devices in the fiction we know, we soon come to a sense of the embarrassing inadequacy of our traditional classification of "point of view" into three or four kinds, variables only of the "person" and the degree of omniscience.
> —*Wayne C. Booth*, The Rhetoric of Fiction[1]

Merely labeling a point of view as "third person, past tense" is far too simplistic for serious literary analysis. Traditional POV categories—like close, distant, or omniscient—are also too vague to be truly useful. The term *omniscient*, in particular, often sparks confusion. As it's commonly defined, it lacks nuance. In reality, the only truly omniscient presence in a novel is the actual author—not the narrator, and not even the implied author—because only the writer has full access to every aspect of the story. But while this is technically true, it's also unhelpful in that it doesn't tell us how the author crafted the varying perspectives within the narrative.

Person, tense, and distance are just starting points for analyzing point of view, but they provide a crucial foundation for understanding how a story is told. In fact, I've devoted the entire "Person, Place, and Time" section in chapter 12, "Language and Grammar" to person and tense. Distance—that is, how close the reader, narrator, and author are in relation to each other—is covered in the "Aesthetic Distance" section found in this chapter, and in the "Position" section of chapter 15, "Voice."

POV is never static

Again, theater and film provide the easiest ways to visualize this concept. No commercial movie ever made had a single point of view.[2] Every camera angle, every dolly, every three-shot, two-shot, and close-up changes the viewer's perspective. Even theater can focus the audience's attention on various parts of the stage through lighting, choreography, costumes, props, sound, and moveable sets.

To demonstrate this fluid POV, I'll use the nursery rhyme "Jack and Jill," which is omniscient and at a distance. It's observational: You never learn *why* they both fetched water or how they felt about their injuries, but you do subtly shift focus from both of them, to wherever Jack fell down, and then over to Jill, tumbling.

Another example of shifting POV is this possible follow-up scene, which I'll reuse a number of times throughout this chapter:

> "I hate you!" Jill shouted, which amplified Jack's already massive headache. "Fetch your own damn water!" And she never went up that hill again.

The passage begins with Jill, so you may initially assume that this is her POV. However, when you learn of Jack's headache, you're inside his head, so the POV cannot be hers. Then you learn that Jill will never again ascend that hill, which could not be known to either Jill or Jack in that moment. So this must be from the POV of either the narrator or Jack—after Jill's death![3]

Although a critical reader may perceive three shifts of POV within this short passage, if we had to choose one, we'd probably agree that it was Jack's. The POV could conceivably be one hundred percent Jill's if the author had added the words *she could see* between *which* and *amplified*.

Your brain in reading mode is innately able to gloss over large chunks of text without considering the ways that a POV is shifting on you, especially if you're not paying close attention. When you are able to focus on POV—because, after all, you're the one creating the movie inside your head—you may find it useful to imagine how a camera operator would capture each perspective. We all have experience watching movies, TV shows, and advertisements, and so we are already familiar with these wide pans, two-shots, and close-ups.

Six narrative levels

At this point we also need to acknowledge three additional actors contributing to POV beyond the three usual suspects (character, narrator, and author). They are the implied author, the implied reader, and you—the actual reader.

> **Implied author:** Think of a cameo in a movie. If you see director Martin Scorsese in a movie, and even if he says, "Hi, I'm Martin Scorsese," what you're seeing is the real person portraying a caricature of himself, willing to play the role of "Martin Scorsese" in a colleague's film.[4] Modern readers who are familiar with social influencers on Instagram and TikTok are better equipped than any other readership in history to recognize that there is a difference between a persona and the real-life person behind it.[5]

> **Implied reader:** When the implied author of *Middlemarch*— George Eliot—signifies his presence in the novel with the pronoun *I*, in real life he is actually a woman author—Mary Anne Evans— addressing an implied reader, one who is certainly not you, whose great-great-grandparents had not yet been born when the book was written. (Phew!)

When reading a novel, you may experience the sensation that an author is speaking directly to you. Remember that the authorial voice is not the author themselves, and whomever they are addressing as "you" is certainly not you in particular. So to read like a writer, you must consider not three but *six* levels of POV: character, narrator, implied author, actual author, implied reader, and you.

Back in the "Self-Assessment" section of chapter 1, I shared with you my personal biases, and in the "Root Cause" section of chapter 4, I shared what motivates me to write. None of those admissions are lies, I assure you, and yet what I've shared is merely a curated view of me, not unlike what you'd find in any online biography, social media profile, or memoir. It's the angle I want to show you, and not the entirety of who I am. To get that, you'd need to actually meet me, and even *then,* there is truth in the adage that you can never truly know another person.

To analyze POV in your reading, therefore, it is essential to consider the interplay among all six of these narrative levels: not only how the characters are portrayed relative to each other, but also how they relate to the various narrators, the implied author and implied reader, the actual author, whose murky presence is buried deep in the background shadows, and of course, you, dear reader, and what you bring to your reading experience.

Rhetorical narration

Rhetoric is the art of using language effectively and persuasively. In a novel, it shows up in how characters speak, how the narrator frames events, and how the author guides the reader's thoughts and emotions. It's used to shape perception, build tension, reveal themes, and move the story forward—sometimes through persuasive dialogue, sometimes through the tone and structure of the narration itself.

All four modes of rhetoric are used within the novel: narration, description, exposition, and argumentation. Most important to POV is narration. In *The Rhetoric of Fiction*,[6] Wayne C. Booth describes ten types of narration, which I've combined into three groups, omitting the topic of person, which is covered in chapter 12, "Language and Grammar." The rest of this chapter addresses POV-related rhetorical techniques:

- **Narration perspective:** Including undramatized and dramatized narrators, observers, and narrator-agents.
- **Aesthetic distance:** Separation that may exist between all six layers of narration, and how it relates to irony, scene, and other rhetorical modes like description, exposition, and argumentation.
- **Privilege:** Access granted to characters. This includes a discussion of interiority.

Let's investigate POV through the lenses of narration perspective, aesthetic distance, and privileges.

Narration Perspective

Every novel is a narrative. And within the narrative someone or something is laying out the information, arranging it into bundles, and relating it to the reader. At any given moment, the narration is going to exist at one or more of four narrative levels: implied author, narrator, one or more of the characters, or the implied reader.[7] To help you identify and categorize each of these levels, let's revisit our postlude to "Jack and Jill" from the perspective of each of these actors.

Implied author

I'll rewrite our story slightly to insert an authorial voice:

> "I hate you!" Jill shouted, which I know would have amplified Jack's already massive headache. "Fetch your own damn water!"

she snapped. And I'll tell ya, she never went up that hill again, the ungrateful wench. End of that fairy tale.

It's the same story, but with the opinionated voice of an implied author, who also happens to be using a more conversational tone. Notice use of the word "I," which is key. In a longer narrative, this "I" could be a narrator or another character in the scene, but because the passage ends with the "end of the fairy tale," it's clear that the "I" stands outside of the story. The implied author is an *intrusive* voice, which could also take the form of a cameo, such as: "I'm Gary McBride, and I approve this fable."

Narrator

"I hate you!" Jill shouted, which amplified Jack's already massive headache. "Fetch your own damn water!" And she never went up that hill again.

This is the same text as the first version I presented above. The sentence, "And she never went up that hill again," could represent the thoughts of an implied author or a character, but without the marker "I" indicating a self, we should assume the default, which is the narrator.

There are different types of narrators: for example, undramatized or dramatized—in other words, narrating within the story or standing outside the story. The original passage uses an undramatized narrator. Here's an example of a dramatized narrator:

"I hate you!" Jill shouted, which surprised me as much as it amplified Jack's already massive headache. "Fetch your own damn water!" she snapped. And I'll tell ya, she never went up that hill again, the ungrateful wench.

Notice how this differs from the implied author example above, in that now the narrator is *in scene*. Such a dramatized narrator is virtually identical to an observer or a narrator-agent—it's the same type of writing for all three. There's no need to split hairs.

Character

This is simply the narrator personified as a named character.

"I hate you!" Jill shouted, which surprised Tony as much as it must have amplified Jack's already massive headache. "Fetch your own damn water!" she snapped. Tony would always look back on this moment as the end of Jill's water-fetching days.

Implied reader

All you need to do here is to change "Tony" to "you":

"I hate you!" Jill shouted, which surprised you as much as it must have amplified Jack's already massive headache. "Fetch your own damn water!" she snapped. You would always look back on this moment as the end of Jill's water-fetching days.

The differences between these four levels of narration are subtle but important to the storytelling. Choosing which narrative voice handles a moment—fine-tuning the POV—depends entirely on what the author wants to achieve in the story.

EXERCISE 1

Reread: Find any scene in any novel and figure out where you are and whose perspective you are in at that moment. Do you have access to one or more characters' thoughts? If it includes backstory, who is conveying it—a narrator, the author, or one of the characters? Does the perspective move from one character to another?

Rewrite: Consider why the author chose this perspective for this scene, and try rewriting it from another perspective. What, if anything, does this new POV change—its meaning or significance, tension, emotional level, character relationships, or something else?

Aesthetic Distance

In any reading experience there is an implied dialogue among author, narrator, the other characters, and the reader. Each of the four can range, in relation to each of the others, from identification to complete opposition, on any axis of value, moral, intellectual, aesthetic, and even physical.
—*Wayne C. Booth*, The Rhetoric of Fiction

Aesthetic distance refers to the difference of opinion, purpose, taste, or style between each of the four primary actors within narration: author, narrator, characters, and the reader. The matter of *physical* distance in a POV is covered in the "Position" section of chapter 15, "Voice."

Let's consider this Jack and Jill coda:

> "You hurt me!" Jill ejaculated, amplifying Jack's already massive headache. "Next time, fetch your own damn water!" she snapped unreasonably, sounding quite the ungrateful bitch.

This version puts distance between all five actors in this story.

- **Jill** is reasonably upset by tumbling down the hill, putting distance between her and **Jack** by blaming him for her accident.
- The **narrator** casts doubt on Jill's judgment, calling her unreasonable and ungrateful.
- Notice the Victorian vocabulary that the **author** put in the mouth of their narrator: "ejaculated" and "quite." "Sounding quite the" has an archaic ring, and implies that the author thinks the narrator is old-fashioned, perhaps even patriarchal and misogynistic.
- This **reader** objects to the narrator's description of Jill, the victim of a fall, as bitchy because she is exercising her agency by standing up to Jack.[8]

Irony

Disagreement is one example of the distance that can exist between key narrative actors. Another is the difference in what each actor knows or understands within the story. You see this in a whodunit, when the detective withholds a crucial clue from a suspect, or when the killer keeps their identity hidden. It also shows up in romance plots, especially when a breakup happens because of a misunderstanding.

A more nuanced example of this kind of distance is *irony*, the gap between what's expected, what appears to be happening, and what's actually going on. When the reader knows more than the characters do, that's called *dramatic irony*.

Beyond narrative voice, distance can also be expressed through the other three rhetorical modes in a novel: description, exposition, and argumentation. An aesthetic distance can also exist between the characters and the scene that contains them. For more on that, see chapter 13, "Context in Scene."

Description

Aesthetic distance in description is about how close or far the reader feels from the scene, emotionally and perceptually. This distance is shaped by the level of detail, the choice of language, and the emotional tone used to describe people, places, or events.

Description includes all the details about characters and the setting, conveyed through the five senses. It can take a poetic form or be more straightforward, like a journal entry. A common technique is to reflect a character's emotions in the way the scene is described—infusing the surroundings with their inner state. These descriptions can either align with the character's feelings or intentionally contrast with them for dramatic effect.

For example, in an early section of Stephen King's 2023 novel *Holly,* one witness to a crime is writing a poem and trying to avoid using the word *halo* to describe the mist surrounding a streetlamp, which she knows is a cliché. The section ends with the narrator describing that same streetlight as having a halo, thereby distancing the narrator from the character. But in this sentence, we can also glimpse King himself winking at the reader in gleeful opposition to his own character's sensibilities. *Let's cut the crap,* I imagine him saying. *We both know* halo *is the most efficient word here.*

Exposition

Aesthetic distance in exposition is expressed by how close or far the narrator feels from the elements that add atmosphere and layers of meaning to a novel, for example: the weather, the village, their community, history, belief systems, hopes, and dreams. When exposition is delivered with emotional detachment, a formal tone, or abstract language, it creates a sense of distance, making the reader observe events from the outside. On the other hand, when exposition is filtered through a character's voice, emotions, or limited understanding, it reduces aesthetic distance, pulling the reader closer into the character's world. The choice of vocabulary, tone, and level of insight all contribute to how close the reader feels to the events or ideas being explained.

In the "Jack and Jill" example above, let's say that the author gives us a long description of their water pail: its construction, its dimensions, what it cost to manufacture, and what it cost to purchase. Perhaps this particular pail has a leak that has been mended with tar, but it's coming loose. The amount of detail given to the pail elevates its importance within our simple story to the level of symbol or allegory. Does the pail represent the agrarian economy, and Jack and Jill's social status within it? Maybe the pail leads to questions about why they need to fetch water at all, given that their neighbors have it piped into their cottages.

Tommy Orange's novel *There There* weaves together character studies of thirteen modern-day Native Americans on their way to a powwow in Oakland, California. At the beginning and again at the midpoint of the novel, this narrative contains two contrasting chapters of pure exposition, which give readers a history lesson about the slaughter of these characters' ancestors and why those events still resonate today. This creates a distance between the characters, who are all aware of this legacy, and the reader, who may not have known about this history. Additional distance is created between the author and the readers, whose ancestors may or may not have been *responsible* for this tragedy.

Argumentation

The rhetorical mode of argument—like a lawyer presenting a case—appears in novels when one character tries to persuade another to see things their way. On a broader level, every novel can be seen as an argument for the author's worldview—that's often the deeper motivation behind the writing. While skilled novelists usually embed their ideas subtly through characters, scenes, and plot, sometimes their message becomes too forceful. When that happens, the story can feel more like polemic—like a sermon or a manifesto—making it preachy rather than persuasive.

This can create distance between the reader and the text, especially if the reader is resistant to the author's position on an issue. Calls to action in recent novels include the "Save the trees!" of Richard Powers's 2019 Pulitzer Prize–winning novel *The Overstory,* and the "Wake up to climate change!" of Jenny Offill's masterful 2020 novel *Weather*.

EXERCISE 2

Reread: Find any passage in a novel and look for aesthetic distance between characters, or between the narrator and the implied reader. How is that distance expressed—through narration, irony, description, or exposition? Does the passage feel like the author has an agenda they're pushing? If so, do you agree with their argument?

How distant or how intimate does the story feel? Is the writing engaging your emotions, or does it feel cold and sterile?

Rewrite: Pick a passage and rewrite it in a more distant or more intimate style, creating aesthetic distance between characters, or between the narrator and the implied reader.

Privilege

We need a good study of the varieties of privilege and limitation
and their function.
　　—*Wayne C. Booth*, The Rhetoric of Fiction

Think of privileges as a set of permissions the author has given a character
that allows them to unlock elements of the narrative. Perhaps a narrator can see
inside Jack's head, but not Jill's. Maybe that narrator has the ability to see into the
future, which gives them the privilege of foreshadowing. Maybe a character has
been given the privilege of wealth, or status, or the ability to see dead people.
Because POVs vary among characters and are constantly evolving, monitoring
the privileges that the author bestows is a much more precise way to understand
POVs, and is therefore extremely valuable to our reading.

Every kind of privilege an author gives to characters—whether it's status,
knowledge, perception, interiority, or something else—can also be understood as
having two key qualities:

- **Fluidity:** It can shift at any point in the story by being granted, increased,
  reduced, or taken away entirely.
- **Scale:** It exists on a spectrum, ranging from minimal to absolute, with
  endless variation in between.

Status

This is the most obvious reading of the term *privilege*. It's the wealth, class,
or occupation of a character that manifests itself outwardly and affects their relationship to other characters. Their point of view is derived from the level at which
they exist, and it colors their perception of the world, their repertoire of options
within that world, and their actions.

This type of privilege has the greatest effect not only on how characters see
themselves but also on how they develop throughout the course of a novel. Status
can dissipate or accumulate within any scene, of course, and this phenomenon is
described in much greater detail in chapter 16, "Character Development."

Knowledge

Knowledge here is defined as characters' access to facts pertinent to their situations. Think of knowledge as the elements involved in a scientific investigation
of a scene. It's not about feelings or perceptions: This is about what can be seen,
smelled, and touched.

Who knows about the pistol hanging on the wall above the fireplace? Who knows that Jack and Jill are not related biologically? Who knows where the body is buried, and the combination to the safe? Knowledge is power and can also be related to the status of a character. Will Jill ever tell Jack that she knows who his real father is?

Knowledge is also fluid, obviously. When Jill finally reveals to Jack the identity of his father, she has ceded some of her privilege to him. When the detective lets slip who was in the kitchen with the candlestick, they may put someone's life at risk. And when a character discovers that something they believed to be true was actually a lie, the balance of understanding—and privilege—shifts again.

The drip-feed of knowledge shared with the reader is also an essential component of the **unspoken contract**.

Perception

Perception is closely related to insight. Jack might notice that Jill is afraid of heights. Jill might pick up on Jack's gambling problem—even if he's unaware of it himself. A narrator can guide the reader's perception, too, by subtly planting clues about what's to come. When you pick up on those hints and the story unfolds as expected, it creates a sense of satisfaction in having seen it coming.

The experience of reading a story shapes how you perceive its characters, their circumstances, and any moral judgments you make about them. If your goal is to re-create those effects in your own writing, then understanding how insight is skillfully and convincingly communicated to the reader is one of the most valuable tools you can develop. This is covered in greater detail in chapter 18, "Pacing," and chapter 19, "Layering."

Interiority

The greatest privilege an author can give a narrator is access to a character's thoughts—the ability to see the world from inside the character's mind. This is the only way the reader can truly understand a character's motivations, which may be hidden from other characters in the story.

While it's possible to obscure a character's true thoughts through an unreliable narrator, it's difficult to do so convincingly. A character can only genuinely deceive themselves if their thinking is somehow impaired—by mental illness, substance use, or some other distortion of perception.

EXERCISE 3

Reread: Open any novel and evaluate the privilege an author grants to the narrator and the characters. What type of privilege has been given—status, knowledge, perception, or interiority—and is the amount of that privilege increasing or decreasing within the scene? What about you? Have you been given access to characters' thoughts, and what clues has the author given you about where the story might lead?

Rewrite: Take away a privilege from any character within the scene you've just read. How does it change their power or agency? Their prospects or opportunities? Does it change the plot?

Notes

1. Wayne C. Booth, *The Rhetoric of Fiction*, 2nd ed. (University of Chicago Press, Illinois, 1983).

2. A movie from a single point of view would be shot from a single stationary camera left on to record from beginning to end, producing a single unmoving perspective, similar to looking through a peephole. Who would want to watch that? On the other hand, a movie shot with a single *mobile* camera, with no visible cuts, represents the most novelistic POV possible on-screen. Two superior examples of this are the films *Rope* (1948) and *Adolescence* (2025), which follow events as they unfold in real time. The camera that follows various characters, lingers on a reaction, takes in a group, or soars over a landscape, mimics the experience of a reader following a novel's narrative thread.

3. Alternatively, we're dealing with an unreliable narrator who is misleading us into thinking they know all about Jill when they don't. The possibilities here are endless.

4. For the most delightfully absurd example of a cameo gone cuckoo, see the 1999 movie *Being John Malkovich*.

5. Although millions of people can't make that distinction, apparently.

6. Booth, *The Rhetoric of Fiction*.

7. We'll omit author and reader for now—they serve other functions within the narrative.

8. I'm not entirely sure whom I am objecting to—is it the narrator, the implied author, or the author? All three could be implicated.

15
Voice

You've probably heard someone say a novel has a *strong voice*—and that's usually one of the highest compliments a writer can receive. But what exactly does that mean?

Voice is the unique personality that comes through in an author's writing. It's made up of tone, mood, register, grammar and language choices—things like word choice, imagery, metaphor, syntax, and rhythm. And most importantly, it's shaped by *point of view* (POV), which acts as the lens through which the story is told.

When all these elements work in harmony, voice is what makes writing feel alive. It creates that magical connection where the story flows effortlessly into your mind. You can see the world clearly, hear the characters speak, and feel like you're right there with them.

In essence, voice is the *composite effect* of all the story's POVs coming together. It's the author's personality, style, and emotional truth, woven into every word.

Voice is the composite effect when all the POVs combine.

When you evaluate a novel's voice, what you're really doing is considering every individual actor's point of view within the text and judging whether you feel they all fit together in an effective way. Beyond the tools you use to dissect a single POV, covered in chapter 14, "Point of View," what elements can you study to tease apart this composite POV? They are, in roughly the order that readers encounter them:

- **Tone:** Register, mood, and themes influencing character development and form
- **Position:** Location in physical space, including time

- **Shift:** Changing POVs and their effect on voice
- **Exposure:** Breadth of the worldview

Because voice is really a manifestation of POV, it's important to understand what goes into it. As discussed in chapter 14, "Point of View," POV can involve anything in a novel that isn't covered by dialogue or scene setting—and that's a lot. So if you haven't already read that chapter, I suggest you do so before tackling this one.

Tone

Tone is the overarching attitude or emotion that a piece of literature conveys to its readers. It's the author's style of expression, delivered through sentence structure and word choice. Tone is also how the writer addresses their implied readers and who they imagine them to be; this includes their education, occupation, sophistication, cultural context, and emotional acuity.

Tone also reveals the aspirations of the author and whether they are trying to entertain, shock, amuse, or educate. So tone exists along different registers or degrees of formality. Authors will use one or more of these registers over the course of their novel:

- **High formal:** Used in professional or academic settings, and to describe life-altering events, like marriage and death
- **Formal:** Characterized by polite, respectful language, often used in business or official correspondence
- **Neutral:** Everyday conversation or general writing
- **Informal:** Casual, relaxed language, often used with friends or found in emails, comments, and text messages
- **Vulgar:** Coarse, colloquial language, typically used in specific cultural or social contexts[1]
- **Static:** Archaic speech, often used to evoke a sense of history or nostalgia

Here are some varieties of tone you may encounter in your reading, and remember also that any of these moods can shift within a single novel:

- **Serious:** High aspirations in a neutral to formal tone, often focused on weighty or profound topics
- **Dramatic:** High aspirations with high energy, often involving high stakes or life-changing events
- **Comedic:** Low aspirations with all levels of energy

- **Satirical:** Using humor, irony, exaggeration, or ridicule to expose and criticize moral failings[2]
- **Grotesque:** Bizarre, with elements of horror or the supernatural
- **Pedantic:** High aspirations in a high formal register that often comes off as stilted

All writing has tone, even a nonfiction work such as this. Consider the tone of this book—can you hear my voice? Picture where we are. Am I behind a lectern addressing you, or are we sitting in two comfy chairs chatting by a fire? I hope you imagine the latter, because that's the tone I've aimed for: a conversation between two peers. Neutral and not at all pedantic.

You'll find more on how word choice and grammar contribute to tone in the "Intonation" section of chapter 12, "Language and Grammar."

Wagging the dog

My choice of tone has heavily influenced the very structure of this book.

I want my book to be accessible to everyone, from the high school student to the doctoral candidate, from the aspiring amateur to the literary professional. To keep it at a digestible length, I have compressed the material and left out a lot of detail. If I had wanted this to be a textbook, I would have been more comprehensive and would have written much longer essays on each topic. But doing so would have dramatically altered the way topics are presented, the length, and the overall form of this book. It would have also necessarily shifted its tone, because the macro and the micro influence each other in a feedback loop.

To make this work easy to consume, I've divided it up into semi-independent chunks—each averaging 4,000 words—that can be consumed in one sitting. I expect that your life is as busy as mine and that you don't have the luxury of time to read this book from beginning to end. For that reason, I've cross-indexed everything; I wanted to make it easy for you to dive in and out of topics as necessary. I've also provided an index as another way for you to find what you need, and I curate a website of additional references and other materials. If you are more academically inclined, I've annotated my sources and provided endnotes for further study.

In these ways, my tone has influenced the form of this book.

Another book in which tone has influenced form is Hernan Diaz's 2022 novel *Trust*. Each of its four sections have different points of view and tone, and is directed toward a different audience, which led to four unique forms: a novel-within-a-novel, the outline of an autobiography, a memoir, and a diary.

Prosody

Sometimes you may notice a shift in tone across a narrative, or a variety of tones, depending on the situation. Here are some reasons to do this:

- **Character differentiation:** Distinguishing the identity of each character is not only achieved through dialogue, but also with visual descriptions, pacing, and of course, narrative tone. Think of the influence of a character on a scene like a star using gravity to pull its planets into its orbit, bending the arcs of the surrounding matter toward itself.
- **Character development:** Sometimes a character's journey is slight—a realization, an awakening; at other times that journey is a lifetime. For example, in a *bildungsroman*, or coming-of-age story, no character passes through adolescence unchanged, and the tone of the narrative may reflect a loss of innocence through language, observations, and the tone of scenes themselves. This is covered in greater depth in chapter 16, "Character Development."
- **Plot points:** Inciting incidents, refusing the challenge, the midpoint, the climax—a shift in tone can indicate a reversal of fortunes, a new beginning, or a door closing forever.

EXERCISE 1

Reread: Open any novel anywhere and identify its tone, taking into account aspiration, mood, register, and its position within the novel. Is the tone formal or informal, emotionally neutral, or florid? Is it underplayed or exuberant and hyperbolic? Serious or jocular? Realistic or artificial? Do you think you're the reader the writer envisioned? If not, why not?

Rewrite: Compare that tone with what you find in any other passage in the same novel. Is the tone in the second passage the same, or does it differ from the tone in the first passage you chose? Why did the author do this, and how would you have done it differently?

Position

The way a narrative voice positions the reader in space and time is much like how a film uses camera angles, lighting, color, and editing. The "camera" of the narrative might be fixed, focusing closely on one character, or it might move fluidly from one perspective to another, like a dolly shot gliding through a scene. It could hover above the action, like an overhead camera at a sporting event, or float freely like a drone, able to go anywhere and see everything.

An author can position the reader anywhere—in any place, time, situation, or worldview. Sometimes, that perspective is nearly godlike, offering a sweeping, satellite-level view of an entire world. When that happens, it's important to consider how the author's own overarching worldview shapes the construction of point of view.

Space

You may find yourself inside a character's head, observing a scene through their eyes. You may be part of a mob, or inside a tree, or floating in space. You may be close enough to the action to feel the cut of a blade, or hear evidence of it through a wall, or zoom away from the main event at the speed of light.

A POV's physical space addresses these three dimensions:

1. **Who:** Who is the subject? Who is at the center of the scene?
2. **Where:** Where are we in three-dimensional space-time? And how far from the subject?
3. **Aperture:** How broad or narrow is the perspective?

Proximity to the subject is an important and easily identifiable aspect of point of view, but it's just one part of a larger picture and shouldn't be overemphasized. Like individual camera angles in a film, each narrative perspective adds something to the story. But the combination of all these "shots" creates the overall atmosphere and shapes the reader's experience.

The combination of near and far, approaching or receding, rising or falling, a frenzy of perspectives evoking vertigo or a slow and steady calm—all of these give us more insight about what the author is trying to communicate and what they want us to experience.

Aperture is the angle of perspective, which can be wide or narrow. A POV can be distant, and yet its aperture can be tightly focused on an individual. An aperture can contain two or more characters at once, reflecting a plural perspective (we or us). An aperture can also be so broad as to cover every character and become omniscient.[3] A scene in a movie that contains only close-ups without any establishing shots of the room feels claustrophobic, while wide-angle landscapes feel expansive. Similar effects are created through the apertures found in a novel.

Time

The fourth dimension of our physical world is time. In a novel, time is being manipulated for the benefit of the storytelling. Time can be sped up or slowed down, and events can be placed out of order.

Novels are made primarily of *scene* and *sequel*, that is, action and reflection upon that action. Or even more simply: Novels are a skeleton of scenes and the connective tissue between them.[4] In any narrative form, the time that elapses between scenes is often massively compacted. Hours, days, years, or centuries can be squeezed into the time it takes to the turn the page and move to the next chapter. Also omitted are the everyday events that don't have any bearing on the story: making the bed, grocery shopping, going to the bathroom. Knowing which elements are necessary to the story and knowing what can be safely cut is also directly related to the art of knowing when to enter a scene and when to exit a scene, cutting everything extraneous.

Conversely, a novelist will sometimes slow time down almost to a standstill. A key moment lasting seconds can be described in such detail that it covers multiple pages and may take the greater part of an hour to read. The reflective prose of sequel passages are musings that exist almost outside of time, thoughts that may take a chapter to describe but may occur within an instant of story time.

Then there's the reordering of time. Some novels begin *in medias res,* and most novels contain some amount of backstory and B-stories, so it's safe to say that almost no novel progresses along a linear timeline from beginning to end. The reader is asked to move forward and backward along a timeline, and is expected to remember whether a passage is in the recent past, deep past, future, or in the primary narrative "present." Some novels take more liberties with time, using alternative structures like retrograde motion, concentric circles, or parallel universes. It's a lot to manage.

Let's group all these manipulations of time under the rubric of *time travel*. And the most important question when finding any type of time travel in your reading is: Does it add to the storytelling, or does it detract from it? In other words, is the time travel necessary, or is it a distraction?

EXERCISE 2

Reread: Take any passage from any novel and pick a scene. How close are we to the protagonist? In the room? In their head? Are we in motion? Or are we changing POV from one character to another?

Is this passage happening in the novel's "present" or in its past? Is it backstory or an out-of-time reflection? Pinpoint exactly when and where you are supposed to be, relative to the "present" and "here." How did the author signal that?

Rewrite: Take the opposite approach to distance that you found in the scene by moving the POV, or changing where the scene happens in time, or altering its pacing. How much have you changed the story's voice?

Contextual frame

> Always push your knowledge of the context as far as you can just to see if aspects of the context are relevant that you might at first have not thought were relevant or if you can discover entirely new aspects of the context.
> —James Paul Gee[5]

Your position in relation to a scene can be measured not just in physical or temporal terms, but also in terms of context—how you relate to what's happening compared to something else. While chapter 13, "Context in Scene" explores context at a smaller, scene-based level, here we look at a broader concept, worldview, and how the worldview in a novel may differ from your own. As a reader, you naturally expect to encounter worlds different from your own, so it's important to stay aware of how close or distant you feel from a character, situation, or the novel's overall perspective.

A novel's *contextual frame* refers to the perspective or viewpoint of the implied author, which we evaluate in relation to our own. This helps us analyze the reliability of the narrator, the believability of the story, and its relationship to the reality we see around us.

When you expand the contextual frame, you begin to reveal the underlying intentions of the author. By including certain key elements in the story, the author may be hinting at deeper themes beneath the surface of the narrative.

One of Gee's examples asks us to imagine a nineteenth-century character suffering from tuberculosis. At first, it may not be obvious how this connects to point of view. But when we widen the context, we discover that TB was far more common in crowded factories and sweatshops than among rural communities or the wealthy. This raises a new question: Could the character's illness be a reflection of the harsh conditions of unregulated industrial capitalism—and could the story, in part, be about that deeper issue?

Another example is to consider the activities of the titular character in Lauren Wilkinson's *American Spy*, who is on a CIA mission to Burkina Faso. But what's really going on, and what are the true motivations of the main character and her author? Beneath the surface derring-do, we discover a plot of colonialist aggression against an independent nation.

Broadening the contextual frame opens the reader up to deeper questions about a novel's ultimate point of view. If you'd like to progress further along this contextual path, you'll find more in chapter 19, "Layering."

EXERCISE 3

Reread: Reflect on a novel you've read recently. How wide or narrow was its contextual frame? Did its voice feel specific, narrow, and confined, or was it broad, expansive, and all-encompassing?

Rewrite: Open or close the aperture of a single scene to refocus on an individual or broaden it to make a social statement. How far from the author's worldview can you travel?

Shift

> You can change point of view, of course; it is your God-given right as an American fiction writer. All I'm saying is, you need to know that you're doing it; some American fiction writers don't. And you need to know when and how to do it, so that when you shift, you carry the reader effortlessly with you.
> —Ursula K. Le Guin[6]

Now that we've covered the basics of voice—tone and position—let's explore what happens when an author shifts point of view mid-story: what that choice involves, how to do it well, and the risks of doing it poorly. As Le Guin reminds us, there are both effective and ineffective ways to handle multiple perspectives. In addition, there are both good and bad reasons for shifting POV.

First, ignore anyone who says a novel should stick to a single point of view, or provides some magic number of maximum POVs. That's hooey. More than half the novels surveyed by *Writers Who Read* use multiple POVs.[7] As you saw in chapter 14, the idea of a single, fixed perspective—the traditional definition of POV—oversimplifies the rich complexity of narrative voice. In fact, when reading like a writer, you'll notice subtle shifts—what we might call micro-POVs—on nearly every page.

When investigating whether a shift of POV is merited or done well, you'll want to look for:

- Clarity
- Consistency
- Necessity

Clarity

You should expect an author to withhold information from you, and you should **assume you're being played**,[8] especially early in a novel. But there's a big difference between guiding a reader down a particular path and writing confusing prose. You may not know initially that the protagonist's ex is working at the local Walmart, or that her sister is having an affair with him, and that's fine if you get that information later, in fulfillment of the **unspoken contract**.

There's a limit to how mysterious or playful an author can be with readers. The line they should never cross is making a scene so vague you can't picture it. Think of it like a movie: Withholding information can be suspenseful—like when we don't know who's behind a door, or we see a character's terrified face before we know what they're looking at. But if the scene itself is blurry—as if seen through a smudged camera lens—it just becomes frustrating. Readers need clear visuals, even if those visuals are intentionally misleading. It's fine to create suspense, but unclear or overly coy scene-setting breaks the reader's trust—and you'll feel it when it happens.

POV needs to be established early, in the first sentence, and sometimes in the first word: "Sally drove her car home from the office, still worried about Charlie." We're getting Sally's POV.

Next chapter: "Charlie opened his laptop, afraid to look at his bank balance." Now Charlie is steering the story.

In both of those admittedly simplistic examples, the focus of the POV was the very first word, and the rest of the sentence remained inside the character's head, further illustrating their perspective. But the point is clear: The story must include markers like this if you are to have any hope of following the story.

Some novels delay revealing the point of view until later on the page, but almost always, that marker eventually appears. The longer a writer waits to clarify whose perspective we're in, the longer you are left unanchored, drifting in uncertainty. Sometimes that fog is intentional, used to create a mood or to convey a protagonist's frustration. But that vagueness comes at a cost: It risks confusing or alienating you.

EXERCISE 4

Reread: Open any novel to the beginning of any chapter. Read until you have a clear idea of whose POV it is. Did you find the indication of POV in the first sentence or paragraph, or further down the page, or on page three? If it was delayed, why? For example, was a character's POV carried over from the previous section, or did you notice a momentary shift to an omniscient narrator?

Rewrite: Clean up any fuzzy POV shifts you find. How can you do it smoothly, in the fewest words, without changing the author's voice?

Consistency

The most consistent point of view is, of course, a single POV. But when a novel includes multiple POVs, what matters is consistency in how those shifts are handled. Here are the most common and clearest ways to signal a POV change:

- **Chapter titles:** When each chapter uses a different POV, authors often name the chapter after the POV character to guide the reader.
- **Subject as the first word:** The clearest signal is starting the new section with the character's name in the first sentence or paragraph. Waiting too long to reveal the POV can confuse readers.
- **Dinkus (section divider):** A visual break, like a dinkus (* * *), signals the potential for a shift in perspective.

Once a pattern is established, good authors stick to it. If POV changes are introduced only at chapter breaks, then suddenly shifting perspective in the middle of a chapter without a clear cue can feel sloppy, unless the author has a deliberate and justifiable reason for breaking that pattern.

This brings us to the issue of *head-hopping*. The problem isn't multiple perspectives—omniscient narrators do that all the time. The issue is inconsistent execution: when one character's thoughts suddenly appear in another character's POV without warning. That inconsistency breaks the reader's immersion in the story and is exactly what writing coaches warn against.

EXERCISE 5

Reread: Using a novel with multiple points of view, investigate how the POV shifts happen throughout the book. Is the new subject's name mentioned as the first word of a new section? If not, then how is a shift of POV being signaled?

Take a look at a number of chapters—is this signaling of POV consistent? And if not, what's going on?

Rewrite: Clean up any inconsistent POV shifts you find in the novel. Does this change the voice of the narrative in any way?

Necessity

The number of POVs in a novel shapes not just how the story is told, but the nature of the story itself.

A single POV often signals a deeply personal journey—one protagonist, one lens, one emotional arc. It's intimate and focused.

With two or three POVs, the story may follow multiple characters individually, explore how their lives intersect, or shift attention from individuals toward a broader narrative.

When a novel contains ten or more POVs, this suggests that the story is no longer just about individual characters. Instead, the focus widens to explore larger themes or systems—social, cultural, or historical. The narrative becomes more fragmented, and tracking any single character becomes harder. Often, this is intentional. For example:

- In *There There*, Tommy Orange uses fourteen POVs to portray the modern Native American experience.
- Mohsin Hamid's *Exit West* includes fifteen POVs to illuminate the global dimensions of migration.
- Luis Alberto Urrea's *The House of Broken Angels* uses twelve POVs to paint a full portrait of a sprawling family.
- Brit Bennett's *The Vanishing Half* offers thirteen POVs to examine race, identity, and generational legacy.
- Jennifer Egan's *The Candy House* uses sixteen POVs—and dozens of characters—to reflect the fragmented, disjointed nature of digital life and social media. The difficulty in tracking the characters mirrors the novel's theme of disconnection.

In each case, the number of perspectives isn't arbitrary but rather supports what the author is trying to say.

EXERCISE 6

Reread: Take any novel you've read and take a rough count of its POVs. Consider why there are so many or so few. Do you think it's the most effective number of POVs to tell that story?

Rewrite: How would the novel's voice change with a greater or lesser number of POVs? Would it become a completely different story?

Exposure

Exposure refers to both the range of what the voice reveals and the depth of the perspective—that is, how much of the author's imagined world is shown to the reader. Like a camera lens, a point of view can zoom in tightly or open wide, with a shallow or deep focus. This selective framing shapes the story by highlighting certain details while hiding others. In this sense, exposure isn't only about what the author chooses to include; it's just as much about what they intentionally leave out.

The reader is like the prisoner in Plato's Cave—facing a wall, unable to see what's really happening behind them. All they can observe are the shadows projected onto the wall, not the actual people or events creating the shadows. This is a powerful metaphor for fictional characters, too. Since characters aren't real, they're made entirely of what the author chooses to show us—no more, no less. It's up to the reader to recognize what's missing and imagine the rest.

From infancy onward, we humans learn to fill the narrative gaps of our lives—it's how our brains make sense of the world. The game of peek-a-boo is very real to a child, and it takes time for them to realize that a person still exists when out of view.[9]

All writers omit, compress, and use shorthand to shape scenes and characters. And that's a good thing—we don't want every "um," "er," or "you know" from real-life speech, nor do we need detailed inventories of clothing, furniture, or bathroom breaks. Readers have been conditioned to accept trimmed-down storytelling that focuses on what's essential.

But because so much is left out, it's easy to overlook the gaps. As readers studying the craft, we need to slow down and ask: What's actually being shown, and what's left to my imagination? Why include this detail and not another? What do I truly know about the characters, plot, and setting—and what's being withheld? These questions lie at the heart of understanding voice.

Remember the **First rule of *Literary Forensics***: **Always ask why**. And because **everything serves a purpose** in a novel, make it a habit to **read** and **reread**. If you don't, you risk misinterpreting the text—filling gaps with your own assumptions and creating a version of the story that the author never intended to write.

Description

Consider two types of world-building: hard and soft.[10] J.R.R. Tolkien's *The Lord of the Rings* trilogy is a good example of hard world-building. Tolkien drew maps, invented creatures, and created an entire language (elvish) in service to the world of his novels. Phew! When Emily St. John Mandel described the twentieth, twenty-first, twenty-third, and twenty-fifth centuries in *Sea of Tranquility*, she did so with a minimum of brushstrokes. The depth and focus of these two authors' world-building efforts give us clues about what their stories are really about. Tolkien is concerned with society, belief systems, and historical trends, while Mandel is focused more on her characters, assuming rightly that people's emotional wants and needs remain constant across the centuries. Her novel leaves much more gap-filling to her reader than Tolkien does to his.

How much detail or how little detail is given to paint the scene? Detail or focus can also sharpen voice. I can say, "A kangaroo goes into a bar and hops up to the bartender…." Or I can say, "In Adelaide in 1867, a kangaroo made its way into the Five Roses bar…." The level of detail signals the difference between the setup for a joke and an account of a confrontation between nature and humans.

Difficulty

How easy or how difficult is the novel to read? The density or inscrutability of the text is another element of a novel's voice. Famously difficult voices include William Faulkner's *The Sound and the Fury*. The first half of that novel is told from the POV of a mentally and emotionally stunted character who doesn't comprehend much of what is happening around him, and so the reader is also at sea. James Joyce filtered his *Ulysses* through the murky lens of Dublin slang and stream of consciousness, making it nearly impossible for most modern readers to penetrate the text. The result is an experience similar to listening to music of contrapuntal complexity: It's challenging to understand, but ultimately rewarding if you're willing to dig in and study it.

How much effort should a novel demand from its reader? Many of us abandon a book at the first sign of difficulty, but we serve our writing selves better when we stop to question *why* the author is making it challenging, and *what* they are trying to achieve. Often, a complex narrative style signals a serious or difficult message beneath the surface. The real test for the reader is whether the effort required matches the weight of the subject matter. If it does, a layered, demanding voice might be the most powerful and appropriate way to deliver the story.

Deception

Remember the **unspoken contract**—the misdirection every novelist employs to direct your focus away from critical information, at least in the opening chapters? I call this "getting played." The author's deception can be deft or heavy-handed. When it's subtle, it's harder to recognize. But every novelist worth reading tries to direct you down a particular path for the sake of the story and its message.

Do you find yourself cheering for the protagonist and booing the antagonist? If so, it's useful to pause your reading to study how the author described each character. A popular manipulative technique is called *Save the Cat!* In a nutshell, it means that readers will sympathize with a character, no matter how sinister, if they help a creature or person in distress. It telegraphs empathy, and it activates our own empathy.

An unreliable narrator is one of the most intriguing expressions of a novel's voice. From the very first page, the voice may present a skewed or counterfactual version of reality, drawing the reader into a specific mindset or emotional state. It's the author's responsibility to craft this voice carefully, by embedding subtle contradictions, inconsistencies, or tonal shifts, to hint at a deeper truth beneath the surface. Without these cues woven throughout, a sudden twist or revelation at the end can feel unearned or jarring. A well-executed unreliable voice isn't just misleading—it's artfully layered, inviting you to question, interpret, and uncover meaning as you read.

EXERCISE 7

Reread: Pick any passage in any novel. Consider how much or how little information is given about the setting, the mood, the characters, and their situations. How do you feel about the primary character in that scene? How did the author make you feel that way?

Rewrite: Fill gaps in the narrative left by the author by changing the exposure of the scene to shift the focus to a different element, or broadening it to include something not related to the primary character. Can you write that in a similar voice to the original?

Notes

1. Every generation believes its vulgarities are coarser than those of previous generations.

2. Here's an informative article on the characteristics of satire: https://www.dbu.edu/mitchell/history-of-comedy/basicssa.html.

3. For a discussion of the widest-possible aperture, omniscience, see also the discussion of "Distance" in chapter 14, "Point of View."

4. Much like movies.

5. James Paul Gee, *How to Do Discourse Analysis: A Toolkit.*

6. Ursula K. Le Guin, *Steering the Craft: A Twenty-First Century Guide to Sailing the Sea of Story,* (Mariner Books, Boston, 1999).

7. When I surveyed the more than fifty novels we covered in my study group between 2018 and 2023, all published between 2017 and 2022, here's what I found:

   - Average number of POVs per novel: Just under five
   - Novels with one POV: Twenty-one (42 percent)
   - Novels with multiple POVs: Twenty-nine (58 percent)
   - Novels with ten or more POVs: Ten (20 percent)
   - Most POVs in a single novel: Twenty-one

     This is a random sampling, of course, but it includes examples of mass-market, thriller, literary, autofiction, speculative, sci-fi, and romance novels.

8. It's one of the **Seven tools**, after all.

9. Some psychologists have attributed the origin of the concept of god to a child's narrative: a placeholder for elements that defy our comprehension.

10. https://www.how-to-write-a-book-now.com/soft-vs-hard-worldbuilding.html

16

Character Development

We live in the world our questions create.
    —David Cooperrider

Around the same time Aristotle was defining the key elements of drama, Theophrastus identified thirty character *archetypes*[1] commonly found in ancient Greek theater—each representing a specific virtue or flaw. When one of these archetypes appeared near the hero or heroine, it signaled to the audience that the challenge embodied by that character would soon hinder the protagonist's progress, sometimes quite literally standing in their way.

In today's novels, these character types have mostly been replaced by a character's internal struggles, but the issues a character faces remain as real as if they were actually confronting another character. A character's intent—what they are trying to accomplish—and how they deal with the obstacles in their way, are critical to the construction of every novel, because *how* a character deals with their struggles reveals to the reader *who they are*.

Character development *is* character.

Let me say that again: The only way we truly understand who a character is comes from seeing what they want and how they respond to challenges. Their desires and the obstacles they face reveal their nature—and from this tension between intent and adversity, the plot emerges. As screenwriter Aaron Sorkin says, this dynamic is the driveshaft of the story.[2,3]

Not every novel is concerned primarily with character development. But even a plot-driven story benefits from clearly defined motivation, obstacles, and decisions that make its characters feel authentic and relatable.

Ultimately, *all* stories are about people, even the ones about beanstalks, spinning wheels, or the *Titanic*. That's because the way we relate to a story is through its characters. So much relies on characters' reactions to events, because ultimately, they represent *us*. As readers, *their* actions and reactions are playing in *our heads*, and as humans, we will always react most strongly to the humanity of any situation.

Any story that doesn't impact the life of at least one character (or some other anthropomorphic being) isn't one worth telling. Example: A meteorite thuds into Mars. No one sees it. Who cares? But if that meteorite alters Mars's orbit and sends it careening toward Earth? Now everybody cares.

In response to the age-old question, "Which comes first, character or plot?" the answer has to be character. What follows are specific character journeys that have been expanded into recognizable plot structures. For each of them, let's consider:

- Does the character begin with health, prosperity, and happiness, or sickness, poverty, and misery, or somewhere in between?
- What motivates the character?
- What obstacles must the character overcome to meet their goals?
- Have the character's strengths, weaknesses, or motivations changed by the end of the novel?

When forming your opinions about plot templates and the characters you encounter in your reading, pay close attention to those four questions. And while you may find the broad-stroke characterizations that follow overly simplistic, they represent useful jumping-off points[4] for analyzing a novel.

Hero's journey: The hero's character is sterling—they are smart or agile or popular—and their strengths will serve them well throughout their journey. Heroes are often altruistic and influential, but something big is holding them back, and this is the dragon that needs to be slain. After every obstacle in their way has been overcome, in the end their internal goodness has not changed even as their external situation has.[5]

Rags to riches: Orphans, outsiders, Cinderella—this character begins without resources or prospects and therefore must surmount obstacles using their wit and pluck. A sense of justice or fairness motivates them—after all, who could be more deserving of happiness? What this character lacks initially is exactly what they will attain by the end of the novel.

Riches to rags: This character begins on the top of the world but has a fatal flaw that will lead to their downfall. Lack of a moral compass or friends and family to guide them will cause this character to make mistake after mistake. Will they see the error of their ways before the end? Maybe. But by then it will be too late.

Icarus: Enterprising Icarus is clever and resourceful, wearing wings his father, Daedalus, made of wax and feathers that take him to the boundaries of the sky. This starts like a rags-to-riches story, but differs midway through, when Icarus flies too close to the sun and his wings melt, causing him to plummet back to earth. His hubris is his downfall; he realizes that he should have trusted others (like his father, Daedalus, who warned him not to fly so close to the sun).

Man in a hole: This is the most popular story type of all time. Joe or Jenny Sixpack is leading a normal, perhaps even virtuous, life when disaster strikes. They spend the rest of the story discovering what happened and learning how to dig themselves out of this horrible fix. They'll end the story a little better off than they started, as cosmic compensation for the ordeal they've been through.

Comedy: Less a form than a style, comedy occurs when a character yearns for base things. While the hero desires peace for humankind, or the man in the hole yearns for a return to the status quo, the comedic protagonist ardently desires silly things: a BB gun, a hot body—anything frivolous or pointless. Comedies rarely end in tragedy, though. Instead, the character learns something truly important about themselves and about life.

Tragedy: This character's journey can begin humbly (as in rags to riches), or on top of the world (as in riches to rags), but it always leads to their death. Tragedy is epic. The tragic character may be moral, but by the end of the story, their convictions have either been utterly corrupted or they have been overcome by forces on the winning side of history.[6]

Checkpoints

A character's archetype or the protagonist's story arc may initially be hidden from the reader's view. But over the course of a novel, their development will become clear to us when we pay attention to the following five checkpoints:

- **Status quo:** Our first view of a character, anchoring their strengths and aspirations
- **Relationships:** How a character is perceived or affected by their friends, connections, and society at large

- **Inciting incident:** Determines a character's aspirations and indicates the level of drama
- **Obstacles and choices:** How a character's character is revealed
- **Denouement**: The final state of a character, in contrast with their initial condition

Status Quo

First impressions are so important.

How a character is introduced—how they initially appear—is probably the most important factor in how the reader will perceive them throughout the novel. In addition to anchoring[7] them in space and time, an opening scene also gives us a hint about the character's motivation, their status relative to others, and their agency. Consider these introductions of three young girls:

- The first girl is late coming down for breakfast, and her mother has to call her three times before she finally tears herself away from writing in her diary.
- The second girl is at school, hiding in an alcove, afraid her enemy will catch her alone and slug her in the arm.
- The third girl is in the park, hears whimpering in the shadows, and frees the puppy caught in a thornbush.

Order matters

We form impressions about each of these three characters before they open their mouths and before we're allowed access to their thoughts. The first girl is dreamy, preoccupied, oblivious. The second has less agency and a low social status. The third is noble and selfless.

These first impressions may also presage different story arcs for each girl. The first may have big dreams but will need at some point to deal with reality. The second will definitely be attempting to overcome her fears. The third may be on her own heroine's journey.

But what if the three passages describe the same girl in different situations? Now the order they are presented to the reader is critical in influencing how we feel about her: her status, her agency, and her prospects. If she is shown to be heroic before she encounters the bully, we know she will eventually overcome her antagonist. If her first appearance is as a dreamer, that will affect our opinion of her prospects. An author can present scenes in any order, so it's important for the reader to be aware of the effects of these deliberate choices.

Hopes and dreams

Editors, agents, contest judges, and your critique group all obsess over the opening chapter of a novel because when introducing a protagonist to the reader for the very first time, every word matters. It's critical for an author to set the tone, to tell you who the important characters are, and at the very least to hint at what makes them tick. The success of any novel hinges on whether or not these characters are believable, sympathetic, or capable.

The establishment of normalcy must come before any sort of inciting incident. This setup is essential to your understanding of any character, in that it gives you enough context to be able to make sense of the character's reaction to change. This requires some insight into their hopes and dreams—that is, what makes them tick.

EXERCISE 1

Pay attention to POV: Pick up any novel you haven't read, read the first few pages of the first chapter, and pause to reflect. Is it clear who the protagonist is, and if not, why not? Have any antagonists been identified? What do we already know about the main character (or any character)—that is, what have they *done*? How were they presented? Is their status high or low? Do they have some degree of control over their lives, and do they have the agency to effect change if needed?

Assume you're being played: Can you identify each character's needs, desires, and intentions? How is the author guiding your thinking? Predict the character arc of the protagonist—how do you think their story will end? (Hint: It shouldn't be obvious.)

Relationships

However many characters may appear in a story, its real concern is with just one: its hero. It is the one whose fate we identify with, as we see them gradually developing towards that state of self-realization which marks the end of the story. Ultimately it is

> in relation to this central figure that all other characters in a story take on their significance. What each of the other characters represents is really only some aspect of the inner state of the hero himself.
> —*Christopher Booker*, The Seven Basic Plots[8]

A character is defined not only by their own actions but also by the characters surrounding them. Their family and their circle of friends and colleagues reveal who they are, the moral and ethical structure of their world, what behavior is acceptable, and even what is possible. Booker says these characters ultimately exist to represent specific facets of the protagonist. The absence of friends and family is also as telling as their presence, and can serve to highlight inclusion or isolation. Author Rachel Cusk took this concept to the extreme in her Outline trilogy, in which the protagonist is defined *exclusively* by the stories that she hears from the people around her.

Character relationships also give a protagonist the opportunity to develop a deeper emotional connection with those around them, demonstrating empathy and understanding.

Hierarchy

No two characters in a novel are equal.

At any point in any story, the relationship between any two characters represents a disparity of status, power, ability, education, agency, empathy, or any other quality you can use to measure and evaluate position and point of view. The other characters in a novel help to define power structures, pecking orders, and social norms, which determine and limit the options available to the protagonist. Cutting against hierarchical norms can trigger a character's greatest fears, further limiting what they believe they can accomplish.

These inequalities provide convincing obstacles in the path of the main character as they try to realize their goals.

Even when two lovers *seem* to be equals—both white, cisgender, middle class, Christian, college graduates, whatever—they come to their relationship with different abilities, aspirations, and perspectives. Otherwise, there's no conflict, no romance, and no story.

Parallel stories

A popular technique in novels, movies, and sitcoms is to have a B-story (and sometimes a C-story) that echoes and reflects the protagonist's journey (the A-story).

It's important to pay attention to every subplot—**everything serves a purpose**—and consider how they color your perception of the protagonist.

The ways in which these secondary stories are similar or dissimilar to the main narrative amplifies or contrasts aspects present in both. When a B-story goes in the opposite direction of the protagonist's, it serves as a cautionary tale. When they progress in parallel, the B-story amplifies the reader's impression that the protagonist is on the right path.

In Curtis Sittenfeld's 2023 novel *Romantic Comedy,* Sally and Noah's budding romance contrasts with the fraught relationship between Sally and her ex, Danny Horst and his many girlfriends, and with the stable relationship between her fellow writers Viv and Henrietta. In Dolly Alderton's 2024 novel *Good Material,* Andy and Jen's breakup is compared with their best friends' exemplary marriage. In Hernan Diaz's 2022 novel *Trust,* the true nature of the relationship between Mildred and Andrew becomes clear only in the section about Ida Partenza's relentless search for her own identity.

Every subplot exists to draw the reader's attention to the most important issues confronting the protagonist, whether as a positive or negative reflection of the main plot.

Friends and foes

> An **objective** is what a character wants from another character during a particular unit…. The second element is the **action**: what one character does to another character to achieve his or her objective.
> —*Robert Knopf,* Script Analysis for Theatre[9]

What one character does to another.

This concise description of what happens when two actors inhabit a stage struck me. The characters are there to do things to each other—not to react to some unseen force offstage, and not to soliloquize about their fate. Every character near the protagonist is there to be *used* by the protagonist to achieve their objectives. Think about it.

This dynamic may be less obvious in novels than onstage, but it's there. Friends and foes alike exist in service of the protagonist's journey; if they're not, they don't belong in the story. With this in mind, it becomes easier to grasp *why* two characters are friends or enemies. They *do things to each other* in very specific ways.

A note on antagonists: They can develop, too! An antagonist's journey may parallel the protagonist's journey, or it may move in the opposite direction. Don't assume that an antagonist will remain static throughout a novel. One person can be an antagonist early on, while another assumes that role later in the story, or the antagonist can shift from a person to a place or to an animal. As a protagonist evolves, they may need to encounter different antagonists to challenge them in different ways.

EXERCISE 2

Reread: Choose a minor character from a novel you've already read and examine their role in the story. Consider their relationship to the protagonist: What trait or aspect of the main character do they highlight or amplify? Are they acting as a support or a foil? Did their relationship with the protagonist evolve over time—and if so, what did that change reveal about the protagonist's development?

Now expand your view to include the protagonist's family, social circle, or the broader culture they live in. How have those people—and social forces like laws, customs, religion, or traditions—shaped the protagonist's identity or limited their choices?

Return to the minor character you chose. How have those same cultural or social pressures influenced that character?

Rewrite: Does the novel include a B-story or subplot? If it does, consider whether it mirrors or contrasts with the protagonist's main journey. If there isn't a clear B-story, imagine one that could serve as a meaningful counterpoint to the protagonist's arc.

Inciting Incident

A novel's inciting incident[10]—the event that upsets the protagonist's status quo and spurs them into action—is one of two unique moments in a novel (the climax is the other) when all the storytelling strands are knitted together. At those moments, not only are a protagonist's characteristics fully on display—who they are, what they fear, and what they desire—but also present are the level of drama, voice, and tone of the entire novel. The relationship between the inciting incident and the climax can also reveal the primary theme of the novel and the very reasons the author wrote their novel. For more on where to find and evaluate the inciting incident and the climax, see the "Pivot Points" section in chapter 17, "Structure," and for more on using them to uncover themes, see the "What the Novel Is About" and "Why the Novelist Wrote It" sections in chapter 20, "The Gestalt."

The level of drama and the level of a protagonist's aspirations are two of the most important elements in the inciting incident. More than any others, these set up the protagonist's development and story arc. They also say a lot about the protagonist's makeup, their morality, their worldview, and ultimately their fate.[11]

High and low drama

Sometimes the stakes in a story are dramatically high: A family member dies, a factory shuts down, a war breaks out, an asteroid hurtles toward Earth, or the fate of an entire galaxy hangs in the balance. High drama is marked by intense emotional experiences, major plot twists, and events that deeply affect the characters—often leading to a powerful, climactic resolution. These stories often follow classic structures like the hero's journey, an Icarus-like downfall, or epic tragedy.

Low drama, by contrast, centers on protagonists who keep a low profile and try to avoid conflict. While the stakes may feel high to the character, they can seem relatively minor to the reader. Stories about characters with modest ambitions who overreact to small setbacks often lend themselves to comedy, satire, or arcs like rags to riches and riches to rags.

High and low aspirations

When characters have high aspirations, their stories take on a certain gravitas.[12] Peace on earth, saving the town, ending the feud with the Capulets. Low aspirations can include more mundane events: overcoming a bad hair day, a broken Slurpee machine, or dandelions studding the lawn. Low aspirations can indicate that the tone of a story is heading toward satire, social commentary, or straight-up humor.

Quality matters more than quantity.

How high or low a character's aspirations are and the size or amount of what's desired do not necessarily equate to higher drama. Wanting to grow the largest pumpkin in the state is no more significant than growing the largest pumpkin in the community garden. The need for a billion dollars may not be any more aspirational than the quest for a million dollars. They're both amounts written on a check, which is meaningless unless the money can be put to good use. Is it to buy a video game? Or a fancy car?[13] Or does the protagonist want to buy enough malaria vaccines to save a nation? Loftier aspirations can elevate the drama and the tone of a novel.

EXERCISE 3

Pay Attention to POV: Start reading a new novel up to the point where you can identify the inciting incident. If you've already read past the 10 percent mark and haven't identified it, you probably missed it. Go back and look for it now so you can work through this exercise.

Once you've identified the event that threatens to thwart a protagonist's existence, ask whether it represents high or low drama. Closely observe the exact words used to describe how the protagonist responds to the event. Are they active or passive? Upset or amused? Curious or annoyed? Does their reaction reveal their aspirations—and does it show what they want, or what they need? Does the protagonist do something in response, or do they refuse the call to action?

Obstacles and Choices

I worship at the altar of intent and obstacle.
—Aaron Sorkin[14]

Once a character's motivation is established, it's the obstacles the author puts in their way, and how the character chooses to overcome those obstacles, that show you who those characters are. In fact, it is *only* through how the character deals with obstacles that you can understand the character's makeup.

Because novels are about characters' journeys, and characters themselves are nothing more than the embodiment of intent and obstacle, then the most important moments in a character's journey are when their intentions are revealed and when we observe them dealing with the obstacles they face.

A character's intention must be something difficult to achieve. If their goal can be attained without difficulty, they would have a very short journey, one not worthy of a novel. That's why there must be a *series* of challenges, both to deepen a reader's interest and investment in the story, but also because those obstacles make the character who they are, and serve to flesh out the character's character.

We know who Captain Ahab is through his struggles to hunt down and kill Moby Dick. What drives Elizabeth Bennet in Jane Austen's *Pride and Prejudice* is finding a man who "must be in want of"… her. Lady Macbeth comes alive because of her obsession with power and through her dealings with those who stand between her and the throne. Elizabeth Zott in Bonnie Garmus's 2022 novel *Lessons in Chemistry* fights an uphill battle to be taken seriously as a female chemist in a man's world. Violet Sorrengail in Rebecca Yarros's 2023 novel *Fourth Wing* so desperately wants to please her mother that she risks almost certain death in her pursuit of this goal.

Each of these character's obstacles makes them resemble a human being that much more.

EXERCISE 4

Reread: Using any novel you've read, consider the protagonist's intent and obstacles. How has the author revealed the protagonist's intent? Are we privy to their thoughts, or are we forced to make assumptions based on the evidence of their actions?

Find at least three obstacles the author has placed in their way, including the final one before the climax. For every choice the protagonist has made, how has it revealed something about who they are? Do they make good choices or bad ones?

Rewrite: Can you think of any additional obstacles you'd like to throw at the protagonist? What elements of character would they reveal? Why?

Denouement

At last, the protagonist has reached the end of their journey. The grail has been found, the dragon slain, the lovers reunited, and our hero has learned something important about themselves and because of it has become a better person. Or not. You close the book with a sigh.

The protagonist's final state must make sense based on everything that has come to pass. Their fate can be the result of a shocking conclusion, but it must also feel inevitable given who they are. If their fate hasn't grown organically from the sum of the parts of the rest of their journey, then the protagonist's position at the end of the story will not feel satisfying. Such conclusions, while frustrating, can also be most instructive to writers who read.

One of my favorite absurdist moments in fiction is the crucifixion scene in Monty Python's *Life of Brian*. As the doomed enter the site of their death one by one, a friendly maître d' casually asks each one, "Crucifixion, or acquittal?" Those who answer "acquittal" are dismissed. Amazed that salvation could be that easy, they drop their crosses and joyfully scamper off.

This is *not* the way to finish a novel. If the protagonist's story is tragic, then they must die. If they are to be redeemed, then there must be a baptism. The ending shouldn't be the result of an author's whim[15] on the final page. It must have proven to be inevitable because of what has transpired over the previous hundreds of pages.

A rushed denouement or a slapdash ending can be the result of the author writing to meet a deadline. Latter scenes are truncated, actions occur without reflection, or too much happens at once or at a much faster pace than elsewhere in the novel. Where the character ends up feels somehow… off. See chapter 18, "Pacing," for more on this topic.

Flat arcs

Not every protagonist reaches the end of their story a changed character. Think of the leads in serial dramas, or most action heroes, who are who they were and who they ever shall be—they remain mostly static. This flat arc, also called a neutral character arc, is a type of character development in which the protagonist does not fundamentally change internally; rather, they remain consistent in their beliefs, values, or identity throughout the story. However, the world or people around them may change as a result of their influence.

The protagonist in a flat-arc story already knows the truth or holds strong, stable convictions at the beginning, and faces external challenges that test their beliefs but ultimately affirm them. A flat arc is less about personal growth and more about affecting others or society, and conflict often stems from the character versus society, character versus antagonist, or character versus environment.

You often find protagonists with flat arcs when the theme centers on inspiring others, exposing truth, or resisting corruption. Novels that are plot- or theme-driven rather than focused on personal growth, and in genres like mystery, satire, fables, or adventure, have main characters who serve as a moral or thematic anchor. Famous flat-arc characters include Sherlock Holmes, James Bond, Atticus Finch in *To Kill a Mockingbird*, and Katniss Everdeen in *The Hunger Games*.

Every member of every society, when attempting to overcome obstacles standing in the way of their goals, chooses an action from a limited repertoire of options. Characters with recurring roles in serial novels have the most severely limited repertoire of all: They're not allowed to change fundamentally, for the good of the franchise. Remember the **unspoken contract** between author and reader: that the novel will conclude in a fulfilling way. The character's final state—whatever it is—must make sense within the context of the story.

EXERCISE 5

Reread: Think about the ending of a novel you've recently finished. Did it feel satisfying to you? Did the protagonist's journey reach a clear resolution, or was it left open-ended with a more philosophical or ambiguous conclusion? What changed—either for the protagonist or those around them? Was the transformation physical, psychological, or spiritual?

Rewrite: How would you have ended the protagonist's journey differently? Why?

Notes

1. https://www.eudaemonist.com/biblion/characters/

2. https://www.masterclass.com/classes/aaron-sorkin-teaches-screenwriting/chapters/intention-obstacle-11ba8c15-7856-490d-85bb-eb0601e02c55

3. Discussing the character of a character is sometimes challenging because the same word is laden with at least two different meanings: a moral virtue, and a fictional representation. David Brooks, who wrote *The Road to Character*, a book about the moral virtue character type, confused these two meanings when he interviewed screenwriter Aaron Sorkin on the topic of character. Brooks was trying to make parallels between some of Sorkin's fictional characters from *The West Wing* and *The Newsroom* who display moral virtue. Brooks assumed Sorkin had modeled some of these characters on real people, but the screenwriter rejected that notion. Sorkin repeatedly made the point that fictional characters are *not* people. Fictional characters wear clothes and speak and move about as though they are real, but it is important to remember that they are nothing more than the embodiment of intent and obstacle. They have no hidden lives offscreen or off the page, or even beyond the choices they make as they encounter obstacles. From "What's Character Got to Do with It?" Aspen Ideas Festival, July 1, 2015, https://www.youtube.com/watch?v=eucVNYQNGAs.

4. The story types I present here are informed more by character arc than by, say, Christopher Booker's list of *The Seven Basic Plots*, which also includes The Quest, Voyage and Return, and Rebirth. https://en.wikipedia.org/wiki/The_Seven_Basic_Plots

5. What about the heroines? In *The Heroine's Journey*, Gail Carriger argues that most Western storytelling focuses on the hero's journey, an individualistic, conquest-driven arc, but there is an alternative narrative: the heroine's journey, based on community, connection, collaboration, and healing, rather than domination or personal glory.

6. Shakespeare's tragedies differ from his comedies primarily in that the protagonist dies.

7. For more on the anchoring effect and why order matters, see the "Anchoring" section in chapter 12, "Language and Grammar," and the "Order" section in chapter 13, "Context in Scene."

8. Christopher Booker, *The Seven Basic Plots: Why We Tell Stories* (Continuum Books, UK, 2004).

9. Robert Knopf, *Script Analysis for Theatre*.

10. Trying to define and identify the inciting incident of any novel has led to many ~~arguments~~ discussions on our *Writers Who Read* podcast. The contention that an inciting incident can occur before the novel begins is more of a craft concept than an account from the reader's perspective. I define the *inciting incident* to be that event, around five to seven percent of the way into a novel, *after* the setting has been established, that propels the protagonist's actions *and* compels

the reader to keep reading. It's not the hook, which entices the reader to *begin* reading, which could occur as early as the first page. Also see https://writers.com/inciting-incident-definition.

11. The literary device that exposes a character's fatal flaw is called *hamartia*. https://en.wikipedia.org/wiki/Hamartia.

12. Sometimes characters are better than we are. Aristotle, in chapter 2 of his *Poetics*, discusses the range of characters we encounter in drama.

13. See my car-buying story in chapter 13, "Context in Scene."

14. https://www.masterclass.com/classes/aaron-sorkin-teaches-screenwriting/chapters/intention-obstacle-11ba8c15-7856-490d-85bb-eb0601e02c55.

15. Also see *eucatastrophe* in the glossary.

17
Structure

Horizontal structure covers the divisions of an entire novel as they appear sequentially from beginning to end. Understanding the elements of structure is a prerequisite for the three chapters that follow, which are all focused on the novel as a whole. Chapter 18, "Pacing," explores the rhythms of form within the structure. Chapter 19, "Layering," is about uncovering and deciphering multiple narrative and thematic threads, and chapter 20, "The Gestalt," considers the novel's overall impact on the reader.

Novelists tend to fall into two general categories: plotters and pantsers. Plotters map out their novel's structure before writing a word. Pantsers—that is, seat-of-the-pantsers—write organically as the spirit moves them, without regard to plot or structure, at least in their initial drafts. But at some point during revisions, pantsers will uncover the shape of their story, and will, either on their own or with the help of an editor, perfect their plot structure.

Regardless of the way the novel was crafted, it will have a recognizable form.[1] This structural shape is of critical importance to the reader who wants to read like a writer, because the form of a novel influences and constrains the options available to the author. Sometimes what we think were incongruent choices made by the author may in fact have been dictated by the novel's form.

We may assume, as readers, that we can only grasp the structure of a novel once we have read it in its entirety, but here we will cover other ways to examine a novel's structure. Our structural tools, roughly in order of ease of observation, are:

- **Major and minor divisions:** Dividing the novel into its structural components, contents, and word count
- **Pivot points:** Identifying the hook, inciting incident, midpoint, and climax
- **Story arcs:** A survey of some common shapes with their variations
- **Structuring time:** Common timeline manipulations and how to spot them

Major and Minor Divisions

> Look once more at the dictionary. There beyond a doubt lie plays
> more splendid than *Anthony and Cleopatra*, poems lovelier than
> the 'Ode to a Nightingale,' novels beside which *Pride and Preju-*
> *dice* or *David Copperfield* are the crude bunglings of amateurs.
> It is only a question of finding the right words and putting them
> in the right order.
> —*Virginia Woolf*

To visualize how novels are organized, let's compare them to the structure of the US Postal Service's ZIP code system. ZIP codes are grouped into 10 zones, 0–9, from east to west. The prefix 8- represents the mountain states, and all of the prefix 80- ZIP codes are within Colorado. Of the 803- ZIP codes, Boulder, Colorado, has five: 80301 through 80305, within which are thousands of ZIP+4 codes, representing portions of neighborhoods, each corresponding to anywhere from ten to twenty street addresses.[2]

You can think of this structure as similar to the way that novels are organized by their authors: Words are grouped into sentences, which are grouped into paragraphs, which are grouped into scenes, sections, chapters, parts, acts, and so on.[3]

Every word in every novel is placed within one of these nested levels or divisions.[4] What we call these nested parts doesn't matter, as long as we recognize the organizational structure itself and understand its importance to the construction of the novel.

Table of contents

Our first structural tool is also the easiest to use. Let's turn now to the table of contents (TOC) and have a look around. Sometimes omitted in the printed version, the TOC is always present in the e-book version.[5] These divisions are of critical importance for electronic indexing and enabling readers to find their place.[6]

Take a look at the TOC's structure. Is the novel divided into *parts* that are subdivided into *chapters*? Or is it more of a flat structure with only chapters? How many chapters are there? About a dozen, or closer to fifty or sixty? The shorter the chapter, the more concise the text within it, which can indicate a more plot-driven narrative, like a thriller. The fewer the chapters a novel has, the more text is found in each chapter, which can indicate a more reflective and emotion-driven narrative.

Let's also look at the relative lengths of chapters and parts.

If a print book TOC includes page numbers, see if the number of pages between the chapters is consistent or varied. If the TOC does not have page numbers, you can also locate the sections manually and note their lengths. In an e-book, observe the percentage of the whole novel each chapter occupies.

Once you've assessed the relative chapter or section sizes, you can make a simple inference: Evenly sized chapters can indicate that the novelist is a plotter, while chapters with inconsistent lengths can indicate a more intuitive construction, as you might find in the work of a pantser author. For a further discussion of the positioning of long and short sections, see chapter 18, "Pacing."

The TOC can also reveal shifts in point of view and the timeline. How are sections and chapters named? If their titles are the names of characters, you are looking at alternating points of view. If marked with dates, that indicates the author has manipulated the novel's timeline, which is covered in more detail in the "Time Structures" section below.

Word count

Amazon's bookselling website is a good resource for top-level statistics pertaining to any novel in publication today. Once upon a time, the website included word counts, but they stopped listing that statistic in about 2010. Today they show the number of pages, which can be misleading, as page count depends on the font, line spacing, lines per page, and cut size. Because we writers are more concerned with word count than page count, we'll cover two methods to approximate a novel's word count.

If you have the print book in front of you, survey a few pages at random to get a sense of how many lines are on each page and how many words are on each line. Multiply these to get the average number of words per page (in printed books, this number is typically between 250 and 300). You can then multiply the number of words per page by the number of pages in the book to get a rough word count.

This also works for e-books, but the math is a little trickier[7] if the e-book application displays only a percentage and no page numbers. Flip through a few pages to see how each page increments the percentage viewed. For example, if it takes five pages to advance one percent, the e-book has about 500 pages total. You can also adjust your e-reader font size to get more or fewer words on the page and find percentage increments that make your math easier. Then you can estimate total word counts the same way you would with a print book.

Another method I like uses audiobook length. Given the sharp rise in popularity of audiobooks in the last decade, these days virtually every major publication has an Audible version. Amazon lists the total time it takes to listen to each title. The novels I've surveyed so far average about 8,900 words per audiobook hour. Slower narrators read approximately 7,800 to 8,000 words per hour, and the faster ones read about 9,000s of words per hour, with the fastest one reading just over

10,000 words per hour. Again, use your calculator to estimate the total word count based on the total number of the audiobook's hours.

EXERCISE 1

Reread: In any novel you're currently reading, examine the section and chapter structure. Estimate the relative sizes of each part, and with this information try to guess whether the author is a plotter or pantser. Search online for video or print interviews in which authors talk about their writing methodologies to see if you were right. Do other clues in the text indicate how the author created their structure?

Then estimate the novel's word count, either by using the average-words-per-page method or by looking up the audiobook length and multiplying the time by 8,900 words per hour. Was the word count greater or less than you expected?

Pivot Points

One of the **Three keys** states that all stories—ancient and modern—contain these three common pivot points: **inciting-midpoint-climax.**

1. **Inciting:** A reason for an audience to pay attention, usually a conflict to be explored, also known as the hook
2. **Midpoint:** An event at the midpoint that changes the course of the story
3. **Climax:** The resolution, or at least the final results or summation of that conflict

In other words, a reason to read, an interesting twist, and a reward for your efforts. We can also think of the novel's narrative structure as a tent: Every novel has at least these three tentpoles, but most have more. For example, the hook and the inciting incident may be different events, and, in addition to the midpoint, many authors further subdivide their novel's structure into thirds or quarters.

These tentpoles together elevate the emotional fabric of the plot:

- **Hook:** The element of interest that compels us to keep reading
- **Inciting:** The protagonist's call to action, an incident that usually occurs within the first five to seven percent
- **Climax:** The plot's resolution, occurring within five percent of the end

- **Midpoint:** Integral to modern storytelling, the midpoint is the fulcrum of the protagonist's teeter-totter journey, in which something shifts at the midpoint that makes us reevaluate what we thought we knew
- **Secondary divisions:** The division of a novel into three or four acts, or into an alternate organizational framework

Hook

This is by far the easiest element to spot. It's what piques your interest or increases your heart rate: a murder, a famous historical moment, or an impending catastrophe. It could be a quiet event, depending on a novel's tone: an email, an unexpected visitor, the first day of school, a new bodega opening on the corner. Whatever it is, it's interesting enough to keep readers turning the page and give them a reason to read the entire novel. Without a hook, a story would seem as irrelevant to us as an asteroid landing on Mars. *Thud.*

Sometimes you can discover a novel's hook before you even start reading. It might be mentioned on the book jacket or the inside cover, and it's almost certainly in every book review or online discussion. The reason to read a novel is never a spoiler, and so it's safe for marketing departments to use its hook to drive sales.

Where within the novel can you expect to find its hook? It had better show up early in the story, because most readers will give a novel only ten to twenty pages to determine whether it interests them enough to keep reading. So if you haven't discovered the hook after reading five to seven percent of the book, you've either missed it or it isn't there. Either way, the author failed to reel you in.[8]

Many modern novels begin *in medias res*, in the middle of the action: the moment a bomb is discovered, a car crash kills a family, a king dies, a volcano erupts. The reason is obvious: If you want to sell books, there's no better place to set the hook than on the very first page. Starting *in medias res* comes with a cost and a set of expectations, though. Learn more about them in the "Time Structures" section below.

The hook may involve the protagonist, or it may not, which we'll cover in the next section, "Inciting incident." You'll know when you've been hooked, though: You keep reading.

Inciting incident

Contemporary novels have abandoned the long prologues of Herman Melville, Thomas Hardy, and James Michener, which certainly set the scene but also delayed the onset of action. Today the inciting incident occurs within the first five to seven percent of every novel. If the scene needs to be fleshed out, the milieu fully explored, or the characters' backstories revealed, that comes later in the text. As a result, a reader may be slightly confused and have unanswered questions when the inciting incident occurs, but like any industrious listicle creator knows, it's better to hook your reader first and save the details for later. It works wonders for click-through (getting readers to click the link to access the story), and quite well for the modern novel.

There are, however, two prerequisites for an inciting incident:

1. An inciting incident follows the establishment of the milieu, the world, or normalcy. Although lengthy prologues are dead, an author must, at a bare minimum, let the reader know what *normal* looks like for the protagonist, before presenting the *abnormal* incident that incites that character to begin their journey. Similarly, you can't understand what a temperature reading means until you understand the range—0 to 100, or 32 to 212—and how normal this temperature is for this location during this season.

2. While the hook may or may not involve the protagonist, the inciting incident *must* involve the protagonist. Can the inciting incident also be the hook? Yes, but not always. The answer is no if the hook is in the opening paragraph, because the hook is an anomaly of a normalcy that has not yet been established. For example, Stephen King's 2023 novel *Holly* begins with a kidnapping—the hook. Holly, the protagonist of the title, doesn't make an appearance until the next chapter, however, and more pages still are needed to establish what her normal is before she makes that phone call—her inciting incident—at the end of that chapter.

Sometimes, especially in more literary fiction, a reader may find it difficult to identify the inciting incident as multiple candidates emerge. How not-normal is the protagonist acting, and what might have made them act this way? Was it the email, or the unexpected visitor, the first day of school, or that new bodega on the corner? And why? Each action reveals different motives. In that case, the author *wants* the reader to ask these questions, because a multitude of possibilities deepens and enriches their narrative.

Climax

Once you've read around 93 to 97 percent of a novel, you'll find its climax. It's the culmination of everything in the novel that has come before, so there's no need to tell you how to find it. You'll know. Sometimes, depending on the genre, the climax may be at the 99-percent mark—the last page—especially if the author feels no need for any further reflection or information about how the protagonist's life was transformed by the experience—that metaphorical cigarette following sex.

The climax is the result of the inciting incident.

This is important: The climax and the inciting incident are bound together more tightly than two sides of the same coin. Whatever the inciting incident disturbed finds its resolution at the climax. Each pairing of question-answer,[9] conflict-resolution, or quest-grail is a product of the **unspoken contract** with another of the **Three keys** of fiction: **inciting-midpoint-climax**. The climax is the result of the inciting incident.

Sometimes, in a literary novel, I can't identify the inciting incident until I've reached the climax—especially if the author presents it subtly or offers several possible turning points. But once I understand what is resolved in the climax, I can look back and recognize what was disrupted by the inciting incident. And in doing so, I uncover something even more important than either: the novel's central theme—the deeper reason the author wrote it. For more on that, see the "What the Novel Is About" section in chapter 20, "The Gestalt."

Consider Lauren Groff's 2021 novel, *Matrix*. Without giving away the plot, I'll describe the inciting incident as "woman in a box," and the climax as "woman in a box." Although the protagonist, Marie de France, accomplishes much in this novel that tells the story of her life, identifying those two pivotal moments and pondering what they signify for women in general gets us closer to the novel's core theme.[10]

"Who brings the cheese?" is the question that kicks off James McBride's 2020 novel *Deacon King Kong*, while the appearance of the literal hand of Jesus at the book's climactic moment gives us the divine answer that reveals the more serious theme underneath the sometimes slapstick plot.

EXERCISE 2

Reread: Go back to a novel you've read recently enough that you can remember the inciting incident and the climax. Consider the implications of what happened to the protagonist at those two most important tentpoles of the novel. How do they relate to each other? Can you combine them to uncover the novel's primary theme?

Was the inciting incident also the hook? Was it at the end of the first chapter, or later? Was the climax on the last page, or did the author provide a chapter or two of resolution after the climax? Why do you think the author did that?

Rewrite: Think about the inciting incident and the climax in your own novel. Do both feature the central theme of your book? When combined, do they provide a key to understanding why you wrote it?

The magical midpoint

One of the most delightful discoveries I have made during my years of analyzing novels is what happens halfway through. Every contemporary novel I have surveyed—every single one—has something structurally significant occurring at or around the fifty percent mark.[11] As a result, I now pay close attention to what I often call the *magical midpoint* in every novel I read. Even if what happens at the midpoint at first appears to be insignificant, I acknowledge the moment and revisit it later. Once I've finished the novel, I go back and look at what happened to the protagonist there, because I know there will *always* be a payoff later on in the novel that's directly related to the events at the midpoint.

I think of a novel's midpoint like the fulcrum of a teeter-totter. Readers walk up one side of the plank to the middle, and, once there, the balance starts shifting to the other side. Similarly, something always happens at the midpoint of a novel—and it can be subtle—that shifts the trajectory of what we thought we knew. We were walking up and now we're walking down. At least subconsciously and sometimes consciously, we perceive the protagonist's journey differently from the midpoint on. Every time.

Here are some examples.

- The marketing for Joshua Cohen's 2022 Pulitzer Prize–winning novel *The Netanyahus* suggests it's a satire of a well-known Israeli political family—and that's what you expect going in. But at the novel's midpoint, the narrator's daughter, Judy, does something startling that pulls the focus somewhere new. Judy becomes a central character and, in the process, exposes the narrator's unreliability. This moment sets the stage for Judy's pivotal role in the climax. Cohen's storytelling shows us how a midpoint shift can change the reader's entire perspective on the novel.
- Tommy Orange's 2018 novel *There There* is structured as a series of vignettes of a dozen Native Americans on their way to a powwow in Oakland, California, each from their own point of view. But exactly at the midpoint, the narrator steps in to give the reader a detailed account of the many injustices heaped upon them and their ancestors. What had previously seemed like everyday events are given gravitas and significance at the midpoint.

- The midpoint of Tana French's 2018 novel *The Witch Elm* is when a catastrophically passive Toby finally takes matters into his own hands to investigate a mysterious murder himself. It's the catalyst for everything that follows.
- At the midpoint of Stephen King's 2023 novel *Holly,* the hunter becomes the hunted.

There are too many examples to name here—that is, every contemporary novel—but I hope this knowledge inspires you to pay attention to the magical midpoint in your future reading.

Semesters versus trimesters

Some novels follow a clear three-act structure, while others break more naturally into four parts. Keep in mind that these divisions—like the midpoint—aren't always found at exact page numbers; they're approximate, because storytelling isn't a precise science. Still, for a novel to hold together, certain structural milestones must be in place—no one can shape 100,000 words without some kind of framework.

The best place to begin your investigation is your old friend, the table of contents.

For example, Damon Galgut's 2021 Booker Prize–winning novel *The Promise* has only four chapters—each is roughly one-quarter the length of the book. Andrew Sean Greer's 2017 Pulitzer Prize–winning novel *Less* has eight chapters, each roughly one-eighth of the total word count. Oh, and multiples of eight are important to Greer because it takes the titular character Art Less roughly eighty days to go around the world. (Literary reference alert!) Katie Kitamura's 2021 novel *Intimacies* has sixteen chapters—four for each quarter of her novel. Do you sense a common thread among these novels' structures?

And now on to the trimesterists. Ocean Vuong's inaugural novel *On Earth We're Briefly Gorgeous* is structured under Part I, Part II, and Part III, each of which is roughly the same length and focuses on a different aspect of an immigrant's experience. Trimesters take on a double meaning in Lauren Wilkinson's 2019 debut novel *American Spy*: the three acts of a coup and the events leading up to the birth of twins.

Sometimes semesters and trimesters serve as markers for different characters' journeys. In Margaret Atwood's *The Testaments*, a sequel to her earlier novel, *The Handmaid's Tale*, embracing the world of the subsequent TV series spin-off, Agnes's pivotal character developments land at one-third and two-thirds through the novel, while Daisy's major plot reveals come at one-quarter, the halfway point, and three-quarters. Mere coincidence? It looks like masterful authorial design to me.[12]

EXERCISE 3

Reread: Take a novel you've read and turn to the midpoint. Poke around for a significant plot point—don't worry, it's there. Recalling your reaction to the overall story, can you remember how this pivot point landed when you first read it? Did it subtly shift your perspective, or did you pass it by?

Study the table of contents and check if the author has organized their novel in multiples of two or three, or by some other set of divisions. If you are reading it on an e-book, you can go directly to the twenty-five percent, thirty-three percent, fifty percent, sixty-seven percent, and seventy-five percent marks to see if anything interesting occurs at those points.

Rewrite: How have you structured your own novel? What happens at its midpoint?

Story Arcs

This discussion of story arcs is here specifically for those of you who have discovered the one true story form that you use to structure all your writing. Don't get me wrong—I have no issue with you following a template or a formula. Whatever works for you is awesome. Where the problem arises is if you also expect to find those same techniques used in every novel that you read and analyze. It just doesn't work that way, because every author does their own thing.

Remember the **Three keys**, which are the *only* elements that *every* novel shares: **inciting-midpoint-climax**, **unspoken contract**, and **everything serves a purpose**. Beyond those constraints, an author is free to construct their novel in any way they see fit. And they do.

This section requires that you are able to identify the key structural moments—or tentpoles—in the novels you read. If you haven't yet read the previous section, "Pivot Points," take a moment to do that first. Here, we'll go further by exploring additional templates and formulas that authors use, giving you more tools to recognize how their stories are built. You might even find that a novel mirrors the structure you use in your own writing—though, as you'll see, that's possible, but not very likely.

We'll cover six frameworks: Eleven-point archplot, Save the Cat! Writes a Novel, Freytag's pyramid, Story circle, Fichtean curve, and Kishōtenketsu. There are many other formats and forms, of course, but I hope these six will be enough to illustrate my point.

Structure *Examples*		Inciting Incident		Midpoint		Climax
Eleven-point archplot *The Hunger Games,* *Gone Girl,* *Life of Pi,* *Ender's Game*	Act One: Status quo	Call to Adventure, Refusal of the Call	Crossing the Threshold, Act Two: Tests, Allies, and Enemies	Midpoint	Approaching Inmost Cave, Act Three: Final Push	Seizing the Sword, Returning with Elixir
Save the Cat! **Writes a Novel** *The Martian,* *Eleanor Oliphant,* *Big Little Lies,* *The Midnight* *Library*	Opening Image, Theme Stated, Setup	Catalyst	Debate, Break in Two, B-story, Fun and Games	Midpoint	Bad Guys Close In, All Is Lost, Dark Night of the Soul, Break into Three	Finale, Final image
Freytag's pyramid *Romeo and Juliet,* *Jane Eyre*	Exposition	Inciting incident	Rising action	Climax	Falling action	Resolution, Denouement
Story circle *Circe*[13]	You	Need	Go, Search	Find	Take, Return	Change
Fichtean curve *The Da Vinci* *Code,* *The Road*		Crisis 1	Crisis 2, Crisis 3	Crisis 4 (midpoint is a twist)	Crisis 5, Crisis 6	Climax, Falling action
Kishōtenketsu *The Tale of Genji*	Ki	Shō		Ten		Ketsu

Eleven-point archplot

Developed by Robert McKee and others, the archplot form is one of the most popular templates for creating modern popular fiction. It's used by writers of all genres, and examples can easily be found in many teleplays and movie scripts as well as novels. On her website, Ingrid Sundberg[14] describes an eleven-point arch-plot along a 120-minute timeline,[15] but her diagram is equally useful to novelists, given today's overlap between the written and visual forms.

Some authors will omit the setup (status quo) and drop readers straight into the action, revealing backstory later, bit by bit. The protagonist may not articulate a clear plan, or have a *dark night of the soul* moment, and some novels end with ambiguity or even cyclical repetition instead of establishing a clearly different status quo by *returning the elixir*. But if, in your investigations, you encounter a purebred eleven-point archplot in the wild, knowing this form will enable you to make a quantum leap in your analysis.[16]

Save the Cat! Writes a Novel

Jessica Brody adapted Blake Snyder's popular screenwriting method *Save the Cat!* for use in writing novels, distilling it into a Beat Sheet of fifteen plot points. It offers more beats than the eleven-point archplot and also differs in other ways: It's focused on marketability and emotional engagement, prioritizing ironic reversals, whereas archplot is concerned more with narrative unity, building themes, causality, and inevitability.

Freytag's pyramid

The nineteenth-century playwright Gustav Freytag identified seven key elements of storytelling. It's an ancient understanding of storytelling that has fallen woefully out of date. While these elements can all be found in contemporary novels, they don't all carry equal weight, nor will we find them in this order. Of these seven elements, *Inciting incident* comes first, and *Exposition* is no longer a standalone element, but rather, is spread across the entire narrative. What was once Freytag's *Climax* has become our *Midpoint*, and his *Denouement* has become our *Climax* in contemporary fiction. *Falling action* appears last, if at all.

I don't think any contemporary novelist uses this form, but you will still see it mentioned in textbooks. *Caveat lector.*[17]

Story circle

Dan Harmon's story circle is a simplified, circular narrative structure based on Joseph Campbell's Hero's Journey, designed to map out character-driven storytelling in eight steps. It begins with a character in a zone of comfort (You), who wants something (Need) and enters an unfamiliar situation to get it (Go). Along the way, You adapt to that new world (Search), You get what You want (Find), but then pay a price for it (Take). You then return to your familiar world (Return), having changed as a result (Change).

The focus is on transformation through conflict, with the circle emphasizing symmetry: descent, challenge, and return. Harmon used this model to create emotionally resonant stories, especially in episodic television series like *Community* and *Rick and Morty*.

Fichtean curve

The Fichtean curve is a narrative structure focused on escalating conflict and rising tension, often used in thrillers, mysteries, horror, and action/adventure stories. Unlike traditional frameworks with evenly spaced exposition and resolution, the Fichtean curve begins *in medias res*—in the middle of the action—to immediately hook the reader. The plot is driven by a series of crises or obstacles that continuously build stakes and deepen character struggles. These crises lead to a climactic turning point, where the central conflict comes to a head. Finally, there's a brief resolution that ties up essential threads, though not always neatly, allowing the emotional or thematic weight of the climax to linger.

Kishōtenketsu

Three- and four-part structures have defined East Asian long-form fiction for centuries. Western readers are most likely to encounter kishōtenketsu, especially those who enjoy Japanese manga. It consists of four parts:

- **Ki:** Introduction of initial idea
- **Shō:** Development or deepening of that idea
- **Ten:** Unexpected twist or incongruous element
- **Ketsu:** Conclusion that blends the *Ki* and the *Ten* in a pleasing way

You don't need to be a Japanese scholar to recognize within this form the inciting incident (*Shō*), midpoint (*Ten*), and climax (*Ketsu*). Also of interest to writers is the Japanese tripartite form *Jo-ha-kyu*[18] (beginning, break, rapid), which is found in theater, poetry, the tea ceremony, and the martial arts of *kenjutsu* and *kendo*.

EXERCISE 4

Reread: Take a novel you have recently read. Can you, from the inciting incident, midpoint, and climax alone, determine which story arc template, if any, was used? If not, how do you think the author organized their story elements? Do some sections not seem to fit? Why do you think the author made the choices they did? Have they introduced you to something new?

Rewrite: If you were to rewrite this novel according to a format you have learned, what elements would you change, add, or omit? How would this alter the story itself? Do you think it would this make the story better or worse?

Structuring Time

Every play needs to have a beginning, middle, and an end. Jean-Luc Godard said, *Not necessarily in that order*, and that's why French movies are so effing boring.
　　—*David Mamet[19]*

Messing with time and presenting events out of order is integral to today's storytellers—think about *in medias res* or the way backstory is often parceled out across an entire narrative. But if that resulting time travel moves the hook and inciting incident too far from the beginning, ignores the positioning of the midpoint and the climax, then I would agree with Mamet wholeheartedly. Effing boring, indeed. Let's explore this further.

One movie that took Godard's suggestion to an extreme is the 2000 film *Memento*. The sequence of events is presented in the reverse order, because the protagonist has amnesia—his memory is wiped clean every day. Each scene takes us further back in time, until we discover the beginning of the story at the end of the film. This film has a dramatic inciting incident, midpoint, and climax, each of which arrives at the expected position within the narrative. The timeline is messed up, but the story form remains the same.

In medias res

If a novel begins *in medias res*, which is roughly at the midpoint of the novel's timeline, a novelist will follow that with alternating chapters or sections of both past and present. The past chapters work their way up to the *medias*, while the present chapters move forward from the *medias* to the climax.

In Lauren Wilkinson's 2019 novel *American Spy*, the protagonist promises to tell her twin children the story of their father. She meets their father at the midpoint, and the climax is the birth of the twins. Of course there's an engaging spy story to keep us enthralled, but the major pivot points, while positioned traditionally, certainly mess with time.

In his 2017 novel *Less,* Andrew Sean Greer plays with dueling timelines between his protagonist and narrator. The protagonist's story moves at a steady pace, but the narrator's is about ten times as slow, his story stretched out over the course of the novel. While the protagonist has moved forward eighty days, the narrator's story progresses forward one week at most. The pivotal event that takes place at the midpoint, therefore, is out of the time sequence, but at the correct position within the narrative.

Backstory

Describing a person, place, or thing requires words, lots of words. Fully explaining how this person, place, or thing came to be, and how they are in the present requires backstory, sometimes lots of backstory.

You can identify backstory in a novel by paying attention to shifts in time, tone, or narrative style that interrupt the forward momentum of the plot. These moments often provide insight into a character's past—experiences, relationships, or formative events—that influence their present behavior and decisions. Backstory may be revealed through a character's memories, internal monologue, conversations, or even a narrator's exposition. Look for phrases that signal a step into the past, such as "She remembered when…" or "Years ago…," as well as entire chapters or scenes that pause the action to fill in emotional or historical context.

Multiple timelines

A novelist might use dual timelines to create suspense and reveal key information gradually, allowing readers to connect past events with present consequences. This structure also deepens character development by showing how earlier experiences shaped their current beliefs, choices, and conflicts. Additionally, dual timelines can offer contrasting perspectives or thematic parallels, layering additional meaning over the narrative.

An amazing example of parallel timelines is found in Lisa Halliday's 2018 novel *Asymmetry*. She takes advantage of rounded binary form[20] to provide alternate versions of her story. To say any more here would be to give away a cunningly clever narrative structure. I urge you to wander down that rabbit hole yourself.

An example of a triple timeline is the sequence of nested narratives[21] found in Emily St. John Mandel's 2022 novel *Sea of Tranquility*. The story begins in 1912 at roughly the same timeframe as the penultimate section begins. Moving inward are pairs of sections taking place in 2020, then in 2203, which enclose the central section, which takes place in the year 2401. But does she displace her inciting incident, midpoint reveal, and climax amidst these temporal leaps? No way.

EXERCISE 5

Reread: Pick up any novel, even one you haven't yet read, and try to decipher how the timeline has been sliced. If the chapters are not explicitly marked with a date, poke around the first few chapters to see how long it takes before the inevitable backstory begins.

Rewrite: Would this novel benefit from an introduction or foreword? Why (or why not)? How would you have included backstory in a different way?

Notes

1. Unless it's experimental fiction, as defined in the glossary, Appendix A.

2. The UK postal codes, which contain 6–7 alphanumeric characters, offer many more possible combinations (36^7 or about 78 billion) than ZIP+4 (10^9 or 1 billion) but they still correspond to about fifteen houses each. If you want to use your postal code *instead* of your mailing address, you'll need to live in Ireland, where each Eircode (Irish postal code) represents one street address.

3. When I started the *Writers Who Read* book critique group, I assumed that diagramming novels would require only two major divisions: *parts* and *chapters* (e.g., part one, chapter one). But then along came Jennifer Egan's *Candy House* with its three major divisions: *parts*, *chapters*, and *enumerated sections*, which forced me to rewrite my algorithm. Now I just refer to them in my code as Levels: Level 0 (topmost), Level 1 (next level down), Level 2, etc.

4. A section sometimes refers to a group of chapters, and other times to a passage within a single chapter. Ugh. Ambiguity. Because the word *section* has multiple meanings, I'll stick to referring to the hierarchical tiers of a novel as levels, and the regional areas as divisions.

5. Even if you are reading the physical book, any e-book viewer that has a "look inside" function should let you view the TOC, so you can use it as a reference without needing to purchase the e-book.

6. As of 2025, both TOC and chapter indexing are missing from most Audible audio books; these would be a most welcome addition. As writers, though, I hope we still read the words on the page. This visual information can aid us greatly, especially for the two-thirds of us who are visual learners.

7. E-books register position using a percentage of the whole, which includes front matter and back matter, so they are less precise.

8. Unless it's a novel you absolutely have to read, I advise you to drop this kind of novel like a rock and pick up another. Life is short, and there are plenty of great novels out there.

9. In question-driven plotting, the same question posed to the protagonist at the inciting incident is answered differently by the protagonist at the climax.

10. This novel may seem to have a flat arc, but it's actually a heroine's journey. See the glossary for definitions.

11. This is either the biggest coincidence in the history of literature, or, more likely, the work of editors and publishers. I would guess it's the latter.

12. I know an author who modified a plot beat sheet into a spreadsheet that they use to calculate the page number where a plot point will occur. They use it to evaluate their story's structure, especially if the pacing feels off, or if they're having trouble identifying a major plot point.

13. The novel by Madeline Miller, written in 2018

14. https://ingridsnotes.wordpress.com/2013/06/05/what-is-arch-plot-and-classic-design/

15. https://ingridsnotes.files.wordpress.com/2013/05/final-revision_traditional-mountain-structure-handout_8-5x14.jpg

16. Note that Eleven-point archplot, Save the Cat!, and Story circle are similar to Joseph Campbell's Hero's Journey, and some of their structures overlap. But while the Hero's Journey is more archetypal and symbolic, archplot, cat, and circle are more goal-driven and plot-focused. The latter three structures describe a transformational journey rooted in cause and effect, with emotional and narrative stakes escalating toward a meaningful resolution.

17. Translation: Let the reader beware.

18. Unlike kishōtenketsu, I haven't included johakyū in the glossary. You can learn more about it at https://en.wikipedia.org/wiki/Jo-ha-ky%C5%AB.

19. https://www.masterclass.com/classes/david-mamet-teaches-dramatic-writing.

20. Mostly used in reference to classical music. See https://en.wikipedia.org/wiki/Binary_form.

21. Director Christoper Nolan took nested timelines to their storyboarded extreme in his 2010 movie, *Inception*. It's worth a viewing.

18
Pacing

The speed of a novel—its pacing—is experienced through the frequency of its *beats*. Narrative beats can include plot points, cliffhangers, emotionally charged reveals, the alternation of action and reflection, or even the flow of sentences within paragraphs. Beats can be small, large, or any size in between; beats can be felt within a sentence, a paragraph, a scene, a chapter, or throughout an entire novel.

Beats can be near one another or spaced far apart. Their varied spacing gives the reader the sensation of speeding up, slowing down, or remaining steady. As Einstein pointed out, all speed is relative to the position of the observer, so when evaluating the pacing of a section, we must also notice what has preceded and what follows. This is especially true in a stage play.

> What we are looking for, overall, is the flow or pulse of the play. For a play with a late point of attack, the pulse is likely to be very driven, with a marked acceleration over the course of the play. With an early attack, the pulse might be more start and stop, as the action moves forward within one scene, only to restart during the next one.
>
> The number of scenes in a play can also reveal the tendencies of the dramatic structure. In plays with very few scenes, the action is more likely to be climactic; in plays with a lot of scenes, the action tends to be episodic.
> —*Robert Knopf, Script Analysis for Theatre*[1]

The study of pacing is the observation of *rhythm*.

Rhythms are all around us: from the annual cycle of seasons, to phases of the moon, to tidal ebbs and flows, down to the beating of our own hearts and every breath we take. Music, for example, comprises layers of rhythms, which, when we listen to it, affects our own internal rhythms. That syncing of rhythms is one reason music can affect us so powerfully.

Rhythm infuses all art forms: from seemingly static visual presentations like oil paintings and architecture, to film editing, conversation, and the written word. Rhythm is what makes art real, what makes it human. In the same way our eyes seek out the human form in clouds and trees and other inanimate objects, we react to expansion and compression, speeding and slowing, all of which mirror our experience of the world.

We intuitively understand a wide repertoire of visual gestures. We signal anticipation by holding our breath, we exhibit panic by speeding up, or we slow down for a moment of introspection. I appreciate the way a dance company's choreography can show thoughts, ideals, a visual sigh, or expressions of joy, or fear, or lust.

These rhythms and gestures are present at all levels of good writing, from the superstructure of chapters and sections down to the construction of a single sentence. And as the micro mimics the macro, so should the overall pacing reflect the rhythms of its components.

Rubber bands

A few years into learning to play the piano, I was introduced to the concept of *rubato*. This is a compression and expansion of the beat, which in classical music is not precisely metronomic. A brief pause after the downbeat followed by a slight rush to get to the next downbeat, *rubato* works something like a rubber band. When one beat is stretched, the others need to be compressed so that the sum total of all the beats remains *in tempo*, that is, in proportion to each other throughout the entire piece. It's this illusion of metronomic beats that allows *rubato* to express any number of human gestures and emotions.

The same principle is at work within a novel.

Dwight Swain described this breathing rhythm across chapters as *scene* and *sequel*. The action and propulsive power expressed in an action *scene* must be offset with a reflective and proportionally slow section following it as its *sequel*. It's like a rubber band that's stretched and then allowed to snap back. Part of the art of storytelling is knowing just how far you can stretch the beats before the rubber band breaks. Readers sense this intuitively.

As Robert Knopf described above, a delayed attack or downbeat of the action requires an acceleration in response. Rhythm can also be expressed in the start and stop between sections or scenes, creating a compelling pulse that will keep viewers and readers interested and engaged. When we apply Knopf's lesson to our novel reading, we observe that novels with very few chapters tend to be climactic, while novels with many chapters tend to be episodic, each pausing with a cliffhanger or other enticement to propel the reader forward into the next.

Rhythms large and small

The very largest and very smallest rhythms within a novel are the easiest to observe. That is, we can scan the table of contents to see whether the number of sections and chapters is few or many. This tells us whether we will be asked to concentrate for long periods or for fifteen-minute intervals, and this influences how we read.

We find the smallest rhythms within individual sentences or paragraphs. Bits of dialogue have their own pacing, down to the cadence of a character's unique speech patterns. Then there are the ratios of short to long sentences, of narrative to dialogue, and the ebb and flow of different elements of storytelling.

In this chapter we will break down our observations of rhythm and pacing into different-sized chunks, from the largest to the smallest:

- **Plot:** The pacing of key events that form a novel's structure and the divisions between sections
- **Chapters:** The spacing of emotional and thematic beats among the major sections
- **Scenes:** Entering and exiting specific locations and the compression and expansion of time within each one
- **Paragraphs and sentences:** The rhythms created within sentences by word choices and the characters' speech patterns

Plot

The orbit of a planet, the cycles of the moon, the tides. How much time does the entire novel cover? A year? A semester? A week? And how is that time divided within its span? Before you start your reading, search the table of contents for anything marking the passage of time. Sometimes the jacket blurb will indicate the total span of a novel: "the McClintock family's dark history" or "summer romance." "Jason must defuse the bomb by 5 o'clock."

Remember that a novel can only hold a finite amount of information. The number of pages within a novel also limits how much information can be conveyed and how much action can transpire, which also sets a limit on *what* any part contains. A 100-page novella isn't large enough to contain a multigenerational family saga, for example. A 500-page novel could contain a single scene, I suppose, but its pacing would be so slow as to render the reader catatonic. Size *does* matter.

Your perception of the pacing of an entire novel falls along two axes: how the novel is split into parts, chapters, and sections, and where the major tentpoles of plot fall: hook, inciting incident, middle, climax.

If you aren't reading this reference sequentially—and I encourage you to hop around—chapter 17, "Structure," has tools to help you recognize any novel's structure. The three most useful sections for pacing are: "Major and Minor Divisions," the most significant beats and their positions in the novel; "Story Arcs," standard dramatic shapes that can also be used to identify primary beats; and "Time Structures," accordion-shaped and circular narratives that bend time to withhold information and manipulate suspense.

While you're dividing the novel by pivot points, or by major or minor divisions, take the time to observe the number of pages per section and per chapter. Are any noticeably longer, or are all evenly spaced? Take note of jumps, lurches, or reverses you find within the novel's timeline. And from your knowledge of novel structure, you should know that from the first word of a novel to its last, time will be stretched, compressed, rolled back on itself, and sliced up.

Withholding information

> I really subscribe to that old adage that you should never let the audience get ahead of you for a second.
> —*Paul Thomas Anderson*

A novel is, at its core, a vehicle for delivering information—whether about characters, settings, relationships, or ideas—and its structure acts as the scaffolding that supports how that information is organized and revealed. The pacing, or beats, of a novel can be understood as the rhythm with which significant pieces of information are released to the reader, guiding our emotional and intellectual engagement with the story. Skilled writers distribute information in carefully measured doses—like the slow, steady drip of an IV—so that curiosity is sustained, tension builds, and readers remain actively involved.

Crucially, not all important information is presented openly. Novelists often mask key details or hint at them obliquely, knowing that what *isn't* said can be just as powerful as what is. By keeping in mind tools like **you're being played** and **what happens is not what's discussed**, you can become more aware of how authors manipulate attention and understanding. Paying close attention to when information is withheld or revealed allows you to recognize the rhythm of the narrative—both within scenes and across entire chapters—and helps you better understand how a story maintains momentum and emotional impact.

Ticking clock

Sometimes a plot's time constraint serves as a tool to shape the pacing and rhythm of a novel. This is often called the "ticking clock,"[2] a narrative device where a deadline or upcoming event drives the urgency of the story. The pacing will accelerate or slow in relation to how close the story is to that moment. In thrillers, for example, this might take the form of a bomb set to explode, a kidnapper's ultimatum, or a critical event scheduled to happen at a specific time.

Sometimes the ticking clock is given away by chapter headings, especially if they include a day, a date, or a clock reading. I've also seen: *Seven days ago*, or *Thursday, 4 p.m.* These cues make the beats easier to identify, especially as the tension increases with proximity to the zero hour.

Note that there's no guarantee that time will move in a single direction or at a steady pace. Take note of where of each tick occurs and check if it is moving steadily forward or whether time jumps forward and backward, or whether there are more pages between certain ticks of the clock. You're observing the author's pacing.

For example, the first half of Curtis Sittenfeld's 2023 novel *Romantic Comedy* spans only one week in the life of a group making a TV sketch comedy show that resembles *Saturday Night Live*. It's hectic, the clock is ticking down to Saturday's live broadcast, and each scene is headed with the day of the week and time of day. In the book's second half, scenes occur over the months and years it takes the two lovers to rediscover each other, dramatically slowing the novel's pacing.

Often the clock is determined by the villain. Stephen King's 2023 novel *Holly* has the antagonists themselves running out of time (that is, nearing the ends of their lives), which is why they turn to crime.

Chapters per beat

Another axis of rhythm we need to consider is the difference between the speed of the beats and the size of the beats. Actions, disclosures, or shifts in relationships may be as subtle as the soft *plink* of a piano, and those beats may happen frequently. That's the *tempo*. Character deaths, battlefield victories, and slayings of dragons will resonate more like a big bass drum, with those booming beats dividing the smaller beats into groups. Pay attention to both the tempo and the *impact* of the beats.

In music, these major and minor beat groupings are called *measures*. Almost all popular music has four beats per measure, yet only one of the four beats is primary. Similarly, novels have major and minor beats that together constitute a novel's *rhythm*.

A novel can't be propelled by big beats alone; there would be too much space between them to hold the reader's interest. Always feel for the subtler aftershocks and the continual heartbeats that move the story forward.

As a starting point, I usually assume there's one big beat per chapter (see the next section, "Chapters"). Even if the chapter is long, I'm still expecting only one major beat, with a number of smaller revelations filling out the rest of the chapter's measures.

EXERCISE 1

Reread: Using a novel you've already read, take a look at the table of contents and map onto that the major plot points of the story. Are they evenly spaced throughout, or are they closely grouped in a recognizable pattern? Do they begin widely spaced and then become closer together, indicating an acceleration? Or the opposite?

Dig in at a wide space between plot beats and skim the text, looking for secondary beats. Can you find any? Or is there an expanse of quietude?

Is there a section where the plot points seem to be bunched up? If so, determine whether all of the beats are equally significant. If not, do the primary and secondary beats comprise a steady rhythm? Take note of the number of pages between the beats, and scan other random sections of the novel. Does the overall tempo remain constant?

Rewrite: How have you organized the beats within a chapter, or the plot points across your entire novel? Is the rhythm steady, slowing down, or accelerating?

Chapters

The purpose of breaking a novel into chapters is to divide the narrative into manageable chunks, giving readers a set of milestones that subconsciously encourage them to continue reading. A new chapter break can also be used to introduce new characters, or locate the narrative in a new place in time and space, which directs the reader to focus on different topics, themes, and plot threads.

A chapter can also exist to help control the pacing of the story, creating beats and building momentum toward the chapter's conclusion. For example, each of the four chapters in Damon Galgud's novel *The Promise* ends with a death. Boom.

No chapter's conclusion, except the final one, answers every question or wraps up every plot thread. On the contrary, although a chapter may be structured like a short story—**inciting-midpoint-climax**—the job of each chapter is to move the characters forward, advance the plot, and ask at least as many new questions as it answers.

Most chapters leave something left unsaid, undone, unresolved. And because every author would like their readers to complete their novels, many chapters end in an enticing way or pose a new question—in the form of a cliffhanger or a hook—encouraging them to read on.

Emotional beats

The term *cliffhanger* dates from the days of the weekly movie serial, a short film that would precede the main feature, and is named after an episode that ends with a character literally dangling from a cliff by their fingernails. The cliffhanger was created to get butts in seats the following week to find out what happened next.

In some genres, especially thrillers, spy novels, and mysteries, authors will leave their protagonist in some sort of quandary at the end of the chapter. Or they will be surprised by an interesting event, or twist, or an unexpected piece of information. A cliffhanger is unfinished business that compels the reader to continue.

Hooks are slightly different, but they will excite readers in the same way. A hook is more subtle, as when an omniscient narrator finishes with, "If Joey only knew what waited for him at lunch," or ". . . and it wouldn't be the last time." In other words, some hint about what the future will bring hooks you into believing that things are about to get a lot more interesting.

Multiple beats

When an author wants the reader to experience two or more big beats in a single chapter, often they will subdivide it into easily recognizable chunks. The most common chapter divider is that comically named typographical symbol, the dinkus.[3]

The dinkus usually looks like three spaced asterisks centered on the page, but it can take a different form—a fleuron, a dingbat, an asterisk, a horizontal line, a number of blank lines, or even a page break. Sometimes a new section is indicated, without fanfare, with a non-indented first line. The first letter, word, or clause may receive special treatment: small capital letters or boldface type, or an initial drop cap.

Whichever method is used, the meaning of the dinkus is clear: Here you will find a new chapter division, and with that, here you will find a new beat.

Just as there is no rule governing the presence or absence of section headings, nor the appropriate number of chapters within each section, there is nothing to prevent an author from subdividing their chapters into as many manageable parts as they desire. Every unusual mark, break, or symbol only makes it that much easier for you to recognize something out of the ordinary. Every dinkus-divided subsection produces a new beat you can use to compare with the other beats within the chapter. And don't forget that even the small and in-between beats in a chapter contribute to a chapter's rhythm just as they do in music.

EXERCISE 2

Reread: Read any chapter in any novel. Test the idea that there is a single big plot beat in that chapter. If you find more than one significant event or emotional peak, ask whether one is larger. If the chapter is divided into subsections, consider the relative importance or emotional power of each of the beats.

Rewrite: Having completed this investigation, do you agree with the author that this chapter stands alone as a chapter, or should it be divided up or combined with another chapter?

Scenes

The scene is the primary building block essential to every dramatic form. All novels contain scenes, and therefore it's important for you to be able to dig into any scene to find its beats. While major events occur at major pivot points or at the chapter level, within the scene you should be able find more subtle elements that still contribute to a novel's pacing. You're looking for the snap of the rubber band and the effects of *rubato*.

When approaching a scene for the first time, always ask what this scene is doing and why it exists. Remember from the **Three keys** of every novel that **everything serves a purpose**—that no scene is superfluous, or is just filling space. Every scene has a reason it wasn't cut during the editing process: It must pull its weight in the whole story.

Reflection

Not every scene describes physical action, but every scene has a physicality—a location in time and space. Scenes in novels are not like essays or newspaper opinion pieces, floating inside someone's head while a philosophical point is made. Proust was eating a madeleine, Captain Ahab was preparing for his voyage, and countless other characters have done mundane things like gardening, sitting in a cafe, or riding a train as their minds wander and they consider their situations.

Such reflection scenes, called sequels, will move at a slower pace than their action-packed counterparts. One thought may lead to another and another in a dreamy daisy-chain, and there may be no heavy beats.

Another special kind of reflection scene at first appears to do nothing to advance the plot or the relationship between characters: Donald Maas calls these *postcards*.[4] While postcard scenes do not move the plot forward, they do deepen the relationship between a protagonist and their environment, or deepen the reader's appreciation of that environment—they enhance a reader's pleasure. Again, a postcard may contain no discernible beats. It's an expansion of a song out of time, like a drum solo or a cadenza.

Entrances and exits

The internal pacing of a scene is marked by characters' entrances and exits, as though they were walking onstage or offstage in a play. In the French Neoclassical period, plays depended on these entrances and exits for structure, an organizational technique also known as *French scene*.[5] Each entrance or exit represented a beat or a distinct unit of action. Every character's presence caused a change to the dialogue, or the subject discussed, along with a signal change in what the characters wanted and what they intended to do to get it.

The way characters enter and exit in a novel can be just as telling as in a stage play. These movements aren't just logistical—they reflect shifts in relationships, tension, and narrative momentum. Each arrival or departure marks a structural beat, and the time between these moments helps establish a scene's pacing.

Time compression

An author's choice of where to begin or end a scene greatly affects how the scene flows, just as film editing shapes the pace of a movie scene. Should the scene start in the parking lot, at the restaurant entrance, when the characters sit down, or in the middle of their conversation? Each choice signals a different narrative focus—parking might allow for introspection, arriving could introduce a new character, scanning a restaurant may reveal relationship dynamics, while jumping into the middle of a conversation shifts our attention from the relationship to the topic being talked about.

Because a picture is worth a thousand words—and a novelist doesn't always want to spend that many—scenes in novels function differently than scenes in movies. In film, a single glance or gesture can convey complex meaning, while a novel must use carefully chosen details to paint the same picture. This means novelists can't introduce as many characters or move through scenes as quickly as filmmakers; they need to set the stage with enough detail for readers to visualize it, which naturally limits how brief a scene can be.

You should also pay attention to what the author chooses to leave out, how time is compressed, and where the narrative slows down. These choices act on a scene the way *rubato* pulls at the tempo in music—flexible timing balances brevity with clarity, ensuring the reader stays engaged while still understanding the scene.

Acceleration

Scenes don't unfold at a constant pace. Time is often stretched or compressed, with the narrative skipping over unimportant moments and expanding on small details to keep the narrative engaging and clear. These shifts in pacing can form patterns: Beats may get closer together to create a sense of urgency, rising tension, or emotional intensity.

Quick exchanges of dialogue and rapid successions of events can make a scene feel faster. But simply describing fast actions, like a character running away, won't speed up the narrative on its own; the rhythm and density of the beats generate the scene's tempo and momentum.

EXERCISE 3

Reread: Isolate a scene in any novel, taking note of where how it begins and how it ends. How many pages is it? How many characters are in the scene? Do these characters remain present throughout the scene, or are there entrance and exit beats? What's the ratio of dialogue to narration, and does this contribute to the pacing? What's the primary beat in the scene, or is there more than one? Does the scene accelerate, slow down, or remain at a constant tempo?

Rewrite: How would you accelerate the scene? Slow it down? Move the focus to something or someone different?

Paragraphs and Sentences

There's a good reason to read your writing out loud: It helps reveal the natural rhythms of speech, especially if you're reading dialogue. Whether or not you have musical ability, you can instinctively recognize the flow and cadence of natural language. You can tell whether characters sound the same, or like toneless robots. Reading aloud also helps analyzing any other element within a novel, especially the subtle pacing of paragraphs and sentences. It reveals the microrhythms of the writing: where the energy builds, where it slows down, and how the flow of language affects the reading experience.

Length and variety

The size of a paragraph or the length of a sentence is most immediately recognizable to readers. Short paragraphs can usually be found in dialogue, or as counterpoint to a number of longer paragraphs. Journalistic writing today, even without quotations, can have paragraphs as short as a single sentence. An author is fully aware of the rhythms these long and short units create in the mind's ear of the reader. To have all sentences and paragraphs the same length would be the tonal equivalent of a robot's voice. We crave variety, but more important than that, variable lengths serve to emphasize the shorter units and provide a welcome break to the flow.

Like this.[6]

Word choice

Veni, vidi, vici. I came, I saw, I conquered. Action scenes use short, punchy words. Depictions of reflection benefit from more contemplative, mellifluous emanations, flowery vocabulary, and longer sentences, clauses, and subclauses set apart by frequent punctuation. The rhythm of a sentence can also influence word choice. Longer words and extended sentences tend to slow the pace of a paragraph, while short, punchy words can speed it up. For a closer look at how Anglo-Saxon versus Latinate words affect tone and pacing, see chapter 12, "Language and Grammar."

Certain words evoke thematic elements woven throughout the text, including references to water, fire, earth, or air; religious allusions; cultural touchstones; and historical figures. Every time one of these key words appears in the text, their presence evokes a faint beat in the mind of the reader, and contributes to the perceived pacing of the narrative. For more on symbolism and themes, see chapter 19, "Layering."

Parallel construction

A group of sentences or a series of paragraphs creates a cumulative effect that shapes the reader's sense of rhythm and pacing within a section of a novel. These rhythms can be subtle—embedded in sentence structure, word choice, or narrative flow—or more overt, such as the repeated use of specific words, images, or phrases that act like callbacks. Repetition can be a deliberate literary device, used to build atmosphere, emphasize a theme, or create a poetic cadence. It can also reveal unconscious habits or patterns unique to the author's voice.

Any recurring motif, whether visual, verbal, or structural, establishes its own rhythm. And just like in music, every rhythm has a tempo that ranges from very slow to very fast. This tempo, in turn, contributes to the overall pacing not only of a scene or a chapter, but of the novel as a whole. Over time, the layering of these rhythms builds the novel's internal pulse, guiding how the reader experiences the unfolding narrative.

Characterization

A character's pacing, pauses, sentence structure, and inflection can subtly reveal who they are, from their emotional temperament to their cultural background or level of education. A character who speaks in clipped, abrupt phrases might come across as guarded or efficient, while another who rambles in winding, lyrical sentences might seem anxious, imaginative, or self-indulgent. These rhythmic distinctions not only help you differentiate voices without constant dialogue tags, but they also enrich the story's texture and bring energy and realism to the page.

When each character speaks with their own natural cadence, the dialogue becomes more dynamic, immersive, and true to life. And reading their words aloud is the best way to feel the beat and the pulse in every phrase. By tuning into this rhythm, you can better understand not only the content, but also the emotional and cognitive experience the writer is creating for you.

EXERCISE 4

Reread: Take a single page from any novel, and read it out loud. Try accenting different words to give different readings, as an actor might rehearse their lines. Do the paragraphs have a natural rhythm?

Rewrite: Apply the same technique to any dialogue in your own novel. Try adding pauses. Do they feel natural, or do they disrupt the flow? Does the exchange read quickly or drag slowly? Consider the tempo of the scene: How do the rhythms and content of the paragraphs shape its overall pace?

Notes

1. Robert Knopf, *Script Analysis for Theatre.*
2. https://tvtropes.org/pmwiki/pmwiki.php/Main/RaceAgainstTheClock
3. Some object to the dinkus's very existence. Google "I hate dinkus" to see what I mean. You can safely ignore these killjoys.
4. Postcards are defined in the "Postcards" section of chapter 10, "You Figured It Out" and referenced throughout this book. See the index for more postcard references. Maass defines *postcards* here: https://writerunboxed.com/2016/06/01/what-makes-fiction-literary-scenes-versus-postcards/.
5. Robert Knopf, *Script Analysis for Theatre.*
6. If you didn't notice the uniform length and similar rhythm of every sentence in the previous paragraph as you first read it in your head, go back and read it out loud. Isn't it monotonous?

19
Layering

Great literature is simply language charged with meaning to the utmost possible degree.
—*Ezra Pound*, How to Read[1]

The layers of meaning we discover in a novel result from the author's deliberate and often lengthy process of editing and rewriting. Symbolism doesn't appear by accident—every metaphor and reference is intentional. Some of these symbols draw on familiar character or plot tropes (as discussed in chapter 16, "Character Development") or recurring themes (see the "Message" section of chapter 20, "The Gestalt"), while others are unique creations specific to the author's story. This chapter explores how to identify all kinds of symbolic layers using semiotic tools.

Semiotics[2] is the study of signs and symbols and how they convey layers of meaning. Complex concepts can be represented by *signifiers*: representations of abstract ideas that convey atmosphere, mood, and tone while imbuing a text with a deeper, richer meaning. Overloaded signifiers[3] that represent more than one concept require you to interpret how their ambiguities impact the narrative.

Powerful signifiers include corporate logos and famous cultural icons. For example, Mickey Mouse represents the ethos of family-friendly entertainment, American global cultural dominance, and when used as an adjective, it also describes a half-assed way of doing something. The Statue of Liberty, *Harley Davidson*, and the Amazon logo are all famous and saturated with meaning, each evoking a range of emotions among different audiences.

Literary signifiers[4] can combine within a narrative to create something completely new, as when toxic elements sodium and chlorine bond into harmless table salt, or when vinegar turns baking soda into a bubbling volcano.

Prefab layers

There's no shortage of existing symbols and literary tropes for authors to draw from, so inventing entirely new ones isn't always necessary. Chapter 16, "Character Development" explores well-established character and story types; in this chapter, we'll broaden the focus to include direct quotations, references, and full retellings of earlier novels.

Lisa Halliday's *Asymmetry* begins with an almost-exact quotation of the opening of Lewis Carroll's *Alice in Wonderland*, both setting the scene and tipping us off that we are heading down the rabbit hole of her imagination. The titular character in Andrew Sean Greer's *Less* imagined himself like the heroic Ulysses, but he wanders the globe much as Don Quixote wandered the countryside, his misguided journey dissolving into comedy and farce. Jessamine Chan's *The School for Good Mothers* owes quite a lot to George Orwell's *1984* and Margaret Atwood's *A Handmaid's Tale*, portraying a realistic world gone wrong by a quarter turn rendering a contemporary hellscape. And Percival Everett's 2024 novel *James* is a direct retelling of Mark Twain's *The Adventures of Huckleberry Finn*, but from the point of view of the enslaved man Jim.

Constructed layers

Authors are, of course, free to invent their own symbols and layers of meaning. In her 2019 novel *Trust Exercise*, Susan Choi uses a three-part structure to subvert readers' assumptions, folding the timeline back on itself and saturating the narrative with meaning that demands a second read to fully grasp. Similarly, Lisa Halliday's *Asymmetry* uses a tripartite form to explore parallel elements that take on entirely different meanings in each section, enriching the reading experience through repetition and subtle callbacks. Jennifer Egan, in *A Visit from the Goon Squad* and *The Candy House*, constructs a multilayered collage using dozens of characters, expanding the story's scope from individual concerns to a reflection on the broader human experience in the modern world.

Everything is metaphor

Do oranges make you think of death? They may if you've watched *The Godfather Trilogy*.

An old man peels an orange. Another man buys an orange. A young man drives his car past a billboard advertising oranges. Each of these scenes precedes a character's death. These symbols have a cumulative effect on any viewer's subconscious, so the next time director Francis Ford Coppola shows you an orange, you may experience a quiver of dread.

In film, this phenomenon is called the *Kuleshov effect*: Two unrelated things that are shown together or in sequence to elicit an emotional response. In psychology, this is known as the *anchoring effect,* or *priming*. That's how symbolic imagery works in novels: by engaging the reader's subconscious and enhancing our reading experience with an emotional or intellectual punch.

Every detail, every element the author has chosen, exists for a reason. And the details that precede or follow other details have also been carefully chosen. We've already explored the power of the positioning of elements within scenes in chapter 13, "Context in Scene," but here we explore the way these contexts and juxtapositions affect the entire novel.

Learn to take nothing for granted or at face value. Assume anything found in a novel could represent something else, and this means anything; symbols have limitless capacity to signify. Here are the most common categories of symbolism found in novels:

- **Names:** People, places, and things
- **The classics:** Anything before the present time, including the Bible, Shakespeare, Greeks, Romans, Toni Morrison, and so on
- **Earth, wind, fire, and water:** The natural elements
- **Cycles and illness:** The seasons, festivals, periodicity, and their disruptions
- **Eating and sex:** Communal activities

Names

For seeing all names are imposed to signifie our conceptions; and all our affections are but conceptions; when we conceive the same things differently, we can hardly avoyd different naming of them.s
—*Thomas Hobbes,* Leviathan

The symbolism of names found in novels is so important that an entire branch of study is dedicated to it: *literary onomastics.*[5] Every proper name of every person, place, and thing a novelist invents has, by definition, filtered through their minds as they are thinking about their stories. Whether subconscious or not, every name has a charge, a context, and a symbolic meaning.

Every one of us has a name, and when we read our name in a book or hear it spoken aloud, something lights up in our brains. My parents named me Gary, unusual even when I was christened. It means "spear" or "spear carrier," and it can suggest someone with a sharp wit. As a child, the only other person named Gary I'd encountered was the actor Gary Cooper, and I was in my midtwenties before I had actually met another Gary. Then Gary Gilmore became famous (yikes!), and when I lived in London, I became aware of Gary Glitter (even worse!). In British drama today, "Gary" is shorthand for a clueless character (and… we're back to infamy!). Thank goodness for award-winning actor Gary Oldman, or I might have to consider changing my name.[6]

It's important, therefore, not to gloss over the proper names we find in the novels we read. They were chosen carefully, either for their banality or uniqueness, for associations with famous people, or for the derivations and archetypes implicit within.

A character name can convey personality traits such as strength, kindness, cunning, or mystery, or foreshadow themes (Faith, Hope, Charity). A place name can also slyly denote a specific culture or an historical era. And proper nouns or invented words act as shorthand for what they symbolize within a novel.

Names matter, and they provide an important symbolic layer to fiction. Look them up—you'll be amazed at the connections you find.

People

We could spend this entire section analyzing the names of Charles Dickens's characters—he seemed to enjoy creating them. The name *Fagin* from *Oliver Twist* (talk about foreshadowing!) means to "collect" (that is, shoplift, or "get the five-finger discount"). *Great Expectations'* wedding dress–wearing *Miss Havisham* sounds like "have a sham," or live a lie, which she is doing. The *Ebenezer* mentioned in the Bible means "stone of help," an ironic depiction of *Ebenezer Scrooge*, until he's visited by a few ghosts and it's no longer ironic.[7]

Atticus Finch's first name is that of the Platonic philosopher and his surname is a bird, calling to mind the mockingbird of Harper Lee's title. Arthur Less, the eponymous hapless writer of Andrew Sean Greer's *Less,* is literally Art-Less. The android Klara in Kazuo Ishiguro's *Klara and the Sun,* although not human, can see humans more clearly than they see themselves.

As Thomas Hobbes reminds us in the above quotation from his *Leviathan*, it's also significant when a character's name changes because of a new job or role, joining a different circle of friends, or an act of self-determination. Consider who views that character differently and who calls the character by their title, their nickname, or some other pet name. Naming can indicate respect and inclusion as much as derision or ostracization.

Places

Yoknapatawpha County, Middle Earth, Hogwarts—every one of those place names was carefully chosen by their authors to evoke a spirit of place and a particular era. Nicknames or alternate names of real places can also signal an author's opinion or a character's viewpoint: the Big Apple, Sin City, the Eternal City, the City of Brotherly Love, the People's Republic of Boulder. Some evocative place names are politically and historically charged and have become shorthand for movements or significant historical events: Waterloo, Avalon, Ferguson, Ludlow, Stonewall, Columbine, Sandy Hook.

Every real place carries its own baggage, which imprints itself onto the reader. What comes to mind when you think of Havana, or Jerusalem, or Bali? Imagine a novel set in Pyongyang, North Korea, Washington, DC, or Silicon Valley. We already have certain expectations about what those stories will be about, just because of the strong associations attached to those places.

Things

The phone booth–like teleportation machine in *Doctor Who*, TARDIS, has entered the UK vernacular to mean something that is much larger inside than it appears to be from the outside. It's a nonsense word now commonly understood. The social media company in Jennifer Egan's *The Candy House*, Mandala, ironically refers to Jungian psychoanalysis and Buddhist imagery. Hari Kunzru's *Red Pill* references an important choice made in a cultural filmic touchstone, *The Matrix*.

The naming of things in a novel can also set the tone of the story. Whimsical names like TARDIS might indicate a lighthearted or fantastical story, while dark or mysterious names like *Red Pill* can set a mood of suspense or foreboding. Objects with ironic or comical names can add levity to serious situations or emphasize certain aspects of their function in the story. I can't think of the "Orgasmatron" in Woody Allen's film *Sleeper* without smiling.

EXERCISE 1

Reread: Think of a character, place, or object name in a novel you've recently read. It was memorable (you just remembered it), but why? Did the name itself evoke an emotion or an image, or had the author worked hard to imbue that name with those characteristics?

Rewrite: Where is your novel set, and why? What are your characters' names? What named objects or entities hold meaning for you?

The Classics

Authors do not need to invent their own symbolism or character types because so much already exists in the public domain. For Western civilization and its authors, the most readily available sources of stories, allegories, fables, and moral lessons are the Christian Bible,[8] the works of William Shakespeare, and mythological and moral tales from many lands, reaching back to the ancient Greeks and Romans.

The Bible

The Judeo-Christian Old and New Testaments have it all: stories of loss and redemption (Eden and Jesus); love and lust (Ruth and Delilah); war and negotiation (Joshua and Jephthah); and global catastrophe (Noah). There are parables (the Prodigal Son, the Talents, the Lost Sheep, the Mustard Seed, the Rich Fool), poetry (Psalms, Song of Solomon), and the precepts and practical advice for living one's life (Ten Commandments, Pauline Epistles).

Generations of writers have looked to the Bible as a storytelling guide, and they have added a quotation or two from that book to their own novels for gravitas. These stories and their lessons are timeless but not unique. Authors of all stripes consult religious and philosophical texts to imbue their writing with a whiff of the eternal.

William Shakespeare

The sixteenth-century bard is *everywhere*. From wholesale reimaginings of his plays (*The Taming of the Shrew* became *Kiss Me Kate*; *Romeo and Juliet* became *West Side Story*), to refactorings (*Hamlet* became *Rosencrantz & Guildenstern Are Dead*; *King Lear* was the seed from which *Succession* grew), to quotations and tropes as novel titles (Gabrielle Zevin's *Tomorrow, & Tomorrow, & Tomorrow*, Eleanor Catton's *Birnam Wood*), William Shakespeare's creations remain relevant to this day.

Screen adaptations of his stage plays are too numerous to mention. Recent titles include *Othello, Richard III, Much Ado About Nothing*, and the perennial favorites: *Hamlet* and *Romeo and Juliet*.

Shakespeare's plays have also been translated into many languages because they contain subjects common to many cultures: power and ambition, jealousy, fate and destiny, betrayal, revenge, madness, loyalty, mercy, greed, and many other aspects of the human condition. As with the Bible, Shakespeare's body of work contains a smorgasbord of themes ready to be applied to modern novels.

Greek and Roman mythology

Every once in a while, a generation of artists decides to reexamine the classics produced by the ancient Greeks and Romans. This was all the rage during the American Revolution, which explains the architecture of Washington, DC. Neoclassical artists, musicians, and writers of the early twentieth century went back to the well, reinterpreting the same two-thousand-year-old works for their own purposes. The ancient stories were howlers, shocking and fantastical, which is why authors continue to borrow their themes today.

Classical scholar and author Madeline Miller turned classicism on its head with her two novels, *The Song of Achilles* and *Circe*, working with the ancient myths in a similar way that Homer and Hesiod compiled oral mythologies not originally their own into stories. Miller has stayed faithful to the original myths while overlaying them with twenty-first-century themes that resonate with modern sensibilities.

As with the Bible and Shakespeare, ancient mythology includes stories about so many aspects of life and interactions between people that there is literally nothing happening today that does not have a parallel story already told in antiquity. It's up to you to spot those references where they appear in the novels you read; doing so will enrich the layers of meaning beyond the plotlines.

Andersen, Grimm, and Aesop

Any child who has chanted "Ring Around the Rosie," "Rock-A-Bye Baby," or "Jack and Jill" is actually relating very dark stories of plague, human frailty, and death. Aesop's Fables and the fairy tales of Hans Christian Andersen and the Brothers Grimm contain many deep and dark themes disguised as harmless children's tales.

Why is this? Was it the goal to traumatize children, or might these catchy couplets actually be coping mechanisms for those who lived through the Black Plague, hundred-year wars, and famine?

The well-chosen parable can reveal much about modern society, as Salman Rushdie did in his 2023 allegory of modern Indian politics, *Victory City*, in which he assembles a cornucopia of Bengali, Hindi, Islamic, and Christian mythology and folklore to enlighten us.

At the very least, we need a cursory knowledge of the most famous fairy tales so we can recognize them and appreciate their meanings when they pop up in our reading.

Modern classics

From the perspective of a contemporary writer, a classic is any work that has preceded their adulthood and continues to endure, quality notwithstanding. *Don Quixote, The Great Gatsby, To Kill a Mockingbird*, and *I, Robot* all qualify as classics to current readers, and so can be mined for archetypes and templates. To portray a disaffected adolescent is to echo Holden Caulfield in *The Catcher in the Rye*, and creating sentient machines calls back not only to Isaac Asimov but also to Mary Shelley's *Frankenstein*. These references endure in the public consciousness to some extent, and can be folded into a novel to achieve deeper layers of meaning.

Including contemporary references or memes can be tricky, however. Some authors try to apply events of the moment as a supporting structure for their thematic material. Unfortunately, no one can predict what events and references will stand the test of time, and which ones will make readers scratch their heads even a few years from now. To remain relevant into the future, authors know it's safer to stick with references that have endured for at least a generation.

EXERCISE 2

Reread: Reflecting on a recent novel you read, identify its themes or use your favorite search engine or ChatGPT to list them for you. Enter "bible," "Shakespeare," "greek [or roman] mythology," or "fairy tale" as a prompt and see how similar themes show up in the classics. Did you find any direct references to those classics in the novel you read?

Rewrite: Is your own novel modeled on a classic story? Do you allude to characters or themes from biblical stories, Greek myths, or Shakespeare's plays?

Earth, Wind, Fire, and Water

The ancients depended on an intimate knowledge of nature and its elements for their survival. They didn't necessarily understand exactly how everything worked, but they did know the importance of air, water, fire, and earth. There's a reason zodiac signs are grouped into these four categories, and that for millennia these were considered to be the essential elements from which everything else was created.

Ceremonies, rites, and festivals arose to celebrate the four elements and to appease their corresponding gods. Acknowledgment and respect for these elements continues today, in sayings and turns of phrase, echoing in our literature, and adding layers of meaning whenever they are used.

Earth

The idea that humankind was formed out of soil and clay is not unique to the Judeo-Christian tradition. People rising from the earth like the crops that feed them made sense for thousands of years. So these ideas continue to exist in modern literature: earthy, grounded, organic, natural, verdant, flourishing, blooming, getting one's hands dirty—these are all attributes related to the ground beneath our feet.

Remember that the earth is not featureless: The mountains rise, and valleys fall. There are paths, vistas, cliffs, deserts, bogs, and bewitching forests. Also look in literature for mud, compost, minerals, stones, and other natural elements to see how they are used. They often indicate a character's condition or a connection to one's heritage. Knowing one's self is understanding where one originates, and where one will eventually return after death. We are but dust to dust, and ashes to ashes.

The protagonists of both Olga Tokarczuk's 2019 *Drive Your Plow Over the Bones of the Dead* and Damon Galgut's 2021 *The Promise* are driven by a need to protect their land, the titular character of Lawrence Wright's 2023 *Mr. Texas* finds inspiration deep within a cave, and in Jesmyn Ward's 2023 *Let Us Descend*, the muddy ground conceals Annis's mother's weapons and eventually traps her (and talks to her!).

Wind

We breathe, we inspire, we expand. Air flows everywhere and through us, nourishing our bodies and our souls. Wind is change and transformation, freedom and liberation, travel and adventure, ideas and creativity—wind represents our very souls taking flight.

But powerful winds can be frightening and destructive, representing emotional turmoil, bad omens, unseen or even mystical powers exerting control over us, and the relentless passage of time.

When we read of extreme weather events, violent storms, hurricanes, and tornadoes, consider these metaphors in the context of the characters involved; they are likely external manifestations of inner turmoil.

In Maggie O'Farrell's 2020 novel *Hamnet*, airborne fleas bring the plague to the title character; the smoke from the Cootings Machine in Kazuo Ishiguro's 2021 *Klara and the Sun* spurs Klara into action to save Josie; and in Benjamín Labatut's 2020 *When We Cease to Understand the World*, toxic gases are created by scientists who are oblivious to the consequences of their discoveries.

Fire

Earth is; air is; water is; but fire must be created. Its discovery was celebrated in the story of Prometheus, who for humanity's benefit stole fire from the gods; he was then punished accordingly. Fire is magical, potent, and hungry. It's the spirit of the gods, passion and desire, the strongest of emotions, and the spark of creativity. It's forbidden knowledge, power, energy, destruction, and as a purifying agent can be the catalyst for phoenix-like renewal.

Fire transforms raw comestibles into food, sinners into saints, and Pompeii into ash. It's dangerous, fickle, and immediate—on us without warning, changing us irretrievably. In our reading we must pay close attention to even the humblest candle's flame, and whether its light is hidden under a bushel.

A fire on a train causes Jivan's life to spiral out of control in Megha Majumdar's 2020 *A Burning*, fire has deformed Eleanor in Gail Honeyman's 2017 *Eleanor Oliphant Is Completely Fine*, and in Angie Thomas's 2017 *The Hate U Give*, the fire that destroys Starr's father's store transforms her personal struggle into a community movement.

Water

Water douses fire. We—our bodies—are mostly water. Humble, nourishing water—essential to life!—is also one of the most destructive elements around us. Just ask anyone whose basement has flooded. We cannot live in water; we will drown.

But if we cross the river, swim from the shipwreck or downpour or flood, and survive drowning, we have been baptized and are reborn, renewed, sanctified. Like wind and fire, water in small doses is positive, but overwhelming and crushing when too much of it flows our way. Therefore, as in life, water in novels is a powerful metaphor that can read as positive or negative according to the context.

A fountain looms large in Laura Lippman's 2019 *Lady in the Lake*, a swim in the sea at the conclusion of Rachel Cusk's 2018 *Kudos* transforms the protagonist, and the rising sea impacts every character's life in Pitchaya Sudbanthad's 2019 *Bangkok Wakes to Rain*.

EXERCISE 3

Reread: Using any novel you have read or are reading now, look for instances of earth, wind, fire, and water. How are those elements portrayed? Who interacts with the element, and what is happening to that character in those moments? Do the elements represent external manifestations of inner turmoil? Or are they being used as metaphors supporting other thematic elements?

Rewrite: How are you using the four elements in your own writing to deepen meaning?

Cycles and Illness

We breathe in and out, our hearts pump rhythmically, we watch the sun rise and fall and the tides ebb and flow, and we observe that life is like a wheel going round and round. We expand our gaze outward to lunar cycles, the seasons, our own birth and death, and when we look back at our parents, their parents, and their parents, our children, their children, and so on, we see these fractals expanding into infinity.

It would all be so gloriously orderly, harmonious, and satisfying were it not for the disruptions, the imperfections, those destructive elements that interrupt our routines, erode our cycles, and shorten our lives: illness, accidents, catastrophes.

Seasons

Our lives are driven by routine. We go to bed; we get up. We eat; we go to work; we come home. In the fall we go back to school; in the summer we play. We compare the phases of our lives to the seasons of the year: spring is our youth, summer our adulthood, autumn our old age, and winter our death.

Other seasons we experience are those on the various sporting calendars, with their periods of hope, challenge, progress, and eventual elevation or playoff elimination. Performing arts seasons usually follow the semesters or trimesters of the academic calendar, except those of summer festivals.

Many novelists use these seasons to organize their material, allowing those changes to amplify or contrast with the growth of their characters. For example, the six-day grind of producing an SNL-like comedy show every week forms the first half of Curtis Sittenfeld's 2023 *Romantic Comedy,* and the academic calendar structures Tom Perrotta's 2017 *Mrs. Fletcher*, Susan Choi's 2019 *Trust Exercise*, and Rebecca Yarros's 2023 *Fourth Wing*.

Festivals

Other societal rituals occur with a regularity that imbues them with the illusion of eternity. The four-year Olympic and World Cup cycles, the (now-endless) American electoral cycle, and the celebrations that follow momentous events:

birthdays, weddings, and funerals, along with Christmas, Easter, Halloween, Labor Day, Mother's Day, Pride Month, Black History Month, and many others.

Many of these holidays, festivals, and remembrances come from darker places, like nursery rhymes do. Pirate Day and Halloween are celebrations of chaos, order upended, and absurdities, all things that would seem to disqualify them for celebration, and yet they thrive as much as their more traditional counterparts.

When a festival is depicted in a novel, it adds at least two layers of meaning for the reader: how the festival on its surface is related to the characters participating in it, as well as the deeper reasons the festival exists and how it influences the world.

For example, the twin festivals of Christmas and Easter anchor both the preacher's family calendar and the plot structure of Jonathan Franzen's 2021 *Crossroads*; a birthday and a funeral form the center of Luis Alberto Urrea's 2018 *The House of Broken Angels*.

Illness

While the cyclical events of the various seasons and festivals point to a never-ending story, they can be interrupted by the intrusion of real life. When watching a movie, notice when a perfectly healthy character coughs for no reason, because that signals they are likely to die before the final scene. Any female character of childbearing age who inexplicably throws up is absolutely pregnant.

Illness can affect anything: crops, societal harmony, academic freedoms, religious authority, artistic expression—in other words, any living being or thing can be brought low by disease and decay.

Think of the killer shark, the lava-spewing volcano, killer bees, global climate change, and pandemics—these anomalies of nature act as plagues on the land and interrupt the harmonious circles of life. They also act as metaphors for the inner lives of the characters who encounter them.

The protagonist's physical diminishment plays a large part in Elizabeth Strout's novel *Olive, Again,* in Taffy Brodesser-Akner's *Fleishman Is in Trouble,* and in Martin Amis's *Inside Story*; in Joshua Cohen's *The Netanyahus,* a character's yearning for a nose job reveals who holds the real power.

EXERCISE 4

Reread: Think of a novel you've read that includes depictions of a season in nature, in sports, or an academic term. Consider how that seasonality was used—to pace the narrative, or to amplify themes, or both? Was an internal, societal, or environmental illness also depicted? If so, how did it reflect the themes of the novel?

Rewrite: How do the seasons and cycles of life figure in your own writing? How about disruptions, plagues, or illness?

Eating and Sex

> Now listen here to the anatomy lecture! This upper story's the brain which is hungry for something called truth and doesn't get much but keeps on feeling hungry! This middle's the belly which is hungry for food. This part down here is the sex which is hungry for love because it is sometimes lonesome.
> —*Tennessee Williams*, Summer and Smoke

We consume and we eliminate. We read books and out of our fingers pop novels. What we take into our bodies determines who we are as humans, as artists, and as lovers. What we hunger for defines the very paths of our lives.

Eating and sex in novels represent communion with others, and are often cathartic experiences revealing deeper truths, sometimes literally stripping away barriers between people and their true emotions. In their most primal, intimate acts—eating and sex—characters show who they really are.

Look for novelistic depictions of meals, and pay close attention to who eats what, where they sit in relation to each other, and precisely what transpires over the breaking of bread. These scenes are often pivotal moments in a narrative.

Ditto for sex scenes. Sex is often a stand-in for rebirth, death, and transformation. Such are sex scenes in Tom Perrotta's 2017 *Mrs. Fletcher*, Ocean Vuong's 2019 *On Earth We're Briefly Gorgeous*, Lauren Wilkinson's 2019 *American Spy*, Elena Ferrante's 2020 *The Lying Life of Adults*, and many, many others.

Cookbooks and erotica

Yes, recipe collections. So many of us love reading about food and its preparation. Why? The popularity of cookbooks underlines the sensual nature of all aspects of food, and its total engagement of the senses: sight, smell, sound, touch, smell, and taste. If we feel so strongly about reading a list of ingredients, how much more powerful is the actual consumption of food within a novel?

The same goes for sex—what's not to love? All the senses engaged to the max. If you love novels about nothing but sex, power to you! But erotica is to sex as a cookbook is to eating. The pleasures are mostly implied in readers' minds as they relate the pleasurable experiences in their own lives to what they read on the page.

Sex is a big deal, of course. But as with food, too much sex is just as unhealthy as too little. This applies to readers as much as it does for the characters in the novels we read.

EXERCISE 5

Reread: Find a meal scene or a sex scene in a novel. How is the meal or the lovemaking moving the story forward? Does it highlight the relationship status between characters, or does it serve some other thematic function? How well has the author invoked the five senses?

Rewrite: How would you change any of the eating or sex scenes to heighten (or dampen) the emotions expressed? Do you write about important meals or sex in your own novel? How do your sex or food-centered scenes amplify the themes in your story?

Notes

1. Ezra Pound, *How to Read* (Haskell House, New York, 1931).
2. Find more background on semiotics in chapter 23, "Academic Disciplines."
3. African American literature, for example, has long embraced what Louis Gates calls *oppositional* signifying. See the Signifying Monkey: https://en.wikipedia.org/wiki/The_Signifying_Monkey.
4. Also see Literary Semiotics: https://en.wikipedia.org/wiki/Semiotic_literary_criticism.
5. Many scholarly articles can be found in the *Journal of Literary Onomastics*. https://soar.suny.edu/handle/20.500.12648/1972
6. Just kidding. Today the plight of Garys is minimal when compared to that of Karens, for example.
7. As I write this chapter, there are active American professional tennis players named Katie Volynets and Tennys Sandgren, whose names, if they weren't real, I would swear were Dickensian creations. See also sprinter Usain Bolt.
8. While many academicians attempt to draw a straight line between the ancient Greeks and Romans and our current culture, others vehemently disagree. Doug Metzger has devoted years of research and written millions of words to support his thesis that the Bible, not the Greeks and Romans, most significantly influenced the education and writings of Anglophone authors over the past five hundred years. I recommend his podcast, at https://LiteratureAndHistory.com, which begins its survey of English literature with Sumerian cuneiform in 3100 BCE; the first hundred episodes progress only as far as St. Augustine in 427 AD. Metzger is nothing if not thorough.

20
The Gestalt

The whole, the "Gestalt," has always meant to me the whole organism and not the phenomena in one field, or merely the "introspective experiences," which in Gestalt psychology play quite
an important part.
—*Kurt Goldstein*, The Organism

Once you've reached the last page of a novel, closed the book, and set it down, you may experience a range of emotions including stimulation, satisfaction, puzzlement, a sense of wonder, or any combination of the above. You are experiencing the novel in full—its *gestalt*—which encompasses both the author's intent and your emotional response to reading it. Gestalt psychology is the study of an entire organism, the idea that *the whole is greater than the sum of its parts*.

While every other chapter in this section is focused on studying a novel's individual components, here we address the cumulative effects of language, grammar, context, POV, voice, characterization, development, structure, pacing, and symbolic layering. Does the gestalt create a satisfying story, or parts that fight each other, are out of balance, or are inappropriate to the novelist's aspirations?

This is where we investigate whether the novelist was successful in molding their novel into a cohesive, organic whole.

After you've completed the novel and have had some time to recover, the inevitable questions arise: What did I get out of it? Was it worth my effort? Why did the author write what they wrote? And what the heck is this novel actually *about*?

What the novel is about

Whether or not an author's story entertained or enlightened, there always exists—as in any organism—a superseding gestalt, an overarching purpose, formulated primarily because *the author themselves* needed a compelling reason to spend years writing and sweating blood. The message is in there, believe me. It could be as innocuous as "Isn't life a gas?" all the way to "We are the authors of our own destruction."

All novels have at their core some very human truth or maxim that readers can relate to. Even a story as entertaining and exotic as that of the lonely astronaut in Andy Weir's *The Martian* has at its core the strong message of the power of knowledge, innovation, and the indomitable human spirit.

As discussed briefly in the "Pivot Points" section of chapter 17, "Structure," the surest way to determine what the novel is about and why the author wrote it is by starting at the climax and figuring out how exactly it relates to the inciting incident. Even if you are initially confused by the novel you just read, studying this **inciting-climax** axis and determining what both have in common always yields the theme. Every time. Here are some examples:

- **Ann Patchett's *Tom Lake*.** Inciting incident: Lara's audition. Climax: Lara's secret procedure. Common element: Declarations of independence. Theme: We define ourselves through stories.
- **Bonnie Garmus's *Lessons in Chemistry*.** Inciting incident: Elizabeth's rape. Climax: Elizabeth's promotion. Common element: Lack of agency. Theme: Women must help each other and accept each other's help.
- **Jennifer Egan's *The Candy House*.** Inciting incident: Bix's social media app. Climax: Gregory's novel. Common element: Synthesizing information. Theme: The novel remains the best snapshot of our society.

Because the message contained in a novel is also such a deep expression of who the novelist is and what they believe most fervently, many novelists revisit the same themes. Nobel laureate Kazuo Ishiguro throughout his novels has written extensively about the complexity of memory, identity, and the search for meaning. In fact, he claimed early in his career to have gotten away with essentially writing the same novel three times.[1] He didn't mean he reused plots, characters, or settings; he meant he had written three different expressions of the way his ideas converged into a whole—the gestalt.

Why the novelist wrote it

Authors use their novels to inspire readers, provoke thought, and reflect on the complexities of the human condition in ways that are relatable and meaningful. Literature is diverse and continuously evolving, but the overwhelming majority of novels' messages focus on positive and aspirational themes.

On the surface, some novels may seem to be breaking the mold and exploring darker themes. Here we find antiheroes, antinovels, and cautionary tales that warn us about humanity's reckless pursuits and our planet's perilous future, but all of them follow a positive moral compass. We recognize the antihero because we know what true heroism is. We understand that the earth is doomed if we do X because we know in our hearts that Y is the right thing to do. Every story of darkness has a positive worldview standing behind it in contrast. Cassandras warn us of our deaths because they understand the preciousness of life.

To illustrate, here's a list of some messages you *won't* find driving a novel (but that may propel an antinovel):

- There is no value in forming meaningful connections with others.
- Hate and discrimination are justified, so intolerance and bigotry should be celebrated.
- Cheating and deception lead to true happiness, and the end justifies the means, no matter the cost.
- Happiness can only be found in material possessions, so being selfish is the key to success.
- Environmental destruction is inconsequential and unimportant.

You get the idea.

While you may find some of these dark themes driving doomsday essays, extremist political screeds, and tweets, they fizzle out upon lengthy examination. Nothing so negative can survive the introspection required by a novelist who must spend months and years examining every aspect and facet of an idea. That's why we find positive themes at the core of a novel's gestalt.

Plot doesn't matter

You may have noticed *Literary Forensics* does not have a single chapter devoted exclusively to plot. This may strike you as strange. After all, the plot is the first thing readers encounter, it's the way readers make sense of the story, and it forms the core of what most readers remember after reading a novel. Try this test on the most recent novel you've read: Describe it to me. Go ahead. Do it now.

Did you just summarize the plot? Most of us would.

But *Moby Dick* is not about a whale—it's about obsession. *The Handmaid's Tale* is not about Offred—it's about misogyny. *Interior Chinatown* is not about kung fu—it's about identity.

The plot of every novel fades into insignificance once you read like a writer. Only then do you realize that this flimsy thing we call *plot* is merely a tarp, a paint job, or a skin wrapped around the vehicle delivering something much, much more important: its message. And through this message we can glimpse into the mind of the author and commune with their spirit. This is heady stuff.

A living organism

> I've learned that people will forget what you said, people will forget what you did, but people will never forget how you made them feel.
>
> —Maya Angelou

Picture someone you know well. What do you see? A face, a laugh, a gesture? Do you remember their clothes, or an event, a touch, a scent? These memory fragments are how our brains store a person's entire being—their preferences, how they act, who they are.

When recalling a novel you have read, you probably remember less of what was written, the details of scene and plot, and more about how it made you feel while you were reading it, and after you finished it. A novel's conception, design, and execution must be consistent, balanced, and relatable, so that it coheres into a unified whole. Only then can the novel come to life in our mind and resemble a living organism.

In all forms of art, the whole becomes greater than the sum of its parts.

That's fine, but it doesn't advance our knowledge of a novel's gestalt. The question remains: How can we hold an entire novel in our head? The answer is: We can't.[2] We are left to consider various aspects of the whole, as we observe light split into colors by a prism. There is no way to study 100,000 words as a single entity, and so we are left once again to consider its aspects. We have powerful tools for doing just that. We'll spend the rest of this chapter investigating a novel's *gestalt* through the lenses of:

- **Completeness:** Pivot points, the **unspoken contract**, characterization, tone, and pacing
- **Balance:** Action and reflection, character scene time, and the pacing of information
- **Morals:** Various constructive and educational story themes
- **Other viewpoints:** Factors external to the novel relating to series, oeuvre, and translation

Completeness

Airplane pilots spend quite a bit of time checking and rechecking the dozens of critical systems on board their planes before they take off. In a similar way, authors write and revise their manuscripts multiple times before editors, proofreaders, and designers help them finish crafting any book, including the one you're reading now.

Think of this section as a checklist we can follow to ensure that the novel we've just read works at all levels. All these items have been covered elsewhere in *Literary Forensics*, but I list them here again so you can review each of these topics as it applies to the novel as a whole.

Pivot points

Every novel has a hook, an inciting incident, something significant that happens at the midpoint, and a climax. Have you identified all four of these pivot points? If you haven't found the climax and the inciting incident, you'll never know why an author wrote their novel. For more about how to locate these critical junctures, see chapter 17, "Structure."

Do you feel that the novel was an appropriate length? Could it have been related in fewer words, or do you feel the author should have expanded the narrative, given the subject matter?

Unspoken contract

From confusion to clarity, darkness to light, question to answer—did the novel resolve the issues presented at its beginning, or were you distracted by missing elements or threads that led nowhere? Did you experience frustration at the novel's end, or were you satisfied that the ending presented a believable conclusion for every character?

Character journey

Did the protagonist follow one of the classic journeys as outlined in chapter 16, "Character Development"? If not, how did their journey differ from these? Identifying how an author has strayed from a well-defined character arc will help you better understand what the real story is about.

If you find a character that is not behaving in a "normal" way, acting inconsistently, or if their motivations and actions seem artificial and contrived, that's usually a good place to start digging. Ask yourself what that character is doing in relation to the protagonist and their journey, why that character has changed, and what purpose that change is serving.

Tone

How would you characterize the overall tone of the novel, as described in chapter 15, "Voice"? Is it more formal or informal, and would you characterize the protagonist's aspirations as high or low drama? Is the story a satire or comedy, or is it more serious? Does the tone change with each POV, or is it consistent throughout? And do you feel that the novel's theme matches its tone?

Pacing

Does the novel flow at a steady rate, or does it speed up or slow down? Do you feel the pacing served the action, or are they incongruent? Does the last part of the novel seem rushed, or does it have the breadth you felt the story deserves? For more about all levels of pacing, see chapter 18, "Pacing."

EXERCISE 1

Reread: Return to a novel you have completed and choose any of the above tests to evaluate a novel's gestalt. Pivot points, **unspoken contract**, character journey, tone, and pacing represent the most critical angles when considering the novel as a whole, but there are others. Think of any other elements you'd like to test (use any chapter or section heading in WHAT YOU NOTICE for inspiration) and give it a go.

Rewrite: Try the same test on your own novel. How does it compare?

Balance

Every scene, point of view, paragraph, and sentence contributes to a novel's gestalt, so every word makes an impression on the reader. And if anything feels out of place, extraneous, or inconsistent, we expect the author to acknowledge these oddities and compensate for them at some point in the novel.

A novel is a balancing act: a mix of action and reflection, slow and fast pacing, and different characters interacting with each other in different combinations and in different ways. As the novel takes shape in our brains, it must make logical sense, at least internally. Whatever pulls a novel off balance must have some other force pulling it back into homeostasis, like the way a steady beat acts on a fluid *rubato*.

My favorite example of a rubber band–like force exerting its pull over a novel is in Stephen King's *11/22/63*, where a time machine makes it possible for the protagonist to go back and try to prevent President Kennedy's assassination. But every time he alters an historical event, objects and events resist this change. The closer he gets to preventing the shooting, the stronger the forces pull against his efforts.

Action and reflection

Remember the classic writing edict, "Show, don't tell." Is the protagonist spending enough time actually doing things to develop their character? Is there a good mix of dialogue and narrative? Are we spending enough time in the present, or is there too much backstory?

Also, think about the scenes as units—how do the scenes balance one another? Is an action scene preceded or followed by something calmer and more reflective, or is it action, action, action? Think also about the chapters, and the pacing of plot points—are they evenly spaced, or bunched together? And if so, how does their distribution in the story affect the narrative?

Consider the use of words: Germanic versus Latinate; poetic versus prosaic; long versus short; standard vocabulary versus slang—how does word usage influence the flow of the scenes, the plot points, and the chapters?

Scene time

Consider the French scene as described in chapter 18, "Pacing," which observes the entry and exit of every character and their impact on a scene. The mere presence of certain characters within scenes has meaning, and the balance of scene time between characters influences how you perceive their significance. Are supposedly important characters present, or mostly absent from the narrative? And if so, what does their presence or absence tell you? Are the absent but influential characters intended to be shadowy or mysterious?

These questions also apply to novels with multiple POVs. It may be worthwhile to count the number of scenes told from each character's POV. The ratios may surprise you and leave you with more questions about the balancing of characters and their development. It is said that the POV should be held by the character with the most to gain or lose within the scene. What do your POV tallies tell you about the status of each of the characters or their importance in the narrative?

Significance

Mysteries and thrillers withhold information or hide critical information in plain sight by burying a few important details within many unimportant details. Listing the items on a banquet table may include the eventual murder weapon, or listing where various suspects were at the time of the murder may eventually reveal the murderer's identity.

How important is the hairbrush? Or the selection of a golf club, or the flavor of jelly in a peanut butter–and–jelly sandwich? Is it part of the background, or is it a thematic element? And how many thematic elements are too many for a reader to take in?

The balance of important and mundane elements is also critical to memoir, autofiction, and historical fiction. I'm reminded of the balance of factual and fictional elements in Colum McCann's *Apeirogon*, a fictional retelling of the stories of two real people. On my first read, I assumed that ninety percent was simply fact, and that McCann was reporting more than he was novelizing. Imagine my surprise on my second read when I tallied the important (factual) and the mundane (fictional) elements and discovered that the balance of fact and fiction was closer to twenty percent factual and eighty percent fictional. As it turned out, McCann had written a novel that read like fact with expertly disguised and obfuscated fictional elements hiding in plain sight.

EXERCISE 2

Reread: Pick a type of balance—action and reflection, scene time, important and mundane, pacing, or significance—and determine its balance or imbalance in a novel you've read. How much did this require you to reread? Could you skim the novel to make your determination? Did you rely on your memory? Sometimes memory is deceiving, as in the *Apeirogon* example above.

Rewrite: Compare what you found with your own novel. How does it differ?

Morals

A novel's primary theme is the message the author is communicating—the reason they wrote their novel. Although superficially a novel may seem to exist merely to entertain, to provoke, or to skewer, these secondary attributes are not enough to sustain a writer through the months and years of writing and rewrites.

A novel may be cautionary and dark—saying billionaires are out of control, we are destroying the planet, or democracy is in decline—but its underlying message cannot fail to be uplifting. Ultimately what inspires an author is their sense of morality—what they believe to be constructive and inspiring.

Below is an incomplete list of messages you may find in the novels you read. I encourage you to discover more.

Flights of fancy

In these adventures, the journey itself may be as important as the destination. The hero may be required to confront their fears as a path to personal growth and liberation, but at the very least they need to embrace change, which is an essential part of the human condition. They will most certainly gain knowledge of themselves, their worlds, their families, and their friends.

Flights of fancy may also employ magical or fantastical elements; imagination has the potential to transform reality and inspire greatness, and, with hope and faith, miracles can occur. These stories implore the reader to pursue their dreams and passions, no matter what obstacles stand in their way, a wise message for writers and readers alike.

Examples include *Alice's Adventures in Wonderland* by Lewis Carroll, *Peter Pan* by J. M. Barrie, and *The Neverending Story* by Michael Ende.

The good fight

This centers on a protagonist or group who takes a stand against injustice, oppression, or overwhelming odds, driven by a moral imperative rather than personal gain. These stories often depict individuals who, despite limited power or resources, refuse to stand by while others suffer. Their struggle is as much about holding on to their values and integrity as it is about defeating a tangible enemy. The stakes are typically high—not just for the hero, but for a larger community or ideal that symbolizes fairness, freedom, or truth.

Fighting the good fight reflects humanity's aspiration to confront evil, even when victory seems uncertain; the fight itself, regardless of outcome, holds inherent value. Examples include tales of civil rights movements, anticorruption crusades, or underdog resistance against authoritarian regimes.

Examples include *The Grapes of Wrath* by John Steinbeck, *To Kill a Mockingbird* by Harper Lee, and *The Handmaid's Tale* by Margaret Atwood.

The right stuff

Determining right from wrong is an eternal struggle and places many a character in a moral quandary. A protagonist or their tribe may fight for justice, but justice is not the same for everyone, and the lines between good and evil may be difficult to discern. Readers want their heroes to be creative and artistic, and motivated by love or devotion more than material gain. Readers want them to strengthen their minds and spirits, and learn from history's lessons to avoid repeating past mistakes.

Examples include *The Lord of the Rings* by J.R.R. Tolkien, *Lonesome Dove* by Larry McMurtry, and *The Martian* by Andy Weir.

Self-actualization

Many novels are about characters who seek mental, emotional, or physical balance in their lives. This often requires self-realization and acceptance of who they are, embracing their imperfections so that they can live their life true to their values and beliefs.

Guides to these authentic lives may be found in nature and the wisdom of the ancients that provide lessons and insights into life's ups and downs. Truth may be found in a Zen-like appreciation of the here and now, taking joy in life's simple pleasures and treasuring the present moment.

Examples include *Jane Eyre* by Charlotte Brontë, *Their Eyes Were Watching God* by Zora Neale Hurston, and *The Catcher in the Rye* by J. D. Salinger.

We are all one

Concerned with relationships and the collective's well-being, these novels may embrace diversity to enrich communities and foster understanding through empathy and compassion. Overcoming bias and prejudice can also foster community harmony and collective growth.

Healing past wounds requires the act of forgiveness, which can be a spiritual cleansing. No one is beyond redemption, and those who choose kindness over fear or hate can have a significant influence on others and their communities.

And finally, the gratitude and appreciation for all the good encountered and the evils overcome brings ultimate contentment and joy.

Examples include *Middlemarch* by George Eliot, *Cloud Atlas* by David Mitchell, and *Small Great Things* by Jodi Picoult.

Love conquers all

The most important and powerful emotion of all is love. Countless stories have focused on the sacrifices made for love and its profound impact on their characters' lives. Stories that center the love of a mate, family, a people, a culture, or an idea celebrate the bonds forged in those relationships.

Love's cousin, friendship, works along the same spectrum, as true friendships are invaluable to sustaining us through life's challenges. Embracing unity of purpose and working toward common goals lead to positive change.

And finally, the people we love and the families we form lead to our most essential partnerships and cherished memories.

Examples include *Pride and Prejudice* by Jane Austen, *The Notebook* by Nicholas Sparks, and *The Fault in Our Stars* by John Green.

EXERCISE 3

Reread: Choose any novel you've read, and based on its climax and inciting incident, identify its theme, its message. You should be able to express it in fewer than a dozen words. Is it a moral message? A positive message? A message of hope?

Rewrite: What is your novel's primary theme or message? Is this made clear in both its inciting incident and climax?

Other Viewpoints

Another way to evaluate the novel as a whole is to broaden your point of view from between a book's covers, out beyond the novel, to view it within a series of novels, or take into account all the works by its author.

This final gestalt evaluation will take advantage of some of the tools described in the following section: WHAT YOU STUDY, which includes the publishing industry, other narrative forms, alternative academic disciplines, and the entire AI toolset currently used in the field of digital humanities. Let's start there.

A wider angle

We learn a lot about something when we look at it sideways, or in the case of Christopher Wren and the dome of St. Paul's in London, upside-down. Faced with a seemingly unsolvable architectural problem, the architect literally flipped his models over to better understand the gravitational forces acting on his new dome.[3] Spanish architect Antoni Gaudí did the same thing when he designed the Sagrada Familia cathedral in Barcelona.

Observing what we think we know from a different perspective is a large part of what this book is about. Today's computing power gives us the tools to understand the novel from an analysis of the data to a depth unimaginable just a few years ago. A novel's data is generally measured along two yardsticks: quantitative and qualitative.

Quantitative analysis refers to the study of numbers within a novel: the number of words, of chapters and sections, the percentage of the novel each section or chapter constitutes, the percentages of past- and present-tense verbs, average sentence and paragraph lengths, and its readability scores.

Qualitative data measures the attributes of a novel, basically what we have spent this entire book learning how to gather. Digital topic modeling, sentiment analysis, and language analysis exist today; I already use them when I study a novel. I can't imagine what other tools will be available to researchers in the near future.

In the past, most of these digital tools were unavailable to average readers, but today, LLM (Large Language Model) tools like ChatGPT are already available to most of us and are ready to answer your novelistic questions. See chapter 24, "Digital Humanities," for more on how to leverage these AI tools.

Body of works

When considering a novel within the broader context of a series, its meaning and resonance often shift dramatically. A standalone novel might appear self-contained, but when situated within a larger narrative arc, it gains layers of significance by foreshadowing future developments, echoing earlier events, or deepening thematic concerns introduced elsewhere. Characters evolve more gradually across multiple books, and what might seem like a small moment in one volume may carry more emotional or symbolic weight in retrospect. This broader scope allows readers to trace arcs not just of individuals, but of ideas, institutions, or even fictional worlds across time.

An example is Stephen King's 2023 novel *Holly*, whose titular character had already appeared in five previous novels, and whose character arc spans all six. You can read *Holly* in isolation, but a full accounting of her character is a multivolume exercise.

Likewise, viewing a novel through the lens of an author's entire body of work can reveal patterns and obsessions that transcend individual plots. Recurring themes—like isolation, redemption, or the search for identity—often take on new shades when seen across multiple works. An author might refine or subvert familiar tropes over time, or return to a particular setting or character type in order to explore it from a new angle. By stepping back to examine a writer's oeuvre, we begin to see how each book functions not only as a singular creative act, but also as part of an ongoing conversation the author is having with their own past work, with their readers, and with the literary tradition itself.

There are also famous authors who represent their own well-established brands, authors who have achieved such a consistency with their writing that their novels are not only internally consistent, but consistent across their entire output. There's a lot of money to be made in consistency.

In both contexts—series and full oeuvre—a novel becomes more than a self-contained story. It becomes a node in a network of meaning, a stepping stone in a creative trajectory. Readers who engage with a novel in this way are rewarded with a richer, more textured reading experience, as they begin to see the subtle echoes, deliberate callbacks, and long-term narrative strategies that might otherwise go unnoticed. The novel becomes not just a destination, but a bridge, linking past and future, part and whole, moment and legacy.

Translations

Novels can be turned into movies; movies in turn can be novelized, and many are. The origin of the novel in your hand could be a video game, a comic book, or a story ripped from the headlines. But the transformation of narratives from one format to another is not seamless and always carries with it the echoes of its original form.

Any story that has been adapted from its original medium automatically acquires another level of pathos, texture, and meaning. The word *text* derives from the Latin verb *texere*, meaning "to weave," and *texus*, meaning "thread." I imagine novels as being interwoven like Arachne's tapestries, incorporating threads from every medium and style that contributed to the novel in your hand.

Novels molded into alternative structures and frameworks are also translations. This includes epistolary novels (written as a series of letters, logs, or diary entries) like Helen Fielding's *Bridget Jones's Diary*, Andy Weir's *The Martian*, and Ocean Vuong's *On Earth We're Briefly Gorgeous*. This also includes novels that do not conform to the standard arch plot, like the tripartite form of Lisa Halliday's *Asymmetry* and Susan Choi's *Trust Exercise*, the 1,001 sections of Colum McCann's *Apeirogon*, the screenplay form of Charles Yu's novel *Interior Chinatown*, and the portfolio form of Hernan Diaz's *Trust*.

Finally, a novel can literally be translated from one language to another. The original author's story still exists, but it has become a secondary layer underneath the new text, which was authored by the translator, who overlays their own beliefs and aesthetic choices onto the original work.[4] The primacy of translators, long hidden in the shadows of literature, is now being acknowledged, as major literary organizations like the Booker Prize and the National Book Award are recognizing translators with their own prizes.

Exploring alternative viewpoints in evaluating a novel reveals that a story's full impact is best understood not in isolation, but within a larger web of contexts—series, the author's body of work, adaptations, and even translations. Ultimately, this holistic approach contributes to the gestalt of a novel—the overall impression that lingers with you long after you read the final page.

EXERCISE 4

Reread: Using your favorite search engine or some of the tools mentioned in chapter 3, "Choosing What to Read," research the novel you have just read to gather more information about the book than you could have found between the covers. This includes YouTube interviews with the author, literary criticism in the form of book reviews, SparkNotes analyses, and anything else that pops up in your search.

See if the novelist has written other novels like the one you've read, or if the novel is part of a series. Does it match an author's brand, or is it different? If so, how? What do other authors have to say about this novel? Where is the author from? What can you find out about their culture or their circle of friends and other authors who act on and react to each other's work?

Has any of your research changed how you feel about the novel's gestalt? And if so, can you pinpoint what has shifted in your understanding?

Notes

1. "Kazuo Ishiguro, The Art of Fiction No. 196," *The Paris Review* 184, Spring 2008, https://www.theparisreview.org/interviews/5829/the-art-of-fiction-no-196-kazuo-ishiguro.

2. It's almost impossible to picture an entire novel in our heads because it's too big to think about as a single thing. Mozart was able to visualize an entire symphony in a moment, and his first-draft manuscripts look like final versions; he was transcribing what was in his head. I have never heard of a novelist with that skill. Perhaps the closest was Jack Kerouac's single-session drug-induced fever-dream of a first draft of *On the Road*, typed onto a continuous roll of paper so that he wouldn't have to stop typing to feed new sheets of paper into the typewriter.

3. Check out how Wren and Gaudí designed their cathedrals using upside-down models at https://en.wikipedia.org/wiki/Catenary and https://www.youtube.com/watch?v=iRv_syz2DAc.

4. A fascinating article highlighting what we English speakers thought we knew about nineteenth-century Russian authors: https://www.nytimes.com/2023/06/28/books/review/constance-garnett-russia-revolution-translation.html.

WHAT YOU STUDY

21
The Publishing Industry

This chapter examines publishing industry resources to learn more about the novels we read and study. We will draw from the life cycle of a novel beyond its content—the editing, publishing, marketing, and distribution—and apply what we learn to your study of the text between the covers.

Publishing is a business, and like any business, it generates a lot of numerical data: the titles currently in distribution and on backlist, print runs, unit prices, number of units sold, and total revenue. Publishers and agents subscribe to Circana BookScan[1] (for print books) and PubTrack Digital[2] (for e-books) to learn how their books are selling, while booksellers and libraries subscribe to Edelweiss+[3] to order the books they put on their shelves. Most of us can't afford subscriptions to any of those services, but luckily, you don't need them.

Successful novels

The question I get most often is: How do I pick the novels we study? My answer is simple: I'm most interested in studying books that are *successful*. And by success, I mean: bestsellers, award winners, book club selections, best-of listers, movie adaptations, and novels that have achieved word-of-mouth buzz.

Anyone can keep up with publishing industry buzz at *Literary Hub*, *Book Riot*, *Electric Literature*, *Book Forum*, the *Reader's Room*, and of course the usual suspects: the *New York Times Book Review*, *Kirkus Reviews*, the *New York Review of Books*, *Chicago Review of Books*, *London Review of Books*, and many more.[4] Buzz also includes my friends suggesting their favorite reads or asking if I've heard of a particular title.

I don't know the exact number of units sold for every novel I read, but I can look up the bestseller lists[5] of the *New York Times* and Amazon. The Goodreads most-popular-by-genre lists, although not perfect,[6] are good enough. By monitoring buzz through popular book lists, I can get a pretty good idea of what's hot right now. Because I'm a nerd, I follow those lists regularly and can get a sense of a novel's longevity—its legs.

Another benefit of following literary influencers is that I am able to stay slightly ahead of the awards committees. It's a rare year I haven't already read one or two selections when the National Book Award or the Booker Prize longlists[7] are announced.

Success for me also means discovering new voices, unique ways of telling a story, and a new perspective from a previously underrepresented group. I'm proud that over 85 percent of the novels we have surveyed in our *Writers Who Read* group so far were written by women, authors of color, and members of the LGBTQ+ community—none of whom would have had an easy path to publication a generation ago.

Industry data

Apart from raw financial numbers, which we can't do much with anyway, a wealth of information is generated for each novel in today's marketplace by authors, publishers, and distributors. Let's see how much we can uncover by working our way backward through the publication process:

- **Distribution:** Discovering your next great read by using alternative search tools
- **Marketing:** Learning about what's inside from book covers, author interviews, book clubs, and prizes
- **Publishing:** A wealth of magical metadata also gives insight into themes and topics covered
- **Editing:** Identifying substantive editors who make novels sing and understanding their contributions

Distribution

When COVID-19 disrupted our world, many restaurants abandoned paper menus in favor of QR codes that open the menus on our phones. This boggles my mind for so many reasons—that everyone now carries a handheld computer for one—but let's focus on the impact QR codes and online menus have on everyone along that information-distribution chain.

For starters, servers are no longer required to memorize a long list of specials or drinks—it's all on the phone. Secondly, because these menus are now all available online, I can preselect what I want *before* I go to the restaurant, or I may choose a different restaurant if their menu is not to my liking, or I may decide to have the food delivered to me instead of going out. The end result is similar to pre-COVID only in that some restaurant will get my money and I will eat a meal, but my dining experience has been radically changed because of this new distribution of information.

So too has our consumption of novels been completely upended by the arrival of e-books and audiobooks, the rise of independent publishers, and the new ways available for us to discover that next novel to read.

Gone are the days of print media's hegemony, when I had to wait outside a bookstore until midnight if I wanted to be the first to read the latest *Harry Potter*. Now I can click a couple of links on my device and start reading, at any time once the book is released.

Any story ever transcribed or recorded can find its way onto my tablet within seconds of me wanting it, which is both exhilarating and trivializing. The instant availability of novels has greatly streamlined the experience of discovering a new novel, but by making something too easy to obtain, that same distribution chain serves to devalue its own product.

We no longer need to visit a bookstore or library to get a novel, just as we don't need to hang out at the record store to find the newest music releases. And yet, paradoxically, most of us are still locked into the same distribution channels that have existed since the printing press.

Why haven't we broken free of this system yet?

Follow the money

As with so many other aspects of our modern lives, understanding how capital is distributed is key to understanding how novels get into our hands. Capital is more than money. John Thompson in his 2012 book, *Merchants of Culture*,[8] listed the five key resources of publishing firms, which apply equally to any digital distribution system today:

- **Economic capital:** the money that flows through the system (thanks to capitalism)
- **Human capital:** from press operators to agents, booksellers, and librarians
- **Social capital:** networks and influence
- **Intellectual capital:** the published content
- **Symbolic capital:** brand value, cultural value

Even with the rise of independent publishers and self-publishing, all five of these key resources retain their primacy. And, as in every age, human and intellectual capital do not have the same leverage as economic, social, and symbolic capital. Marshall McLuhan famously proclaimed that "the medium *is* the message,"[9] meaning the way a story is delivered can be as relevant or more so than the story distributed in that medium.

While the media has evolved dramatically, the one thing that has remained constant throughout the ages is the supremacy of distribution channels over content. Without an audience to read or hear them, even the greatest stories die a lonely death.

Today, the distribution channel still determines the ultimate reach of a novel. How can you read a book if you can't find it—either online, at your local bookstore, or at your library? These days, you can't depend on buying chapbooks off some random guy on a street corner.

Stocking shelves

I spent the better part of a decade traveling all over the world for work, and for a time I enjoyed taking photos of airport bookstore displays. I was interested in the ratio of local to international titles, and curious about which American novels had taken hold abroad.

Bookstore managers and librarians try to be as proactive as possible when they order books to stock their shelves, so they must place their orders well in advance of actual demand. Where do they go to find their next purchases if not their usual distribution channels? It's convenient and efficient to stick with the major publishers and their offerings. Unfortunately, it also serves to perpetuate the existing channels, making it close to impossible for some independent authors to get their books shelved.

Recommendation engines that generate the ads you see online work in a similar way. Based on your shopping and your reading habits, novels are recommended to you that originate from the usual distribution channels. Because they are based on your previous picks, this works similarly to the social media echo chamber that is Facebook, Twitter, Instagram, and TikTok. On those platforms your options appear to be narrowing, not broadening. They only care about optimizing your eyeballs to make money.

Alternatives

If you can't beat the distribution system, why not learn how to game it? Four of the online tools librarians and researchers use to find books for themselves are not influenced by advertising algorithms:

- **NoveList:** Booksellers use the NoveList[10] database of book recommendations to find titles with similar themes, styles, and characters. You can, too!
- **WorldCat:** Anyone with a library card can search WorldCat,[11] a large network of library content and services, to locate books and check availability at nearby libraries.
- **BookFinder:** The search engine BookFinder[12] taps into the inventories of over 100,000 booksellers worldwide, allowing booksellers to find out-of-print books, first editions, and cheap textbooks.
- **Library of Congress catalog:** As of this printing, the Library of Congress's digital collection[13] of books provides access to millions of items, including books, serials, manuscripts, maps, music, recordings, images, and electronic resources.

EXERCISE 1

How do you choose what novels you read? Friends? Reviews? Where do you buy the novels you read? Local bookstore? Online? Your assignment is to mix it up. If you read *New York Times* book reviews for inspiration, check out *Kirkus Reviews,* your local newspaper, or Goodreads.com. If you purchase books online, try a different e-tailer, or pop out to visit your local new or used bookstore in person.

Or try one of the book search engines recommended above and discover something new.

Marketing

Marketing gives us our first glimpse of a novel. We gaze upon the marketing department's cover art and read the novel's title, which may have also been created by the marketing department.

And where did we first see this novel's title and maybe its cover? Whether it was in a book review, an ad, a mention in a blog, tweet, video, or article, or it was a finalist for a prize, these impressions are all part of the same marketing engine.

Marketing is both the incessant nagging that puts an author's story in front of us and the sugarcoating that gets us to swallow it.

31 Flavors

But we all have different tastes, don't we?

In America one of the rituals of attaining majority is ordering your first (legal) cocktail. It's usually a painful process to discover which of the five alcohol types you prefer (or that your body can tolerate): whiskey, rum, gin, tequila, or vodka. And then, after a few false starts, you land on a flavor profile, and off you go for the rest of your life, ordering up your favorite cocktail as confidently as James Bond. The conceit of Starbucks is that it allows coffee drinkers the same level of refinement and snobbery.

What if we don't want to drink alcohol, or caffeine, or eat ice cream? We drink mocktails, or decaf, or eat frozen yogurt. It only takes a few moments to realize that the cocktail-mocktail, coffee-decaf, ice cream–yogurt pairs aren't really choices at all—they're essentially the same things, slightly repackaged.

Don't underestimate the role that marketing has played in your choice of beverages or the novels you read. We make our selections from the limited number of options available to us, whether we realize it or not. Marketers know that, and by limiting our choices, they manipulate our tastes.

614 Genres

In 2025, the Book Industry Study Group listed 351 adult fiction[14] genres (and subgenres) and an additional 263 young adult fiction[15] genres. Called *BISAC* (Book Industry Standards and Communications) *codes* or *BISAC subject headings*, these codes help a bookseller know where to shelve a book, and they are included in the data transmitted from the publisher to the retailer with the rest of a novel's *metadata*, which we'll examine in more depth in the "Publishing" section below. Genre and subject also intermingle in the Library of Congress catalog's *LCGFT* (Library of Congress Genre/Form Terms) entries, which are similar to the BISAC subject headings.[16]

Amazon categorizes the books it sells into over 16,000 genres (I don't know how many of those are fiction) that map roughly, but not exactly, onto the BISAC codes that the publisher provides. You can easily see a novel's sales ranking among a number of categories (Amazon lists only three on their public site) to get a sense of its genres. Amazon's algorithm sometimes categorizes a novel into some wildly incorrect genre that has little or nothing to do with either its content or themes, so take their genre information with a grain of salt.

As you can tell by now, the idea of genre in publishing, distribution, and retail equals a categorization to make a book easier to locate, order, stock, and shelve. We can also put this information to our advantage as we analyze the novels we read. For more on genres and categories, please take a look at chapter 3, "Choosing What to Read."

Yes, you *can* judge a book by its cover

I remember the initial explosion of interest in the *Harry Potter* series in the UK. So many adults were reading this YA fiction that Bloomsbury printed editions with adult-themed noir covers so that commuters wouldn't be embarrassed to read them on the Tube.

Novel cover art does more than target and attract audiences. Well-crafted examples also hint at what awaits readers inside. Without showing you illustrations, I'll bet you can recall covers from various genres: romance, fantasy, literary fiction, YA, thriller, etc.

But covers contain more than just depictions of dragons, houses, or faceless women.[17] They feature blurbs (a short review from a noted author), an indication of bestseller status, and the emblem of a prestigious award or book club associated with the novel or its author. When the author's name appears in larger type than the title, or above the title instead of below it, this indicates the author's draw in the literary marketplace.

The best covers capture not only the major themes of their novel, but also the tone and spirit of the writing. Multiple portals of diminishing light tempt us into Jessamine Chan's dark 2022 novel, *The School for Good Mothers*. Eight-bit graphics surround the title of Gabrielle Zevin's 2022 novel about game designers, *Tomorrow, and Tomorrow, and Tomorrow*. Charles Yu's 2020 novel on race relations, *Interior Chinatown*, lightheartedly resembles a Chinese takeout menu.

Cover art warrants as much study as a painting at a museum. Take note of the color palette: Is it subdued, garish, neon, earthy, plastic? What are the predominant shapes you notice, and does the art direct your eyes to one place or another? What is being depicted—is it found in the natural world, or is it artificial, or geometric? And is the style modern, retro, cartoonish, abstract?

What about the font? Is it bold and large, or does it have curlicues or serifs? And which is more prominent: the title or the author's name? Like any movie poster, the size and placement of a name matters greatly.

EXERCISE 2

What genres do you avoid? Take a stroll through your local bookstore or a virtual stroll through any bookseller's website and find a dozen novels in those genres. Then using only the covers—don't peek inside just yet—try to predict as many details as you can about the story inside. Based on the cover alone, evaluate whether or not you'd want to read that book.

When you look up some reviews of those novels, were your assessments correct? When you consult the Amazon category tags, do their designations surprise you?

Do any of these novels interest you now? I'd be surprised if you weren't tempted to read at least one of them. Want to know why? Because their covers caught your eye in the first place.

Marketers are sneaky that way.

Publishing

The products created by a publisher include more than the book: There is also the *metadata*. The information communicated electronically to libraries, distributors and retailers contains everything the publisher wants anyone to know about the book, from the title, author, cover images, size, weight, and price of a book, to its availability, promotional events, blurbs, reviews, extracts, and prizes won, to territorial rights[18] and links to websites.

There's an awful lot of information in the metadata to interest writers who read.

Metadata

ONIX (ONline Information EXchange) is the international standard for representing and communicating book industry product information in electronic form. ONIX 3.1.2 (the most recent version at the time of this writing) allows a publisher to describe a novel with hundreds of fields.

Of primary interest to us are the book content descriptions, which can get quite detailed, including:

- Summary
- Subjects (BISAC codes and plain-English descriptors)
- Themes
- Notes
- Table of contents
- Excerpts, which could be an entire chapter
- Keywords
- Relationships between titles: comparable titles in the genre (also called "comps"), the author's other books
- Citations: professional reviews and endorsements

The easiest and most accessible way to access a subset of a novel's metadata is to navigate to Amazon's landing page for that novel. The different pages for hardcover, Kindle, and audiobook yield slightly different data, as their ISBN numbers are different and their metadata is also slightly different.

But Amazon isn't the only provider of metadata. Every user of metadata displays the hundreds of possible fields in slightly different ways.[19] You can observe this by comparing the websites of Google Books, Barnes & Noble, Powell's Books, eBay, Better World Books, BooksRun, CampusBooks, Bowker, Ingram, and Open Library.

I like to use my free WorldCat[20] subscription, which links me to libraries around the world, to get a slightly richer set of data than I can find at Amazon. I used it to study the metadata for 2024 National Book Award winner *James* by Percival Everett.[21] Its subject list includes: Huckleberry Finn (fictitious character), male friendship, fugitive slaves, Mississippi River, action & adventure, humorous fiction, and more, in case you didn't know what the book was about. In other words, this data provides a plethora of thematic information about any book you're investigating.[22]

ISBNdb[23] offers an ISBN search engine and my search there for *James* yielded a slightly different list of subjects, which included Historical, Satire, Literary, and this curiosity: English & College Success → English → Fiction. I suppose *James* has already been targeted for scholarly study. It's a natural fit.

I also visited the *James by Percival Everett* page on its publisher's website, Penguin Random House,[24] and there I found a reading guide, with a four-paragraph introduction and fifteen questions and discussion topics.

Converging on a topic

Every year, new genres and subgenres are created as a result of market research. (More dragons! Fewer grumpy old men!) Every year, new BISAC genres are proposed, and many are adopted by the industry.

At a traditional publishing house, the editorial department consults their financial department and various cultural soothsayers, and from their inputs they compile a wish list of what they believe will sell two years from now. Sometimes they tell agents exactly what they're looking for. Have you ever wondered why sometimes you'll see a handful of books published at the same time on the exact same topic? That's why.

And we know that publishers bring to contract only those manuscripts that they believe are topical and interesting enough that readers will multiply their investment. Their output represents the huge amount of time and effort they have spent trying to understand what people were interested in reading eighteen to twenty-four months ago, when they first acquired those properties.

Self-publishing is able to respond to the latest trends faster than traditional publishers. When a genre like romantasy or cozy fantasy blows up, many authors can jump on the bandwagon quickly because they're able to write and publish a story in a matter of weeks or months rather than years.

For readers, this means that the books hitting shelves—whether traditionally published or self-published—are often a direct reflection of shifting cultural tastes and market demand, offering a snapshot of what stories people craved months or even years ago, and revealing how deeply reader interest drives the kinds of stories that get told.

EXERCISE 3

If you don't already have a library card, get one. In addition to being able to borrow books,[25] movies,[26] (and sometimes waffle irons and guitars[27]), you also get access to WorldCat[28] and other library-centric metadata resources. Using WorldCat, or the Library of Congress database, or the publisher's novel landing page, research a novel you're interested in. See how much metadata you can glean from those sites and from commercial retailers like Amazon.

Do these resources give you a better sense of how the publisher has positioned the novel? Does learning more about this make you more or less likely to read this novel?

Editing

I'm always looking for the best books to read, both for myself and for the literary analysis group I lead. While I value the opinions of individuals and organizations I respect, I don't always trust their taste. As a result, I end up reading every single novel *before* it goes on the *Writers Who Read* study list. I've encountered a number of duds, even from the most highly regarded best-of lists. Amazing, right?

I usually don't find fault with a novel's editing and proofreading, which represent the lowest bar to clear in today's published works. Misspelled words and bad grammar are easy to discover and to fix. Mistakes are still made, but they don't generally bother me. Words that are spelled correctly and the names of people, places, and things that are consistent are great, don't get me wrong, but they themselves don't ensure a well-crafted story.

The problems, even in some highly regarded novels, are located deeper within the text; they include issues with thematic organization, presentation, and clarity, and the organization of chapters, sections, and paragraphs to form a coherent whole. These flaws can result in a tone that's too preachy, weak characterizations, an ending that feels tacked on, or stilted writing that does more telling than showing. None of these issues could have been corrected by proofreaders; they're all structural flaws created during the novel's development that should have been fixed further upstream in the editing process.

Quality

Does a novel's availability or popularity correspond to its quality? Of course not. I give you *Fifty Shades of Grey*.[29] It has ever been thus.

When the *National Book Awards* debuted in 1950, the fiction prize went to Nelson Algren's *The Man with the Golden Arm*, which was the favorite in that genre. But was it well written? That didn't seem to matter much to the nominating committee. The *New York Times* that year described *Golden Arm* as being "obtrusively poetical… [with] the use of periods where commas are normally called for,"[30] and "hard to read,"[31] and reported, "One of the judges, peppery, Irish-born Mary Colum, commented, 'Half of the books suggested for the prize should never have been published.'"[32]

The truth is that the publishing industry is concerned less about publishing quality novels, and more concerned with publishing novels that will sell. And what sells is the illusion of the new, polished to a high gloss, masquerading as quality. Does this surprise you?

Any novel published by one of the major publishing houses will have superior cover art and manuscripts that have benefited from in-house editing services. The major houses also want to cover their asses and will check for factual accuracy, hire sensitivity readers, and stamp out libelous content. They don't want to be ridiculed, canceled, or (most importantly) sued.

But poor writing exists everywhere, and not even the best editor can save subpar execution.

The other huge obstacle to major houses publishing quality writing was the fact that for many decades they were all run by white males who favored White male writers. Women, people of color, and minority groups were almost never represented. It's for this reason I rejoice not only in the recent elevation of non-White non-male executives to publishing leadership positions, but also to the rise of the alternative publishers—the indie presses and do-it-yourselfers—who contribute to a much richer variety of voices.

We've been missing out on some of the best writing for far too long.

Acknowledgments

A good editor is worth their weight in gold. Short of contacting the publisher to get an editor's name, I often hit pay dirt in the acknowledgments section of a novel I admire. Authors reward the people who have contributed substantially to the creation of their passion project.

In addition to the names of the various editors, publicists, and their agent, you can also get a sense of the author's process. They may credit their mentors, or beta readers (I always count these), or reading groups, or even other authors who have influenced and befriended them.

In years past, this collection of authors would have been called a "school." In some future decade, a literary historian may group them together and label them as exactly that.

EXERCISE 4

Find a novel you admire and look at the acknowledgments section. If no editor is listed, then go to the publisher's website and see who they list on staff, or go to the author's website and poke around. You can always try to contact the author or their publisher directly to ask them for a list of editors, but don't expect a quick answer.

Notes

1. BookScan is a data provider for the book publishing industry that compiles point-of-sale data for book sales, owned by Circana in the United States and NIQ in the United Kingdom, Ireland, Australia, New Zealand, India, South Africa, Italy, Spain, Brazil, Mexico, and Poland.

2. https://www.ibpa-online.org/page/circanapubtrack

3. https://www.edelweissplus.com/

4. Every organization listed here has an RSS news feed, which I monitor frequently. I currently use the Feedbro RSS browser plugin to monitor all of my news feeds on one page. And yes, I know about #BookTok.

5. Constance Grady, "The convoluted world of best-seller lists, explained," *Vox*, September 13, 2017, https://www.vox.com/culture/2017/9/13/16257084/bestseller-lists-explained

6. Emily Temple, "8 Notable Attempts to Hack the *New York Times* Bestseller List," *Literary Hub*, September 26, 2017, https://lithub.com/8-notable-attempts-to-hack-the-new-york-times-bestseller-list/.

7. Nobel and Pulitzer prizes are trickier to predict. The closest I came was in early 2019, when I told anyone who would listen that Tommy Orange's *There There* would win the 2019 Pulitzer Prize for Fiction. It was a runner-up.

8. John B. Thompson, *Merchants of Culture: The Publishing Business in the Twenty-First Century*, second ed. (Plume, New York, 2012).

9. Marshall McLuhan, *Understanding Media: The Extensions of Man* (McGraw-Hill, New York, 1964).

10. https://www.ebsco.com/novelist/find-my-organization

11. https://search.worldcat.org/

12. https://www.bookfinder.com/

13. https://catalog.loc.gov/vwebv/searchBrowse

14. https://www.bisg.org/fiction

15. https://www.bisg.org/young-adult-fiction

16. I don't know why the Library of Congress has its own set of non-industry codes.

17. "Faceless woman" was a common trope on literary fiction covers in the early 2020s.

18. A country's rights are of interest to publishers who want to translate a novel to sell it in that country.

19. A great overview of book metadata and where to view it: https://isbndb.com/blog/book-metadata/

20. https://search.worldcat.org/topics/welcome

21. https://search.worldcat.org/title/1385322570

22. The Library of Congress catalog also has its own data for *James*: https://catalog.loc.gov/vwebv/holdingsInfo?bibId=23022867; you can find three LCGFT (Library of Congress Genre/Form Terms) entries: Action and adventure fiction, Humorous fiction, and Novels.

23. https://isbndb.com/

24. https://www.penguinrandomhouse.com/books/738749/james-by-percival-everett/9780385550369/readers-guide/

25. https://libbyapp.com

26. https://www.kanopy.com

27. https://www.libbylife.com/2024-07-25-75-surprising-things-you-can-borrow-from-the-library

28. https://search.worldcat.org/topics/welcome

29. Some of the worst writing I've read, and also one of the most massive bestsellers ever. Its sixty million copies sold are more than any individual volume of the *Harry Potter* series.

30. https://timesmachine.nytimes.com/timesmachine/1949/09/11/96471434.html?pageNumber=109

31. https://timesmachine.nytimes.com/timesmachine/1950/03/17/87154557.html?pageNumber=21

32. https://timesmachine.nytimes.com/timesmachine/1950/03/26/90485083.html?pageNumber=204

22
Other Narrative Forms

Can we study other narrative forms that aren't novels to help us to write novels? Absolutely, yes! But before we do that, we should be aware of how these other forms are similar to novels and how they are different from novels—how their components overlay or map to the novelistic form, or how they don't. We don't want to waste any time looking for novelistic elements that aren't there.

So let's first agree on what a novel is.[1] When does a novel become a novella or a short story? Or a memoir? Or nonfiction? Or something else entirely? Here's my best definition of the novel, created by highlighting six key characteristics:

1. **Fictional narrative**—explores characters, plot, and themes through prose.
2. Involves human experiences, relationships, and societal issues that affect a **protagonist**.
3. Uses **literary techniques** like character development, symbolism, and immersive settings.
4. **Long-form**—typically has 40,000 to 100,000 words.[2]
5. Contains the **inciting-midpoint-climax** pivot points.
6. The **unspoken contract** between author and reader is that the ending will contain a resolution or answer to the themes and conflicts explored within.

Although this definition is somewhat prescriptive, I believe it works well enough to define novels written today in America, two hundred years ago in Europe, and five hundred years ago in East Asia. For each of the six characteristics, I'll use the key phrase I've highlighted in bold as its title below when we explore how other narrative forms differ from the novel.

Pushing Boundaries

Novels are defined by the age that creates them. Because today's culture is evolving, so too are contemporary novels. And because novels already cover a big tent of narrative forms, the issues of today sometimes push authors into uncharted territories, pushing at the boundaries of one or more of the six key characteristics listed above. The following sections discuss recent examples.

Long-form

Novelist and poet Jenny Offill has chosen a minimalist approach to her novel writing, in which each word is carefully chosen and each sentence has a purpose. Her writing is lean and direct, and this can make her work feel very intense, as every sentence is laden with meaning, with no room for unnecessary embellishment. When writing, Offill says she uses a collage technique, printing out disparate passages—quotes, excerpts, musings, pieces of advice, and even trivia—then laying them all out on the floor or sticking them onto poster boards—then taking months, even years, to assemble them into a novel. Her 2020 novel *Weather* is constructed from these bits of information: facts, anecdotes, snippets of conversation, and musings on a wide range of topics like environmental collapse, personal trauma, and the political landscape. This technique makes her writing feel alive and constantly in flux, mirroring the disorientation many of us feel in our contemporary world. *Weather* length is about 31,000 words, but it feels like a complete novel distilled into novella length, providing a full novelistic experience.

Compare *Weather* with short-story master George Saunders's 2017 novel, *Lincoln in the Bardo*. Most of the novel takes place over the course of a single evening, following Abraham Lincoln into a graveyard crypt, where he holds his dead son, Willie. Although *Bardo has* approximately 20,000 more words than *Weather,* it does not feel as long, due to its single narrative arc.[3]

Protagonist

Many novelists have experimented with protagonists who are *not* an *individual human* beings, such as a non-human protagonist, or multiple protagonists, or the absence of a protagonist.

Klara, the protagonist of Kazuo Ishiguro's *Klara and the Sun*, is an AI robot, while the narrator of *The Book Thief* by Markus Zusak is Death. Jeffrey Eugenides's *The Virgin Suicides* is narrated in the rare first-person plural from the POV of an anonymous group of teenage boys who struggle to find an explanation for the Lisbons' deaths.

Jennifer Egan, in her 2022 novel *The Candy House*, employs multiple narrators or a group consciousness, shifting the focus from an individual to shared experiences. It's impossible to identify a single protagonist because of the sheer number of characters and story threads. Egan did this to give the reader the sensation of the social consciousness multiverse that acts on our brains in the twenty-first century.

Another way to mess with the novelistic concept of having an individual human being at its center is to omit the protagonist altogether. Rachel Cusk accomplishes this in her *Outline* trilogy of novels, in which the reader is given almost no physical information about the protagonist, nor is allowed access to her thoughts. All we know about her is what others tell her about themselves. The protagonist is an empty shell, an outline around which others project themselves onto her.

Inciting-midpoint-climax

Every novel has a beginning, a middle, and an end (inciting incident, midpoint pivot, and climax), but there's nothing preventing a novelist from having more than one of each. Two recent novels that play with pivot points both use a three-part form: 1) the story; 2) the story restated; 3) a coda.

The A-story in Lisa Halliday's 2018 novel *Asymmetry* has an inciting incident, a midpoint pivot, and a climax, which only takes us to about the midpoint of the novel. The B-story also has an inciting incident, a midpoint pivot, and a climax. At first glance, these two stories have nothing to do with each other, but the C-story—the coda—reveals everything and ties them together.

The A-story in Susan Choi's 2019 novel *Trust Exercise* also has an inciting incident, a midpoint pivot, and a climax. Unlike in *Asymmetry*, the B-story is clearly related to the A-story, but it's told from a different point of view, and in the tradition of the film *Rashomon*,[4] gives us an alternative narrative. The C-story, from yet another point of view, clears up the confusion. As with *Asymmetry*, we are given more than one archplot in a single novel.

Fictional narrative

> The fiction-versus-nonfiction question doesn't really have an answer anyway, for the good reason that the novel has always, since its inception, been a hybrid, impure form, stranded (as the most cursory glance at Defoe, Behn or Sterne, never mind Acker, Burroughs or Heti, will demonstrate) between the various stools of epic poetry, the essay, theological-cum-personal confession

and so on. It is, to borrow Gödel's term, incomplete, right down to its (missing) core.
    —*Tom McCarthy*[5]

And then there's the biggest bugaboo of all: mixing fact with fiction. While this third-rail topic is usually focused on invented elements in writing that purports to be nonfiction,[6] it also creates controversy for novels that contain real-life nonfiction characters.

McCarthy's essay is referring to the novels of Benjamin Labatut, who has fictionalized the lives of real-life scientists, including Werner Heisenberg, Alexander Grothendieck, and John von Neumann. Labatut's 2020 novel *When We Cease to Understand the World* uses Heisenberg and Grothendieck as fictionalized characters in his narrative, inventing character traits and inner monologues for them that could not possibly be based in fact. As readers of fiction, we may rebel when we find real people masquerading as characters, and yet we also rebel when these same characters deviate from their real-life selves.

Another example of real people's stories intruding into a fictional narrative is Colum McCann's 2020 novel *Apeirogon*. McCann (the author) interacts with the two main characters, a Palestinian, Bassam, and an Israeli, Rami, both fathers of children who have been killed as a result of the Palestinian-Israeli conflict. All three are real human beings, and the story McCann presents is also real. On my first reading, I wondered how could this be a novel and not a memoir?

On my second reading, I took note of the passages that could have been invented—thoughts, observations, references to poems and other external things— and I discovered that only about 13 percent was the Rami/Bassam narrative; the remaining 87 percent was invented. This absolutely satisfies the fictional narrative requirement of a novel.

EXERCISE 1

Can you think of a novel you've read that has pushed the boundaries of what a novel is? If it hasn't pushed the boundaries of any of the six key elements listed above, in what other way did it seem un-novelistic? Have you read any autofiction?[7] Do you think that an author fictionalizing their own life into novel form counts as a true novel?

Other narrative forms

The remainder of this chapter investigates the characteristics of other narrative forms and catalogs how they differ from novels in the six key characteristics of a novel as listed above. There is much to learn from other narrative forms that we can apply to our novel writing, but at the same time, it is important to remember what can transfer from one form to another and what cannot.

These narrative forms fall into two broad categories: fiction and nonfiction:

Fictional narratives

- **Drama:** Stage plays, radio plays, films, and graphic novels
- **Episodic drama:** Television serials, miniseries, comic books
- **Short stories and novellas**: A concise narrative, typically under 20,000 words, focused on a single incident or character
- **Narrative poetry and novels in verse**: Stories told through verse, using meter, rhyme, and symbolism
- **Interactive narratives and video games**: Interactive narratives in which players' choices influence plot, character development, and world-building

Nonfictional narratives

- **Memoir and biography:** Memoirs, autobiographies, letters, diaries, and essays expressed in first person, and biographies and profiles told in third person; focused on key events or moments that shaped their subject's identity
- **Historical narrative:** Incorporates elements of New Journalism to make real people and events seem more novelistic

Each fictional and nonfictional narrative form listed above is discussed in its own section, below. At the end of each section, you'll find a chart comparing that narrative form to the novel across six categories:

- Fictional narrative
- Protagonist
- Literary techniques
- Long-form
- Inciting-midpoint-climax
- Unspoken contract

If a category aligns with the novel form, the cell in the chart contains light gray. If it differs, the chart explains the difference between them.

Drama

This category encompasses all dramatic forms acted on the stage, screen, or as an audio presentation. I included graphic novels here because they descended from storyboards, which are a series of cartoons, each one representing a single camera shot, an essential tool for filmmakers.

Acts and scenes

Dramas follow the traditional three-act form of novels: inciting incident, midpoint pivot, climax. While the three-act structure (or eleven-point archplot) is almost always used in screenplays and radio plays,[8] most modern stage plays follow a two-act structure with a single audience intermission. Despite the differences between two-part and three-part construction, this aligns perfectly with novel structure, as both forms have an inciting incident, a midpoint pivot—which in a stage play happens right before the intermission—and a climax. Novels are also often split into thirds, halves, or quarters, so they are also consistent with dramas in this way.

Another similarity between dramas and novels is in scene structure. The two types of scenes resemble each other so closely that I have frequently used movie scenes as examples throughout this book. Many of today's novelists have clearly been influenced by the dramas they have witnessed when they wrote their novel's scenes. The imaginary camera of POV, with its wide shots, pans, and close-ups, is evident in today's novels, and readers have benefited greatly from this visual shorthand.

Thoughts and senses

The presentation of a drama's narrative is where it differs most starkly from the novel. Movies and graphic novels are primarily visual, while stage plays and radio plays are primarily auditory. All of these forms favor one sense over another, which makes them less immersive than written novels, which require a reader's inner eye, inner voice, and memories of touch, smell, and taste to make them come alive.

Where the novel shines over any form of drama is in its ability to get inside the head of the protagonist, or in the head of any other character the author chooses. Novels also have a narrative voice, which has no direct parallel in visual media. The closest thing is the director's and editor's point of view, characterized by camera angles and shot selections. This is similar to a novel's *voice*, but it still lacks a novel's unique interiority. The characters in graphic novels can share their thoughts via thought bubbles, just as stage and screen actors can break the fourth wall to share an aside with the audience, but neither of these techniques gets in the head of a protagonist quite the way a novelist can.

Compression

Dramas are also highly compressed storytelling vehicles, completing their narratives within two to three hours. Every scene, gesture, and action is essential to the story. Quick visual edits allow for the transmission of a large amount of information in a short period of time; something that could take a chapter or two in a novel can be communicated within a few minutes.

How drama differs from the novel

Fictional narrative	Similar to novels
Protagonist	Limited interiority, primarily experienced by external actions and words
Literary techniques	Primarily visual or auditory, not engaging senses of touch, smell, taste
Long-form	Compressed to two to three hours (from eight to twenty-four hours for reading a novel)
Inciting-midpoint-climax	Similar to novels
Unspoken contract	Similar to novels

EXERCISE 2

Rewrite: Pick a movie and stream it. Pause after the opening scene and imagine how you would write it as a chapter. Pause at any moment during the movie to ask questions about the scene you've just finished viewing—why was it there? About the scene you're analyzing, ask what's going to happen, and why. Again, imagine how you would write it.

For a stage play, see if you can find the script. Remembering that a script is only dialogue and stage directions, think about how you would write the opening scene to portray what the set only hints at, to introduce all the characters, and to describe how they feel about what's happening. You may need a lot of words to do this.

Episodic Drama

Episodic drama differs from one-off drama primarily in characterization, form, and length. Similarities include the media (film, streaming services, broadcast television, and print, for comic books), a fictional narrative, and the primary focus on the visual (and auditory). The television series, thirteen to one-hundred-and-fifty episodes—one to fifteen seasons—of drama or comedy, differs from the multipart miniseries primarily in length (at four to ten episodes), but also in form and scope, and we will address their differences and similarities as they apply to our studies.

The closest parallel found in episodic television drama and comic books to novels is when a novel is part of a series, or is a sequel or a reimagining of a previously published work, reintroducing established characters, locations, and scenarios for new purposes.

It's the art of reusing previously established elements and deepening our understanding of characters, relationships, places, and things that makes this form unique and worth studying.

Archetypes

To convey a story in less than an hour, many shortcuts are taken to paint scenes, scenarios, and characters. Most characters' beliefs, attitudes, and quirks are painted in broad strokes, to make who they represent easily recognizable: the stoic cop, the concerned parent, the crazy ex. Characters in situation comedies—The Fonz, Urkel, Sheldon—are more caricature than character, resembling Theophrastian archetypes. See chapter 16, "Character Development," for more detail.

Character development is something fairly new to episodic drama. For most of the twentieth century, every situation comedy contained well-established characters that remained static for the duration of their existence. Mary Tyler Moore never got married; Archie Bunker remained a bigot; Seinfeld never grew up; Ross, Chandler, Joey, Phoebe, Rachel, and Monica lived in their New York City bubble.

But in the late 1990s, cracks emerged—Murphy Brown got pregnant and became a single mother; Ellen DeGeneres came out as gay—and their characters changed irrevocably.

The early twenty-first century is a golden age of the television serial for two reasons: 1) the rise of streaming services and the money available to make innovative programming; but much more importantly for our studies, 2) the restriction that characters remain static is *gone*.

The characters in today's serials are expected to evolve. That's *huge*. These developing and evolving characters bring situation comedies and police procedurals closer to the graphic novel and further away from the comic book.

Long form

TV serials and miniseries are both in it for the long run, but they differ in form. A situation comedy or a police procedural acts like a mini-novel: There is an inciting incident, followed by a few plot pivots, and then a climax and resolution conclude the episode. A miniseries needs to maintain a dramatic arc over the course of an entire season or series, so episodes may end not with a resolution but with a cliffhanger, much like the chapters of a novel.

While the single episode is a self-contained mini-drama, the six- to ten-episode miniseries actually resembles the amount of time it takes to read a novel (eight to twenty-four hours). The most significant difference in form between say, an episode of *Young Sheldon* and the entire span of *The Queen's Gambit* is the length of the narrative: twenty-two minutes versus seven hours. Both have clear protagonists, inciting incidents, B-stories, character development, pivots, and climaxes.

How episodic drama differs from the novel

Fictional narrative	Similar to novels
Protagonist	Features the same characters over episodes and seasons, constraining their growth; limited interiority, primarily experienced by external actions and words
Literary techniques	Primarily visual and auditory, not engaging senses of touch, smell, taste
Long-form	Situation comedies and police procedurals compressed to individual episodes an hour or less in length
Inciting-midpoint-climax	Similar to novels
Unspoken contract	All story threads are usually tied up at the end of TV serials, but in multipart dramas, including soap operas, multiple threads can be left dangling until the final episode

EXERCISE 3

Reread: Pick a situation comedy you're unfamiliar with, watch the first five minutes of any episode, and pause. Who are the main characters? How does each behave? What are the character's relationships with each other? What are their likes and dislikes?

If you can't answer all these questions, then the writers haven't done their job.

Rewrite: Go back and watch again, this time noticing how their characteristics are being portrayed. A word, a gesture, a look? Think about how you would write these introductions.

Short Stories and Novellas

Novellas and short stories are to novels as whiskey is to beer.[9] Both are enjoyable, but the former has a higher concentration of alcohol that is guaranteed to make you feel tipsy much more rapidly. Although these two forms of narrative are shorter than novels, they are condensed in different ways, so we'll need to study each in turn.

Novella

Merriam-Webster defines a *novella* as "a work of fiction intermediate in length and complexity between a short story and a novel." Wikipedia's *novella* entry[10] has a wonderful table of submission lengths for novella entries to various competitions: The lower range is between 15,000 and 20,000 words, and the upper range is from 20,000 to 40,000 words. The shorter *novelette* is deemed to be between 7,500 and 17,500 words. That's darned close to the *short story* range, which can be as high as 15,000 words but is typically between 1,000 and 4,000 words.

Okay, it's short. But what *is* a novella?

> [The novella] is one of the richest and most rewarding of literary forms…. [I]t allows for more extended development of theme and character than does the short story, without making the elaborate structural demands of the full-length book. Thus it provides an intense, detailed exploration of its subject, providing to some degree both the concentrated focus of the short story and the broad scope of the novel.
> —*Robert Silverberg*, Sailing to Byzantium[11]

A novella, therefore should contain everything a novel does. It's just much, much shorter, that's all.

Short story

The word count for a short story limits what it can accomplish. Of limited scope, a short story often has a twist or a moment of revelation, which equates vaguely to the midpoint pivot we expect to find in a novel. But given the low word count, short stories prioritize brevity over deep exploration, and they usually only have room for a single theme or central idea.

A short story can have a number of scenes, but formalistically it equates more to a single chapter of a novel than to anything else. A single theme, a twist or revelation, and we're out.

As a result, short story writers, like poets, pore over every word and must be concise in their scene setting, characterizations, and interactions. Every gesture and every word matters, so much more than in a novel. You'll never find a postcard[12] in a short story—there simply isn't room.

How short stories and novellas differ from the novel

Fictional narrative	Similar to novels
Protagonist	Similar to novels
Literary techniques	Similar to novels
Long-form	Novella is short form; short story is chapter form
Inciting-midpoint-climax	In a short story, the midpoint and climax may be combined, and the inciting incident subtle
Unspoken contract	Short stories typically pose a philosophical question, and may not give a definitive answer

EXERCISE 4

Reread: Read a short story and try to identify the inciting incident, the midpoint pivot, and the climax. What did you find? Were any of these missing? Think about the theme—was it clear, or nebulous? Why was this written as a short story and not a novel?

Narrative Poetry and Novels in Verse

Narrative poetry is poetry that tells a story, through the voice of one or more characters. Traditionally this form was reserved for classical stories, ballads, and epics, due to the elevating nature of verse on any subject. Fables, myths, and legends that have been passed down to us, often with moral lessons, also fit into this category. This form is rare to find today, though, so it's difficult to generalize about how it relates to the novel.

Poetry's superpower, present in all its forms, is carefully curated words and their unique placements in feet within meters—the rhythmic structure of lines—to create similes, metaphors, and unusual images undergirded with the propulsive power of rhythm. When we praise a novel for being poetic, what we are primarily referring to are: clever word choices, brevity, and passages with a discernible rhythm. We're not thinking about the bits of poetry that take multiple scans to parse, and months or even years to internalize fully.

Unfortunately, on this point poetry and prose are at odds: While poetry contains multitudes, prose needs to be quickly and easily comprehensible on the first pass. The poetic turn of phrase that we praise can be confusing in a novelistic narrative. In spite of that, some novelists have written entire novels in verse, most famously two from 2018: Elizabeth Acevedo's *The Poet X* and Robin Robertson's *The Long Take,* both of which received critical acclaim.[13]

Sometimes poets write novels, too. It must have been particularly challenging for Ocean Vuong to write *On Earth We're Briefly Gorgeous*, or for Patricia Lockwood to write *No One Is Talking About This*, which were both successful novels. Kaveh Akbar, in his 2024 novel, *Martyr!*, sidestepped this issue by making his main character a poet, and presenting the protagonist's poetry in separate sections, parallel to the main narrative.

Interactive Narratives and Video Games

Long before video games came Vladimir Nabokov's 1962 novel *Pale Fire,* the earliest example of a novel threaded through itself like the path of a doomscroller clicking on every hyperlink. Fourteen years later came the *Choose Your Own Adventure* series of children's books. Charles Dickens's final novel, *The Mystery of Edwin Drood*, was left unfinished at his death, with no notes, opening the door for many authors, including Dickens's own son, to try to complete it and solve the mystery. In 1985, Rupert Holmes adapted it for his musical theater work of the same name, writing eight different endings, one for each of the characters who could be Dick Datchery—and the ending that gets the most audience votes is the one performed.

Christmas melodramas and oral storytelling traditions are fluid and can change with each telling. They may include elements like audience participation, music, or other forms of performance to enhance the narrative.

> Gamers co-author the games they play by the choices they make and how they choose to solve problems, since what they do can affect the course and sometimes the outcome of the game.
> —*James Paul Gee*[14]

These attempts at interactive narrative look puny when compared with what any video game can do, however. The fact that two-thirds of Americans play them underlines the massively powerful appeal of being the protagonist in a fantastical adventure. This is literally the stuff dreams are made of.

Some video games have highly intricate, cinematic narratives (e.g., *The Last of Us*, *Red Dead Redemption 2*), while others have more emergent storytelling. Narratives are most developed in adventure games and least developed in first-person shooter games. Beyond those broad statements, however, video games are so varied that I don't want to make too many generalizations. Any game in which the player can die and be reborn again with a game restart more closely resembles episodic television than a novel. Adventure games that progress from level to level also resemble miniseries or entire seasons of television more than they do the relatively compact form of the novel, which only takes eight to twenty-four hours to consume.

Memoir, Autobiography, and Autofiction

Memoir

Although memoir and autobiography are considered separate genres, for the purposes of our study, let's consider their similarities. A memoir does not necessarily encompass the writer's entire life, but it can. Autobiographies typically follow a chronological order, while a memoir can begin anywhere and may not adhere to a linear timeline. Outside of those differences, the two forms overlap nicely.

Comparing memoir with autofiction is a useful exercise, as the two narrative forms are polar opposites in some aspects. Both autofiction and memoir use similar storytelling techniques but to different ends. Although both forms feature the author as the main character and are written in first-person POV, both contain character development, and are concerned with pacing and the layering of themes:

- Autofiction presents daily minutiae; memoir encompasses a lifetime.
- Autofiction may not lead to specific moral or philosophical conclusions; memoir often recounts the hero's or heroine's journey.
- Autofiction can be vague and does not pretend to be literal; memoir is packed with precise details and can be fact-checked.

I'll admit that I'm a cynic: I don't believe in a fully nonfictional memoir. Writing about oneself objectively is an impossible task, as even with the best note-taking we all have faulty memories and a very human need to turn unrelated events into a story. It's in our nature to make things up. We tell ourselves stories about ourselves to survive and to stay sane in this crazy, mixed-up world.

Reflections

Included here are diaries, essays, or collections of letters that offer reflections and intimate insights. Some of the most famous examples of this type are *The Diary of Anne Frank,* Joan Didion's essays in *Slouching Towards Bethlehem,* and Rainer Maria Rilke's *Letters to a Young Poet.* These are nonfiction narratives that blend personal history with broader societal or cultural themes and include reflections on personal growth, identity, and major life events.

What binds these forms together is their episodic nature, demarcated by a single day, a single letter, or a single topic. Each of these segments may resemble the shape of a scene or a chapter, but the collected whole often lacks a recognizable structure (such as the archplot of creative fiction).

Biography and profile

A biography is a detailed account of a person's life, typically including information about their experiences, achievements, and personal background, and offering insight into their character and their impact on the world. When a biography has been written by the subject (autobiography), the author often has an agenda—that is, a reason for repackaging their life in a way that addresses some perceived issue or deficit. When a biography is written by someone other than the subject, it hews to topics the author thinks will be of interest to the general public.

A profile is an article, usually published in a periodical, that features a day in the life of a famous person. Its form is somewhat similar to a single chapter taken from a biography. A profile is not intended to span a person's entire life, but it still must give the reader a clear picture of who the subject is.

A profile is to a biography as a short story is to a novel.

New York Times Magazine staff writer Taffy Brodesser-Akner is a master of the celebrity profile who has made the leap to writing successful novels.[15] One key difference between the two forms, which are both narratives, is in character creation.

> [H]er concern, when starting the novel, was that as all journalists know, life is much stranger than fiction. "The thing about people is that they're so bad at being consistent," [Brodesser-Akner]

says. "And that is the joy of writing about them. What if you can't make that up? That's the anxiety I had."[16]

Real people are full of amazing quirks and inconsistencies that make reading their biographies and profiles interesting and insightful. Fictional characters are not famous, of course, and do not exist outside of the novel. They therefore require some level of consistency for readers to recognize who they are and what drives them. This is the same conundrum all fiction writers face: how to make characters believable *and* compelling to observe closely.

How memoir and biography differ from the novel

Fictional narrative	Nonfiction
Protagonist	Similar to novels
Literary techniques	Similar to novels
Long-form	Episodic format of life events that often form a hero's journey
Inciting-midpoint-climax	Will always have an inciting incident; the midpoint pivot often involves the life event that is also the reason they are famous enough for you to be reading about them; the climax may be a moment of insight or the subject's greatest achievement
Unspoken contract	Intended to be revelatory, and therefore may be missing a novel's initial obfuscation

EXERCISE 5

Reread: Read any profile, essay, or a chapter of a memoir. Read it again, looking for an inciting incident, midpoint pivot, and moment of insight. Were any of these three elements missing? Think about the theme—its message. Why was this piece written in this form?

Rewrite: Would it be possible to rewrite it as a short story? Why or why not?

Historical Narrative

We all experienced, during our school days, the turgid prose of the history textbook. Names and dates, wars and alliances, facts upon facts until our heads spun from information overload. And then we pick up *The Power Broker* by Robert Caro, or *Seabiscuit* by Laura Hillenbrand, or *Assassination Vacation* by Sarah Vowell, and we wonder: Where did these writers come from?

In 1965 Random House published *In Cold Blood*[17] by Truman Capote, which the author referred to as a "nonfiction novel," blending techniques from fiction and journalism to tell the true story of a brutal murder in Kansas. This book is widely regarded as a landmark in the development of New Journalism, the American literary movement in the 1960s and '70s that pushed the boundaries of traditional journalism and nonfiction writing.

The genre combined journalistic research with the techniques of fiction writing in the reporting of stories about real-life events. The writers often credited with beginning the New Journalism movement include Capote, Hunter S. Thompson, Gay Talese, Joan Didion, Terry Southern, and Tom Wolfe, who coined the phrase.

The key novelistic elements of New Journalism are:

- **Emphasis on personal perspective:** Modern historical nonfiction often includes the author's perspective and voice, allowing readers to connect with the story on a more personal level.
- **Focus on character development:** Historical figures are portrayed with depth and complexity; their motivations, emotions, and personal struggles are explored within the larger historical context.
- **Scene-setting and vivid details:** Writers use descriptive language to immerse the reader in historical settings and events.
- **Accessibility for broader audiences:** By incorporating narrative elements, historical nonfiction has gained appeal to a readership beyond academic circles.

How historical narrative differs from the novel

Fictional narrative	Nonfiction
Protagonist	The author as narrator or a character within the narrative
Literary techniques	Similar to novels
Long-form	Similar to novels
Inciting-midpoint-climax	Similar to novels
Unspoken contract	Similar to novels

EXERCISE 6

Try reading a historical narrative by Robert Caro, Laura Hillenbrand, or Sarah Vowell. I can't recommend their books highly enough, and I think they represent the pinnacle of the form. Try also David McCullough, Jon Krakauer, and other best-selling authors writing about historical subjects that interest you.

Take note of the key elements of novels as you find them in these historical narratives—believe me, they will all be in there!

Notes

1. https://en.wikipedia.org/wiki/Novel
2. Plenty of novels exceed 100,000 words, but 40,000 is the absolute minimum, beneath which lies the novella and the short story. The average novel is somewhere around 80,000 words.
3. Most novellas have one main character and a handful of secondary characters, and explore a single, compelling central conflict without any subplots. Because of length constraints, most of the character development will be focused on the protagonist. For a discussion of the difference between the novella and the novel, see https://en.wikipedia.org/wiki/Novella.
4. https://en.wikipedia.org/wiki/Rashomon
5. Tom McCarthy, "The Miracle and Madness of Science That Changed The World," *New York Times Book Review*, September 29, 2023, https://www.nytimes.com/2023/09/29/books/review/benjamin-labatut-the-maniac.html.
6. Read about the *A Million Little Pieces* "memoir" debacle here: https://en.wikipedia.org/wiki/A_Million_Little_Pieces#Doubts_on_its_authenticity.
7. See examples at https://en.wikipedia.org/wiki/Autofiction.
8. Any radio plays that exist at all in the twenty-first century are aired primarily on non-commercial radio. The NPR clock requires a station break at the twenty- and forty-minute marks of every hour, making a three-act form almost a necessity. *This American Life* host Ira Glass announces the sections of his program as acts one, two, and three.
9. In the early stages of production, beer and whiskey follow the same process up to the creation of the wort. Distillation and aging transform the fermented liquid into whiskey, much as prose is distilled into poetry.
10. https://en.wikipedia.org/wiki/Novella
11. From the introduction to Silverberg's novella anthology, *Sailing to Byzantium*.
12. Donald Maass, "What Makes Fiction Literary: Scenes versus Postcards," Writer Unboxed website, June 1, 2016, https://writerunboxed.com/2016/06/01/what-makes-fiction-literary-scenes-versus-postcards/.
13. Note that, although written in verse, these novels contain the **Three keys** and adhere to everything else we know about novelistic form.
14. James Paul Gee, "10 Truths About Books and What They Have to Do with Video Games," *HuffPost*, May 10, 2011, https://www.huffpost.com/entry/ten-truths-about-books-an_b_859469.
15. Charles Duhigg, "How a First-Time Novelist Wrote a Bestseller in Six Months," *Slate.com*, July 3, 2020, https://slate.com/culture/2020/07/taffy-brodesser-akner-on-how-to-write-a-novel.html.
16. Emma Brockes, "Profiling the Profiler: An Interview with Taffy Brodesser-Akner," Fiction, *The Guardian*, June 18, 2019, https://www.theguardian.com/books/2019/jun/18/taffy-brodesser-akner-profile.
17. *In Cold Blood* failed to win the Pulitzer Prize, which greatly disappointed Capote. Fifteen years later, Norman Mailer, covering essentially the same territory with his *Executioner's*

Song, did win the prize. At 1,136 pages, almost 800 pages longer than Capote's taut account, *Executioner's Song* is proof that if you want to win a prize, you need to write a longer novel. See F.P. McGowan, "The rule of tome? Longer novels are more likely to win literary awards," *Journal of Cultural Economics* 48 (2024), 311–329. https://doi.org/10.1007/s10824-023-09488-5.

23
Academic Disciplines

Literary Forensics focuses on investigative techniques from a large variety of academic disciplines, including hermeneutics and literary theory, epistemological philosophy, social psychology, cultural anthropology, discourse and narrative analysis, pedagogy, dramaturgy, linguistics, semiotics, and close, distant, and critical reading. Some of these elements are presented overtly, while others have been woven throughout the text.

You do not need to go beyond this book to understand the principles of how to read like a writer. It's all here. This chapter catalogs the academic disciplines I've borrowed from, so if you're interested you can investigate further and return with even richer insights that you can apply to your reading and your writing.[1] The bibliography (Appendix C) lists some of the titles I have read to ground me in these topics and others.

Silos of knowledge

If *Literary Forensics* is such a great methodology, you may be thinking, then why haven't these disciplines been assembled and applied to literary studies before now? That's an excellent question, and one I asked myself often during my research.

For much of academia's history, disciplines were seen as self-contained domains with distinct methodologies, epistemologies, and vocabularies. Researchers stepping outside their field were sometimes perceived as "diluting" scientific or scholarly rigor.

University departments also control their own hiring and funding, basing tenure and promotion decisions on metrics specific to a discipline. "Publish or perish" remains the primary measure of an academician's output, and interdisciplinary research spanning different departments can be harder to evaluate, as it often falls between the expertise of reviewers in a single discipline. Questions about which department or discipline should own a project or manage its resources can also create administrative hurdles.

Today, thankfully, the walls between departments are starting to come down and cross-disciplinary work is becoming much more common, even expected, making it easier for their scholars to get funded, published, and promoted. But a lot of practical information about how to approach a novel is still cloistered within these silos of knowledge.

Holistic studies

> The hip bone's connected to the back bone,
> The back bone's connected to the neck bone,
> The neck bone's connected to the head bone,
> Now shake dem skeleton bones!
>   —*from* "Dem Bones"[2]

My wife, Deb, is a Gyrotonic instructor.[3] Gyrotonic is a holistic approach to body awareness that recognizes that everything is connected. While physical therapists may focus on a single limb or body part, Gyrotonic always focuses on the whole. Pain in one part of your body is likely a symptom of something going on in another part of your body. Give and take. Push and pull. Yin and yang.

More and more medical professionals are recognizing the value of holistic medicine. After all, we are not machines; we are living organisms with a complex array of strategies to adapt to our surroundings and compensate for our physical and mental ailments. In our bodies, everything relates to everything else.

This is true of the novels we read.

As New Criticism gave way to deconstructionism, academic literary theory expanded from the narrow critical study of a *few* canonical texts, broadening into a study of how society has shaped *every* text. Concurrently, the essential skill of critical reading was shunted off to its own special corner, focused more on following footnotes than on learning how to read current literature with a writer's eye. As the scholarship of one advanced, the other retreated.

When I started researching *Literary Forensics,* I was amazed to find this green field of study that *no one else seemed to have integrated*. I found a huge gap between literary studies and the skill of reading. While there exist various lagoons around the edges of this vast lake of discovery, no one had done more than dip a toe into the water.

You and I, dear reader, are swimming across its entire breadth.

I invite you to study chapter 20, "The Gestalt," in its entirety, and use its simple tools to uncover why an author wrote what they wrote. Take advantage of the entire WHAT YOU FEEL section that investigates your emotional reactions to a text to show you where to begin your studies. Use the WHAT YOU NOTICE section to focus on craft, but from the opposite end of the telescope from every other book about writing.

You hold in your hand a holistic approach to reading.

Fruitful disciplines

Turning back to the other academic fields I have used in this book, disciplines that were not necessarily intended for the purposes to which I have applied them, but have proven to be very useful nonetheless, include:

- **Hermeneutics and literary theory:** The basics of the reader's relationship to the text, and how to peel back the layers of meaning
- **Epistemology and social psychology:** Understanding the limits of our knowledge and how we interact with the world; how we influence others and how they influence us
- **Applied linguistics and semiotics:** Stylistics, translation, and the interpretation of symbols and signs
- **Discourse and narrative analysis:** Cultural anthropological methods of parsing spoken and written narratives for their underlying messages
- **Pedagogy and dramaturgy:** Teachers', directors', and actors' analysis and presentation of drama and narrative
- **Close, distant, and critical reading:** Includes literary criticism and media literacy

Hermeneutics and Literary Theory

Reading—reading just anything—is a complex and potentially almost unlimited activity. That's one of the good things that theory teaches us.
    —*Paul Fry*, Theory of Literature[4]

First things first. When approaching a narrative work, you need to understand that there are gaps between you (the reader), the implied reader, the implied author, and the real author. We do not share the same mind, nor the same situation in life, nor the same background; that would be impossible and absurd. So before you dive into a text, it is essential to first understand how you, the reader, differ from these other personae and how those differences show up in the author's text.

Hermeneutics

Luckily there is an entire branch of academia dedicated to the study of those differences, and I have relied heavily on its scholarship to inform the first section of this book, WHAT YOU BRING. Modern literary theory owes a lot to the work of the nineteenth-century German philosopher and theologian Friedrich Schleiermacher. Although focused initially on religious texts, Schleiermacher's great inspiration was to focus his framework, known as hermeneutics, on how people—including us—understand texts in general.

The hermeneutic circle, the centerpiece of hermeneutics, is an iterative process that focuses in on specific parts of a text, then on the text as a whole, then on the parts, then the whole again, etc. Every alternation of this close and distant reading, switching contexts again and again, leads the reader to a deeper understanding of the text. The processes in this book, especially the chapters on context, point of view, and the gestalt, owe a lot to the hermeneutic circle.

Literary theory

How is hermeneutics is applied to modern literature? It's all about the context, and texts exist in so many contexts! Any text can be interpreted through the lens of class struggle, or its stance on gender identities, racial bias, or colonial hierarchies. This leads to the studies of racial criticism, feminist criticism, queer criticism, and many others. It is essential that we understand who we are—our history, upbringing, education, class, society, religious and political beliefs, and every other bias we hold—because we bring all the baggage of our unique selves to every novel we read.

I have relied heavily on the studies of reception theory, a flavor of reader response criticism that treats every reader as an individual and acknowledges that unique interpretations of text will arise based on those differing points of view. In other words, your experience and worldview color how you understand what's on the page; furthermore, there is no such thing as a text that can be separated from the culture within which it was written or where it is read.[5]

I also incorporated encoding/decoding theory into *Literary Forensics*. Content creators encode messages into their presentations that rely on readers (or, in Stuart Hall's seminal paper,[6] television viewers) to be able to decode those messages. Millions of dollars of research have been spent by advertising and marketing agencies to ensure that their expensive thirty-second TV ads make lasting impressions on viewers. In broadcast and streaming media, reception theory is taken seriously. And because the novel is merely a set of encoded messages with a different packaging, it's a framework that we can employ in our understanding of the novel. We may as well take advantage of what we can learn from those corporations who spent so much money on what turned out to be a gigantic research project. (Yay, capitalism.)

As with the other disciplines in this chapter, you can certainly further explore any of these topics. This book only skims the surface of this deep subject for the sole purpose of keeping our focus on point. We're here to read books, after all.

EXERCISE 1

Learn the basics of hermeneutics—I used Richard E. Palmer's *Hermeneutics*,[7] a classic overview of the work of Schleiermacher and others. For an overview of literary theory, I can recommend Jonathan Culler's *Literary Theory*,[8] and Paul Fry's Yale University course, "Theory of Literature," every lecture of which is available on YouTube.[9] Fry is comprehensive, precise, and entertaining.

I have always found Camille Paglia's takedowns of Foucault and other deconstructionists to be insightful and amusing; her collection of essays *Sex, Art, and American Culture*[10] was revelatory to me as an outsider to her world.

Epistemology and Social Psychology

> We move from the idea that literature is in some sense caused by language, to the idea that literature is in some sense caused by the human psyche, to the idea that literature is in some sense caused by social, economic, and historical forces. And there are corollaries for those ideas in terms of the kinds of effects that literature has and what we might imagine ourselves to conclude from them.
>
> —*Paul Fry*, Theory of Literature

How we come to know ourselves and how we interact with the world are two of the most important skill sets that we develop throughout our lives. Understanding the limits of what we can know and the influence we have over others (and they have over us) will also help us to better understand the mindsets of the characters—and their social circles—that we read about and want to write about.

Epistemology

Epistemology is a branch of philosophy that focuses on understanding the essence, origins, and boundaries of knowledge. Often referred to as the *theory of knowledge*, it examines fundamental concepts like belief, truth, and justification. It's also about how we acquire knowledge, through sensory perception, self-reflection, memory, and reasoning.

Epistemology is an important field of study for readers, because there are so many things in this world that we think we know that simply aren't so. We're most often fooled by the very language that we use and how we use it. Philosophers like Bertrand Russell, Ludwig Wittgenstein, Walker Percy, and Noam Chomsky have advanced our understanding of language itself and how critical it is to the formation of our perceptions and belief systems.

Social psychology

> New customs, Though they be never so ridiculous—Nay, let 'em be unmanly—yet are follow'd.
> —*William Shakespeare*, Henry VIII, *act 1, scene 3*

This discipline focuses on how we perceive, influence, and relate to one another. People's attitudes, social awareness and influence, prejudice, stereotypes, and interpersonal relationships also determine group behavior. As readers, we have an intuitive sense of how we expect characters to behave in certain situations, but novels often deal with extraordinary situations outside of our normal experience. Psychological research into what actually makes people behave the way that they do in any situation can illuminate whether or not the characters we read are behaving in a believable, if not immediately recognizable way.

Also because of the unique way a novel interacts with our brains, as we create a movie in our imaginations representing the emotions found in our reading, we are more psychologically involved in the consumption of a novel than many of us realize.

I have benefited from decades of scientific research to inform the WHAT YOU FEEL section of this book. Studies on boredom, agitation, and confusion yield insights into what needs to be present in our minds for us to feel those and other emotions. If what I have presented piques your interest to go deeper, then do your own research.

EXERCISE 2

The epistemological overview I have used is *Epistemology* by Robert Audi,[11] but there are many others to choose from. Alternatively, you can go directly to the classic texts written by the philosophers themselves: *An Enquiry Concerning Human Understanding* by David Hume, *The Theory of Knowledge* by Bertrand Russell, or *Tractatus Logico-Philosophicus* by Ludwig Wittgenstein, to name just a few. Fair warning: This field is both broad and deep, so be careful not to turn into a philosopher and stop writing novels altogether.

The seminal work for social psychology is Elliot Aronson's *The Social Animal*,[12] first published in 1972 and now in its twelfth edition. It covers all the bases. It has also influenced the authors of a generation of books on social influence and social persuasion. A popular example of the genre is Robert B. Cialdini's *Influence: The Psychology of Persuasion*, which reads like a self-help book. But it contains lessons that may help you to understand the behavior of some of the characters you read.

Applied Linguistics and Semiotics

From grammar, to philology, to linguistics, to semiotics. The progression of the study of language over the centuries has led to today's focus on the *nature* of symbols and their meaning. While linguistics focuses on words—their structure within language—semiotics examines the broader system of signs and totems that convey meaning.

Ferdinand de Saussure and Charles Sanders Peirce were two of the most influential thinkers who laid the groundwork for modern linguistics and semiotics, and their work has greatly influenced this book. Peirce's triadic model of communication (object, sign, and interpretant), originally applied to philosophy, has such an obvious application to linguistics that it has been widely adopted.[13]

Applied linguistics

Applied linguistics is a broad interdisciplinary field, spanning artificial languages, language acquisition, multilingualism, forensic and culinary linguistics, and language teacher pedagogy, among others. In *Literary Forensics*, we are predominantly concerned with the disciplines of translation, *stylistics* (the study of vocabulary, syntax, metaphor, tone), and discourse analysis, which is significant enough to merit its own section below.

Stylistics are covered primarily in chapter 12, "Language and Grammar," and chapter 15, "Voice," but as with other disciplines, it has informed most of the topics in this book. Translation is covered in chapter 20, "The Gestalt," but the concept of translation—morphing an idea or a concept from one set of symbols into another—is also woven throughout this book.

Semiotics

While linguistics focuses on language as a specific coded system, semiotics examines a broader range of signs and symbols, including nonlinguistic ones like images, gestures, and objects. Of course, even visual semiotic symbols are represented by words and are peppered throughout every novel we read, sometimes doing double duty as themes and motifs. See chapter 19, "Layering," for a more in-depth look at the importance of recognizing semiotic signs in our reading.

EXERCISE 3

Start your study of linguistics with one of the seminal texts: Ferdinand de Saussure's *Course in General Linguistics*.[14] As for semiotics, Charles Sanders Peirce never wrote a treatise on his triadic model—only journal-published articles—so the best introduction to his thinking comes from studies of his work. The classic text *Peirce on Signs*[15] edited by James Hoopes is a good outline of Peirce's ideas.

Discourse and Narrative Analysis

Discourse analysis is the study of language-in-use. Better put, it is the study of language at use in the world, not just to say things, but to do things.
—*James Paul Gee*, How to Do Discourse Analysis: A Toolkit[16]

In a way, we are all anthropologists.

As children and adolescents, we learn about the world by observing the behaviors of the society around us and making assumptions about what motivates people to do the things they do. This process begins the moment we realize we are not the center of the universe and we need to interact with people who are different from us. That's also when we pay closer attention to what people say, and we become more careful about what we say to them. What we hear and what we say matters.

Narrative analysis is a subset of discourse analysis, which is itself is a subset of applied linguistics. Together these analysis toolkits comprise a systematic methodology of qualitative research—grounded theory—that's conducted by social scientists to parse the meanings hidden within the stories we tell each other. Through this discipline, we can arrive at what an author *means*, in spite of what they have *written*.

We encounter the novel through its words and sentences, much like an anthropologist encounters an unfamiliar culture. The act of reading a novel in this way is akin to the twentieth-century anthropologist Margaret Mead encountering Samoans and trying to make sense of their worldview by studying how they communicate. We readers benefit greatly from a contextual framework to organize our investigations, and, luckily for us, scholars have been working for decades to create the very tools we require.

I have used the framework of discourse and narrative analysis to organize the material in the WHAT YOU FEEL section.

EXERCISE 4

Check out the works of James Paul Gee, who has authored a number of authoritative texts on discourse analysis, especially his accessible *How to Do Discourse Analysis: A Toolkit,* which I have consulted frequently while writing this book. Also take a look at Stanton Wortham's *Narratives in Action: A Strategy for Research and Analysis*[17] for further study.

If you plan to conduct a qualitative survey of the books you read, some good tools are available online.[18] If you're looking for a textbook, *The Handbook of Narrative Analysis* by Anna de Fina and Alexandra Georgakopoulou is a recent introduction to the discipline.

Pedagogy and Dramaturgy

Understanding the methodologies of professionals whose job it is to consume, analyze, and present narratives to their audiences also benefits our studies. Just as English teachers and actors learn to present works of fiction for audiences, so too do we become both presenter and audience as we create the movie of a novel in our heads.

Modern pedagogy—the discipline of how to instruct others—is rooted in constructivism, which acknowledges that learners bring prior knowledge and experiences that are shaped by their social and cultural environment. Readers (and all students, everywhere) "construct" knowledge based on their experiences. Therefore, it is important for us to understand how this process works so that we can learn not to stray from what's written in the text.

Dramaturgy is the study of the social, cultural, and historical context of a play, film, or other performance. It involves analyzing the text, researching the background, and understanding the themes, motifs, and character arcs to gain a deeper understanding of the script. Does this sound familiar?

As the template for a drama is really an outline—dialogue and stage direction only—a script leaves many gaps for directors and actors to fill. So, too, fictional narrative leaves many gaps for readers to fill in, and therefore the way we receive these details is commensurate with how much we *already know* about the topics discussed.

In writing *Literary Forensics,* I have drawn not only from novels but also from film, television, and theater for my examples of characterization, motivation, conflict, theme, and scene work. And because we're here to peel back the layers—however we can—studying the crafts of pedagogy and dramaturgy can pay useful dividends.

EXERCISE 5

The principles outlined in chapters 1 through 5 of the pedagogical textbook, *How Learning Works: 8 Research-Based Principles for Smart Teaching*[19] informed the WHAT YOU BRING section of this book, and I when I lead my Writers Who Read study group, I adhere to what you will find in chapters 6 through 8. I also learned a lot about modern writing workshop facilitation from Matthew Salesses's *Craft in the Real World.*[20]

Among the dramaturgy texts I can recommend for further study: Robert Knopf's *Script Analysis for Theatre,*[21] Melissa Bruder's *A Practical Handbook for the Actor,*[22] and John Willett's *Brecht on Theatre.*[23]

Also important to our studies is the crossover between stage and screen tropes with those found in today's novels, which are increasingly cinematic. For example, I frequently refer to Blake Snyder's *Save the Cat!*[24] series, but there are many, many more books on scriptwriting techniques.

Close, Distant, and Critical Reading

Close, distant, and critical reading are quite different from one another, but each has something valuable to offer the inquisitive reader. I've purloined elements of all three and infused their techniques into this entire book, so what follows is a quick summary of each discipline to give you a sense of what awaits if you decide to study any of them further.

Close reading

You may already be familiar with this term. It's big in academia. Unfortunately, if you want to learn the mechanics of deep reading today, you'll need to pore through hundreds of academic papers. And that's because the target audience is not you, the lay reader, and it's not writers, either. It's teachers, primarily elementary school English teachers, who are the modern-day beneficiaries of close reading scholarship, because it's currently applied to instructing children in the basics of reading comprehension.

Close reading, as it was developed in the early decades of the twentieth century, was initially intended to parse poetry, but it quickly morphed into a technique used by New Historicists to parse the great works of literature.

But it came with a caveat.

Because the close reading of poetry and literary novels expected a certain layering of meaning and use of symbolism, it was assumed that it would and should only be applied to the canon of great works. This is where close reading stalled for decades. It wasn't assumed to be applicable to *all* works of literature, and so it was never developed to apply to any text.

Distant reading

This approach to the text—coined by Franco Moretti—was developed in the mid-twentieth century as a reaction to close reading and the somewhat-snobbish approach to literary criticism at the time. Distant reading is all about context, and a consideration of how that text might be received to a wider readership. This evolved concurrent with the development of many of the group-specific flavors of modern criticism: feminist, postcolonial, Marxist, and others. No text exists in a vacuum, so distant reading is the polar opposite of close reading, which holds that words and phrases have absolute meanings and can be studied in isolation.

Critical reading

Critical reading is closely related to critical thinking. Unfortunately, this discipline as taught today is focused exclusively on sniffing out false or spurious factual content: namely, the inspection of footnotes and original sources found in academic papers. While enormously useful to the scholar, I believe that a similarly rigorous approach can and should be used by any reader who wants to get beneath the surface of the text, as we do.

Another parallel discipline that's useful to us can be found in media literacy education. In this age of unverifiable social media content and "fake news," the goal of media literacy is to teach news consumers—members of the general public—how to spot bullshit. It's similar to critical reading but with a different focus.

Both of these disciplines have much to teach any critical reader of fiction.

EXERCISE 6

One of the classic texts on close reading, I. A. Richards's *Practical Criticism*,[25] provides a solid overview and is a good place to start. Current scholarship is both dense to read and scattered across many journals, so I suggest continuing with one of the reading technique compilations. There are many to choose from, including titles by Charles Van Doren,[26] Ezra Pound,[27] Terry Eagleton,[28] Stanley Fish,[29] and Thomas Foster.[30] I can also recommend two delightful books about close reading: Francine Prose's *Reading Like a Writer*,[31] and George Saunders's *A Swim in a Pond in the Rain*.[32]

Distant reading: I have used the writings of Franco Moretti both to inform my reading analysis and also the topics covered in chapter 24, "Digital Humanities." I learned many lessons from Moretti's *Graphs, Maps, Trees*,[33] and so can you.

Critical reading: I prefer the practical advice given in Steven Novella's *The Skeptics' Guide to the Universe* over the more academic literature on the subject. This is also a good guidebook for media literacy.

Notes

1. If you're successful, I'd love to hear from you for possible inclusion in future revisions of this book. See the afterword, "The Next Edition."
2. I'm quoting from the children's version that is focused on learning anatomy, not the original spiritual, which is about the apocalypse. Yikes. https://en.wikipedia.org/wiki/Dem_Bones
3. Her studio can be found here: https://bodySpan.com.
4. Paul H. Fry, "Theory of Literature," *Open Yale Courses* series (Yale University Press, Connecticut, 2012).
5. To further pinpoint the origin of this framework, reception theory is part of the individualist branch of reader response criticism and uses psychology as a starting point. The other two branches of reader response criticism are experimenters and uniformists. Uniformists claim it's

possible to understand a text objectively—that is, while remaining immune to one's own culture, status, and personality. To this, I say, "Ha!" As you may have guessed, this theory informs my understanding of the reader's relationship to the novel, and as such I oppose those parts of formalism and New Criticism that discount outside influences we bring to our reading. A formalist, for example, believes that a text stands in complete isolation to the world around it; the formalist would have no use not only for this chapter, but the entirety of WHAT YOU BRING. To this, I just shake my head in wonder, because this type of thinking contradicts almost every Goodreads review ever written.

6. Stuart Hall, "Encoding and Decoding in the television discourse."

7. Richard E. Palmer, *Hermeneutics: Interpretation Theory in Schleiermacher, Dilthey, Heidegger, and Gadamer* (Northwestern University Press, Illinois, 1969).

8. Jonathan Culler, *Literary Theory: A Very Short Introduction* (Oxford University Press, New York, 1997).

9. https://www.youtube.com/playlist?list=PLD00D35CBC75941BD

10. Camille Paglia, *Sex, Art, and American Culture: Essays* (Vintage, New York, 1992).

11. Robert Audi, *Epistemology: A Contemporary Introduction to the Theory of Knowledge* (Routledge, New York, 1998).

12. Elliot Aronson and Joshua Aronson, *The Social Animal*, 12th ed. (Worth Publishers, New York, 1972).

13. I find it interesting that neither de Saussure nor Peirce published a definitive book in their lifetime, and their scholarship comes to us via acolytes who have compiled their writings into the texts we use today. Does this represent a meta-application of their own disciplines?

14. A compilation of de Saussure's lecture notes by his students following his death. Published in French in 1916, and translated numerous times over the years. I used Roy Harris's version: Ferdinand de Saussure et al., *Course in General Linguistics*, 3rd ed., trans. and annotated by Roy Harris (Bloomsbury, UK, 2013).

15. James Hoopes, ed., *Peirce on Signs: Writings on Semiotic by Charles Sanders Peirce* (The University of North Carolina Press, North Carolina, 1991).

16. James Paul Gee, *How to Do Discourse Analysis*.

17. Stanton Emerson Fisher Wortham, *Narratives in Action: A Strategy for Research and Analysis* (Teachers College Press, New York, 2001).

18. See: https://delvetool.com/blog/narrativeanalysis and https://delvetool.com/blog/codebook.

19. Marsha C. Lovett and Michael W. Bridges, Michele DiPietro et al., *How Learning Works: 8 Research-Based Principles for Smart Teaching*, 2nd ed. (Jossey-Bass, New York, 2023).

20. Matthew Salesses, *Craft in the Real World: Rethinking Fiction Writing and Workshopping* (Catapult, New York, 2021).

21. Robert Knopf, *Script Analysis for Theatre*.

22. Melissa Bruder, et al., *A Practical Handbook for the Actor* (Vintage Books, New York, 1986).

23. John Willett, *Brecht on Theatre* (Hill and Wang, New York, 1964).

24. Especially Jessica Brody, *Save the Cat! Writes a Novel* (Ten Speed Press, California, 2018).

25. I. A. Richards, *Practical Criticism: A Study of Literary Judgment* (Kegan Paul, Trench, Tubner & Co. Ltd., UK, 1930).

26. Adler and Van Doren, *How to Read a Book*.

27. Actually, two books by Ezra Pound: *ABC of Reading* (1934) and) *How to Read* (1931).

28. Terry Eagleton, *How to Read Literature* (Yale University Press, Connecticut, 2013).

29. Stanley Fish, *How to Write a Sentence: And How to Read One* (Harper Paperbacks, New York, 2012).
30. Thomas C. Foster, *How to Read Literature Like a Professor* (HarperCollins, New York, 2003).
31. Francine Prose, *Reading Like a Writer*.
32. George Saunders, *A Swim in a Pond in the Rain*.
33. Franco Moretti, *Graphs, Maps, Trees: Abstract Models for a Literary History* (Verso Books, New York, 2005).

24
Digital Humanities

Tomorrow's illiterate will not be the man who can't read; he will
be the man who has not learned how to learn.
—*Alvin Toffler*, Future Shock

Digital humanities is an academic discipline at the intersection of digital
computing and the humanities. It spans digital archiving, analysis, publishing,
and scholarship, and includes the digital tools that we can use to help us study the
novels we read. Investigating critical theories or examining power dynamics? Sift
through every publication ever digitized to find trends and test hypotheses. In the
past such studies would take years; today, they take minutes.

So much information and computing power is available to us that it's less,
what *can* we do? and more, what *should* we do? And, most importantly for us,
how can these tools make us better readers and better writers?

The best tools are the ones that help us learn how to learn.

Objective literary analysis

My entry into literary analysis—when I hosted my first *Writers Who Read*
meeting back in 2018—was through digital humanities. I wanted to lead a writer-
focused survey of today's novels, but without being able to find scholarly analyses
of any of these titles, I was wary of presenting subjective opinions that were not
authoritative or reliable. My search for a way to present novels in an objective,
opinion-free way led me to quantitative analysis: numbers. In the absence of
qualitative criticism, I counted words, chapters, and sections, compared present
and past tense, enumerated points of view, and gave a sort of numerical overview
of a novel. In those early days, I wasn't attempting to say how the novel worked,
or even what worked, or why. I was listing the results. At this point, I have accrued

enough data from my surveys to consider these works as a group, using them to uncover trends from this small sample set.[1]

I also embraced statistical analysis and natural language processing, with its subdisciplines of sentiment analysis and topic modeling. This led me to create software and begin analyzing books, one at a time. I was performing, in microcosm, some digital humanities functions. I was looking for a way to dissect novels free of human bias—essential elements of literary criticism that don't require the critic's judgment. I thought: Wouldn't it be useful to have the ability to list all the characters, and label all the POVs and themes, before you even start reading?

Pandora's box

In hindsight, I should have been careful what I wished for, because artificial intelligence (AI) is already changing the way we study and learn.[2] What's referred to as AI is really an amalgam of technologies, but the two strands most relevant to *Literary Forensics* are: statistical analysis, which has been around for decades, and generative AI chatbots, which are front-ends to Large Language Models (LLMs) and which burst into the public consciousness in late 2022 with the release of ChatGPT.

Statistical analysis is at the core of *data science*, which is the art of wrangling large amounts of data and finding trends within. Since their inception, digital humanities departments have been studying texts by purely statistical analysis of large bodies of texts—thousands of novels in a single investigation. I, on the other hand, have been working with individual novels and have applied statistical tools to each in turn for the purposes of analyzing sentiment, story shapes, and topics. I'm not trying to make any statements about *literature* in general. I'm more interested in what I can learn from a single novel.

There is a limit to what statistics can do for us. In their 2016 book, *The Bestseller Code,*[3] Jodie Archer and Matthew L. Jockers trained a statistical model on all the bestselling novels over the past few decades with the purpose of helping editors evaluate slush-pile manuscript submissions for their bestseller potential. One of the key features their model identified was the optimal number of times the word *the* appeared in the text. That may be interesting information for editors, but it's absolutely useless for our purposes.

Generative AI chatbots

Statistical analysis is primitive indeed when compared to the insightful power of LLMs. LLMs understand the rules of the English language as it is used by humans, which in itself represents a quantum leap over any form of AI that has come before.

In 1949, mathematician Alan Turing—who famously led a team during WWII to crack Germany's Enigma code—created a thought experiment he called the

"Imitation Game."[4] We know it today as "the Turing Test," which tests a computer's ability to exhibit intelligent behavior indistinguishable from that of a human. Turing realized that it was not important whether the nascent science of artificial intelligence would ever create a sentient machine; what mattered was whether AI could fool a human into believing that they were communicating with another human.

The answer is yes. That's the leap forward LLMs represent.

Green intern

LLMs are trained on enormous corpora—virtually everything ever published digitally—and so their knowledge base is comprehensive. However, the chatbots we interact with are using purely statistical analysis to determine *how* to answer our queries, and so they sometimes put the wrong words together and end up inventing new things. This is known as *hallucinating*.[5]

LLMs are flawless when prompted to answer a direct question, such as, "Who wrote Huckleberry Finn?" They produce interesting answers when queried about their opinion or when asked to gather information. An example prompt of this type is, "Name the five most influential novels." But that's also where LLMs shine; their ability to synthesize information and create mostly literate responses represents a giant leap forward for our research.

The moral and ethical issues that arise when we use LLM chatbots comes with how we use them. If we get a chatbot to write our term paper, that's not only ethically wrong, but it's also a missed educational opportunity. We are here to learn to read like writers. If we use chatbots to do our reading for us and form opinions based on its reading, we have gained nothing.

The most useful way to engage with AI chatbots, then, is to take advantage of their ability to give us a running start on what we want to learn: to recommend a novel similar to another we have enjoyed, for example, or to hint at the themes we might find inside. The best analogy I have yet heard compares an AI chatbot to an inexperienced intern. *Go and fetch X,* we might order our intern, and they return with *something*. But it's up to us to judge whether what they found was accurate, complete, or even useful.

The delight of using this technology comes when it sparks a new idea, or opens the door to another line of inquiry we had not even considered pursuing.

A moving target

The technology is moving too quickly for me to feel confident that what I write here will be accurate or even relevant in a few months or years. Rather, I'm sticking with introducing important principles and lines of inquiry, which you can then apply to whatever this technology morphs into. I hope it's the digital equivalent of giving you a fishing pole instead of handing you a fish.

So here are four ways to take advantage of the latest technology in your digital humanities pursuits that should be quite useful to readers for the foreseeable future.

- **Grammar and readability:** Text parsing, diagramming, and readability metrics
- **Novel dissection:** Themes, writing styles, and story arcs
- **Literature trends:** Surveys, big data, and the impact of AI chatbots
- **Cultural analytics:** Trends, movements, power dynamics, and interdisciplinary collaboration

Grammar and Readability

Tired of looking up words? Most e-readers have built-in dictionaries, or you can turn to online tools like this one[6] to provide every possible meaning of every word in a given sentence. Voyant Tools[7] can analyze entire chapters, showing you a word cloud, term graphs, trend lines, collocates, contexts, and a dozen other indices that make a word nerd like me happy.

Are these tools useful for our purposes? Kinda sorta. And there are other tools out there—too many to list—and more are being created every day. In fact, there seems to be a tool for everything you can imagine. If you're curious, try them out! Just don't let them distract you from your reading.

Grammar

Sometimes a novel proves difficult to read, which could indicate grammar issues. If a sentence isn't yielding up its meaning, then one approach is to diagram it, just like we did back in grade school. Remember how to do that? No, neither do I, but a generative AI chatbot can diagram with ease. Here's a sample prompt:

```
Diagram this sentence: "The quick brown fox jumped over
the lazy dog."
```

This is one result:

```
This sentence is a well-known pangram, a phrase that
uses all the letters of the alphabet at least once. Here's
a diagram of the sentence:
The: The definite article, indicating a specific noun.
quick: An adjective describing the noun "fox."
```

brown: An adjective describing the noun "fox."
fox: A noun, the subject of the sentence.
jumped: A verb, describing the action of the fox.
over: A preposition indicating the location of the action.
the: The definite article, indicating a specific noun.
lazy: An adjective describing the noun "dog."
dog: A noun, the object of the sentence.
Here's a simple diagram of the sentence structure:

```
S
|
|— NP (The quick brown fox)
|      |
|      |— Det (The)
|      |— AdjP (quick brown)
|      |    |
|      |    |— Adj (quick)
|      |    |— Adj (brown)
|      |— N (fox)
|
|— V (jumped)
|
|— PrepP (over the lazy dog)
|      |
|      |— Prep (over)
|      |— NP (the lazy dog)
|           |
|           |-- Det (the)
|           |-- AdjP (lazy)
|           |    |
|           |    |— Adj (lazy)
|           |— N (dog)
```

This also works for more complex sentences, too. Some chatbots even draw pictures for you to make sentence diagrams easier to comprehend, and I have never seen a single mistake in one of these diagrams. This makes sense, once you remember how these chatbots work. Knowledge of grammar is at the core of their design. It's the one thing AI chatbots will never get wrong or hallucinate about. Finally! A technology made for readers—even if the readers are primarily the chatbots themselves.

Readability

You may also ask yourself: Is it just me? Am I the only one having trouble making sense of the writing in this novel? That's where readability tools are useful.

Sixth grade is the average reading level in the United States, and even the most literary fiction is written at or around that level. The Gunning Fog Index, used by technical writers and English teachers to determine the level of education required to comprehend a text, is the most popular readability test for English writing. If you submit text to the tool and it returns a higher grade level than sixth or seventh, then it's not just you struggling with comprehension—it's the writing level.

There are, of course, other tests used to determine the grade level of a text, among them Flesch-Kincaid, Coleman Liau, ARI (Automated Readability Index), and SMOG. You can also use readability indices, scaled from 0 to 100: Flesch Reading Ease, and the Lexical Density Index. Other useful indices to determine lexical complexity include average number of characters per word, average number of syllables per word, and average number of words per sentence. I use many of these informative metrics in the contour map[8] that I create for every novel we survey.

EXERCISE 1

Try diagramming sentences using an AI chatbot, starting with a prompt similar to the one above. Then calculate the readability of various texts through a *Gunning Fog Index* tool. You can use this one,[9] or just enter a prompt like this into an AI chatbot: "Calculate the Gunning Fog score for this text: [insert text to be analyzed here]." If the text scores at a high grade level, try editing the text to lower the score. This tool[10] and this tool[11] generate specific editing suggestions.

Novel Dissection

I have tried to bring scientific thinking to literary criticism and there has been very little gratitude for this.
—*Kurt Vonnegut*[12]

When I first started writing fiction, I had so many questions. I didn't know the average word count for novels being published that year, or if those numbers varied according to genre. I wanted to understand the structure of the novel, the size and shape of its parts, chapters, sections, and paragraphs. Should I be writing in first person or third? What's normal, and what's unusual? I needed to understand the boundaries so I could gauge how to measure my own work against other works. At that time, I couldn't find any of this critical data, especially for novels published within the past few years.

In the past, this esoteric knowledge resided inside the heads of a select few: literary editors. Literary editors work with authors to finalize their manuscripts, keeping track of plot points, character arcs, themes, structure, and, of course, word counts.[13] Many literary editors prepare spreadsheets[14] for every book they edit, keeping track of the appearance of every character, all the thematic threads, and the plot points.[15] By carefully noting exactly where each occurred within the text, editors are able to also track the lines of rising and falling tension that map a novel's emotional journey.

Sentiment analysis

Author Kurt Vonnegut had an idea for a master's dissertation when he was enrolled in the University of Chicago's anthropology department after World War II, he wrote in his autobiography, *Palm Sunday*:[16]

> The thesis has vanished, but I carry an abstract in my head, which I will here set down. The fundamental idea is that stories have shapes which can be drawn on graph paper, and that the shape of a given society's stories is at least as interesting as the shape of its pots or spearheads.

Vonnegut used a chalkboard to demonstrate his story shapes in an entertaining lecture[17] at Case Western Reserve University in 2004, which was the inspiration for a 2016 academic study by a team led by Andrew J. Reagan at the University of Vermont. The outcome was a paper, "The emotional arcs of stories are dominated by six basic shapes,"[18] which provided the first scientific proof of Vonnegut's theory.

I was inspired by that paper to contact Reagan, who shared his notebooks with me as I began my own investigation into story shapes through natural language processing (NLP) sentiment analysis and topic-modeling technology. Since analyzing dozens of recent novels with my software, I've confirmed what Vonnegut suspected and what Reagan and his team proved using a few thousand Project Gutenberg public-domain novels: Our stories do, in fact, conform to these six basic shapes. The last two appear most frequently:

1. **U**   Person falls into a hole and digs their way out
2. **∩**   Icarus story: Person flies too high, then falls down
3. **/**   Rags to riches

4. \ Tragedy (or riches to rags)
5. **M** Double-peak journeys, starting and ending low
6. **W** Double-valley journeys, starting and ending high

Notice that some of these shapes map directly onto the character arcs covered in chapter 16, "Character Development."

Themes

There are no shortcuts in our personal education. The way to learn is to seek, to struggle, and to persevere. In *Literary Forensics,* the primary way to uncover a novel's themes is by necessity *to read the book* and follow the advice laid out in chapters 19 and 20.

We live in the age of AI, however, and sometimes the answer to these questions is as easy as writing the appropriate prompt. I won't discourage you from using these tools, but I suggest you do so in a way that *aids* your reading, and doesn't *replace* your reading. For decades, struggling students have been able to use a number of shortcuts: CliffsNotes, SparkNotes, LitCharts, and others. They still exist, but rarely for the most recently published novels.

Chatbots rely on the data they find at these study sites; failing to discover anything there, the bots scour the Internet for anything they can find, most of it dubious. But in 2025, when I prompted a chatbot for the themes in Percival Everett's 2024 novel *James,* the bot returned a detailed—and accurate—list. I suppose it helps to ask about a bestselling novel that also won the National Book Award. Texts like those tend to get fast-tracked onto the study sites, which the LLMs slurp up.

Writing styles

Stylometry is the dark art of evaluating the style of a text to identify its author using vocabulary, word frequency, sentence length, and other metrics. A magical combination of these elements creates an author's style. How can we put this qualitative linguistics methodology to good use?

Again, AI chatbots come to the rescue. When I entered the prompt, "What is the writing style of Percival Everett?" I learned that his writing style is characterized by:

- A blending of genres
- Playful use of language
- Experimentation with narrative structure
- Themes of identity, racism, and classism
- Critiques of societal norms

I can confirm from my reading that the bot wasn't hallucinating. Furthermore, I learned that Everett's writing style compares to that of Thomas Pynchon and Don DeLillo. Again, I exhort you to take advantage of the wealth of knowledge out there to add richness and context to the novels you read.

If you're looking for the raw numbers I sought above—word counts, numbers of chapters, genre—again, AI chatbots are your friend.

EXERCISE 2

Pick a recent novel you've read and jot down your impressions of what you can quantify or qualify, and whether you think those metrics are high, average, low, or rare. This includes: word count, number of chapters, dramatic arc, themes, or any other characteristic that interests you. Now use a chatbot to enter some prompts about the book, and see what you can learn from the results of your query.

Literature Trends

> The literary scholar of the twenty-first century can no longer be content with anecdotal evidence, with random "things" gathered from a few, even "representative," texts. We must strive to understand these things we find interesting in the context of everything else, including a mass of possibly "uninteresting" texts.
> —*Matthew Jockers*, Macroanalysis: Digital Methods and Literary History[19]

Modern weather forecasts are created by using the Monte Carlo method. Just input current data points into a prediction model and run it a thousand or a million times. If rain is the outcome in 70 percent of the simulations, then a 70 percent chance of rain is forecast. Very simple, very accurate, but it relies on lots of fast computers to be able to run all these simulations.

Your mileage may vary

As recently as ten years ago, statements about trends in literature were based on very few data points—namely, the number of novels that researchers were able to read, which numbers in the dozens per year, so those statements were not very reliable. As a result, our knowledge about the larger trends in literature was always spotty. Were novels getting longer or shorter in the aggregate? We didn't know. Were multi-genre works of fiction on the increase, decreasing, or holding steady? Again, we didn't really know.

I have run my own analyses of length and genre based on a very small dataset of Pulitzer Prize, National Book Award, and Booker Prize winners in fiction over the past fifty years. I noticed a very slight downward trend in number of words in the American award winners, and a slight upward trend in Booker Prize winners. As for multi-genre prize-winning novels, there has been a slight increase in novels by Americans, but it's holding steady at none for Booker Prize winners. My conclusion? There's not enough data to claim movement in any direction.

Enter big data. In 2022, *WordsRated*[20] conducted a survey[21] of 3,444 *New York Times* bestselling titles and found that between 2011 and 2021, average book length decreased by 51.5 pages, from 437 to 385 (−11.8 percent). This list included fiction and nonfiction titles, so it's not conclusive that novels are getting shorter, but the trend is evident. Seven years previous, *Flipsnack* conducted their own survey[22] of 2,515 fiction books from the *New York Times* Best Sellers and Notable Books lists published between 1999 and 2014 and found that they were getting *longer*—from 320 to 407 pages—an increase of 27.2 percent!

Does this mean that nobody knows about the length of novels?

No. It means that comparing those two studies is like comparing apples and oranges. Although both took their lists from the *New York Times*, they included different types of books, from different years, gathered from three different subjective lists. It's no wonder they got different results.

42

One of the big jokes in Douglas Adams's *The Hitchhiker's Guide to the Galaxy* involves asking a deep-thinking computer to reveal the answer to life, the universe, and everything. After hundreds of years, the computer spits out the answer: 42. Disappointed, the data scientists want to know why. Next time, the computer replies, ask a better question.

Fortunately, most of us are not aspiring to become philosophers, historians, or data scientists, so the veracity of what we discover in our studies does not matter as much as that our discoveries be thought-provoking. What topics and themes and genres are publishers favoring this year? A quick chatbot prompt will give you a brief overview based on any question you can formulate.

We no longer need to rely on grant-funded multiyear studies to get our answers, and our knowledge can remain fairly up-to-date, if we ask the right questions.

The new reality

The biggest trend in literature at this time is the move towards AI-enhanced digital creation, which is growing larger and becoming more influential every year.

ChatGPT was made available to the public on November 30, 2022. By mid-February 2023, Amazon's e-book store reported[23] that more than two hundred titles openly listed ChatGPT as an author or co-author. A few months later, author Stephen Marche used ChatGPT to help him write[24] the novella *Death of an Author*, which he published in May 2023 under the pseudonym Aiden Marchine.[25]

Publishers are receiving too many AI-written submissions,[26] and tech companies are getting into publishing, with at least one "publishing platform" hoping to disrupt (and devalue) the entire industry by flooding the market with new AI-designed books.[27]

AI-generated content has one gigantic flaw: All of it echoes the biases of the material on which its underlying model was trained. By design, AI synthesizes new content out of existing ideas, but it cannot innovate or create new ideas. When AI chatbots attempt to innovate, we call this output *hallucinations* for good reason. It's machine-driven gobbledygook that is not at all related to the human experience.

When cell phones arrived, thriller writers were worried their characters would never be unreachable again. Later, when everyone got a smartphone, mystery writers feared that too many facts would be available to their detectives, killing the whodunit.

Neither of those things happened, did they?

Today we fear AI will take our jobs, write our stories, and make novelists obsolete. And to this I say, probably not. The one thing that has remained constant throughout history is that we humans are very adaptable to our changing situations and will always find a way to express ourselves. AI didn't suddenly render us mute, but it is already changing our lives in ways that we absolutely *will* write about and read about.

Remember, no machine can write more convincingly about the human experience than we can. It's our jam.

EXERCISE 3

Try writing some AI chatbot prompts that return information about the average word count of contemporary YA novels, or the most common themes found in the works of John Green, or Rebecca Yarros, or Gabrielle Zevin. How about the average number of chapters per genre, percentage of novels using first-person

POV, or any other question about the novelists and the genres you want to study that's relevant to your reading and writing? Go crazy.

Keep in mind that the most important things we glean from our investigations are what help us write our own novels. It's easy to slip into the rabbit hole of big data, so be careful what you ask for.

Cultural Analytics

One of the best uses for big data is to reveal the largest trends—the big picture—that no single researcher has the time, money, or inclination to synthesize. The contours of our entire culture are now at our fingertips, so we have no excuse not to learn everything we can.

Anything you need to know so you can better understand what you read is a chatbot prompt away, so use it. What follows are some ideas for further study, based on current digital humanities curricula.

Cultural trends

Societal values, biases, and new ways of thinking can all be found with the right prompts, which can take advantage of millions of words from literature, media, and social discourse across time. From these large datasets of books, social media, and newspapers emerge societal values, biases, and historical shifts in thinking.

Also mirroring our society are the words and terms we coin, use, and redefine—our language is constantly changing. Regionalisms enter the mainstream, grammar does evolve, although slowly, and words change their meanings over time. Another way to analyze cultural trends, therefore, is to track word and phrase usage over the past few centuries. In addition to AI chatbots, a comparative graphical interface is available on the Google Ngram Viewer.[28]

Movements and power dynamics

MeToo, Black Lives Matter, global warming, pandemic behavior, the rise of fascism, and every other social movement you can think of is being documented and evaluated every day, and AI technology can offer a window into their trends. Unfortunately, chatbots themselves are limited by the biases built into the algorithms that generate their responses. Traditional voices of power still occupy a position of prominence. Relying too heavily on this new technology may further solidify the cultural norms that have led to various voices being repressed while others are overrepresented.

The ethics of how to properly use AI in our daily lives are still evolving, and we can't simply ignore these dilemmas and hope that they will go away. AI is here to stay. We will be participating in the discussion about AI's rightful place in our society for years to come.

Interdisciplinary collaboration

Data is topic-agnostic, so the inventiveness of your prompts can generate some interesting cross-discipline insights. Here's but one example: the intersection of philosophy and artistic aesthetics.

The final proposition of Ludwig Wittgenstein's 1921 book *Tractatus Logico-Philosophicus* famously states: "Whereof one cannot speak, thereof one must be silent." In other words, because all philosophical issues arise from misunderstandings and the ambiguities of language, once we understand language, philosophy is no longer useful. But philosophers stubbornly refused to stop philosophizing, and eventually Wittgenstein admitted he may have underestimated the complexity of language itself.

Not only that, but philosophical studies have also progressed beyond the study of language to encompass the study of culture, epistemology, and even artistic aesthetics.[29] No single discipline can adequately explain how we view the world and our place in it, and the world is a richer place for it.

Every study we make is greatly shaped by the culture in which we live, the questions we ask—or don't ask, and the language we use to formulate our thoughts. So when we think we are finally finished and have reached the limits of our studies, we are most assuredly mistaken.

We are only just beginning.

EXERCISE 4

Explore recent cultural topics with an AI chatbot, realizing it may not yet be up-to-date, and its algorithms were created by humans and so contain a measure of bias. Can you modify your prompts to correct for the bias?

Notes

1. Common newbie author questions include: How many words should I write? How many chapters? Sections? POVs? I now have a lot more information from the novels I've surveyed to share with my Writers Who Read group.

2. As a society, we were completely unprepared for the impact AI would have on our daily lives, and at the time of this writing, we still have yet to deal with the legal, moral, and ethical ramifications of what LLMs can do for us and to us. But we're not here to focus on the robot apocalypse.

3. Jodie Archer and Matthew L. Jockers, *The Bestseller Code: Anatomy of the Blockbuster Novel* (St. Martin's Press, New York, 2016).

4. Watch the award-winning movie of the same name to learn more about Turing's contribution to data science and cryptography.

5. I expect this will continue to improve.

6. https://www.lexisrex.com/English/Sentence-Study

7. https://voyant-tools.org/

8. https://literaryforensics.org/novel-contour-map/

9. http://www.gunning-fog-index.com/

10. https://www.online-utility.org/english/readability_test_and_improve.jsp

11. https://hemingwayapp.com/

12. Kurt Vonnegut, "Kurt Vonnegut, Shape of Stories." From a lecture delivered on many occasions, including on February 4, 2004, for The Case College Scholars Program. Video clip: https://www.youtube.com/watch?v=GOGru_4z1Vc.

13. To get a sense of what different types of literary editors do, see: https://janefriedman.com/comprehensive-guide-to-finding-working-with-editors/.

14. Here is one editor's methodology: https://storygrid.com/story-grid-101/.

15. Many authors do the same to keep track of their stories. You can see a page of J.K. Rowling's personal story grid here: https://www.openculture.com/2014/07/j-k-rowling-plotted-harry-potter-with-a-hand-drawn-spreadsheet.html.

16. Kurt Vonnegut, *Palm Sunday* (Dellacorte Press, New York, 1981).

17. Kurt Vonnegut, "Kurt Vonnegut, Shape of Stories."

18. Andrew J. Reagan, Lewis Mitchell, Dilan Kiley, Christopher M. Danforth, and Peter Sheridan Dodds, "The emotional arcs of stories are dominated by six basic shapes." EPJ Data Science 5, no. 31 (2016). https://doi.org/10.1140/epjds/s13688-016-0093-1.

19. Matthew L. Jockers, *Macroanalysis: Digital Methods and Literary History* (University of Illinois Press, Illinois, 2013).

20. https://wordsrated.com/books-stats/

21. https://wordsrated.com/bestselling-books-have-never-been-shorter/

22. https://web.archive.org/web/20201213214532
    https://blog.flipsnack.com/flipsnack-study-are-books-getting-bigger-and-better/

23. https://www.popsci.com/technology/chatgpt-books-amazon/

24. https://www.nytimes.com/2023/04/20/books/ai-novels-stephen-marche.html

25. https://www.amazon.com/Death-Author-Novella-Aidan-Marchine-ebook/dp/B0C364BMNZ/

26. https://neil-clarke.com/a-concerning-trend/

27. https://www.thebookseller.com/news/new-publisher-spines-aims-to-disrupt-industry-by-using-ai-to-publish-8000-books-in-2025-alone

28. https://books.google.com/ngrams/

29. Experimental philosophy of art and aesthetics focuses on the nature of beauty, creativity, and how we perceive art and literature. It blends traditional philosophy with cognitive science and psychology to broaden our understanding of the world. Does this sound familiar?

25
Your Own Study Group

Find a group of people who challenge and inspire you, spend a lot of time with them, and it will change your life forever.
—*Amy Poehler*

If your goal is to avoid other people, you can't do much better than choosing to be a writer. Once you've locked yourself in isolation for a few hours per day, if you also want to avoid interacting with other humans during your leisure hours, putting a book in front of your nose is almost foolproof. So, dear readers and writers, I am about to propose an activity that may change your lives.

How about reading a book—or ten—as a group activity? Studying novels as a group is much more fun than studying in isolation—and we *always* learn more when we learn with the support of others.

The group I founded out of desperation back in 2018, *Writers Who Read,* has changed my life forever, and I'm not exaggerating. In relating the story of forming my group, maybe you will be inspired to lead your own.

Starting a new study group does require adhering to a few simple rules:

- Be organized
- Create a safe space
- Stick to the book
- Make an agenda
- The drinking comes later
- Rinse and repeat

Be Organized

Before you can meet, a few preparations will smooth the way to facilitating a good discussion group. I'll share here the mistakes I made when I first started out so that you don't have to make them yourself.

Get the venue first

The first step is to find a suitable venue and pick a regular date and time to meet. If you skip this step and choose a book and a day before you secure a venue, you may end up meeting in someone's living room and competing for attention with noisy family members. Not ideal.

I love public libraries. Many libraries have meeting rooms that residents can reserve, but remember that this is a limited resource and that those rooms usually go quickly. At the Boulder Public Library, I have to reserve my room six months in advance to make sure I can get the date and time I want. That takes planning.

Churches sometimes allow secular meetings in their basements, but usually only to parishioners and with a donation. Since I don't want to charge a fee for my group, and I don't want to lose money either, I have been very happy using library meeting rooms.

When I first started my *Writers Who Read* group, we met at the Boulder Bookstore, which was great for marketing the events, but it wasn't ideal as a meeting space because they didn't have a quiet room with a door. Patrons were shopping for books in and around my group for our first four meetings.

I've attended book groups that met in coffee shops, which have the added benefit of caffeinated beverages—yay! But there's always a lot of noise and no privacy. That makes it challenging to hear what's being said and makes any group discussion next to impossible if people are spread out. I often say that the most important piece of equipment in my home office is my door; this also holds true when you're leading a group.

You need peace and quiet so you can hear yourself think.

Same time, same place

You can meet as frequently or infrequently as you'd like, but I've found that once a month suits most people—and their reading schedules—the best. Meeting on the same day of the week at the same time of day also helps but isn't required. At the Boulder Book Store, we met on the first Wednesday of the month at 7 p.m. Now we meet at the Boulder Public Library on the first Sunday of the month at 2:30 p.m.

Wherever we meet, I try to make it at the same place at the same time on the same day of the month for an entire season (I pause the group for the summer months). If you're trying to grow your group, it helps it become a habit for your attendees. If you're constantly moving around, let's say from living room to living room, and changing the day or the time, you're more likely to lose members.

I have also found that it takes between 90 and 120 minutes to have a satisfying discussion about any book, so remember to factor that into your room reservations.

I like using meetup.com to coordinate and publicize events. Once people join your Meetup, they can sign up for as many meetings as they like, and you can keep track of who is planning to attend. They'll also get regular notifications leading up to the event, so you won't need to take the time to remind each individual to come. Posting events is not free, however, so if you can find another group to join, you might be able to share the cost. That's how I found the Boulder Writers Alliance. They host my group, and I manage their website, a fair exchange in my opinion.

Stay three or four books ahead

It's important to lead with some initial decisions on book titles. I always take suggestions for future books to make it clear that we as a group can determine what we read, but someone has to take charge. It can be so annoying when the organizer isn't sure what book will be covered next month and opens the floor to discussion.

That wastes people's time, and it's poor leadership.

I plan my books about half a season in advance, and sometimes I will list possible books I'm thinking about for next year as a way to generate some discussion if we finish a meeting early. But my group always knows at least the next three or four books on the list. That gives members time to reserve a library book if they don't want to buy it, and to decide ahead of time whether that title will induce them to attend.

In person or online

After far too many years, Meetup has *finally* embraced the post-COVID reality that a lot of people would prefer to remain in their homes and not join a group of strangers in a public place. I'm lucky that BWA lets me use their Meeting Owl,[1] which is the perfect tool to facilitate hybrid in-person and online meetings. If you do lead hybrid meetings, though, it's essential to keep a few additional things in mind.

First of all, you'll need a computer and a large display that everyone in your meeting room can see easily. The Boulder Library's meeting rooms come equipped with presentation displays that are large enough to be seen even from the back of the room.

Wi-Fi is essential for broadcasting your hybrid meeting online. Be sure that your meeting place has adequate connectivity, and that the meeting room itself gets a strong signal. There's nothing worse than losing your signal midway through a discussion and having to try to reestablish a link while managing the room.

If you're presenting slides or sharing any other content besides your live audio and video, you'll need to consider that in-person attendees and online attendees see different views. I share only the application I'm presenting, and not my entire screen, and then I position that application on my desktop so that those of us in the room can also see the online attendees. This usually takes some juggling, and after dozens of these meetings, I'm still working on perfecting the layout.

It's a lot to ask to run a meeting, operate a computer, and keep track of what's happening online. And over time, I've realized that I just can't notice everything I need to, so I always make sure to ask my in-person attendees to keep an eye out for online chats or attempts by online attendees to be heard. Prompt responses from those of us in the room keep the remote attendees engaged in the discussion.

Create a Safe Space

Another reason I like to meet at the library is because it's a neutral location. Your living room, as inviting as it seems to you, can be equally intimidating for others, and might keep them away. Also, visiting your house may feel less like a study date and more like a social call that requires bringing a gift or taking off one's shoes. And if any of your participants have pet allergies, your lovely dogs and cats will only scare them off.

Be inclusive

The only request I make is that people finish reading the novel before coming to the meeting. Even then, I still allow people who haven't finished the book to attend. That's okay for the group, so long as everyone in the room is aware that we will talk about the ending and that there will be spoilers. We have to consider the book as a whole, and we can't be constrained in our discussion. What's the fun in holding back?

Other than that, everyone is welcome: all beliefs, all genders, all readers. We're here to have fun learning!

Every emotion is valid

Monitoring how we feel about the novels we study is an important tool to be able to identify where within the books we want to start digging. But just as every reaction is valid, assigning values to someone else's emotions is out of bounds.

There's a saying among writers: When someone tells you that your writing doesn't work, they are usually correct. But when they try to tell you how to fix it, they're usually wrong. Anyone can identify a problem, just as anyone can experience an emotion. But it's up to the reader and the writer to understand why they felt that way, and to decide what they will do about it.

Discussion is key

Your job as moderator is to generate discussion, not to push your personal opinions. A good start to creating the right environment is to embrace all points made. Like a good brainstorming session, there are no bad ideas. The fact that someone has the courage to state an opinion means that there is some logic or at least a gut feeling behind it, and *that* process can also be discussed.

And if there is disagreement, it goes without saying that it's important that members debate the *ideas*, and not attack the *people* for having the ideas.

Leave your religion at home

I was taught that it was never polite to bring up religion, politics (which is a form of religion), or money (which can also be worshiped), and I believe that rule still holds true today. Although a novel under discussion may be political, or discuss religious beliefs, it's important to always bring the discussion back to whether or not the author has been effective in making their points. It is *not* okay to use any of those topics as a springboard to launch an ad hominem attack on any of the members or the author.

Stick to the Book

The easiest way to create a safe and open space for discussion is: to insist that every point made is backed up by specific references to the text itself. That takes the focus off individual members and puts it back onto the book, where our attention belongs.

This also helps to defuse any strong feelings that may arise during discussion, and it helps the moderator to be a neutral arbiter.

No one cares what you think

I learned this valuable lesson about crafting convincing arguments in the years when I wrote white papers. It's simple: No one cares what Gary thinks. A great way to turn people off the message is to make bald assertions without any proof. However, if authority A says this, and authority B concurs, and authority

C makes a different point about something else, then it's logical and satisfying to draw these three experts together in a new way to craft a convincing argument.

At no point would I write that *I* assert this or that, because *I* wouldn't be believed. Instead, I let the experts speak for me, which has proven to be very effective.

The same principle is true when you moderate discussions. Authority A, B, and C in this case are: the text of the book, the author's own words, and maybe an outside authority on the topic or the genre. At no point should you ever resort to the phrase, *I think this*, unless it can be backed up with proof in the novel itself. I've found these ratios to be about 90 percent novel, 5 percent author's words, and 5 percent outside authorities, but your mileage may vary.

A great tool to keep members focused on the text is to ask everyone to bring their favorite sentence from the novel to the meeting. Discussing why they chose what they did is both enlightening and helpful to keep the discussion squarely on the book. Finding the exact phrase that elicits a feeling, reveals a theme, or foreshadows a plot element also nicely fixes other potential problems that could derail a discussion:

- It prevents people from going off topic into the personal anecdotes that form a large portion of traditional book club discussions.
- It focuses the group on digging into the text instead of relying on the fuzzy thinking of their own opinions.
- It takes focus off of the moderator, who should remain neutral.

Read and reread

Before presenting any book to my group, I have already read the entire novel twice, and I encourage my members to do the same. It's quite difficult to pick up on most of the important structural or thematic elements the first time through, when the story is new to you. Only on subsequent readings can you begin to notice the hints embedded early in the text, the foreshadowing, and the clues that lead to a deeper understanding of what the novel is really about.

I also use the first reading to take note of my impressions of the flow of the story. After all, this is my only opportunity to approach the novel cold, and it's useful to record exactly how it lands in the moment. In other words, I read for *effect* before I read for *craft*.

I always make sure to read the novel *before* I put it on our reading list, to ensure quality control. This is because some wildly hyped books do not live up to their press, while other under-the-radar books turn out to be gold mines of information about craft.

It's impossible to know what's most useful for your group until you do the reading yourself.

Author interviews

Over the years, I have gotten into the habit of watching YouTube videos of authors being interviewed about their novels. I do this between my first and second readings of the book, because I will almost certainly learn something new about the book that I would not have gleaned by reading the book itself, and I can apply that additional knowledge to my next reading. If an author names an outside reference or source that influenced them in their writing, I may also be inspired to do some additional research before I discuss the book with my group.

I will watch a number of interviews, but the best ones, I have found, are the one-on-one: two chairs, two microphones, and usually on a university stage or in the corner of a bookstore. The best interviewers are other authors—not talk-show hosts—who have been through the experience of writing a novel themselves. They are the most sympathetic and insightful interviewers.

Some bookstores host a lot of author interviews: Politics and Prose and Barnes & Noble have the most videos online. Literary vloggers can also produce excellent online discussions, especially when the interviewer has novel-writing experience.

I tend to stay away from watching critiques of the novel I'm studying, most of which exist primarily to feature the preferences and biases of the critic themselves. The exception I make is when I'm studying a novel in a genre I'm not familiar with. A critic who reads only within their genre can give me, as an outsider, a pretty good idea of how this work fits alongside similar popular works. But of course, this criticism also needs to be evaluated for what it is: one opinion, not a majority ruling.

Which book?

Here's how I decide which novels to present to my group. Traditional book clubs get bogged down when they discuss a book's theme or plot line at the expense of discussing what's in the book itself. Let's say the book is about familial relationships. It's easy to imagine the conversation veering off course as members recount similar relationship issues in their own lives.

Although I'm looking for novels that generate discussion, I'm more interested in keeping that discussion focused on structural elements of the book itself. For example, when a novel presents an interesting use of time, or a unique POV, or any of a hundred other things that spark writers' interest in their craft, I focus the discussion on that. So if I have to choose between a novel about a current issue and one that subverts the form in a subtle way, I almost always go for the latter.

Make an Agenda

And now the time has come: The novel has been read, the group has assembled, and it's time to begin the discussion. I suggest you have an agenda, both to set expectations about how you'll be spending the next few hours, and also to keep your discussions on track.

I have dozens of examples of books[2] my group has already covered, and I've developed what I think is the most efficient and enjoyable way to organize your time. I prefer to use a projector, which focuses everyone's attention on a single point, but you can also present everything orally, or share paper copies of your agenda that everyone can consult.

1. The agenda

Yes, the first item on the agenda is to present the agenda. This gives everyone an idea of what to expect, how to budget their discussion time, and also when the group will get into the topics that interest them the most.

The agenda also includes the name of the novel, a brief overview of why the group is meeting, and what we hope to accomplish, and for the benefit of new members I sometimes pepper the introduction with these words:

> The one question I will never ask you is: Did you enjoy the book? Because I don't give a damn whether or not you enjoyed the book. That's not the point, and that's not why we're here. We're here to learn from novels you may enjoy, but we can learn just as much from novels we hate.

Feel free to temper this statement into something gentler.

2. WHAT YOU BRING

This mirrors the WHAT YOU BRING section of this book. I like to ask everyone to introduce themselves with a few words about what biases they bring to the text. This accomplishes three things: It gives everyone a chance to speak, it allows others to learn a little something about each member, and it immediately gets everyone focused on the spirit of discovery. This usually takes about ten to fifteen minutes, depending on how many people are in attendance. I follow this up with a brief bio of the author, to give everyone a sense of their background, and to hint at any agenda the author may be pursuing in their novel.

3. WHAT YOU FEEL

This is the part where everyone gets the chance to share what they really feel about the book. Some love it; others hate it. But I insist that everyone always refers back to the text to discover and share exactly what engaged or provoked their emotions.

This is not easy, because most people are not used to systematically peeling back their emotions. But WHAT YOU FEEL is critically important, partially because an emotion triggered is a great signal that something within the writing is doing its job (or not).

It's also extremely important to shut down personal anecdotes. Most book clubs (don't call this a book club!) make these emotional discoveries the center-piece of their discussions. We do not. I can't stress enough how important it is to direct everyone's attention on the book.

A rule of thumb: All emotions are valid. However, the conclusions you make may not be. In other words, maintain a safe space. Encourage dissenters. But use participants' interest to steer further investigation back to the text. After all, this is why we're meeting.

4. WHAT YOU NOTICE

Discussions about the craft of writing cover observations such as interesting word usages, sentence structures, or point-of-view choices. Analyzing craft can reveal an unexpected structure, plot point, or character flaw. Identify the inciting incident and the climax; discuss themes, symbolism, and pacing. WHAT YOU BRING and WHAT YOU FEEL are the necessary preludes; WHAT YOU NOTICE is the *meat* of what we can learn from the text. Be sure to give these topics the majority of your time.[3]

5. WHAT YOU STUDY

I use this section to discuss any background information I've learned from authors' interviews and the references they've made to outside topics. This is where I present my Contour Map (see chapter 24, "Digital Humanities"), reading metrics, marketing categories, and information about the audiobook, prizes won, and other recognition this book has received in the marketplace. See WHAT YOU STUDY for more on these topics.

6. Next month

I always close by thanking everyone for bringing their ideas to the discussion and alerting them about our next meeting. I hope for continuity and want these meetings to become habitual. That's why I plan months in advance. That's also why I always send a follow-up thank-you email the next day. I want every member to know how valuable they are to me, and that I hope these study sessions become valuable to them.

The amazing thing that I've discovered is that, without fail, I learn more about each novel after meeting as a group than I knew coming in, no matter how much research I've done.

It's a virtuous circle.

The Drinking Comes Later

Another reason I like meeting at the library is that they don't allow alcohol. It's an environment that feels more like a classroom, and after all, we are there primarily to learn, not to socialize.

But these discussions do create a sense of camaraderie, and after two hours, we can get mighty thirsty, so most of us repair to a nearby bar immediately afterward.[4] That's also why, in our *Writers Who Read* podcast, we pair every novel with a cocktail. Find a complete list of pairings here.[5]

Clear eyes, full hearts, can't lose.[6]

Rinse and Repeat

There is no shortage of wonderful writers. What we lack is a dependable mass of readers.
—*Kurt Vonnegut*, Palm Sunday[7]

The way to really get the most out of a study group is to meet on a regular basis. So once you've got the train on the tracks, you might as well keep it running as long as you can. It can take half a year for members to get into the groove and really start finding interesting things in the novels you read together.

Please use this book as a guide.

My website[8] also contains a wealth of information, including presentation materials for each book we've studied, every one published since 2017, that I've used to lead our discussions.

Oh, and one last thing: Please don't call this a book club. This isn't a book club. We go much deeper than that.

EXERCISE 1

Do any reading study groups exist in your area? If so, look at their reading lists to see if any of the titles interest you. It's rare to find one focused on reading like a writer, but they do exist. You may want to start attending. And if one doesn't exist where you live, start your own!

Notes

1.   https://owllabs.com/products/meeting-owl-3
2.   https://WritersWhoRead.com/LIVE
3.   You may discover that, because the topics of WHAT YOU FEEL and WHAT YOU NOTICE tend to blur into each other, you may cover these two sections simultaneously. But remember that if the discussion falters, you can always ask the group questions specific to craft, such as: Is there unusual language? How many POVs appear in this novel? What is this character's function in the story? How was the pacing? Was the ending satisfying?
4.   I have observed firsthand how much work and devotion is required for authors to maintain their well-deserved reputations for being able to put it away.
5.   https://WritersWhoRead.com/the-drinks
6.   I always did enjoy *Friday Night Lights*.
7.   Kurt Vonnegut, *Palm Sunday*.
8.   https://WritersWhoRead.com

AFTERWORD

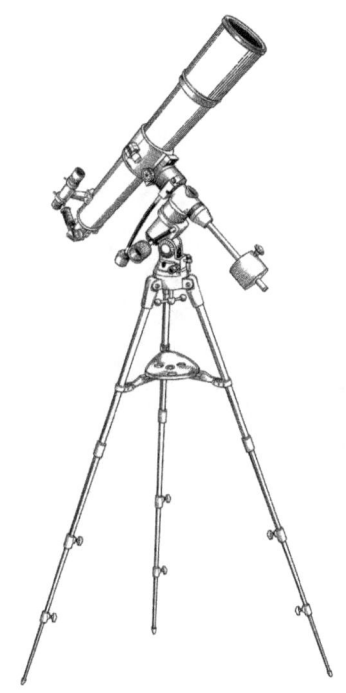

The Next Edition

The book in your hands represents my first attempt to cover a lot of ground, namely, everything there is to know about how to read like a writer. While other books have focused on topics at the periphery of this subject, I believe that mine is the first comprehensive synthesis. Because of that, I know it is highly unlikely I got everything right on my first attempt.

This is a work in progress, meaning that I will continue to expand and refine it as long as I am able to read books. Because I value the experiences and opinions of serious writers and readers, I ask you to share your thoughts with me.

Feedback

I have no doubt you will find omissions, better ways to express ideas, and sometimes flat-out errors. For all of these, I apologize.

I do my best to avoid social media, mostly to maximize my reading and writing time (and avoid online trolls). I understand that any book, including this one, will likely be discussed in public forums, but don't expect me to engage with you there.

I'm a believer in the old one-on-one—what we quaintly call "conversation." So if you feel you have something interesting to say and you're interested in dialogue, then by all means please contact me using the information at the back of this book. I promise to give all constructive feedback the attention it deserves. (But a message like "U suk" will go directly to a spam folder.)

Collaboration

By the time this book goes to press, it will already be out of date because I'm continually adding new novels to my website both for my reading group and for your use as well. I add on average ten new titles per year, but I hope to collaborate with other authors and readers to increase that number.

Here's my ask.

If you have analyzed other novels using the techniques outlined in this book, I am interested in talking with you. I'm not sure yet how to ensure quality control on the new titles, but adding books I have not personally vetted and reviewed is definitely on my to-do list. I have only two eyes and one brain and can't read everything I want to, so in the future I hope to rely on a network of readers who can help me with this.

A Final Word

I hope this book will find its way into enough writers' hands and will sell enough copies to merit a second edition. If that comes to pass, I know there will be additional examples and more than enough improvements in the text to justify a rewrite. I enjoy collaborating in the study of literature, and I would love to have a reason to add your names to the acknowledgments section of the next edition.

In literature, as in life, there is no destination. The reward is the journey. For me, and I hope for you, that journey is one of constant exploration and joyful discovery.

To everyone: Happy reading and happy writing!

Acknowledgments

For a few glorious months in 2016, my writing coach, Lori DeBoer, curated a reading study group for her writers. Inspired by Lori and hungry for more after that group disbanded, I decided in May of 2018 to start one myself at the Boulder Bookstore. Initially, I didn't know what I was doing, so I'd like to thank the Boulder Writers Alliance for giving me a home in 2019, especially BWA presidents Rick Killian and Laura Border. Curating literary discussions almost every month since has taken me on an educational and deeply rewarding journey.

It was Laura who first whispered to me those magic words, "You really ought to write a book," and she has been my tireless champion ever since. Thank you, Laura!

My next guardian angel is Mira Landry, who organized the Rocky Mountain Fiction Writers 2022 Colorado Gold Writers Conference and is a member of my *Writers Who Read* study group, and one of my podcast co-hosts. She encouraged me to present my work at the Rocky Mountain Gold Conference, which started the chain of events that led to this book. I wrote a seventy-two-page book proposal, and because of that I met my agent, Amy Collins of Talcott Notch.

One night when Rick Killian came over to my place for tennis and beers, he advised me that to build a platform for this book, I ought to do something that I'm good at and that I enjoy, as the process of publishing a reference book can take years. He knew I was a radio producer, so he said, "You should do a podcast with Whitney." This led me to create the *Writers Who Read* podcast with Whitney Pinion and Mira Landry in November of 2023.

I first met Whitney at John Dunn's wonderful Boulder Bookies book club, and when I started my book group, she was on board, attending almost every meeting and reading every book. She is the quote queen, and I rely on her to find the best *bon mot* in every novel we survey. It's her love of spirits that inspired our cocktail pairing with each book. "We Are Writers Who Drink" is her catchphrase.

Special thanks to *Writers Who Read* members Chelsea Pennington, whose insights have enriched a number of our podcasts, and Mary Bridges, who stuck around after that very first *Writers Who Read* meeting and who, after the Boulder Bookstore kicked us out, continued our discussion on the corner of 11th and Spruce for almost another hour that August night in 2018—*and* who made sure I knew how important she felt our discussions would be to her writing. It meant the world to me then and it still does. I had originally planned to survey only four novels and then call it quits, but Mary, Whitney, and others encouraged me to keep going.

Next I'd like to thank the intrepid members of *Writers Who Read*, some of whom have been with me since our first book, *The Hate U Give*, and most of whom have been beta readers for various chapters of this book: Whitney Pinion, Laura Border, Susan Flakes, Risë Keller, Paula Weinberger, Mary Bridges, Susan Stanish, Dan Lang, Elizabeth Tait, Charlie Vavra, Chelsea Pennington, Jim Hensinger, Mira Landry, Eben Johnson, Jane Imber, Stephanie Roth, Jim Ringel, Jennifer Swallow, Lindsay Allison, Diana Hoguet, Susan Ferguson, Harry Kennedy, Willyn Webb, Dani Coleman, and many, many others. My tribe. Drinks all around!

I am deeply indebted to those who beta-read the entire manuscript, both providing essential insights and keeping me from looking foolish: Laura Border, Susan Stanish, Chelsea Pennington, and Rachel Chamberlain. Rachel, especially, steered me in the right direction many times and offered me continuous encouragement, as did my dear friends William Wilson and Frank Nowell.

To Risë Keller, my sterling copy editor who has been with *Writers Who Read* from the very first book—and who even came up with the name *Writers Who Read:* I couldn't have done this without you!

Many thanks also to my awesome indexer, Cheryl Landes; cover designer, Debbie Lewis; graphic designer, Amanda Sari; proofreader, Christy Phillippe; and to the team at Illumify Media—Michael Klassen, Jen Clark, Geoff Stone, and Valerie Morris—who helped *In Res Media* get this book across the finish line.

Finally, and most importantly, I'd like to thank my patient wife, Deb, who abides my early morning typing in bed and behind my closed office door, whose taste in books is exquisite and in husbands not so exacting—thank goodness for that!

APPENDICES

Appendix A: Glossary

A-story The primary plot of a novel.

See also B-story.

agency A character's ability to make choices and take actions that drive the plot and shape their own destiny. Agency involves having control over their decisions, motivations, and behaviors, which in turn influence the story's outcome. A character with high agency is proactive, making deliberate choices that affect the narrative.

See also stuck character.

Always ask why The **First rule of *Literary Forensics*.** The rule from which all the others derive. Explained in detail in the YOUR FIRST CLUE section.

analytical reading A critical reading approach that involves breaking down a text into its components to understand its meaning, structure, and underlying themes. It requires the reader to make successive passes through the text to analyze the text's language, literary devices, and authorial intentions, to uncover deeper meanings.

See also close reading, WHAT YOU NOTICE.

anchoring effect The cognitive bias that occurs when a reader relies too heavily on the first piece of information they encounter within the text (the "anchor") when making decisions or judgments about the text that follows. This initial information can influence subsequent emotions and opinions about people, places, things, and situations encountered in the novel, even when the initial information is irrelevant or unreliable.

See also priming.

Anglo-Saxon words Old English words originating from Germanic languages that were first used by the Anglo-Saxons in England from the fifth to the eleventh centuries, derivations of which English speakers still use today. In contrast to Latinate words, words of Anglo-Saxon origin tend to be shorter and more emphatic, which make them suitable for concise, direct communication. Authors often use shorter words like these to increase the pace of a narrative, especially in action scenes.

See also Latinate words.

antagonist
A character, group of characters, institution, or force acting in opposition to the protagonist—the main character—throughout the novel. The antagonist's actions, motives, or presence create conflict and tension, driving the plot forward.

See also protagonist.

aphantasia
A neurological condition in which a person is unable to visualize mental images, which makes reading a novel and trying to imagine a scene, a person, or an object and "play the movie in one's head" impossible.

applied linguistics
A branch of linguistics that focuses on the practical application of linguistic theories and methods to real-world problems, such as how to read like a writer. Applied linguistics draws from linguistics, psychology, sociology, and education, and is employed in discourse analysis, narrative analysis, and when evaluating the grade-level difficulty of a text.

appropriation
The act of taking or using someone else's cultural, intellectual, or artistic property without permission, credit, or compensation. Appropriation in literature includes using racist stereotypes and the vernacular of a culture not one's own. Sensitivity readers can be employed to provide feedback to authors who want to treat another culture with respect.

See also sensitivity reader.

archplot
A story structure that follows a traditional linear narrative arc, characterized by a three-act structure, with a protagonist, an antagonist standing in their way, and a clear resolution or climax that ties up loose ends and provides a sense of closure. Some archplots have eleven distinct plot points: The Ordinary World, The Call to Adventure, Refusal of the Call, Meeting the Mentor, Crossing the Threshold, Tests and Allies and Enemies, Approach to the Inmost Cave, The Ordeal, Seizing the Sword, The Road Back, and The Return with the Elixir.

argumentation
A rhetorical device that focuses on the art of persuasion through language and communication. Argumentation appeals to emotions, logic, and ethics, to convince readers of a particular point of view or to persuade them to take a specific action. Although some novels may use rhetorical argumentation, rhetorical narration is the novel's primary form of communication.

See also narrative.

autofiction
A literary term that describes a blend of autobiography and fiction. This narrative form combines the author's real-life experiences

with fictional elements, blurring the lines between fact and fiction. In an autofiction novel, the author recounts events from their own life but with modifications, inventions, or reinterpretations, creating a unique narrative that defies categorization as memoir.

B-story

A secondary narrative that runs concurrently with a novel's main storyline, involving secondary characters with their own goals, conflicts, and resolutions. A B-story either enhances the main narrative by providing additional depth, complexity, and character development, or it contrasts with the A-story by providing alternative outcomes or by showing negative behavior.

See also A-story.

backstory

The events that occur before the main narrative begins that have shaped the characters, their motivations, and the world they inhabit. Backstory can be revealed through flashbacks, reflection, and within dialogue and narrative description.

backward design

A planning framework originally created to develop educational curricula that starts with the end in mind, setting goals before choosing instructional methods and assessments. This technique is used in *Literary Forensics* to develop a novel-studying plan by: 1) identifying the gaps in your writing technique, 2) developing your learning strategy, and 3) studying novels that represent good (and bad) examples of the craft to improve your own writing.

See also reading worksheet.

beat

A significant occurrence or event within a novel that changes something, propelling the narrative forward or revealing crucial information about characters. It is a fundamental unit of storytelling, often described as a "micro-moment" or a "heartbeat" of the narrative.

See also pacing.

Bechdel test

Named after American graphic novelist Alison Bechdel, this is a measure of representation of women in fiction and other narratives. A work passes the Bechdel test if it features at least one scene with two female characters discussing something other than a man.

bildungsroman

A novel that focuses on the moral and psychological growth of its protagonist from youth to adulthood. The term originates from German, *bildung* meaning education or formation, and *roman* meaning novel. This literary genre explores the protagonist's journey of self-discovery, learning, and maturation as they navigate the challenges of adolescence and young adulthood.

binary form

Binary narrative structure presents two opposing or contrasting perspectives, themes, or ideas, often to explore the complexities of a particular issue or concept. This can take the form of two seemingly unrelated stories, presented in sequence, each of which improves the reader's understanding of the other.

canon The literary canon refers to the collection of works considered to be the most important, influential, and representative of a particular literary tradition or period, which are often studied, taught, and revered in academic and literary circles. The canon includes works from ancient civilizations, established authors, and influential movements. The canon is often criticized for being Eurocentric, exclusionary, and static.

character A constructed figure who resembles a human being in thought, emotion, and behavior, but is not a real person. What a character does reveals who they are, and their motivations, decisions, and growth inform the story's shape, meaning, and emotional impact.

See also intent versus obstacle.

character: ethos Refers to a dramatic character's moral character or reputation, which is often established through their words and actions. Aristotle's concept of ethos is closely tied to his theory of drama, as outlined in his *Poetics,* and is one of the three key elements of persuasion described in his *Rhetoric*.

Chekhov's gun Chekhov's gun is a literary principle named after Russian playwright Anton Chekhov that states: "If you show a gun in act 1, it must be fired by act 3." This means any element introduced in a story, including characters, plot points, or objects, should serve a purpose and be resolved or explained by the end of the story.

See also **Everything serves a purpose**.

chronotope A literary concept introduced by Mikhail Bakhtin to describe the way time and space are represented and interconnected within a narrative. It refers to how these dimensions shape the structure of a story, influencing both the characters' actions and the overall meaning of the text.

climax The moment of highest tension and conflict at which the protagonist faces their greatest challenge or the central issue reaches its peak. It is a turning point that often determines the outcome of the story and leads to its resolution, offering a moment of catharsis for the reader.

See also denouement, inciting incident, magical midpoint.

close reading A literary analysis technique that involves a detailed and systematic examination of a text to uncover its meaning, structure, and literary devices. It involves reading the text multiple times to identify and analyze the language, imagery, and syntax. Close reading evolved from the Romanticism of the eighteenth and nineteenth centuries, which emphasized the individual experience and subjective interpretation, into the more objectively rigorous and scientific methodologies utilized by the New Criticism movement of the 1920s.

See also analytical reading, distant reading, WHAT YOU NOTICE.

code switching
A linguistic phenomenon where a speaker or writer switches between two or more languages, dialects, or language varieties in a single conversation or text. It indicates coded and layered meanings expected to be interpreted differently by different groups.

cognitive linguistics
A branch of linguistics that examines how language is processed and stored in the mind, and how it is used to convey meaning and communicate with others. Cognitive linguistics draws on insights from psychology, philosophy, and anthropology to understand the complex relationships between language, thought, and culture.

cognitive poetics
A branch of literary theory that applies insights from cognitive linguistics to the study of poetry and other forms of literature. It examines how readers process and interpret texts, and how the mind constructs meaning from the linguistic and formal features of those texts.

See also cognitive linguistics.

comedy
A literary and dramatic genre that uses humor, irony, and exaggeration to create a lighthearted and entertaining effect, often with a happy ending, as in Shakespeare's comedy plays. The protagonist's flaws and mistakes are typically used to create humor and satire, and the story often features a resolution that is both satisfying and humorous. Comedy can take many forms, including satire, farce, and irony, and is often used to comment on social issues, politics, and human nature.

See also irony, satire.

commercial fiction
Fiction that is written with the primary goal of entertaining and engaging a wide audience, often with a focus on plot, character, and marketability. It is typically written in a straightforward and accessible style, with a clear narrative structure and a focus on storytelling. In contrast, literary fiction is a type of fiction that prioritizes artistic merit and literary value over commercial appeal, often featuring complex and experimental writing styles, nuanced characterizations, and a focus on themes and ideas.

See also literary fiction.

context
A linguistic concept that refers to the surrounding circumstances, including the physical environment, social situation, and cultural background that influence the meaning and interpretation of language. In linguistics, context is a crucial factor in determining the meaning of words, phrases, and sentences, as it provides the necessary information to disambiguate and clarify the intended

meaning. The principle of context emphasizes that language is not used in isolation but rather is embedded in a complex web of social, cultural, and situational factors that shape its meaning and interpretation.

See also contextual frame.

contextual frame   A psychological term that refers to the mental framework or schema that individuals use to interpret and understand a situation or context. It is the set of assumptions, expectations, and knowledge people bring to a situation, which influences how they perceive and process information. The contextual frame is shaped by an individual's past experiences, cultural background, and social environment, and it can be thought of as a mental filter that influences how one interprets and makes sense of the world.

See also code switching, context.

critical reading   Actively engaging with a text by questioning its arguments, evaluating evidence, and considering its context, purpose, and assumptions. It emphasizes not just comprehension, but also interpretation, analysis, and synthesis, assessing the validity of claims, identifying biases, and recognizing the author's underlying message or perspective. Critical reading also teaches how to analyze various forms of media, considering how content is constructed, who produces it, and for what purpose, fostering an awareness of the role that media plays in shaping public opinion and societal norms.

See also analytical reading, close reading, media literacy, reading like a writer.

cultural anthropology   The study of human cultures, past and present, with a focus on understanding the social, cultural, and linguistic practices of different societies. It examines the ways in which people live, think, and interact with one another, and seeks to understand the complex relationships between culture, power, and identity. By studying the diversity of human cultures, cultural anthropology aims to gain a deeper understanding of what it means to be human and to develop a more nuanced appreciation for the complexities of human experience.

cut size   Also called trim size, the final width and height of a printed book or novel after it has been bound and the excess paper has been trimmed away. Common cut sizes include: 5 x 8 inches (US standard trade paperback); 6 x 9 inches (often used for literary fiction or nonfiction); 7 x 10 inches (reference books, like this one).

deconstructionism   An approach to literary criticism rooted in the work of French philosopher Jacques Derrida in the 1960s that seeks to reveal and challenge the inherent contradictions and instabilities in texts. It argues that meaning is not fixed but is always shaped by the interplay of language, context, and interpretation, thereby resisting the idea of absolute or singular truth. Deconstruction destabilizes the traditional hierarchies and binaries (e.g., presence/absence, speech/writing) of New Criticism, suggesting that these structures are constructs rather than natural truths.

See also formalism, New Criticism.

deixis

Words and phrases that require contextual information to be fully understood, such as *this*, *that*, *here*, *now*, *you*, and *me*. These terms *point* to something specific, but their meaning changes depending on who is speaking, when, and where, anchoring characters and readers in the time, place, and perspective of the narrative.

denouement

The final resolution or conclusion of a story, play, or novel, in which plot threads are tied together and the characters' fates are revealed. The denouement typically answers any remaining questions, resolves any conflicts or tensions, and provides a sense of finality and completion to the narrative.

description

The use of language to create a vivid and detailed picture of a character, setting, object, or event in the story. It is a literary device used by an author or narrator to engage the reader's senses and imagination, drawing them into the world of the narrative and helping them to visualize and understand the story. Effective description can be used to create a sense of atmosphere, mood, and tone, and to reveal character traits, backstory, and motivations.

See also dialogue, scene, sequel.

deus ex machina

A plot device in which a sudden, unexpected event or character is introduced to resolve the conflict or problem in a story, often in a way that feels contrived or unearned. This device is often used to resolve a plot twist or to provide a convenient solution to a problem, but it can feel like a cheat to the audience. The term *deus ex machina* comes from ancient Greek theater, where a machine or god would be lowered onto the stage to resolve the conflict and provide a satisfying ending.

See also eucatastrophe.

dialect

The unique language patterns, vocabulary, and grammar used by a particular group of people, often reflecting their regional, social, or cultural background. Dialect is used in novels to create a sense of authenticity and to convey the distinct voice and perspective of a character or community. By incorporating dialect, authors can add depth, nuance, and realism to their writing, making the story more engaging and immersive for readers.

dialogue   Conversations between characters, which serve to reveal character traits, relationships, and backstory, which also helps to advance the plot, create tension, and provide exposition in a more engaging and natural way. Effective dialogue should sound authentic and unique to each character, while still conveying necessary information to the reader.

diction: lexis   In Aristotle's *Poetics*, diction (or *lexis*) refers to the choice of words and phrases used in a literary work. It encompasses the style, tone, and language employed by the author to convey meaning and create a specific effect on the audience. Aristotle considered diction to be a crucial element of poetry, as it can make or break the emotional impact and artistic value of a work.

digital humanities   An academic discipline at the intersection of digital computing and the humanities. It spans digital archiving, analysis, publishing, and scholarship, and includes the digital tools that we can use to help us study the novels we read.

dinkus   A small, decorative element used in printing and typesetting, often appearing between paragraphs or sections of text. It can take various forms, such as a small icon, a line of dots, or a decorative border, and is used to visually separate and enhance the layout of a document or publication. A typical dinkus is three asterisks separated by spaces: * * *

discourse analysis   The study of language in use, examining how language shapes and is shaped by social contexts, power relationships, and cultural norms. It involves analyzing the structure, meaning, and function of language in various forms of communication, such as conversations, texts, and media, to understand how language constructs and reflects social reality. This approach can reveal how language is used to create, maintain, or challenge social identities, relationships, and institutions.

See also narrative analysis.

distance   The level of agreement, intimacy, familiarity, or detachment between the implied author, narrator, characters, and the implied reader, which can be adjusted by the author to create a specific narrative effect. These distances form complex relationships, with the implied author's intentions and the implied reader's expectations influencing the narrative, while the actual reader brings their own interpretation and understanding to the text.

distancing effect   A dramatic storytelling technique developed by Bertolt Brecht in the 1920s and 1930s, which aims to disrupt the audience's emotional engagement with the performance by creating a sense of detachment or alienation. By using techniques such as breaking the fourth wall, using unconventional settings, and highlighting the artificiality of the narrative, an author can encourage the reader to think critically about the social and political issues presented in the novel, rather than simply identifying with the characters and their emotions.

distant reading

A literary analysis method that involves analyzing large collections of texts using computational tools, focusing on patterns, trends, and relationships rather than detailed analysis of individual works. Coined by Franco Moretti, *distant reading* contrasts with *close reading* by prioritizing quantitative approaches, such as word frequency and network analysis, to uncover broader cultural and historical insights across vast literary bodies of work.

See also close reading.

distorian

A false representation or manipulation of historical figures or events, often contorted to correspond with an author's point of view or their modern-day sensibilities.

eisegesis

The process of interpreting a text by projecting one's own beliefs, ideas, or biases onto it, rather than deriving meaning objectively from the text itself. It contrasts with *exegesis*, which seeks to understand the original intent and meaning of the author or text based on its historical and cultural context. This term was originally intended to describe certain religious studies but now applies to any interpretive work.

See also exegesis.

elementary reading

The foundational stage of learning how to read that focuses on basic skills such as recognizing letters, associating them with sounds (phonics), blending sounds into words, and deriving basic meanings from those words. This level is critical for developing literacy and sets the groundwork for more advanced reading and comprehension. This basic reading skill level is insufficient for reading like a writer.

See also analytical reading, inspectional reading, syntopical reading.

encoding/ decoding theory

Developed by cultural theorist Stuart Hall, this theory explains the communication process in media, suggesting that media producers encode messages with intended meanings, but audiences decode these messages differently based on their own cultural contexts, experiences, and perspectives. This model identifies three decoding positions: dominant/hegemonic, where the audience accepts the intended message; negotiated, where the audience partly agrees but adapts it to their context; and oppositional, where the audience rejects the intended meaning.

epistolary novel

A novel consisting of a series of letters written between fictional characters. More recent epistolary novels include references to electronic documents such as emails, blogs, podcasts, and social media posts.

eucatastrophe   A sudden and favorable resolution of events in a story, often bringing about a joyful and unexpected ending. Coined by J.R.R. Tolkien, the term contrasts with *catastrophe* and is seen as a pivotal moment of hope or redemption, often in the face of despair.

See also deus ex machina.

everything serves a purpose   A feature of modern novels that arises from an author's need for every element to serve double or triple duty to condense the story and help minimize page count. The *Literary Forensics* tool derived from this principle is the **First rule of *Literary Forensics*: Always ask why**.

exegesis   The critical interpretation and explanation of a text, originally applied only to religious or classical works, to uncover its intended meaning within its original historical and cultural context. This method seeks to objectively analyze the text, focusing on its language, structure, and context to derive insights free from personal biases, and is now used on texts of all kinds.

See also eisegesis.

experimental fiction   Literary works that push the boundaries of traditional narrative structure, style, or form, often challenging readers' expectations. While the novel has always seen innovation, experimental fiction makes novelty its primary mode, often at the cost of clarity and emotional resonance. Ignoring the **Three keys** of what fiction is results in a narrative that transports the reader as effectively as a car without wheels.

See also **Three keys**.

exposition   A narrative device used to provide background information necessary for understanding the story. This includes details about the setting, characters, and prior events that establish the groundwork for the plot and its conflicts. Effective exposition is often woven seamlessly into the narrative through dialogue, description, or flashbacks, avoiding overt information dumps to maintain the reader's engagement.

exposure   Describes both the breadth of voice and the depth of perspective: how much or how little of the author's universe is revealed to the reader. Like a camera lens, a point of view's aperture can be narrow or wide, and the depth of focus can be shallow or deep.

First rule   The primary investigatory tool used in *Literary Forensics*, derived from the principle that **everything serves a purpose**, is **Always ask why**. If a word, character, scene, or chapter is in a novel, it must be there for a reason, and it's the reader's job to ponder why the author included it and the function it serves in the story.

flat arc   Also called a neutral character arc, a type of character development in which the protagonist does not fundamentally change internally; rather, they remain consistent in their beliefs, values, or identity throughout the story. However, the world or people around them may change as a result of their influence.

focus shifting   The way a character or narrator changes emphasis from one part of a sentence to another, often to highlight new or important information. This can be done through changes in intonation, word order, or stress, helping listeners understand what the speaker considers most relevant at that moment.

formalism   A literary movement that emerged in the early twentieth century, focusing on the form and structure of a work rather than its content, context, or the author's intentions. It emphasizes close reading, analyzing the elements of a text such as language, meter, rhyme, narrative techniques, and literary devices to understand how they contribute to the work's meaning. Formalist critics argue that a text should be analyzed as a self-contained entity, and that its value lies in the way these formal aspects function together, independent of external influences like historical context or biographical details. This movement influenced New Criticism, which similarly prioritized textual analysis over context, marking a shift from earlier approaches like historical or biographical criticism.

See also deconstructionism , New Criticism.

four stages of discovery   The four sections of *Literary Forensics*, each representing a different level of a reader's interaction with a novel, in order: WHAT YOU BRING, WHAT YOU FEEL, WHAT YOU NOTICE, and WHAT YOU STUDY.

fourth wall   The imaginary barrier between a fictional story and its audience, typically separating the characters from directly acknowledging viewers or readers, like the invisible wall between the front of the stage and the seats in a theater. When a character "breaks the fourth wall," they step out of the narrative to address the audience directly, often for humor, commentary, or dramatic effect.

French scene   A structural unit in a play or screenplay that begins and ends with a character's entrance or exit. Unlike traditional scenes defined by location or time, French scenes are determined by shifts in onstage character dynamics, often highlighting power changes, new conflicts, or evolving relationships. This technique helps writers and directors analyze the emotional and narrative flow of a story in finer detail.

Freytag's pyramid   A narrative structure model developed by nineteenth-century writer Gustav Freytag that outlines the typical progression of a dramatic story. It divides a plot into five distinct parts: exposition, rising action, climax, falling action, and denouement (or resolution), illustrating how a story builds tension before resolving its conflicts. This model is especially useful for analyzing classical works of literature and is often applied to understand the traditional arc of tragedies, in which a protagonist experiences a downfall due to a flaw or fate.

gaslighting   A form of psychological manipulation where one person deliberately distorts or denies reality to make another person doubt their own perceptions, memory, or sanity. This tactic often involves subtle, persistent actions such as denying facts, minimizing experiences, or presenting false information, leading the victim to question their own judgment. The term originated from the 1938 British play *Gas Light* by Patrick Hamilton, and was made more famous by the 1944 film version *Gaslight*, directed by George Cukor and starring Ingrid Bergman, Charles Boyer, and Joseph Cotton.

genre   A category of literary composition characterized by shared conventions, themes, or styles, such as fiction, poetry, drama, or nonfiction, with further subdivisions like mystery, fantasy, or romance. This classification helps readers and critics categorize and interpret works based on their distinctive features and narrative structures. Some genres are also defined by the tastes or identities of their intended readership—such as young adult, new adult, upmarket, or literary fiction—where audience expectations shape both content and style.

grounded theory   A qualitative research method that involves generating theories through the systematic collection and analysis of data. It focuses on building theory inductively from observations, allowing patterns and concepts to emerge organically from the data rather than testing existing hypotheses.

See also close reading, discourse analysis.

hamartia   A character's tragic flaw or error in judgment that leads to their downfall, commonly found in Greek tragedies.

head-hopping   Shifting abruptly between different characters' points of view (POVs) within a single scene or paragraph, which can confuse readers about whose thoughts or emotions are being presented. While switching perspectives can enrich a narrative, excessive head-hopping can disrupt the flow of the story and lead to a disjointed or unclear reading experience, making it difficult for readers to connect with the narrative voice, which can lead to a lack of emotional depth or clarity in the storytelling.

hermeneutic circle   A concept in interpretation theory that describes how understanding a text involves a dynamic relationship between the whole and its parts. To comprehend the entire text, one must interpret its individual elements, but to interpret those elements, one must have some sense of the whole. This circular process reflects how meaning is gradually constructed and refined through repeated interpretation.

hermeneutics The theory and methodology of interpretation, particularly focused on understanding texts, language, and symbols within their historical and cultural contexts. Hermeneutics emphasizes the interplay between the interpreter's preconceptions and the text's meaning, aiming to bridge the gap between the author's intent and the reader's understanding.

heroine's journey A narrative framework developed by Maureen Murdock that explores a woman's inner journey toward healing, self-acceptance, and integration of the feminine and masculine within. Unlike the hero's journey, which emphasizes external conquest and individual triumph, the heroine's journey centers on inner transformation, beginning with a rejection of the feminine and culminating in a return to wholeness. Murdock developed this model to address the psychological and spiritual needs unique to women's experiences, offering an alternative path to empowerment and self-realization.

hero's journey A narrative structure identified by Joseph Campbell that outlines the common stages of an archetypal hero's adventure, starting from their ordinary world, through trials and self-discovery, to their eventual return with newfound wisdom or power. This form is widely used in novels, memoirs, and modern film. Stages include the Call to Adventure, the Refusal of the Call, the Meeting with the Mentor, Crossing the Threshold, Trials, Approach to the Inmost Cave, the Ordeal, Reward, the Road Back, Resurrection, and Return with the Elixir.

hierarchy of needs A psychological theory proposed by Abraham Maslow positing that human beings have a set of needs organized in a five-level pyramid. The base of the pyramid represents basic physiological needs like food and water, followed by safety, love and belonging, esteem, and at the top, self-actualization, which is the realization of one's full potential.

hitting pause An essential skill for reading like a writer, this is the ability to interrupt your flow state while reading to notice writing craft as you encounter it. A complete description of how to do this, with exercises and games, fills chapter 11, "You're Engaged." It's also described in chapter 2, "How You Read."

hook A narrative device used to immediately engage readers, creating an initial excitement or curiosity that compels them to continue reading, and other devices like cliffhangers—which leave the narrative at a critical or suspenseful moment—that keep readers hooked by prompting them to read on in search of resolution.

horizon of expectations The set of cultural, historical, and personal expectations a reader brings to a text based on their prior knowledge and experiences. This concept, developed by philosopher Hans Robert Jauss and fundamental to reception theory, suggests that readers interpret and evaluate a work through the lens of these expectations, which evolve as they encounter new genres or styles. Authors may play with or subvert these expectations to surprise or challenge their readers, often creating deeper meanings or new interpretations of the text.

See also reader response criticism, reception theory.

Icarus story
A narrative arc in which a character rises toward success or greatness, only to fall dramatically as a result of overreach or hubris, much like the myth of Icarus in Greek mythology. The inverted-U shape of this arc contrasts with other story shapes, such as rags to riches, where the protagonist's growth leads to an eventual positive outcome. It is used to explore themes of ambition, pride, and the fragility of success.

See also hero's journey, man in a hole, rags to riches, tragedy.

implied author
The version of the author that is constructed by the narrative voice, style, and structure of a text, distinct from the actual person who wrote it. This concept, developed by literary theorist Wayne C. Booth, suggests that the implied author reflects the author's narrative choices and values as perceived through the text itself, rather than being a direct representation of their real-life identity or intentions.

See also implied reader.

implied reader
The ideal or hypothetical reader constructed by the text itself, as envisioned by the author. This reader embodies the values, knowledge, and expectations that the author assumes, guiding how the text is interpreted, without necessarily representing a specific or actual person. The idea, introduced by philosopher Wolfgang Iser, highlights the relationship between the text and the reader, focusing on how the author implicitly suggests the appropriate response to the narrative or ideas within the work.

See also implied author.

imposter syndrome
A psychological pattern in which individuals doubt their accomplishments and fear being exposed as a fraud, despite evidence of their competence and success. This feeling of inadequacy often affects high-achieving individuals and can lead to anxiety, stress, and a constant fear of failure.

in medias res
A Latin term meaning "in the midst of things" that refers to a narrative technique where a story begins in the middle of the action or events, rather than starting at the beginning. This technique draws readers or viewers into the plot immediately, creating intrigue and often requiring them to piece together prior events through dialogue, flashbacks, or other narrative devices.

inciting incident
The event that disrupts the status quo in a novel, propelling the protagonist into the main conflict or journey of the narrative. This

key moment often occurs early in the plot and serves as the catalyst for the unfolding of the story's events, sparking action and setting the protagonist on their path of change or struggle.

inciting-midpoint-climax One of the **Three keys**, this asserts that the inciting incident, the magical midpoint, and the climax together form the primary structural tentpoles of every novel.

See also climax, inciting incident, magical midpoint.

inspectional reading The eyes-open-wide reading technique I hope all of us use on our first pass through a novel. Useful for evaluating a text's relevance or value without committing to an in-depth, analytical reading.

See also analytical reading, syntopical reading.

intent versus obstacle The sum and depth of what a character is—all the reader knows of them—which is the conflict between a character's goals (intent) and the challenges or hindrances (obstacles) they face in achieving them. This tension not only propels character development but also engages the reader, making the story dynamic and emotionally resonant.

interiority The depiction of a character's inner thoughts, emotions, and mental processes, providing readers with insight into their psychological state. This technique is commonly used in first-person or limited third-person point of view, where the narrative focuses on the subjective experience of the character, often conveyed through introspective monologues, stream-of-consciousness, or reflective passages.

intonation The context of point of view (POV) that refers to the subtle variations in voice that convey emotional tone, emphasis, and the speaker's attitude. It affects how a narrative feels to the reader by influencing how a character's internal state or external perceptions are communicated.

See also point of view, voice.

irony A literary device that involves a discrepancy between expectation and reality, where events or statements turn out contrary to what one would logically expect. Dramatic irony is where the reader knows more about a situation than the characters do.

kishōtenketsu A narrative structure commonly used in East Asian storytelling, particularly in Japanese and Chinese literature, that consists of four key parts: Ki (introduction), Shō (development), Ten (twist), and Ketsu (conclusion). This structure emphasizes an unexpected shift or resolution in the third part (Ten), which contrasts with Western narrative structures that typically focus on conflict and resolution. The form is well suited for stories that focus more on mood, character, or theme than on action-driven plots.

Kuleshov effect   In film editing, where viewers derive meaning from the juxtaposition of two unrelated shots, attributing emotion or intent to a character based on the context of the surrounding images. This effect was demonstrated by Soviet filmmaker Lev Kuleshov in the 1910s, who showed that a neutral expression could be interpreted as conveying different emotions (e.g., sadness, hunger, or desire) depending on the images that followed it.

lampshading   Also called *lampshade hanging*, this is when an author draws attention to a plot inconsistency, cliché, or trope within the story by explicitly acknowledging it within the narrative. This self-aware moment allows the author to call attention to something that might otherwise be seen as a flaw or predictable, often through a character's dialogue or inner thoughts.

Latinate words   Words derived from Latin, which tend to have longer syllables and a more sophisticated feel compared to Anglo-Saxon words, which are typically shorter and simpler. Latinate words are often associated with a higher level of diction and are used for precision, formality, or to convey abstract concepts, and are typically found in passages of reflection.

See also Anglo-Saxon words.

legal doublet   A pair of synonymous legal terms used together for emphasis or clarity, often derived from different linguistic sources, such as Latin and Anglo-Saxon, in order to provide precision in legal language. Examples: assault and battery, aid and abet, null and void.

literary criticism   The study, analysis, and interpretation of literature, often focusing on themes, forms, historical context, and the author's intent. It encompasses various schools of thought, such as formalism, feminism, Marxism, and psychoanalysis, each offering a different lens through which to understand and evaluate literary works. Through literary criticism, scholars explore how texts reflect or challenge societal values, and how they use language, symbols, and structure to convey meaning. This critical approach helps readers engage more deeply with literature, providing insights into both the text itself and the world in which it was created.

literary fiction   Works of fiction that focus on character development, thematic depth, and stylistic complexity, often exploring the human condition and social issues. Unlike genre fiction, which prioritizes plot-driven narratives, literary fiction emphasizes artistic expression, intellectual engagement, and emotional resonance, aiming to provoke thought and evoke a deeper understanding of life and society.

See also commercial fiction, genre.

Literary Forensics	The title of this reference, meaning the art of reading like a writer, combining and repurposing the analytical tools of hermeneutics and literary theory, epistemological philosophy, social psychology, cultural anthropology, discourse and narrative analysis, dramaturgy, linguistics, semiotics, and close, distant, and critical reading techniques.
	See also the four stages of discovery: WHAT YOU BRING, WHAT YOU FEEL, WHAT YOU NOTICE, and WHAT YOU STUDY.
logline	A one- or two-sentence summary that captures the essence of a novel, including the main character, their goal, the conflict, and the stakes. It is designed to hook readers or industry professionals by conveying the core premise in a concise and compelling way. The term originated in the film industry.
MacGuffin	An object, event, or device in a story that drives the plot forward but is often of little inherent importance to the narrative, serving mainly as a catalyst for the characters' actions. Popularized by Alfred Hitchcock, the MacGuffin's primary function is to motivate the characters or create suspense, while its true nature or significance remains secondary to the story itself.
	See also red herring.
magical midpoint	A significant turning point or shift that occurs midway through a novel that redefines the direction of the story, intensifies the stakes, and forces the protagonist to confront deeper challenges, often changing the character's motivations or goals. This shift can create a sense of urgency or introduce a new obstacle, energize the narrative, and steer the characters toward their final confrontation or resolution.
major/minor divisions	Sections, chapters, and chapter partitions—essentially, every division within a novel marked by a new section or chapter heading, or demarcated by a dinkus.
	See also dinkus.
man in a hole	A narrative structure, as defined by Kurt Vonnegut in his famous diagram of story arcs, where a character starts in a relatively stable or positive situation, falls into a challenging or difficult predicament (the "hole"), and climbs to a better or resolved state by the end of the story. This arc focuses on the character's struggle, loss, and ultimate redemption or resolution, where the "hole" symbolizes the obstacle or conflict the protagonist faces.
	See also hero's journey, Icarus story, rags to riches, tragedy.
mass-market fiction	See commercial fiction.
media literacy	The ability to access, analyze, evaluate, and create media in various forms, including print, digital, and visual content. It involves understanding how media messages are constructed, recognizing

biases or manipulations, and being aware of the impact that media has on society, culture, and individual perception.

melodrama

A dramatic genre characterized by exaggerated emotions, clear moral dichotomies, and sensationalized plots, often focusing on the struggle between good and evil. In melodramatic works, characters are typically portrayed in extremes—heroes are virtuous and noble, while villains are deeply malevolent, and the narrative often relies on heightened emotions and events designed to provoke intense reactions from the audience. This genre frequently emphasizes visual spectacle and emotional appeal over complex character development or nuanced storylines, as seen in many classic Hollywood films or stage plays of the nineteenth century.

melody: melos

According to Aristotle, melody plays an essential role in evoking emotions, setting the tone, and reinforcing the mood of a scene, helping to deepen the impact of the narrative. Originally referring to music and song, within novels this dramatic element relates to the poetry and rhythm or dialogue and narrative, as well as the structure and pacing of the plot.

metafiction

A literary technique where the text self-consciously addresses its own fictional nature, often drawing attention to the act of storytelling or the conventions of literature. This can involve characters who are aware they are in a story, the author directly interacting with the narrative, or the story blurring the lines between reality and fiction. Metafiction challenges the reader's perception of narrative structure and reality, often creating a more self-aware and playful reading experience.

See also fourth wall.

mise-en-scène

A French term in film and theater meaning "placing on stage," this refers to the arrangement of all visual elements in a scene, including sets, lighting, props, costumes, and actors' movements. In novels, this concept is crucial for setting the tone and atmosphere, and conveying the themes or emotions of a scene, as it shapes the reader's perceptions and enhances storytelling.

mood

The atmosphere or emotional ambiance that the writing evokes in the reader, shaped by setting, tone, and language choices. Mood is the sensory and emotional experience that immerses readers, influencing how they feel as they engage with the story.

See also point of view, tone, voice.

multiculturalism

The inclusion and exploration of multiple cultural perspectives, identities, and traditions within literary works. It emphasizes the representation of historically marginalized or underrepresented communities, fostering understanding and dialogue between different cultural groups and experiences. Multicultural literature can broaden readers' horizons, encouraging empathy and a nuanced appreciation of global and local cultural dynamics.

narrative The structured account of connected events and experiences, typically conveyed through a sequence of scenes, actions, and dialogue. It forms the backbone of the novel, shaping how characters, settings, and plots are presented to engage the reader and convey the author's themes or messages.

narrative analysis A method of examining stories or accounts to understand how they are structured, the themes they convey, and the ways they reflect cultural, social, or psychological meanings. By focusing on elements such as plot, characters, and narrative voice, narrative analysis seeks to uncover deeper insights about the storyteller's intentions and the audience's interpretations, making it a valuable tool for understanding human communication and storytelling across contexts. This approach is often used in fields like literature, sociology, and psychology to study how narratives shape perceptions, communicate values, and construct identities.

narrative poetry A form of poetry that tells a story and contains characters, a plot, and a setting.

narrator The voice or entity that tells the story, guiding the reader through the events, characters, and settings of the narrative. The narrator can exist in various forms, such as a character within the story (first-person narrator), an outside observer with varying degrees of omniscience (third-person narrator), or even an unreliable perspective that challenges the reader's interpretation of events. The choice of narrator greatly influences the tone, perspective, and depth of the story, shaping how the reader connects with the plot and characters.

New Criticism A twentieth-century literary movement that emphasized close reading of texts, focusing on their formal elements—such as imagery, symbolism, and structure—rather than historical or biographical context. Originating in the United States and Britain, it advocated for the idea that a literary work should be analyzed as a self-contained entity, with meaning derived solely from the text itself rather than external factors.

novel A long-form narrative work of fiction that explores characters, settings, and events in depth, typically through a structured plot and prose style. It allows for the detailed development of themes, emotions, and relationships, offering readers an immersive experience into imagined or sometimes semirealistic worlds. As a literary form, the novel has evolved over centuries and continues to evolve today.

See also **Three keys**.

novella
A highly condensed novel form, typically one-quarter to one-half the length of a full-length novel, which still contains the **Three keys** of a novel.

See also novel, **Three keys**.

omniscience
A narrative perspective in which the narrator has unlimited knowledge and access to the thoughts, feelings, and experiences of all characters, as well as events happening in multiple locations. This point of view allows the narrator to present a comprehensive understanding of the world within the story, offering insights that no individual character could know. The omniscient narrator can provide commentary, predict outcomes, or shift between various characters' perspectives, giving readers a broader social understanding or philosophical commentary.

onomastics
The study of names, including the origin, meaning, and use of personal names, place names, and other identifiers.

Overton window
A political theory that refers to the range of ideas and policies that are considered acceptable or mainstream within a given society at any given time. It highlights how public opinion can shift, making previously unthinkable ideas more acceptable or vice versa, depending on political discourse and advocacy efforts.

pacing
The speed at which the novel unfolds, determined by the balance between action, dialogue, description, and reflection, and affecting the reader's emotional engagement and the narrative's tension. It is a key element in controlling suspense, character development, and the overall flow of the plot, with faster pacing often used in action scenes and slower pacing for introspective or emotional moments.

pantomime
A theatrical performance that combines exaggerated gestures, music, and audience interaction, often blurring the lines between drama and spectacle. British *panto*, performed at Christmastime, is a comic, family-friendly stage show with cross-dressing, slapstick, and call-and-response routines, while American melodrama often focuses on heightened conflict and sentimentality. Similar elements appear in Thai *Likay* and Chinese opera, where stylized movement, musicality, and role reversals serve both to entertain and to convey moral or folkloric themes.

pantser
As opposed to a plotter, a novelist who writes by *the seat of their pants*, that is, by instinct rather than to an outline.

See also plotter.

parallel construction
The repetition or consistency of grammatical structures, word choices, or sentence patterns to create a sense of balance and rhythm within the text. It is used to enhance clarity, emphasize ideas, and create a sense of cohesion within the narrative.

phatic expression A type of speech or communication used primarily to establish or maintain social relationships, rather than to convey specific information. These expressions serve as a form of social interaction that confirms the speaker's presence, checks on the listener's well-being, or fosters connection, without necessarily offering substantive content.

pivot point A significant event or moment in the novel that drives the narrative forward and often leads to a shift in direction or character development. The most important three pivot points are the inciting incident (which sets the story in motion), the midpoint (where the stakes or character motivations shift), and the climax (where the central conflict reaches its highest tension).

See also climax, denouement, inciting incident, midpoint.

plot: mythos The plot or narrative structure of a story, central to its emotional impact and thematic depth. Aristotle emphasized that the plot should have unity, meaning that all actions and events must be logically connected and contribute to the overarching narrative. *Mythos* is not just the events themselves, but also their dramatic arrangement, key in eliciting emotions like fear and pity, and ultimately leading to a satisfying resolution.

plotter A novelist who writes to an outline.

See also pantser.

point of view (POV) The perspective from which the story is told, determining how the reader experiences the events, thoughts, and feelings of the characters. It shapes the narrative by defining the narrator's position—whether they are inside or outside the story—and the level of knowledge they have, with common POVs including first-person, second-person, and third-person (limited or omniscient). The choice of POV affects a novel's intimacy, focus, and reliability, influencing how much information is revealed to the reader.

See also mood, tone, voice.

postcard Coined by literary agent Donald Maass, a *postcard* refers to a reflective passage found most often within literary fiction that deepens our understanding of characters and relationships without advancing the plot. These powerful, evocative sequels are intended to leave a lasting impression on the reader, often evoking an emotion or visual image.

See also sequel.

presentism A concept in historical analysis and literary criticism that involves interpreting past events, texts, or phenomena through the lens of contemporary values, beliefs, or concerns. This form of bias can lead to anachronistic judgments, where historical figures or works are evaluated based on modern standards, potentially distorting their original context. Presentism is often contrasted with historical contextualism, which emphasizes understanding the past within its own historical framework.

priming
A psychological phenomenon where exposure to one stimulus influences the response to a subsequent stimulus, even if the person is unaware of the connection. In the context of reading, when two descriptions are placed near each other, the first description can "prime" the reader's perception or interpretation of the second, shaping how the second description is understood or felt.

See also anchoring effect.

privilege
A set of permissions an author grants a character or narrator, allowing them access to knowledge, power, or structural control within the story. Privilege is fluid and can be granted, broadened, or taken away at any time. Examples include a narrator's knowledge of future events, a character's thoughts, or a character's awareness that they exist within a narrative by addressing the reader directly.

probable impossibility
The idea, first stated by Aristotle, that a narrative can include things that could never actually happen in real life—as long as they feel believable within the world of the story. This is much preferred over its opposite—a possible improbability—which, although possible, is so unlikely to happen that it makes a story seem inauthentic.

protagonist
The central character around whom the plot revolves, typically facing challenges or conflicts that drive the story's development. This character is often the one the reader is meant to empathize with or root for, although the protagonist's role and traits can vary depending on the genre and narrative perspective.

See also antagonist.

qualitative linguistics
The study of language that focuses on understanding meaning, context, and social interactions rather than numerical (quantitative) data. It examines how language is used in real-life situations, exploring patterns, cultural nuances, and subjective experiences conveyed through communication.

question-driven plotting
The idea, espoused by author Chuck Wendig and others, that the questions asked by characters and the questions posed to readers are the driving force of a novel's plot and are what keeps the reader reading.

rags to riches
A narrative story arc in which the protagonist starts in a position of poverty, hardship, or low status and rises to wealth, success, or high social standing through their actions, perseverance, or chance. This arc is often used in tales of personal transformation where the protagonist overcomes significant challenges and

achieves their desires, symbolizing hope, resilience, and the potential for change.

See also hero's journey, Icarus story, man in a hole, tragedy.

readability test   A tool or formula used to evaluate how easy or difficult a piece of writing is to understand, based on factors like sentence length, word complexity, and vocabulary. Common readability tests include the Flesch-Kincaid Grade Level, Gunning Fog Index, and the SMOG (Simple Measure of Gobbledygook) index, which provide numerical scores indicating the educational level required for comprehension.

reader response criticism A literary theory that emphasizes the role of the reader in interpreting a text, arguing that meaning is not solely inherent in the text itself but is co-constructed by the reader's personal experiences, emotions, and cultural background. This approach contrasts with traditional theories that focus primarily on the author's intent or the text's formal elements. The reader's engagement with the text is seen as an active process, shaping the meaning rather than merely discovering it.

See also deconstructionism, horizon of expectations, reception theory.

reading like a writer   Reading with intent and being present enough while you read to be aware of the craft behind the text, in the same way that an author would read as they evaluate and edit their own writing. Essentially the same thing as critical reading.

See also critical reading.

reading worksheet   Found in *Appendix B*, this worksheet can help guide a writer who reads in their study of novels using the following steps: 1) introspect—uncover biases and technique gaps, 2) strategize—create a learning plan, and 3) read lots of novels.

See also WHAT YOU BRING, WHAT YOU NOTICE, and WHAT YOU STUDY.

reception theory   A literary theory that focuses on how different audiences interpret and respond to a text, emphasizing the active role of readers in shaping the meaning of a work. Developed by theorists like Hans Robert Jauss and Wolfgang Iser, reception theory argues that a text's meaning can change over time as it is interpreted by different audiences, and is shaped by a reader's "horizon of expectations," the set of cultural and historical expectations that shapes their interpretation.

See also horizon of expectations, reader response criticism.

red herring   A literary device or plot element designed to mislead or distract the reader from the actual focus or solution in a narrative, often used in mysteries or thrillers.

See also MacGuffin.

register   The level of formality or informality in a character's language, shaped by their social context, background, and relationship to others. It influences word choice, sentence structure, and tone—ranging from casual and conversational to formal or academic. Used to make dialogue and narration feel authentic and to reveal deeper aspects of a character's personality, education, and status.

rhetorical modes   *Rhetoric* is the art of using language effectively and persuasively, which includes the strategies and approaches used in writing to achieve specific purposes, such as informing, persuading, or entertaining the reader. The four primary rhetorical modes are: narration (relating the story), description (painting a picture), exposition (explaining or informing), and argumentation (convincing an audience).

satire   A literary genre or technique that uses humor, irony, exaggeration, or ridicule to criticize or expose the flaws, vices, and absurdities in society, politics, individuals, or institutions. Satire often aims to provoke thought, encourage social change, or simply entertain by highlighting hypocrisy or injustices in a way that is both entertaining and enlightening.

See also comedy, irony.

Save the Cat   Originally developed by Blake Snyder for screenwriting, this storytelling technique refers to a key moment early in the story where the protagonist does something endearing or heroic, like saving a cat, which establishes their likeability and moral alignment.

scene   A distinct unit of narrative that takes place in a single location and time, typically characterized by a change in action or emotional tone. It usually involves characters interacting with one another, making decisions, or reacting to events that drive the plot forward. Each scene is usually followed by a transition to the next moment in the story, whether through a sequel, a passage of time, or a change in location, depending on the pacing and structure of the novel.

See also scene and sequel, sequel.

scene and sequel   Two key components of narrative structure, popularized by writer Dwight Swain, that balance action with reflection to maintain pacing and emotional engagement throughout a story. A scene is an event or sequence in a story that is driven by action or conflict, usually taking place in real time and moving the plot forward. A sequel, in contrast, is a quieter, reflective section that follows a scene and deals with the aftermath of the events.

See also scene, sequel.

semiotics   The study of signs and symbols, their meanings, and how they communicate in both language and nonverbal forms. This framework, introduced by Ferdinand de Saussure, examines how meaning is constructed and understood through various cultural and societal systems, encompassing everything from words and images to gestures and rituals. In semiotics, a sign is anything that communicates meaning, and it is broken down into three main components: the signifier (the physical form of the sign, such as a word or image), the signified (the concept or idea the sign represents), and the referent (the real-world object or event the sign refers to).

See also signifier, symbolism.

sensitivity reader   A person who reviews a manuscript, story, or piece of writing to ensure that it portrays certain groups of people or cultures accurately and respectfully. Sensitivity readers are often hired to identify and address potential issues related to stereotypes, cultural appropriation, harmful language, and misrepresentation, particularly when the author does not share the same background or identity as the characters or subjects they are writing about. The goal is to create more inclusive, accurate, and thoughtful narratives that reflect the experiences of those outside the author's own lived reality.

See also appropriation.

sequel   A quieter, reflective section that follows a scene and deals with the aftermath of the events. It is more focused on internal processes like a character's thoughts, feelings, and decisions. The sequel provides space for characters to process what has just happened, reassess their goals, and make plans for the next course of action. This section often connects one scene and another, slowing the pace of the narrative before the plot resumes moving forward.

See also postcard, scene, scene and sequel.

serendipity   The phenomenon of finding something valuable or fortunate when you are not actively seeking it. It highlights the idea that sometimes the best things in life happen when you're not looking for them, suggesting that openness to the unknown can lead to unexpected joys or discoveries.

Seven tools   Deriving directly from the **Three keys** found in every novel, the most powerful and frequently used tools in *Literary Forensics*. The **Seven tools** are: **use structure to identify themes; assume you're being played; pay attention to POV; what happens is not what's discussed; reread; rewrite**; and the **First rule of *Literary Forensics*: Always ask why.**

See also **First rule, Three keys.**

short story A short-form fictional narrative that corresponds in length and scope to a single chapter from a full-length novel.

signifier In semiotics, the *signifier* is the physical form of a sign, such as a word, image, or sound that represents something else. The signifier is the element that conveys meaning and is paired with the *signified*, which is the concept or idea the signifier points to.

See also semiotics.

sound symbolism The idea that certain sounds in language can convey inherent meaning or evoke specific associations beyond their conventional linguistic use. It suggests that the sounds of words, especially the phonetic qualities like pitch, tone, or consonant-vowel combinations, can influence how people perceive and interpret those words.

spectacle: opsis *Opsis* refers to the visual elements of a play or dramatic work, including the setting, costumes, and stage effects that contribute to the overall experience. Aristotle describes it as one of the six key components of tragedy, which serves to enhance the emotional impact of the story. In a novel, this refers to any extravagant settings, fabulist plots, celebrity cameos, or any other showy elements that an author uses for dramatic effect.

status The social, emotional, or psychological position of a character in relation to others within the story. It can involve the character's rank, power, wealth, or influence, as well as more abstract elements like self-perception or emotional resilience. Status shapes how characters interact with one another and can be fluid, shifting throughout the narrative as characters experience challenges, successes, or growth.

stichomancy Using a randomly chosen line of text in a book to gain insight or guidance about specific questions. Finding inspiration wherever we look for it is a core component of serendipitous learning. Synonyms include *bibliomancy* for sacred texts, and *rhapsodomancy* for poetry.

See also serendipity.

stream of consciousness A narrative technique that attempts to capture the continuous flow of a character's thoughts, feelings, and perceptions, often in an unfiltered or disjointed manner. This method seeks to mimic the natural flow of thoughts, which can jump from one idea to another without clear transitions, creating a more intimate and fragmented portrayal of a character's internal world.

stuck character When a character is experiencing an internal or external conflict that prevents them from progressing in their personal journey or achieving their goals. This could manifest as emotional stagnation, a lack of agency, or a situation where the character is trapped by circumstances, choices, or their own psychological barriers.

See also agency.

stylistics
The study of style in language, analyzing how choices in vocabulary, syntax, and rhetorical devices contribute to meaning, tone, and effect. It bridges literary analysis and linguistics by examining how language patterns influence interpretation and reader response.

See also reader response criticism, reception theory.

stylometry
The data science technique of evaluating the style of a text to determine authorship using vocabulary, word frequency, sentence length, and other metrics.

suspension of disbelief
When a reader consciously accepts the implausibility or fantastical elements of a novel to more fully engage with the narrative. The suspension of disbelief allows the reader to accept events, characters, or settings that may not be realistic, as long as these elements serve the emotional or thematic purpose of the story. Essential for enjoying genres like fantasy, science fiction, and horror, in which the audience needs to temporarily set aside skepticism to fully immerse themselves in the world of the story.

See also probable impossibility.

symbolism
The use of symbols—objects, characters, or events—that represent larger ideas, concepts, or themes within the story. These symbols often carry deeper meanings that extend beyond their literal function, providing a way for authors to convey complex ideas or emotional states indirectly.

See also semiotics.

syntopical reading
Reading that involves comparing and analyzing multiple texts on the same subject to gain a broader and deeper understanding of a topic. Rather than reading a single text in isolation, syntopical reading allows the reader to examine various perspectives, synthesize different viewpoints, and draw connections between ideas across sources. This approach is often used in research or academic settings, where reading multiple works on a theme or question helps to develop a more comprehensive view of the subject matter.

See also WHAT YOU STUDY.

theory of mind
A psychological concept that refers to the ability to attribute mental states—such as beliefs, desires, intentions, and knowledge—to oneself and others, and to understand that these mental states can differ from one individual to another. This cognitive skill enables individuals to predict and interpret the

behavior of others based on their understanding of those mental states and is crucial for social interactions and empathy.

thought: dianoia   The intellectual aspect of a narrative, encompassing the ideas, themes, arguments, and reasoning expressed through the dialogue and actions of the characters. It is how the novelist communicates the moral, philosophical, or thematic messages of the story, often reflecting the characters' motivations and the underlying principles driving the plot. This dramatic element, defined by Aristotle in *Poetics*, is closely linked to persuasion and logic, aligning with the rhetorical techniques found in Aristotle's *Rhetoric*.

Three keys   The three components common to all novels: **inciting-midpoint-climax**, the **unspoken contract**, and **everything serves a purpose**. Explained in detail in the YOUR FIRST CLUE section.

three-point rule of oration   1) tell them what you're going to say, 2) say it, 3) summarize what you said.

ticking clock   A narrative device that introduces a time constraint or deadline to create urgency, tension, and increase the stakes for the characters. Common in thrillers and action genres, the ticking clock could take the form of a literal countdown, such as a bomb timer, or a figurative one, like a critical decision needing to be made before an impending event.

tone   The author's attitude or emotional stance toward the subject matter, characters, or audience, conveyed through word choice, style, and narrative voice. Tone is a key element in establishing the mood and thematic depth of a narrative. It shapes the reader's emotional response to the story and can range from serious or somber to humorous, sarcastic, or hopeful.

See also mood, point of view, register, voice.

tragedy   A novel genre that explores human suffering, typically through the downfall of a noble protagonist, often due to their own flaws and external circumstances. Tragedy aims to evoke a cathartic response in readers, and its tone is typically serious and dignified.

trope   A recurring or overused literary and rhetorical device, motif, or cliché in novels and other narrative forms. Tropes include frequently used plot devices, stock characters, euphemisms, and common themes. A trope can also refer to a figure of speech like a metaphor.

unspoken contract   A reader's expectation that the end of a novel will include some form of resolution or explanation of what has happened in the novel, and that the author has provided a satisfying ending and is worthy of a reader's trust. A set of tools arises from this, grouped under *You're Being Played*. See YOUR FIRST CLUE for a full description.

vernacular   Informal spoken language, as opposed to more formal written language. Vernacular includes dialect, slang, idioms, nonstandard grammar, code switching, and in novels is found most frequently in dialogue.

voice   The unique tone, style, and perspective an author or narrator brings to the novel. Voice is a distinctive way of communicating, expressing thoughts and emotions, and conveying the story that includes word choice, grammar, syntax, and rhythm.

See also intonation, mood, point of view, tone.

WHAT YOU BRING   A reader's preconceived opinions of a novel that are formed before reading it. Recalibrating expectations requires consciously acknowledging and compensating for a reader's background, education, culture, real-life experience, and previous readings, so that they can approach and evaluate the novel in as balanced a way as possible.

See also contextual frame, four stages of discovery.

WHAT YOU FEEL   Emotions that a novel evokes in the mind of a reader, which often marks the exact passage within the text to investigate craft most effectively.

See also four stages of discovery, melodrama, melody: melos, spectacle: opsis.

WHAT YOU NOTICE   Categories of craft that a reader consciously encounters in the text, which include language and grammar, context in scene, point of view, voice, character development, structure, pacing, and layering.

See also analytical reading, close reading, four stages of discovery.

WHAT YOU STUDY   Resources outside a novel that a reader consults to gain greater insight into the craft of the novel that include publishing industry resources, other narrative forms, academic disciplines, the digital humanities, and study groups.

See also four stages of discovery, syntopical reading.

wheel of craft   A visualization of the nine chapters in the WHAT YOU NOTICE section, representing different entry points a reader can use to study an author's craft. Each topic relates most closely with its neighbors, and there is some bleed-through from one chapter to the next.

wheel of emotions   A psychological model created by Robert Plutchik that visually represents a range of human emotions and how they relate to each other. The model is structured as a wheel with eight primary emotions arranged in opposing pairs: joy versus sadness, trust versus disgust, fear versus anger, and surprise versus anticipation. These primary emotions can combine to form more complex emotions, which are represented as mixtures of adjacent colors on the wheel with varying degrees of intensity for each emotion.

whodunit A subgenre of mystery fiction centered on solving a crime—typically a murder—through clues, deduction, and logical reasoning. The narrative often follows a detective or amateur sleuth as they investigate suspects, uncover secrets, and ultimately reveal the culprit, usually in a climactic scene. Hallmarks of the genre include red herrings, a closed circle of suspects, and an emphasis on fair play, inviting readers to solve the puzzle alongside the protagonist.

Writers Who Read The monthly novel study group in Boulder, Colorado, that Gary has led since 2018. Also, the name of the monthly podcast that features novels discussed by the study group.

Appendix B: Reading Worksheet

Literary Forensics Reading Guide

What I Bring

- My history
- My biases
- My reading habits
- My writing needs

Technique Gaps

Skill Acquisition Strategies

- Root cause / Motivation-driven
- End-means / Goal-driven
- Heuristics
- Serendipity

Reading List / Study Schedule

What I Bring
What I Feel
What I Notice
What I Study

Appendix C: Bibliography

Adler, Mortimer J., and Charles Van Doren, *How to Read a Book,* revised and updated edition (Simon and Schuster, New York, 1972). First published 1940.

Archer, Jodie, and Matthew L. Jockers, *The Bestseller Code: Anatomy of a Blockbuster Novel* (St. Martin's Press, New York, 2016).

Aristotle. *Poetics,* trans. Malcolm Heath (Penguin Classics, UK, 1996). Written c. 335 BCE.

Aronson, Elliot, and Joshua Aronson, *The Social Animal,* 12th ed. (Worth Publishers, New York, 2018). First published 1972.

Audi, Robert, *Epistemology: A Contemporary Introduction to the Theory of Knowledge* (Routledge, UK, 2003). First published 1998.

Bakhtin, Mikhail M., *The Dialogic Imagination: Four Essays,* trans. Michael Holmquist and Caryl Emerson (University of Texas Press, Texas, 2010). First published 1981.

Baldick, Chris, *The Oxford Dictionary of Literary Terms,* 4th ed., (Oxford University Press, UK, 2015).

Booker, Christopher, *The Seven Basic Plots: Why We Tell Stories* (Continuum Books, UK, 2004).

Booth, Wayne C., *The Rhetoric of Fiction,* 2nd ed. (University of Chicago Press, Illinois, 1983).

Brody, Jessica, *Save the Cat! Writes a Novel: The Last Book on Novel Writing You'll Ever Need* (Ten Speed Press, California, 2018).

Bruder, Melissa, Lee Michael Cohn, Madeleine Olnek, Nathaniel Pollack, Robert Previto, and Scott Zigler, *A Practical Handbook for the Actor* (Vintage Books, New York, 1986).

Burroway, Janet, and Elizabeth Stuckey-French, *Writing Fiction: A Guide to Narrative Craft* (Pearson Longman, New York, 1996).

Chomsky, Noam, *On Language* (The New Press, New York, 1998).

Coyne, Shawn, *The Story Grid: What Good Editors Know* (Black Irish Entertainment LLC, 2015).

Croft, William, and D. Alan Cruse, *Cognitive Linguistics* (Cambridge University Press, UK, 2004).

Cron, Lisa, *Wired for Story: The Writer's Guide to Using Brain Science to Hook Readers from the Very First Sentence* (Ten Speed Press, California, 2012).

Culler, Jonathan, *Literary Theory: A Very Short Introduction* (Oxford University Press, UK, 1997).

de Certeau, Michel, *The Practice of Everyday Life,* trans. Steven Rendell (University of California Press, California, 1984). First published 1980.

de Saussure, Ferdinand, Charles Bally, Albert Sechehaye, and Albert Riedlinger, *Course in General Linguistics,* 3rd ed., trans. and ed. Roy Harris (Bloomsbury, UK, 2013). First published 1916.

DiYanni, Robert, *You Are What You Read: A Practical Guide to Reading Well* (Princeton University Press, New Jersey, 2021).

Eagleton, Terry, *How to Read Literature* (Yale University Press, Connecticut, 2013).

Ferrante, Elena, *In the Margins: On the Pleasures of Reading and Writing*, trans. Ann Goldstein (Europa Editions, New York, 2022).

Fish, Stanley, *How to Write a Sentence: And How to Read One* (Harper Paperbacks, New York, 2012).

Foster, Thomas C., *How to Read Literature Like a Professor* (HarperCollins, New York, 2003).

Foucault, Michel, *Power/Knowledge: Selected Interviews and Other Writings, 1972–1977*, trans. Colin Gordon (Pantheon Books, New York, 1980).

Fry, Paul H., *"Theory of Literature," Open Yale Courses Series* (Yale University Press, Connecticut, 2012).

Garner, Bryan A., *A Dictionary of Modern American Usage* (Oxford University Press, UK, 1998).

Gee, James Paul, *How to Do Discourse Analysis: A Toolkit* (Routledge, UK, 2005).

Hall, Stuart, *"Encoding and Decoding in the Television Discourse," The CCCS Selected Working Papers* (Centre for Contemporary Cultural Studies, Alabama, 1973).

Hawker, Libbie, *Take Off Your Pants! Outline Your Books for Faster, Better Writing* (Running Rabbit Press, Washington, 2015).

Hoopes, James, ed, *Peirce on Signs: Writings on Semiotic by Charles Sanders Peirce* (University of North Carolina Press, North Carolina, 1991).

Jockers, Matthew L., *Macroanalysis: Digital Methods and Literary History* (University of Illinois Press, Illinois, 2013).

Jonuska, Kate, *The Dictionary of Fiction Critique: How to Read Like a Writer in Order to Give and Receive Constructive Critique* (CreateSpace Independent Publishing, California, 2018).

Kahneman, Daniel, *Thinking, Fast and Slow* (Farrar, Straus and Giroux, New York, 2011).

King, Stephen, *On Writing: A Memoir of the Craft* (Scribner, New York, 2000).

Knopf, Robert, *Script Analysis for Theatre: Tools for Interpretation, Collaboration and Production* (Methuen Drama, UK, 2017).

Lovett, Marsha C., Michael W. Bridges, Michele DiPietro, Susan A. Ambrose, and Marie K. Norman, *How Learning Works: 8 Research-Based Principles for Smart Teaching*, 2nd ed. (Jossey-Bass, New Jersey, 2023).

Maass, Donald, *Writing the Breakout Novel* (Writer's Digest Books, Ohio, 2001).

Maass, Donald, *The Emotional Craft of Fiction: How to Write with Emotional Power, Develop Achingly Real Characters, Move Your Readers, and Create Riveting Moral Stakes* (Writer's Digest Books, Ohio, 2016).

Moretti, Franco, *Graphs, Maps, Trees: Abstract Models for a Literary History* (Verso Books, New York, 2005).

Novella, Steven, Bob Novella, Cara Santa Maria, Jay Novella, and Evan Bernstein, *The Skeptics' Guide to the Universe: How to Know What's Really Real in a World Increasingly Full of Fake* (Grand Central Publishing, New York, 2018).

Orwell, George, "Why I Write," in *Why I Write* (Penguin Books, UK, 2004). First published 1946.

Paglia, Camille, *Sex, Art, and American Culture: Essays* (Vintage, New York, 1992).

Palmer, Richard E., *Hermeneutics: Interpretation Theory in Schleiermacher, Dilthey, Heidegger, and Gadamer* (Northwestern University Press, Illinois, 1969).

Percy, Benjamin, *Thrill Me: Essays on Fiction* (Graywolf Press, Minnesota, 2016).

Percy, Walker, *The Message in the Bottle: How Queer Man Is, How Queer Language Is, and What One Has to Do with the Other* (Picador, UK, 1975).

Plutchik, Robert, *The Emotions* (University Press of America, Maryland, 1991). First published 1962.

Plutchik, Robert, *Emotions in the Practice of Psychotherapy: Clinical Implications of Affect Theories* (American Psychological Association, District of Columbia, 2000).

Pound, Ezra, *ABC of Reading* (New Directions, New York, 1934).

Pound, Ezra, *How to Read* (Haskell House, New York, 1971). First published 1931.

Prose, Francine, *Reading Like a Writer: A Guide for People Who Love Books and for Those Who Want to Write Them* (HarperCollins, New York, 2006).

Prose, Francine, *What to Read and Why* (HarperCollins, New York, 2018).

Reagan, Andrew J., Lewis Mitchell, Dilan Kiley, Christopher M. Danforth, and Peter Sheridan Dodds, "The emotional arcs of stories are dominated by six basic shapes." *EPJ Data Science* 5, no. 31 (2016). https://doi.org/10.1140/epjds/s13688-016-0093-1.

Richards, I. A., *Practical Criticism: A Study of Literary Judgment* (Kegan Paul, Trench, Trubner & Co. Ltd., UK, 1930).

Salesses, Matthew, *Craft in the Real World: Rethinking Fiction Writing and Workshopping* (Catapult, New York, 2021).

Saunders, George, *A Swim in a Pond in the Rain: In Which Four Russians Give a Master Class on Writing, Reading, and Life* (Random House, New York, 2021).

Sellars, Wilfrid, *Empiricism and the Philosophy of Mind* (Harvard University Press, Massachusetts, 1997). First published 1956.

Shawl, Nisi, and Cynthia Ward, *Writing the Other: A Practical Approach* (Aqueduct Press, Washington, 2005).

Smith, Barbara Herrnstein, "What Was 'Close Reading?': A Century of Method in Literary Studies." *The Minnesota Review 2016*, no. 87 (2016), 57–75. https://doi.org/10.1215/00265667-3630844.

Stockwell, Peter, *Cognitive Poetics: An Introduction*, 2nd ed. (Routledge, UK, 2020).

Swain, Dwight V., *Techniques of the Selling Writer* (University of Oklahoma Press, Oklahoma, 1965).

Theophrastus, *Theophrastou Charakteres*, trans. Richard Claverhouse Jebb and John Edwin Sandys (Macmillan, UK, 1909). Written c. 319 BCE.

Thompson, John B., *Merchants of Culture: The Publishing Business in the Twenty-First Century*, 2nd ed. (Plume, New York, 2012).

Tufte, Virginia, *Grammar as Style* (Holt, Rinehart and Winston, Inc., New York, 1971).

Tufte, Virginia, *Artful Sentences: Syntax as Style* (Graphics Press LLC., Connecticut, 2006).

Vonnegut, Kurt, *Palm Sunday: An Autobiographical Collage* (Delacorte Press, New York, 1981).

Wallace, David Foster, "Tense Present: Democracy, English, and the Wars over Usage," *Harper's Magazine*, April 2001.

Wendig, Chuck, *Damn Fine Story: Mastering the Tools of a Powerful Narrative* (Writer's Digest Books, Ohio, 2017).

Willett, John, ed., *Brecht on Theatre: The Development of an Aesthetic* (Hill and Wang, New York, 1964).

Wittgenstein, Ludwig, *Tractatus Logico-Philosophicus*, trans. David Pears and Brian McGuinness (Routledge Classics, UK, 2001). First published 1921.

Wood, James, *How Fiction Works* (Farrar, Straus and Giroux, New York, 2008).

Wood, James, *Serious Noticing: Selected Essays, 1997–2019* (Farrar, Straus and Giroux, New York, 2019).

Wortham, Stanton Emerson Fisher, *Narratives in Action: A Strategy for Research* (Teachers College Press, New York, 2001).

INDEX

www.ingramcontent.com/pod-product-compliance
Lightning Source LLC
Chambersburg PA
CBHW082246120626
46555CB00009B/2983